The German Contribution to the Building of the Americas

The German Contribution to the Building of the Americas

Studies in Honor of
Karl J. R. Arndt

Edited by Gerhard K. Friesen
Wilfrid Laurier University
Walter Schatzberg
Clark University

Published by Clark University Press
and
Distributed by the University Press of
New England,
Hanover, New Hampshire, 1977

Contents

In Appreciation of
Karl J. R. Arndt

Was man in der Jugend wünscht,
hat man im Alter in der Fülle.

Goethe, *Dichtung und Wahrheit*, Part 2

A brief laudation like this cannot possibly do full justice to so dedicated and productive a life as that of Karl Arndt. Better than any commentary, the long list of important publications bespeaks his life-long devotion to the scholarly pursuit of truth in the area of German-American cultural relations. Only the highlights of his career may therefore be traced here.

Born in St. Paul, Minnesota, in 1903, Karl John Richard Arndt resided in China from 1913 to 1919, where his father was a Lutheran missionary for the Missouri Synod. After attending St. John's College in Winfield, Kansas, and Concordia Seminary in St. Louis, Karl Arndt in 1928 obtained his M.A. degree at Washington University in St. Louis, where Otto Heller was directing a number of substantial studies on Charles Sealsfield. At the Johns Hopkins University, Karl Arndt continued his studies in Germanistics. Under William Kurrelmeyer, whose uncompromising standards were responsible for the discovery of the so-called *Doppeldrucke*, he received the rigorous philological training for which this institution was then famous. After receiving his doctorate in 1933 (following a dissertation on Ernst Wildenbruch), Karl Arndt taught Greek and German at Hartwick College in Oneonta, N.Y. It was here, at the headwaters of the Susquehanna and in the setting of Cooper's life and works, that Karl Arndt began his continuing discovery of the fascinating field of German-American affinities. His move to the Louisiana State University in 1935 brought him into the sphere of Count Leon's American activities and initiated decades of historical research into the utopian ventures of the Harmonists from Swabia.

From 1945 to 1950, Karl Arndt served with the U.S. Military Government in Germany, where he was in charge of the Office of Church-State Relations. One of the first to arrive in devastated Berlin, he immediately began his search for the manuscript of the monumental Sealsfield biography by Eduard Castle, with whom he had managed to correspond via Siberia for part of World War II. Having located the manuscript, Karl Arndt's efforts to gain the American authorities' assistance toward its publication were frustrated by a top official who believed that Germans already had too many "goddam books" to read. In order to assist in the orderly transition to constitutional government in Western Germany, Karl Arndt resigned his Louisiana professorship in 1947.

In 1950 he accepted an appointment at Clark University, where he served as Head of the German Department until 1969. From here he was able to effect the 1952 publication of Castle's work with the support of the American government. Karl Arndt's research in the archives of the American Antiquarian Society in Worcester (which had elected him a member) brought to light a great amount of crucial evidence about Sealsfield's American career. Years of patient and painstaking research in collaboration with Miss May E. Olson of the Louisiana State University Library in Baton Rouge resulted in their joint publication of *German-American Newspapers and Periodicals 1732 to 1955* (1961) and its sequel, *The German-Language Press of the Americas* (1973). This two-volume work represents, in the words of the *Neue Zürcher Zeitung*, "an admirable accomplishment, and for a long time it will be the starting point for all research in the field of German-American history and culture."

Far in advance of most other preparations toward the commemoration of the American Declaration of Independence, Karl Arndt organized the publication of Sealsfield's *Sämtliche Werke* (a venture that had twice been defeated in our century) as a bicentennial project. Under Karl Arndt's continuing editorship, fourteen of the planned twenty-eight volumes have appeared, and reviews have been gratifying.

The common denominator in Karl Arndt's work of a lifetime—epitomized by his publications on the Harmony Society, the German-American Press, and Charles Sealsfield—is scholarship of the highest order coupled with a genuine sense of humanitarian values. Nowhere in his publications has his passion for factual objectivity and historical accuracy belied his belief in the prerogative of personality. In good German-American tradition, he is not a believer in *übertünchte Höflichkeit* and cherishes the freedom of individual expression. With a directness rare among younger Germanists, he has consistently upheld the causes of the important American minority of German heritage, without courting popularity or becoming political. As he is religious without being intolerant, he is proud of his German roots without being boastful.

Two world wars and their irreparable damage to the potential development of a German-American identity as well as the failure of the American democratic messianism in a world polarized by hostile ideologies have led Karl Arndt to a certain skepticism about our political future. Like Sealsfield, he is conscious of the forces impeding the progress of intellectual enlightenment and is fond of quoting St. Paul's Epistle to the Ephesians (VI:12): "For we wrestle not against flesh and blood, but against principalities, against powers, against the rulers of the darkness of this world, against spiritual wickedness in high places." All this has convinced Karl Arndt that "the world of libraries and archives is the one place of refuge and strength for the sincere scholar," and has also instilled in him a sense of urgency about his projected work.

The bicentennial year finds him as energetic and enterprising as ever. Apart from the continuing Sealsfield edition, two other current bicentennial projects attest to his undiminished productivity. A documentary history of the Indiana activities of the Harmony Society will accompany the ongoing renovations of their original settlement in that state. Furthermore, a special bicentennial edition of volume I of *The German-Language Press of the Americas* is forthcoming, and a third volume (entitled *German-American Press Research from the Time of the Revolution to the Bicentennial*) will round off the entire work.

It is altogether fitting that with this book (whose title circumscribes the area of Karl Arndt's own distinguished contributions) his friends and colleagues in the universal *Gelehrtenrepublik* honor him in the American bicentennial as one of the foremost German-American scholars. It is also most fitting that the Clark

University Press produce this volume in honor of Professor Arndt, who has brought and continues to bring so much honor to his university. At Clark he has inspired generations of students with the ideals of the German cultural heritage and with a love of learning. For his colleagues he has been and continues to be the very embodiment of the teacher-scholar in the best sense of the German university tradition, a tradition which has guided Clark University from its inception.

Gerhard Friesen
Walter Schatzberg

Bibliography of Publications of Karl J. R. Arndt

ABBREVIATIONS

AGR	*American German Review*
AL	*American Literature*
CL	*Comparative Literature*
GR	*Germanic Review*
GQ	*German Quarterly*
IMH	*Indiana Magazine of History*
JAH	*Journal of American History*
JEGP	*Journal of English and Germanic Philology*
LHQ	*Louisiana Historical Quarterly*
MLJ	*Modern Language Journal*
MLN	*Modern Language Notes*
NYH	*New York History*
PH	*Pennsylvania History*
PMHB	*The Pennsylvania Magazine of History and Biography*
PMLA	*Publications of the Modern Language Association of America*
PAAS	*Proceedings of the American Antiquarian Society*
WPHM	*Western Pennsylvania Historical Magazine*
ZDP	*Zeitschrift für deutsche Philologie*

1932
"Nikolaus Lenau's American Experience." *Monatshefte* 24:241–244.

1934
"Poe's *Politian* and Goethe's *Mignon*." *MLN* 49:101–104.

1935
"Should Americans Teach Foreign Languages?" *School & Society*, March 28.

1937
"New Letters from James Fenimore Cooper." *MLN* 52:117–120.
"Cooper comments on Goethe." *GQ* 10:91–92.
"John Christopher Hartwick, German Pioneer of Central New York." *NYH* 18:293–303.

1940

"A Bavarian's Journey to New Orleans and Nacogdoches." *LHQ* 23:485-500.
"The Life and Mission of Count Leon." (Part I: Germany) *AGR* 6:5-8.
"The Life and Mission of Count Leon." (Part II: America) *AGR* 6:15-19.
"Toennies—The Concept of Law and Human Progress." *Social Forces,* October.
"George Rapp's Petition to Thomas Jefferson." *AGR* 7:5-9.

1941

"The Genesis of Germantown, Louisiana." *LHQ* 24:378-433.
Heller's *Sealsfield Bibliography. GR* 16:151-152.
"Die Anfänge einer deutschen Ansiedlung an den Quellen des Susquehanna." *Deutsches Archiv für Landes- und Volksforschungen* 5:58-71.
"Herder and the Harmony Society." *GR* 16:108-113.
"Sealsfield, The 'Greatest American Author'." (Co-author with Henry Groen) *AGR* 7:12-15.
Review of Heller's *The Language of Charles Sealsfield. Monatshefte* 33:335.
Early German-American Narratives. New York: American Book Company, 358 pp.

1942

"The First Song to the Wabash." *IMH* 38:80-82.
"New Light on *Sealsfield's Cajütenbuch und Gesammelte Werke.*" *JEGP* 41:210-222.
"New Light on the Harmonists." *WPHM* 25:3-4, 168-174.

1943

"The Cooper-Sealsfield Exchange of Criticism." *AL* 15:16-24.
"Sealsfield's Claim to Realism." *Monatshefte* 35:271-285.
"Sealsfield's Early Reception in England and America." *GR* 18:176-195.
"George Rapp Discovers the Wabash." *WPHM* 26:109-116.
Review of John S. Duss' *The Harmonists. A Personal History. WPHM* 26:159-166.

1944

"The Harmonists and the Mormons." *AGR* 10:6-9.
"The Harmonists and the Hutterians." *AGR* 10:24-27.
"Lenau's Lost Poem 'An die Ultraliberalen in Deutschland'." *GR* 19:180-185.

1945

"American Incitement to Revolution on the Eve of the Frankfurt Parliament." *AGR* 11:24-25.
"American Utopias and Internationalism." *CL News-Letter* April.
"The Harmonists as Pioneers of the American Silk Industry." *AGR* 11:27-29.
"The Harmonists as Pioneers of the American Oil Industry." *AGR* 12:7-9.

1946

"Mozart and Schiller on the Wabash." *Monatshefte* 38:244-248.

1949

"World War II and the Russian Co-Religionists of the Harmonists." *AGR* 15:10-11.

"Der Begriff der humanistischen Bildung in den Erziehungssystemen der Vereinigten Staaten." *Paedagogische Provinz* 4:237-242.

1951

Review of A. E. Zucker's *The Forty-Eighters: Political Refugees of the German Revolution. GR* 26:303-304.

1952

"Sealsfield and Strubberg at Vera Cruz." *Monatshefte* 44:225-229.

"Sealsfield's Command of the English Language." *MLN* 67:310-313.

1953

Review of E. Castle's *Der Grosse Unbekannte.* (Das Leben von Charles Sealsfield.) *Monatshefte* 45:153-155.

"Charles Sealsfield and the *Courrier des Etats-Unis.*" *PMLA* 68:170-188.

"The Harmony Society from Its Beginnings in Germany in 1785 to Its Liquidation in the United States in 1905. Research Report." Philadelphia: *Year Book of the American Philosophical Society,* pp. 188-194.

1954

"Charles Sealsfield in Amerika." *ZDP* 72:169-182.

"Recent Sealsfield Discoveries." *JEGP* 53:160-171.

"Plagiarism: Sealsfield or Simms?" *MLN* 69:577-581.

1955

"Three Hungarian Travelers Visit Economy." *PMHB* 79:197-216.

1956

"Early Impressions: An Unknown Work by Sealsfield." *JEGP* 55:100-116.

1957

Review of Eduard Castle's *Der Grosse Unbekannte. Briefe und Aktenstücke. JEGP* 56:455-456.

1958

"The Effect of America on Lenau's Life and Work." *GR* 33:125-142.

"The Harmony Society and *Wilhelm Meisters Wanderjahre.*" *CL* 10:193-202.

1960

Review of *Anglo-German and American German Crosscurrents.* Vol. 1. Ed. by Philip Allison Shelley with Arthur O. Lewis, Jr., and William W. Betts, Jr. (University of North Carolina Studies in Comparative Literature, No. 19) Chapel Hill, 1957. *JEGP* 59:378-379.

1961

German-American Newspapers and Periodicals, 1732-1955. History and Bibliography. (With May E. Olson.) Heidelberg: Quelle & Meyer, 794 pp.

1962
Review of Günter Schulz' *Schillers Horen. Politik und Erziehung: Analyse einer deutschen Zeitschrift*, Heidelberg. *MLN* 77:108–109.

1963
Review of *Anglo-American and American German Crosscurrents*. Vol. 2. Ed. by Philip Allison Shelley. Chapel Hill, 1962. *JEGP* 62:821–822.
"The Litigious Mr. Sealsfield." *MLN* 78:527–532.

1964
The Ernst Steiger Collections of German-American Newspapers and Periodicals in Heidelberg and Vienna diligently compared and cataloged for co-operating libraries as a guide to microfilm copies of the Heidelberg collection. Worcester, Mass., 51 pp.
Review of William I. Schreiber's *Our Amish Neighbors. GQ* 37:90–91.
"Zu den Lücken in der Gretchentragödie." *Monatshefte*, May:173–177.
"Charles Sealsfield, 'The Greatest American Author'." *PAAS* 74:249–259.

1965
German-American Newspapers and Periodicals 1732–1955. History and Bibliography. (With May E. Olson.) 2nd Revised Edition with Appendix. New York: Johnson Reprint Corporation, 810 pp.
Microfilm Guide and Index to the Library of Congress Collection of German Prisoners of War Camp Papers Published in the United States of North America from 1943 to 1946. Worcester, Mass., 63 pp.
George Rapp's Harmony Society, 1785–1847. Philadelphia: University of Pennsylvania Press, 682 pp.
Review of Klaus G. Wust's *Society for the History of the Germans in Maryland, Thirty-First Report. GQ* 38:113–114.
Review of William F. Roertgen's *The Frankfurter Gelehrte Anzeigen, 1772–1790. MLJ* 49:336–337.

1966
Review of Gerhard H. W. Zuther's *Eine Bibliographie der Aufnahme Amerikanischer Literatur in Deutschen Zeitschriften 1945–1960. MLJ* 50:442.

1967
Review of George Fenwick Jones' *Henry Newman's Salzburger Letterbooks. JAH* 54:110–111.
Review of Hermann J. Weigand's *Survey and Soundings in European Literature. Symposium* 21:353–355.

1968
Review of Gilliam Lindt Gollin's *Moravians in Two Worlds. PH* 35:316–318.
"Biography and Bibliography of Ernst Steiger, German-American Publisher and Collector of Americana." Philadelphia: *American Philosophical Society Year Book 1967*, 453–456.

1969
"Pragmatists and Prophets: George Rapp and J. A. Roebling versus J. A. Etzler and Count Leon." In 2 Parts. (With P. R. Brostowin.) *WPHM* 52:1-27; 52:171-198.

1971
George Rapp's Successors and Material Heirs, 1847-1916. Rutherford: Fairleigh Dickinson University Press, 445 pp.
"Harmonist Music and Pittsburgh Musicians in Early Economy." In 3 Parts. (With Dr. Richard D. Wetzel.) *WPHM* 54:125-157; 54:284-311; 54:391-413.
"The Indiana Decade of George Rapp's Harmony Society: 1814-1824." *PAAS*, 1-25.

1972
George Rapp's Harmony Society, 1785-1847. Rev. edition. Rutherford, N.J.: Fairleigh Dickinson University Press, 713 pp.
Charles Sealsfield (Karl Postl 1793-1864) Sämtliche Werke. Unter Mitwirkung mehrer Fachgelehrter herausgegeben von Professor Dr. Karl J. R. Arndt, Clark University, Worcester, Mass. Kritisch durchgesehene und erläuterte Ausgabe. 28 volumes. Volumes 1-14 published. Hildesheim: Olms Presse.
"'Dauer im Wechsel': Grimmelshausen's Ungarische Wiedertäufer und Rapp's Harmoniegesellschaft." München: *Traditions and Transitions, Studies in Honor of Harold Jantz*, 78-86.
"The 'Pittsburgh Leader's' Analysis of the 1890 Crisis in the Harmony Society and its International Repercussions." *WPHM* 55:319-346.
"Newly Discovered Sealsfield Relationships Documented." *MLN* 87:450-464.

1973
The German Language Press of the Americas, 1732-1968. History and Bibliography. Volume 2: Argentina, Bolivia, Brazil, Canada, Chile, Columbia, Costa Rica, Cuba, Dominican Republic, Ecuador, Guatemala, Guyana, Mexico, Paraguay, Peru, USA (addenda), Uruguay, Venezuela. (With May E. Olson.) Pullach/München: Verlag Dokumentation, 708 pp.
"Koreshanity, Topolobampo, Olombia, and the Harmonist Millions." *WPHM* 56:71-86.
"The Peter Rindisbacher Family on the Red River in Rupert's Land: Their Hardships and Call for Help from Rapp's Harmony Society." Toronto, Canada: *The German-Canadian Yearbook*, 1:95-106.

1974
"The Strange and Wonderful New World of George Rapp and His Harmony Society." *WPHM* 57:141-166.

1975
A Documentary History of the Indiana Decade of the Harmony Society,

1814–1824. Volume 1: 1814–1819. Indianapolis: Indiana Historical Society, 837 pp.

"A Former Harmonist Describes his Civil War Experiences, Including Parade Before Lincoln." *Historical Society Notes and Documents* 57:279–281.

Review of Lois T. Henderson's *The Holy Experiment,* Flo Morse's *Yankee Communes. Another American Way,* Alex Carmel's *Die Siedlungen der Württembergischen Templer in Palastina 1868–1918,* and Erwin Roth's *Preussens Gloria im Heiligen Land. Die Deutschen und Jerusalem. WPHM* 58:83–85.

1976

"Bismarck's Socialist Law of 1878 and the Harmonists." *WPHM* 59:55–69.

"Steigers Sammlung amerikanischer Zeitungen in der Weltausstellung zu Wien, 1873, und das Internationale Echo der Presse." At request of AACHENER GESCHICHTSVEREIN for *Festausgabe Bernhard Poll.* (In press.)

To be published:

A Documentary History of the Indiana Decade of the Harmony Society 1814–1824. Volume II: 1820–1824.

The German Language Press of the Americas (with May E. Olson). Volume I will be published as a Bicentennial Edition.

Volume III will bear the sub-title: *German-American Press Research from the time of the Revolution to the Bicentennial.*

Oswald Seidensticker's The First Century of German Printing in America, 1728–1830. Greatly amplified by the research of Wilbur H. Oda, Ph.D. Revised and prepared for publication by Karl John Richard Arndt, Ph.D.

"German as the Official Language of the United States of Amerika?" In: *Monatshefte,* Bicentennial Issue, Summer 1976.

1. "… beschreibung eyner Landtschafft der Wilden / Nacketen / Grimmigen Menschfresser Leuthen": The German Image of America in the Sixteenth Century
Duncan Smith

… beschreibung eyner Landtschafft der Wilden/Nacketen/Grimmigen Menschfresser Leuthen …—*The German Image of America in the Sixteenth Century*

German involvement in the exploration of the New World began immediately after the first voyage of Columbus in 1492. Although German mercenary adventurers may well have accompanied subsequent early expeditions across the Atlantic, the primary involvement of the Germans was in the financing of expeditions setting sail from Spain. The southern German banking houses, notably the Fuggers and the Welsers,[1] had long maintained extensive connections with the house of Habsburg, and both Maximilian I and his nephew Charles V were heavily in debt to these two concerns. When Charles was chosen to be King of Spain after the death of Philipp the Handsome and Ferdinand's removal from the regency, he brought with him to his new kingdom large numbers of Flemish counselors and agents of the major German banking firms with whom he regularly did business. These firms were all very interested in the results of the explorations of the New World, particularly since the trade in eastern goods via Venice and Genoa was becoming increasingly difficult due to the conquests and mercantile intransigence of the Ottoman Turks. Naturally enough, the first concern of these commercial and finance companies was the discovery of a new route to the original sources of the valued spices and other goods, and only subsequent to the failure of Magellan and later of Cabot to discover a practical route to the East Indies did these firms show any great interest in the actual discoveries of the Spanish and Portuguese expeditions to the New World. It was largely the rumors of the enormous gold resources, the legend of El Dorado, which eventually restimulated interest on the part of the two largest German banking companies, the Fuggers and the Welsers, in acquiring rights to some of the lands in the New World. When the first treasure galleons began to arrive in Spain, particularly after the conquests of Cortes in Mexico, the interest of these two firms grew greatly. The Fuggers particularly, who had contributed over half a million gold ducats toward the election of Charles to the throne of the Holy Roman Empire, derived very direct benefit from these galleons, because much of the gold was to be taken from Spain and delivered to Fugger's agents waiting across the border in France or in the harbor of Ghent.

The interest of the Fuggers in the actual financing of expeditions and the acquisition of lands in the New World was, however, short lived. After Jakob Fugger's death, his nephew Anton did contract with Charles V in 1530 to "discover, populate, and fortify the islands and lands extending from the Straits of Magellan to Pizzaro's territory."[2] Despite the intense isolationism of the Spaniards who constantly objected to any foreign presence, the Emperor and King of Spain was inclined to accept the Fuggers' terms which were scarcely generous to the monarchy and which made Anton Fugger governor and owner of much of what is now Venezuela, Colombia, Brazil, and Argentina. But though the temptation was very great, Anton eventually rejected the agreement. A first expedition financed by the Fuggers returned in 1532 or 1533 without any success at all, having been heavily damaged by an Atlantic hurricane. In addition, the religious strife in southern Germany had occasioned Catholic Anton a brief period of imprisonment in Augsburg, an experience from which his pride, at least, never recovered. But above all it was Fugger's awareness that his position depended upon a consistent ability to finance the house of Habsburg's needs which turned him away from risky and hitherto unproductive ventures in the New World. Instead, he directed the firm's attention to continental matters of importance, to the house of Habsburg and to himself, namely the defense of his Hungarian trading interests and to the financing of the Spanish conquest of Tunis and offensive against Algiers in 1535. Eventually Fugger liquidated his factories and agencies in the New World, including a profitable undertaking in Haiti. Whether the firm maintained its active interest in the African slave trade, of which Augsburg was for a time a financial center, is uncertain but not unlikely.

Far better known is the involvement of the smaller Welser firm in the exploration and colonization of what is now Venezuela and Columbia.[3] This firm, also with close financial and personal connections to Charles V and the Spanish Monarchy, took a very early and more lasting interest in reports of the New World. The firm owned land in the Canary Islands and soon after the discovery of the New World opened an office in Santo Domingo. The expertise of the Welsers in mining and their experience and interest in overseas trade made them very important to the Spanish Monarchy, which rewarded the company with Venezuela in 1528. For eighteen years from that date the Welsers continually made attempts to colonize and more especially to reap profit from that enormous possession, and it was in this effort that we have our only evidence of the earliest direct German involvement in the exploration and colonization of the New World. This direct involvement consisted of financing expeditions upon contract and approval by the Council of the Indies in Spain and the appointment of a governor or captain-general. The recruits to man the ships and form the army were largely Spanish, though a few German arquebusiers occasionally accompanied the expeditions, since Spanish soldiery was not at that time sufficiently acquainted with the new weapons. By unusual agreement with the Spanish Monarchy, the Belzares, as they were known in Spain, had the right to appoint their own governor who officially was always a German during those eighteen years, though such confusion often reigned, that Spaniards technically governed the colony a number of times in that period. The names of the German expedition leaders are Ambrose Ehinger, often known as Alfinger, 1529-1533; Georg Hohermuth or Jorje de Spiro, 1535-1540; Nikolaus Federmann, 1534-1539; and Philipp von Hutten, 1540-1546, with Bartholomäus Welser, Junior, as one of his captains.

Opinions vary on the effectiveness of the German governors in Venezuela according to the nationality of the historian recording those times. The most valuable studies on this period are Colombian, Venezuelan, and German;[4] the former give a negative view based largely on reports of 16th-Century Spanish writers like Bishop Bartholomo de las Casas who were uniformly quite anti-German. The German work, written in 1938, is equally fierce in its positive assessment of the individual German efforts and negative in its view of all things Spanish, although the writer is obliged to concede that the brutal disunity among the Germans themselves was much responsible for the failure of the German colonization in Venezuela.

The first of the governors, Ambrose Ehinger, whose older brothers were partners of the Welser firm in Saragossa, arrived at the colony of Coro on the northern coast of Venezuela on February 24, 1529. He planned, among other things, to increase the productivity of the mines in that region by importing German miners to the colony. Additionally he was to oversee the development of an export trade of the raw materials—metals, cotton, sugar, drugs, and wood—to Spain from which trade the Welsers expected to draw great profits. More intriguing no doubt to Ehinger and to his Spanish friend, García de Lerma, the governor of Santa Marta farther to the west, was the opportunity to discover in Venezuela what Cortes had discovered in Mexico, and it seems from available evidence that Ehinger and subsequent German governors were rather uninterested in colonization. Ehinger met with continual opposition to his plans from the Spanish government in Santo Domingo, partly due to national antagonism, and largely due to the prevalent envy and greed of all the *conquistadores* regardless of nationality. Appeals for help to the Council of the Indies in Spain were not very effective since communications with Europe were few and far between, and Ehinger was accordingly left very much dependent upon his own wiles to avoid the pitfalls engendered by the opposition of the Spaniards. Even during his early days as governor there was a rebellion against his authority led by Juan de Ampies which Ehinger, however, successfully put down.

Ehinger's first expedition to the west in 1529 led to the founding of the town of Maracaibo and was but the first of numerous efforts to relocate the original Coro settlement away from the unhealthy coastal location.

Spanish opposition to the German's plan for self-enrichment was, for all its fierceness, not as dangerous as the plottings of Ehinger's own brothers who had decided to replace Ambrose with brother George, who sailed with that intention to Coro in 1530 after the Ehingers had dissolved their partnership with the Welsers. George's efforts to remove Ambrose proved futile, and he returned to Spain where he attempted to stir up animosity against Ambrose in the Council of the Indies and in the royal court. Heinrich, the oldest brother and chief plotter, had gained a position at the court as financial advisor to Charles V, but the emperor was not fooled by the campaign against the Venezuelan governor and the Welser firm. Instead Charles awarded all rights previously accorded to the Welser-Ehinger partnership exclusively to Bartholomäus and Anton Welser. With their power assured, the Welsers appointed their agents Nikolaus Federmann and Hans Seissenhofer leaders of a new expedition to the colony. Their four ships carried not only supplies and soldiers but also the first European women (Germans among them) to arrive as colonists in the New World. This expedition arrived in Coro on April 28, 1530 and increased the complexity of the situation to the bewilderment of the Spaniards who now were convinced that every newly arrived ship would inevitably bring with it a new German governor, or even two. But the difficulty was this time solved in an amicable manner, according to some historians at any rate, and Seissenhofer's death occurred about a full year after his voluntary withdrawal from the administration of the colony, removing much suspicion that the solution was less than amicable.

Seissenhofer had appointed Federmann his deputy in Coro, before Ambrose Ehinger, the real governor, who was away at Maracaibo, had returned to renew his claims to authority in the colony. Ehinger, ill with the usual assortment of tropical ailments, confirmed Federmann in that position and returned for rest and recuperation to Santo Domingo, instructing Federmann not to undertake any expeditions in his absence. This sort of instruction was not given out of any regard for the dangers which Federmann or any deputy might face, but simply because possession was nine-tenths of the law, and anything which Federmann discovered would increase Federmann's—not Ehinger's—wealth and prestige. Federmann was quick to disobey these instructions and set out for the interior of the colony, penetrating as far as Barquisimeto. He returned to Coro on March 17, 1531 where an unsmiling Ehinger awaited him. With his deputy back and covered with much glory and wealth, Ehinger organized his own expedition to the interior, which left the Coro settlement on September 1, 1531 and which was, by the standards of the *conquistadores,* quite successful. The largest part of the plunder was to be taken back to Coro ahead of the main force by Ehinger's lieutenant, de Vascuna. The latter's small force became lost in the jungle and was eventually constrained to bury the gold and try, each man for himself, to return to Coro. Only one man made it, and he could not remember where the gold was buried. Search parties were sent out from the main body but also failed to locate the missing de Vascuna (one can imagine that the motives of the search parties were not entirely those of the Good Samaritan), and Ehinger's own efforts to continue his exploration ended with his death from a poison arrow of an Indian at the beginning of 1533. Ehinger's comrades returned to Coro bringing with them substantial treasure, enough so that the Welser firm might have been expected to show pleasure. But the firm reacted strangely, for it made no effort to refill the vacant governorship which the anti-German government at Santo Domingo had filled with governor *pro-tem* Rodrigo de Bastidas.

Federmann had returned during Ehinger's absence to Europe and was in Spain when the news of Ehinger's death reached him. He went at once to Augsburg and received from the Welsers the promise of the governorship of Venezuela and was later confirmed in this position by the Spanish crown on July 19, 1534. But the Spanish interests in Santo Domingo succeeded in blocking the realization of Federmann's plans, and his governorship was taken from him. The Spaniards claimed Federmann's treatment of the native and the colonial population was intolerable, a charge which was never proven though in view of the general behavior of *conquistadores,* not difficult to believe.[5] The Welsers did, in this instance, react with more speed, perhaps because news of Pizarro's successes was beginning to arrive in Europe, and they appointed Georg Hohermuth governor in Federmann's place, with Federmann, now cleared of the charges against him, as his second in command.

Federmann arrived at Coro on December 5, 1534, and Hohermuth on February 6, 1535. If indeed, as Federmann claimed, the Welsers had meant Federmann to be the governor and not the provisional governor, Hohermuth did not believe it. Not even a second royal investiture of Federmann as governor of the colony, issued November 5, 1535, was able to convince him, though it convinced Federmann. Hohermuth had promptly set out for the interior on May 13, 1535 ignoring (one can understand his suspicion) Federmann's advice and warnings that he was going the wrong way. Federmann, not to be outdone, resumed his own exploring in 1536 and reached his El Dorado, the city of Bogotá in 1538, only to find Gonzalo Jimínez de Quesada already there and in far better condition than Federmann and his tattered band.

The exploration of the New World had been given new impetus by the news of Pizarro's conquest of Peru in 1535, and the *conquistadores* all dreamed of another Inca Empire awaiting them. Federmann and Quesada, both full of these not unjustifiable dreams, decided to let their potential argument as to the possession of the treasure of Bogatá be settled in Spain and set out for that country in July of 1539. Federmann had not even bothered to visit the colony of which he was supposedly governor. Hohermuth's expedition had in the meantime been totally unsuccessful, and of the 400 who had set out only 160 returned, including Hohermuth, who did not, however, long survive the rigors of his experiences. He died in Coro on June 11, 1540[6] just after the arrest of Federmann by Bartholomäus Welser in Ghent.

Federmann's downfall appears to have been the result of continual accusations of cruelty and bad government made against him from Santo Domingo and by Hohermuth's reports on his behavior, for the brotherhood of nationality meant nothing to the disappointed Hohermuth. In addition, the Welser agent in Santo Domingo had reported that Federmann had grown very wealthy on money rightfully belonging to the Welser firm, whose employee he was. It was this latter charge on which, by old Bartholomäus' order, Federmann was imprisoned in Ghent in 1539. Federmann had the good sense to insist on a trial in Spain on all the charges, a request which was granted because of his position as a Spanish governor and by virtue of the fact that the charges of the Audiencia in Santo Domingo were more important to the Spanish Monarchy than Bartholomäus Welser's accusing purse.[7] Federmann returned to Sevilla where he died on February 27, 1542 while the trial dragged on. The charges against him were never proven, and though he did settle with the Welser firm just before his death, the settlement does not seem to have been overly harsh towards him.

The Welser firm lost, of course, their claims through Federmann to the Kingdom of Bogatá which proved to be almost as wealthy as the Inca Kingdom and which went to Quesada in 1547. In a very real sense this loss meant the end of the Welser colony in the New World. But Bartholomäus Welser Senior did not yet know this, though he, like the more cautious Fuggers before him, began to withdraw from his involvement in the New World, closing down the factory in Santo Domingo in 1540. Anti-German sentiment of the Spaniards accounts for some of the difficulties of the German attempts to colonize the land, but the low rate of profit (estimated for the eighteen years at nine percent) and continued high cost of equipping expeditions to supply the colony probably played the largest role in the Welsers' decision.

Bartholomäus Welser equipped one more large expedition under the command of his son, Bartholomäus Welser Junior. This expedition left Spain for Venezuela in 1540, where the governor *pro-tem* appointed by the Audiencia in Santo Domingo was Bishop Bastidas. The latter had named Philipp von Hutten, Ulrich's equally tragic older brother and previously a member of Hohermuth's ill-fated expedition, governor general and appointed Pedro de Limpias and Bartholomäus Welser Junior his captains.[8] Hutten promptly set out for the interior on August 1, 1541, betraying again the German lack of interest in colonial development, undoubtedly the real reason behind the ultimate failure of the German venture in Venezuela. The expedition, which lasted five years, was a fiasco, for Hutten insisted on setting off in the wrong direction, an inauspicious start from which the expedition never recovered. The control which Hutten exercised over the Spanish soldiery was apparently slight, and the eventual mutiny and desertion of Pedro de Limpias and a force of men not only went unpunished but had to be overlooked entirely even after the mutineers were obliged to return to the main force. When the remnant of the expedition did finally return to the region around Coro, they had long been given up for dead, and a deputy of Bishop Bastidas, Juan de Caraval, had assumed complete command of the colony. Caraval had finally led the majority of the colonists, all but the old and infirm, away from the fever-ridden region of Coro to a new settlement at Tocuyo in 1545.

The Audiencia in the meantime had been obliged several times to send investigators to the Venezuelan colony to look into the constant complaints of the colonists against the government, and thus were compiling a file by which the Welser grip on the region could be removed. On December 3, 1545 the royal judge, de Frías, arrived in the ghost town of Coro to begin a full inquiry into the conditions in the entire colony. This resulted in an abrogation by the Audiencia in Santo Domingo on January 28, 1546 of all the Welsers' rights to the colony which then reverted to the Spanish Crown.[9] Although this judgment was later set aside in a subsequent major investigation under Tolosa, its substance was set into action at once, and the judgment itself was renewed in Spain by the Council of the Indies on April 13, 1556. Caraval had, shortly after Hutten's departure from Coro in 1541, begun to assume all the responsibilities for the administration of the colony and named himself royal commissioner on January 1, 1545. Although more complicated than its end may seem, the result of this action and Hutten's miraculous reappearance near Coro in 1546 led to a conflict with Caraval, who eventually murdered Hutten, Welser, and their Spanish comrades near Quibore outside Coro. Caraval was later brought to trial and executed in vivid Spanish style on September 17, 1546, but the German colony in Venezuela was finished.

Although the Welsers did attempt to regain their rights to the colony, Juan de Villasinda was appointed governor of Venezuela in the King's name in 1554 without consultation with the Welsers. The repeated accusations of the Spaniards against the German firm and its governors concerned the lack of responsible help in the development of colonies on the land, and indeed there is much evidence which supports this view. The Welser firm did not long survive the failure of its American venture. Grown overcautious perhaps because of the venture in the New World, the firm refused to make loans to the pope and then to the emperor at critical moments, and its leaders failed to give clear indications of support for the "true religion." When, at the death of Charles V, the impoverished empire suffered another financial collapse, it took much of the Welsers' fortune down with it. The Spanish crown went bankrupt in 1557, and the Welsers were able to collect only five percent of their credits. Paul and Marcus Welser were imprisoned, the former to die in jail in 1620 and the latter to die in poverty at the age of eighty in 1633.

For all the activity of German banking houses in the New World from 1529 until the collapse of the Welser firm at the conclusion of the reign of Charles V, few Germans actually were ever directly involved in the expeditions themselves, and of those few only three published accounts of their experiences for the world at home in German lands to marvel at. Two of those who did publish accounts of their activities were German mercenary soldiers of no particular distinction within their expeditions. Only one high-ranking German, sometime governor Nikolaus Federmann had his account published posthumously by his brother-in-law in 1557. Even then, Federmann's *Indianische Historia*[10] dealt only with his first voyage with Georg Ehinger in 1529.

Federmann's account of his own rather successful expedition, undertaken illegally in September 1530 while proper authority was unable to intervene, reads like an uninspired Xenophonic anabasis, for Federmann dwells long on the number of miles covered and the names of Indian tribes met, but seldom gives any description of customs or of events which are not of essential military importance. It is easy to see why this slim volume did not have more than one edition in 16th-century Germany and is now among the most difficult of the three first-hand German accounts of the conquest to obtain. Federmann does mention the calamitous epidemic of "viroles," presumably smallpox, which had reduced the total Indian population of the area from 500,000 to a mere 20,000 according to Federmann's Indian sources. He also admits that inter-tribal warfare and the charity of the Christians particularly, put an end to many more:

> ain grosser thail (seyent gestorbn) auss übertribener arbait/ darzu sie die Christen/ in den Goldbergwercken/ genöttigt/ welches doch wider ihre gewonhait ist/ dan sie von art/ ain zart un wenig arbaitent volck gewest ist/ . . . (B II versa — B III)

Federmann's treatment of the Indians, for which among other things he was twice brought to trial, he himself characterizes as fair, and by Spanish standards it probably was, though occasionally one reads between the lines, as for example when he writes:

> Unnd zwo meil von dannen/ erraichten wir einen Pueblo oder flecken/ darinnen ein reicher Cacique oder landtherr wonen

solte/ denen vermainten wir zu überfallen/ un auch also wie die
andern zu freünde zubringen/ . . . (D II)

In yet another case he writes:

Sandte ich einen haubtman mit fünffzig der bas gerüsten männern zufuss/ sampt ainen Tolmetschen diser Nation/ das sie die
Zwergen mit lieb unnd freindschafft/ und wa nicht füglich/ mit
gewalt für mich zubringen/ . . . .
aldar wartet ich biss an den andern tag/ das was auff den fünfften
tag Octobris/ der aussgesandten/ die khamen abendts spat/
brachten ob die hundert und fünfftzig personen/ manne und
weiber/ welche sie in einem flecken/ bei fünff meil von dem
flecke da ich innen lage/ hetten uberfallen/ unnd als sie sich zu
wehr gestelt/ und freiwillig mich haimzusuchen/ un für mich zu-
khumen/ nicht wolten begeben/ gefangen/ ettwa vil im scharmützel erschlagen/ und auch der Christen etlich von ihnen auch
gewundet . . . . (E II).

Genuine concern for the souls of these Indians unfortunate
enough to be befriended by the white men characterized most of
the *conquistadores,* though Federmann's description of the pragmatic side of this problem of soul-saving is more honest than that
which can be read in many tracts. Of the aforementioned absent
Cacique or lord, who was, of course, found, he writes:

Disen Cacique oder herren/ sampt allem seinem mitgebrachtem
volck/ liess ich täuffen/ und sovil sichs lasst einbilden/ vom
Christlichen glauben sagen/ Dann was ist nott/ ihnen lang zu-
predigen/ und zeit mit ihnen zuverlieren/ dann solchs muss/
. . . . (D IV).

Of the incredible hardships, hunger, thirst, disease, etc., Federmann makes little mention. He was hard on his troops, as we know
from the charges brought against him, but equally hard on himself—the ideal soldier. He appears to have contracted malaria but
allowed himself little notice of it other than to take an occasional
rest when the hot and cold spells came over him. Seldom does he
mention the appearance of the Indians, though on one occasion he
remarks of the Caquetios:

Ist ein volck vast gutter lenge un proportz/ auch starcker

dispusion and glidmässig/ Auch vast schöne gerade weiber/
(N III)

But Federmann had been in the jungle a long time at this point,
and there were no laws against fraternization, as the population of
Brazil testifies to this day. His recollections carefully include descriptions of his attempts to be fair to the Indians, not to incite
them against him (cf. F III, G II/III, etc.), though his usual methods for making initial acquaintance included the forcible seizure of
a few Indians from the tribe about to be visited. The coastal
Indians were already well aware that the appearance of a strange
looking ship meant capture and enslavement for them.

> Wir kundten aber die selbige nacht nichts erwarten/ dan die
> Indios/ als sie das schiff ersehen/ hetten sie sich in ihre flecken
> un gewarsam gethon/ besorgend alls offt von Santo Domingo
> auss beschehen/ ain raubschiff were/ und umb sie auffzuheben/
> zufahen und zuverkauffen aldar komen/ (B III)

Only once does a bit of cynical humor escape from Federmann's
pen and then only to describe the perils of a monk accompanying
the expedition who rashly attempted to drive a jaguar away from
his prey so that he might have it for himself and who was saved by
a thick jungle vine of which Federmann remarks laconically:

> welches dieses Münchs glück was/ dann sonst were ihm seiner
> zuvil fraidigkait gelonet worden/ . . . (O III)

More impressive as a documentary account of 16th-century
America is the often published work of Ulrich Schmidel of
Straubing, like Federmann a Bavarian who spent twenty consecu-
tive years in the New World as a gunner, first with Pedro de
Mendoza's expedition to the River Plata, which contemporaries
prayed might be the long-sought passage to the Indies. After
Mendoza's death while returning to Europe, Schmidel continued
his mercenary service with whomever his immediate troop captain
obeyed. His book, *Neuwe Welt: Das ist/ Beschreibung aller schönen
Historien* . . .[11], was first published in 1567 and several times again
in the 16th and also in the 17th centuries. Schmidel's odyssey began in 1534 when he left home and joined Mendoza's large force of
2500 Spaniards and "150 Hochteutsche, Niderländer und Sachsen"
(B I) sailing to Brazil in fourteen ships.

Unter diesen 14. Schiffen hat eins zugehört/ Herren Sebastian Neidhart/ und Jacoben Welser zu Nürnberg/ ... Mit denen bin ich und andere/ als Hochteutsche und Niderländer ungefehrlich biss in die 80. Mann wolgerüst/ mit Büchsen unnd gewehr/ nach Riodellaplata gefaren. (B)

Schmidel spent his years experiencing all the incredible hardships of those first explorers, being several times shipwrecked and constantly attacked by "treacherous" Indians. He seems never to have minded either hazard very much. Like all those early soldier-explorers he faced enormous odds with great self-confidence relying largely on the guns and horses to drive away the Indians. His account too suffers from the shortcomings of Xenophonic travel accounts, though he is far more personal and observant than Federmann. He relates the story of Amazons, and accompanies an unsuccessful expedition to find the fictional maidens behind this sly Indian legend.

Dieser Amazones Weiber haben nur eine Brust/ und komen zu jren Weibern die Männer 3. oder 4. mal im Jar/ und so sie mit einem Knaben/ von dem Mann schwanger wirdt/ so schicket sie denselben nach der geburt jhrem Mann heym.

Ist es aber ein Mägdlin/ so behalten sie es bey jhnen/ und brennen jhnen die rechte Brust auss/ damit sie nicht wider kan wachsen. Dessen aber is die ursach/ das sie köndten (und meynen) jre gewehr un Bogen brauchen/ dann es seind streitbare Weiber/ und führen Krieg wider jhre feinde. (D I)

He of course, plunders, though at times tactfully:

Wir hetten gern mehr von jhnen begert/ durfttens aber nicht thun/ dan es waren unser Christen zu wenig/ mustens derohalben fürchten/ (D II)

The Brechtian vagaries of the mercenary soldier's life, encompassing brutal eroticism and excessive cruelty, are well reflected in the following two passages in the first of which he relates the misadventures of a captain who was presented with three young girls by a native chief:

Darnach hin/ umb mitternacht/ hatte unser Hauptmann seine 3. Metzen verloren/ hatt sie villeicht nicht alle drey zufriden stellen können/ dann es war ein Mann von 60. Jaren/ hette er sie under uns knechte gelassen/ villeicht weren sie nicht darvon gelauffen/ In suma es war derowegen ein grosse auffruhr im läger/ (D IIII)

In the second anecdote he tells of the fate of an Indian tribe mistaken for a tribe which had previously attacked an expedition:

Also fanden wir am 3. tag die Maijaijos bey einander/ Mann/ Weib unnd Kinder/ in einem Wald/ aber sie waren nicht die rechten Maijaji/ sonder ihre freunde. Diese besorgten sich unser gar nicht/ das wir zu jhnen kommen würden/ also must der unschuldig des schuldigen entgelten/ dann da wir zu diesen Maijajiis kamen/ schlugen wir sie zu todt/ und namen gefangen/ Mann/ Weib/ unnd Kindt/ biss in die 3000. Personen/ unnd wenn es tag wer gewesen/ als nacht/ so were jhr keiner darvon kommen/ . . . .
Ich brachte in diesem Scharmützel mehr dan 19. personen/ Mann und Weiber/ die nit fast alt waren darvon/ (E)

After nineteen years of soldiering, Schmidel was reluctantly released from Spanish service through the help of a Fugger agent in Sevilla, and he left the expedition December 26, 1552, with twenty Indian slaves among his plunder. He spent six months journeying through Brazil from Buenos Aires to Sao Vincente from where he took a Portuguese ship and reached Europe only after numerous storms and other troubles which culminated when a ship bearing most of his plunder was accidently wrecked off the Spanish coast. He arrived in Holland whence he had set out, on January 26, 1554. Schmidel's tale was a publishing success and must have been a well known piece of travel literature in the second half of the 16th century, contributing significantly to the popular image of the New World in Germany.

Far less influential, to judge by the lack of editions, was the most amazing and interesting story of Hans Staden's *Warhafftig Historia und beschreibung eyner Landtschafft der Wilden/Nacketen/ Grimmigen Menschfresser Leuthen/ in der Newenwelt America gelegen.*[12] Staden made two voyages, the first with the Portuguese from April 1547 to October 1548, and describes his motivation for this first trip as follows:

Ich Hans Staden von Homberg in Hessen/ name mir vor/ Wens Gott gefellig were/ Indiam zu besehen/ zoge der meynung von Bremen nach Holandt/ zu Campen kame ich bey schiffe die wolten in Portugal saltz laden . . ./ (G)

His first voyage, as a gunner with two other Germans in a Portuguese trading vessel was uneventful by comparison with what was to come. That second voyage, in Spanish service, left Spain in 1549 four days after Easter and arrived after difficulties with weather and navigation in Portuguese Brazil on November 24, 1549. The expedition's ships, separated by storms, did not reassemble. Staden was to spend two miserable years on the Island of St. Catharine off the Brazilian coast until help was secured from the nearby Portuguese colony at Sao Vincente. He took up Portuguese service on the Island of St. Marco as a gunner in the beleaguered fortress of the small settlement where he lived for a time in relative comfort, a seeming idyll which ended when he was captured by cannibalistic Indians. He was to remain their captive until 1554.

Staden's narrative power is considerable as is his abiding trust in God's mercy. He describes his capture by the Indians as follows:

Wie ich nun so durch den waldt gieng/ erhub sich uff beyden seiten der wegs ein gross geschrey auff der wilden leut gebrauch/ un kamen zu mir ingelauffen/ da erkante ich sie/ und sie hatten mich alle rund umb her bezirckt/ und jhre bogen uff mich mit pfeilen gehalten/ schossen zu mir ein. Da ruffet ich/ Nun helff Gott meiner seelen. Ich hatte das wort kaum so bald aussgesagt/ sie schlugen mich zur erden/ schossen und stachen uff mich/ Noch verwundeten sie mich/ (Gott lob) nit mehr/ dann in ein beyn/ und rissen mir die Kleyder vom Leib/ . . . . Dan so wolten sie mich Kawewi pepicke töten/ Das ist/ sie wolten gedrencke machen/ und sich versamlen/ ein Fest zumachen/ und mich dann mit eynander essen/ (C III)

Immediately threatened with death and with being eaten, he never lost his keen power of observation or his "gift of gab" which together with chance or "God's mercy" saved him again and again from the pot. His nightmare continued the entire time of his captivity, and the meal, at which he was to be both host and main course, was constantly a part of his anguish. He was reassured at the outset that he was not to be eaten right away. But he was made on several occasions to observe the rites at which he was eventually to be slaughtered and vividly describes those rites. He also records poignantly his attempts to comfort two Christian Portuguese who were eventually to be killed and eaten.

The second part of his book is a fine description of the New World by a writer with a gift for expression unusual in 16th century German. The following two passages describe America in general and the rites at which Staden was to be consumed:

> America is eyn grosses Land/ hat vil geschlecht Wilder leut/ . . . .
> Es hat im landt etliche früchte der erden unnd beume/ darvon
> sich die leut und Thier erneren/ die leuthe des landes sein rod-
> brauner Farbe am Leibe/ der Sonnen halben/ welche sie so ver-
> brennet/ ein gerades volck/ listig zu aller bossheyt/ sehr geneigt
> jhre feinde zu verfolgen un zu essen/ (P)

The second passage is the general description of the slaughter and cannibalization of their enemies:

> Darnach kompt eyn fraw mit den holtz Iwera Pemme gelauffen/
> keret die Fedderquesten inn die höhe/ kreuschet von freuden/
> lauffet vor dem gefangenen uber/ das er es sehen sol. Wann das
> geschehen ist/ so nimpt eyn Mans person das holtz/ gehet mit
> vor den gefangenen stehen/ helt es vor jnen/ das ers ansihet/
> dieweil gehet der/ welcher jnen todtschlagen wil/ hin/ selb 14.
> oder 15. und machen jre leib graw mit äschen/ denn kompt er
> mit seinem zucht gesellen uff den platz bey den gefangenen/ so
> uberliffert der ander so vor de gefangnen steht/ diesem das
> holtz/ so kompt dann der Künig der hütten/ und nimpt das
> holtz/ und steckts dem/ der den gefangenen sol todtschlagen/
> eynmal zwischen den beynen her/ welches nun eyn ehr unter
> jnen ist/ Dan nimpt der widerumb das holtz/ der den todt-
> schlagen sol/ und sagt dann/ Ja hie bin ich/ ich wil dich tödten/
> dann die deinen haben meiner freunde auch vil getödtet und
> gessen/ antwortet er/ wann ich todt bin/ so habe ich noch vil
> freunde/ die werden mich wol rechen/ darmit schlecht er jnen
> hinden auff den Kopff/ das jm das hirn darauss springt/ als bald
> nemen jn die weiber/ zihen jn auff das fewer/ kratze jm die haut
> alle ab/ machen jn gantz weiss/ stopfen jm den hindersten mit
> eynem holtze zu/ auff das jm nichts entgehet. (T II/III)

It is strange to note that Staden's book, contrary to its modern vogue, was not to enjoy much success in his own time. Three printings were made of it, all in 1557, but no others followed.

If it is valid to assume that 16th-century German interest in America was reliably reflected by contemporary authors, we may conclude that it was indeed slight, a fact which alone is worthy of comment and explanation. German political and economic interests in the 16th century were largely inwardly directed, and the Fuggers' withdrawal from the overlordship of half the South American continent in favor of relatively minor Hungarian trading interests is but symptomatic of this continental European interest. The rigors of the Reformation, Counter-Reformation, mid-century economic troubles, and the events leading eventually to the Thirty Years' War all contributed to German neglect of America at this time. That same Thirty Years' War eliminated a precondition for colonization which Carl Bridenbaugh has found for early 17th-century Englishmen—overpopulation of the land.[13] What interest Germans did take in the New World was financial, ending when a northwest or southwest passage proved unfindable, and the whole Welser colony failed. Thereafter America represented for a very few an interesting natural wonder about which cosmographers and navigational enthusiasts were excited. For many, America meant travel literature about a place one would only like to read about. It is sad to speculate that Staden's report of a land of savage, naked, vicious people-eaters has not lost all of its applicability to this continent and that there may still be many people, particularly those in Asia who would be compelled in light of modern happenings to agree with Staden's assessment.

NOTES

1. Cf. Richard Ehrenberg: *Capital and Finance in the Age of the Renaissance*, trans. H. M. Lucas (New York, 1928).

2. Germán Arciniegas: *Germans in the Conquest of America* (New York, 1943), p. 47.

3. Arciniegas; Juan Friede: *Los Welser en la Conquista de Venezuela* (Caracas, Madrid, 1961); Karl Panhorst: *Los alemanes en Venezuela* (Madrid, 1927); Erich Reimers: *Die Welser landen in Venezuela. Das erste deutsche Kolonialunternehmen* (Leipzig, 1938); Karl Rossmann: *Vom Handel der Welser um die Wende zum 16. Jahrhundert* (München, 1933); Hugo von Waldeyer Hartz: *Die Welser in Venezuela* (Berlin, 1927); Josef Weiss: "Süddeutsche Kaufleute und Feldhauptleute in Venezuela, 1528–1556," in *Bayernland*, 24/1-4 (München, 1912); Jules Humbert: *L'Occupation Allemand du Venezuela au XVIe Siècle* (Bordeaux & Paris, 1905).

4. Arciniegas, *op. cit.;* Friede, *op. cit.;* Reimers, *op. cit.*

5. Friede writes of Federmann and the Germans generally: "Nosotros, con el propósito que tenemos de narrar y explicar los trechos, sin emitir juicios personales sobre su vida y obra, no podemos, menos de exaltar el importante papel que jugó aquel alemán en la historia del descubrimiento y conquista de las actuales repúblicas de Colombia y de Venezuela. Sus expediciones pusieron las bases para la futura colonización de varios territorios. Su arrojo y valor personal fueron ejemplares. . . . Los delitos que ciñeron a las circunstancias que encontró el Nuevo Mundo. . . . Su valerosa oposición a la poderosa casa monopolista de los Welser merece admiración; actuó como el hombre renacentista, que revindica el derecho del individuo para recoger los frutos de sus trabajos y desvelos." p. 335.

6. Friede quotes the epitaph of Hohermuth (Formut):

En aquesta sepultura
yace George Formut, vaso lleno e virtud
mas vacío de ventura.
Ser varón de fuerte pecho,
su nombre nos lo decía,
mas a su nombre vencía
la grandeza de su hecho.
Fué de la ciudad de Espira
de alemana parentela
y dentro, de Venezuela
le llegó la fatal ira. p. 373

7. Cf. Friede, pp. 441 ff. Cf. also Hieronimus Benzoni: *Historia von der newen Welt* in De Bry (Frankfurt/M., 1594), "Das ander Buch Das Sechste Capitel; Wie ettlich Teutschen der Spanier Exempel und Sitten seyen nachgefolget/ und die Indianer auch auff mancherley Weg geplaget. Durch deren Schmachheit die Indianer seind verursachet worden von jhnen abzufallen/ un

jnen selbs den Todt angethan." This chapter contains evidence from contemporaries of the ill-will of the Spaniards against the German *conquistadores*.

8. Cf. Friede, pp. 375 ff.

9. Cf. Friede, pp. 47–48.

10. Niclaus Federmann: Indianische Historia, Sigmund Bund (Hagenau, 1557).

11. Ulrich Schmidel: *Neuwe Welt: Das ist, Wahrhafftige Beschreibung aller schönen Historien von erfündung viler unbekannten Königreichen,* Sigmund Feyrabend (Frankfurt/M., 1567).

12. Andreas Kolben (Marburg, 1557).

13. Carl Bridenbaugh: *Vexed and Troubled Englishmen.* New York, 1968.

2. Deutsche Einwanderung nach Mexico in vier Jahrhunderten
Marianne O. de Bopp

Schon im Jahrhundert der Eroberung kamen Deutsche nach Mexico; sie kämpften unter den Soldaten des Cortés, halfen als Mönche verschiedener Orden bei der Christianisierung der Indianer und arbeiteten als Handwerker, Bergleute und Drucker. Um 1510 bereits hatte Spanien seine Kolonien hermetisch gegen jeden ausländischen Einfluß abgeriegelt. Ein königliches Dekret beschränkte die Einwanderung aufs strengste und machte sie von Nationalität und Religion abhängig. Angst vor kriegerischen Einfällen und der Wunsch, die mühselige Christianisierung der Indianer von den damaligen theologischen Wirren Europas frei zu halten, führten dazu, daß jeder Passagier auf spanischen Galeeren eine besondere Erlaubnis erlangen und nachgewiesenermaßen blut- wie ideenmäßig frei von ketzerischer Ansteckung sein mußte. Von 1518 an wird die Einreise in die Kolonien verboten: für jeden *reconciliado,*[1] jeden neu bekehrten Mauren oder Juden, seine Kinder oder Enkel, alle jemals zum Tragen des *Sambenito*[2] Verurteilten, alle Kinder oder Enkel, in männlicher oder weiblicher Linie, eines auf dem Scheiterhaufen der Inquisition Gerichteten, für jeden wegen ketzerischer Ideen Verdammten, für alle Zigeuner, sowie ihre Kinder und Diener. Am Ende des 16. Jahrhunderts werden illegale Passagiere zu vierjähriger Galeerenstrafe verurteilt, wenn sie Plebejer, und zu zehn Jahren Gefängnis in Oran, wenn sie adlig sind. Auch der Schiffskapitän, der sie mitnimmt, wird bestraft. Das Dekret wird im 16. und 17. Jahrhundert mehrmals erneuert. Von 1660 an dürfen weder Untertanen des Königs noch Ausländer ohne ausdrückliche Erlaubnis und Prüfung durch Richter der "Casa de Contratación" in die Kolonien reisen; von 1600 an kein Ausländer mit Mexico Handel treiben, kein ausländisches Schiff in einem Hafen Neuspaniens landen, und alle Fremden ohne Spezialerlaubnis sollten, nach der "Recopilación de Indias," ebenso mit dem Tode bestraft werden, wie die Kaufleute, die mit ihnen Geschäfte machten; ihre Güter wurden eingezogen. Nicht einmal die Kolonien untereinander durften Handel treiben. Die spanische Politik stützte sich auf ihr Handelsmonopol, dessen Folgen auf die Dauer den Ruin der Kolonien bedeuteten. Aber kein Dekret konnte verhindern, daß trotzdem Ausländer in die Kolonien kamen. In diesem Zeitalter der Entdeckungen wanderten zahlreiche Deutsche nach Spanien und Portugal, vor allem nach Sevilla, neben Cadiz Ausgangshafen aller überseeischen Unternehmen. Die Häuser der Fugger und Welser, denen Karl V. verpflichtet war, beteiligten sich an spanischen und portugiesischen Expeditionen. In Sevilla bildete sich eine große deutsche Kolonie von Angestellten der Handelshäuser und Seeleuten. Schon 1528 reisten deutsche Bergknappen aus Joachimsthal nach Santo Domingo, Venezuela und Columbien, ebenso wie 1536 nach Mexico. Dazu holte die Kolonialverwaltung spanische, flämische, italienische und deutsche Handwerker in die Kronländer, die mit indianischen Gesellen arbeiten und ihre Fertigkeiten dort heimisch machen sollten. Zwischen den europäischen Nationalitäten der Eroberer zu unterscheiden, fiel den Indianern allerdings ebenso schwer wie den Kolonisatoren die Unterscheidung der Indianerstämme. Zur Feier eines zehnjährigen Waffenstillstands zwischen dem französischen König und dem Kaiser führen Indianer in Mexico 1539 eine "Eroberung Jerusalems" auf; in der Prozession des spanischen Heeres mit den Fahnen der einzelnen Länder marschieren auch Deutsche und Italiener—die aber, da die Indianer niemals wissentlich Deutsche gesehen hatten, alle als spanische Soldaten auftreten.

1531 wurde das königliche Dekret verkündet, das die Einfuhr von "romanhaften Büchern, wertlosen oder profanen Geschichten, wie etwa des Amadís und anderer" verbot, "da sie den Indianern ein schlechtes Vorbild bieten und es schädlich ist, daß sie sich damit beschäftigen oder sie lesen." Aber es sind vor allem die ketzerischen Gedanken, deren Eindringen verhindert werden soll. Auf Erlaß Philipps II. durfte nach 1558 in Spanien kein gedrucktes Werk mehr ohne Genehmigung des *Consejo Real* erscheinen. Jedes Buch erforderte kirchliche und Inquisitions-Erlaubnis, über die erst nach Eingabe des Werkes mit eingehender Inhaltsangabe und Begründung seiner Tendenz entschieden wurde. Dabei hatte sich die Kunst des Buchdrucks bereits erstaunlich schnell in den Kolonien des spanischen Reiches verbreitet. Schon am Anfang des 15. Jahrhunderts gab es deutsche Drucker in Spanien. In der deutschen Kolonie von Sevilla arbeiteten neben anderen die Druckereien der drei Cromberger aus Nürnberg. Jacob Cromberger sollte schon 1525 mit offizieller Genehmigung in die neue Welt fahren, konnte aber seine Pläne nicht durchführen. Sein Sohn Johann lernte in Sevilla den späteren Erzbischof von Mexico, Fray Juan de Zumárraga, kennen, der ihn veranlaßte, in Neuspanien eine Druckerei einzurichten, in der wahrscheinlich (um 1539) das erste Buch auf amerikanischem Boden gedruckt wurde.

Aber trotz mancher Ausnahme blieben die Kolonien weitgehend isoliert, für lange Zeit ausgeschlossen von der industriellen, wissenschaftlichen, technischen, politischen und künstlerischen Entwicklung der europäischen Länder, ahnungslos oder spät unterrichtet von den Erschütterungen der Welt. Die Kolonialregierung wollte nicht nur die Indianer in Abhängigkeit halten, sondern auch verhindern, daß das gedruckte Wort zum gefährlichen Instrument der Gedankenfreiheit werden könnte. Deshalb schürte der religiöse Fanatismus der Inquisition auch den Haß gegen die Einwanderer aus Europa, die wegen der Verfolgungen von Juden, Morisken und Protestanten Zuflucht in der neuen Welt suchten. Bereits 1593 wurde ein deutscher Bergmann, Michel Redlich aus Guben in Böhmen, ins Gefängnis der Inquisition eingeliefert, als Lutheraner zum öffentlichen Abschwören seines Glaubens, vier Jahren Klostergefängnis und Tragen einer Mönchskutte verurteilt und sein Vermögen (23 Mark 5 Unzen Silber) konfisziert.

Unter den englischen, französischen und holländischen Piraten, deren unaufhörliche Einfälle an den Küsten für die vizekönigliche Regierung problematisch blieb, waren Protestanten mit deutschen Namen, die 1572 der Inquisition überantwortet werden. Noch 1682 erhielt der Virrey, Conde de Paredes, die alarmierende Nachricht, daß der Bischof von Brandenburg sieben Kriegsgaleeren nach Neuspanien ausgesandt hätte, um sich für den Sold der im Flandrischen Krieg Spanien zur Verfügung gestellten Hilfstruppen zu entschädigen; nachdem er ein spanisches Schiff in Ostende gekapert hatte, wollte er tatsächlich unter der Maske des Verbündeten, einige Häfen Neuspaniens besetzen. Der Virrey bereitete sich zur Verteidigung vor, aber die brandenburgische Armada kam nur bis zum Kanal von Bahama und kehrte dann nach Europa zurück.[3]

Am Ende des 16. Jahrhunderts kommt der heute noch etwas mysteriöse Kosmograph und Drucker Enrico Martínez nach Mexico, der wahrscheinlich aus Hamburg stammte, und 1589 mit dem Titel eines Königlichen Kosmographen seine wissenschaftliche Tätigkeit aufnimmt, der Inquisition als Dolmetscher dient und vor allem eine wichtige, wenn auch undankbare Rolle bei der Entwässerung des Tales von Mexico spielt. Obwohl sein Werk noch Humboldts Bewunderung hervorruft, wird er als Direktor der Arbeiten zweimal eingekerkert. Gleichfalls unsicher ist die Herkunft des Jesuitenpaters Francisco Eusebio Kino (Kühn?), der am Ende des 17. Jahrhunderts zwanzig Dörfer im Norden Mexicos gründet und damit große Bedeutung für die mexikanische Kolonisierung der Nordprovinzen gewinnt.

Anfang des 17. Jahrhunderts gibt eine *Cédula Real* Ausländern mit Spezialerlaubnis die Genehmigung, sich in den Provinzen ihrer Wahl (ausgenommen die Seehäfen) anzusiedeln und Handel zu treiben,[4] wenngleich 1670 versucht wird, mittellose oder Kaufleute mit geringen Mitteln für legitimen Handel an der Einwanderung zu verhindern, "da sie nur den Handel schädigen und die Kolonien mit unerwünschten Vagabunden bevölkern." Soweit ausländische Einwanderung nicht völlig untersagt war, wurde sie möglichst erschwert, und in der Zeit des Virreinats bleiben die meisten Einwanderer anonym. Der fanatische Kampf um die koloniale Traditionen gefährdenden Ideen ist noch im 18. Jahrhundert in vollem Gange, auch wenn die strengsten Vorschriften langsam gelockert werden und katholische Ausländer sich niederlassen dürfen. Der Einfluß der Kirche, von der der stärkste Widerstand ausgeht, beginnt vor den Ideen der Aufklärung zurückzuweichen. Noch immer waren alle Bücher strengster Zensur unterworfen, die wenigen Schulen und Druckereien von Regierung und Kirche kontrolliert. Aber die Schriften Voltaires, Rousseaus und der Enzyklopädisten gelangten trotz aller Verbote, heimlich in Weinfässern und Kisten eingeschmuggelt, in die unruhig werdenden Kolonien.

1780 werden deutsche Bergleute aus Freiberg von der spanischen Krone nach Mexico gesandt, um die Methoden der Silbergewinnung zu verbessern. Fausto de Elhuyar, Direktor und Gründer des *Colegio de Minería,* hatte in Freiberg studiert und holt Friedrich Sonnenschmid, Fischer und Lidner ins Land, die durch ihre metallurgischen Entdeckungen und Verfahren bekannt werden. Beiträge von Sonnenschmid erscheinen seit 1793 immer wieder in den Zeitungen; 1805 veröffentlicht er ein "Tratado de amalgamación de la Nueva España" und lehrt am Colegio de Minería, ebenso wie Lidner, der am Bergbauseminar als Professor und Lehrer für Chemie und Mineralogie arbeitet.

Im Jahre 1790 leben 2335 Europäer in Mexico;[5] Humboldt zählt 2500 weiße Europäer,[6] aber die Zahl der Deutschen darunter bleibt unbedeutend. In der Hauptstadt wohnt Don Enrique Kors, Orgel- und Klavierbauer, der auch andere Instrumente repariert und stimmt; 1790 berichten die "Gacetas de México," daß alle Christen über Juan Samuel Suhr in Sombrerete jubeln, der im deutschen Kaiserreich, im Elektorat Sachsen, im protestantischen Glauben geboren, den Irrtümern des Luthertums abgeschworen hat und zum katholischen Bekenntnis übergetreten ist.

Eine Persönlichkeit wie Humboldt trägt natürlich dazu bei, das Interesse Europas auf Mexico zu lenken. Seine Empfehlungen an den Vizekönig Iturrigaray, seine Beziehungen zu den Gelehrten Mexicos öffnen ihm alle Türen, und er gibt Geschichtsschreibung, Geographie und wissenschaftlicher Erforschung aller außereuropäischen Kulturen neue Anregungen. Auch Goethe interessiert sich für seine Beobachtungen in Mexico. Später erweitert Johann Moritz Rugendas, der ursprünglich als offizieller Zeichner und Maler sechs Jahre lang die amerikanischen Länder bereist und im Mai 1831 begeistert die Landschaften und Denkmäler der alten Kulturen festhält, Europas Kenntnisse über Mexico.

Aber das alles sind Sonderfälle. Die napoleonische Invasion Spaniens erregt eine Welle von Intoleranz, die alle Ausländer trifft. 1809 veröffentlichen die "Gacetas de México" ein Dekret des Virreys Garibay, wonach "gehorsam unseren weisen Gesetzen, die Einreise von Ausländern, besonders Franzosen, zu verhindern ist, da die meisten von ihnen entweder Atheisten, aufklärerische Freimaurer, Sansculotten oder Jacobiner, auf jeden Fall Feinde von Altar, Thron und Eigentum sind ... und blinde Anhänger jenes blasphemischen Ungeheuers der Unordnung und Pestilenz, Napoleon Bonaparte...." Weder im Haven von Veracruz noch in den übrigen Häfen Neuspaniens darf ein Ausländer landen, vor allem aber keiner, der in einem der jetzt von Napoleon beherrschten Länder geboren wurde, selbst wenn er aus spanischen Häfen und mit Pässen spanischer Gouverneure in Amerika versehen, oder als Diener spanischer Bürger oder der Schiffskommandanten kommt. Alle Ausländer müssen sich registrieren lassen, und ihre Angaben werden überprüft. Noch 1814 fürchtet man "Vertrauensleute von Bonaparte, die mit dem Auftrag kommen, die Seele der Mexicaner zu vergiften."[7] In der Stadt Veracruz läuft das Gerücht um, daß ein bekannter Militär-Agent heimlich an Land gegangen sei, so daß die Regierungspolizei einen armen Schneider aufgreift und ins Gefängnis wirft. Noch 1824 erleidet der Deutsche Wilhelm Stein bei seiner Ankunft das gleiche Schicksal, für einen französischen Spion gehalten und verhaftet zu werden.

Die Trennung vom Mutterlande wandelt aber die Stimmung zumindest der Gebildeten Mexicos, die geistige Verbindung mit Europa fordern, obwohl Morelos in der Konstitution von Apatzingan (1814) nur den Ausländern mexikanisches Bürgerrecht zugestehen will, die Anhänger der Unabhängigkeit des Landes und katholisch sind. Ob auch Spanier als Ausländer gelten, bleibt dabei offen. Auch die Monarchie Iturbides neigt zu liberalen Ideen hinsichtlich der Einwanderung. Schon seit 1819 kommen schweizerische und deutsche Kolonisten. Auch nach der Entthronung Iturbides 1824 sind die Intellektuellen und Politiker der neuen Republik überzeugt von der Notwendigkeit der Kolonisation durch Fremde, die die Bevölkerung vermehren, verbessern und die menschenarmen Landstriche für Mexico sichern kann; liberale Gesetze würden zweifellos große Gruppen von Europäern nach Mexico führen, in die mächtigste, größte und liberalste Republik Amerikas, und das gleiche Resultat wirtschaftlichen und kulturellen Fortschritts erreichen wie bereits in den Vereinigten Staaten.[8] Die Konstitution von 1823/24 verweigert aber Einwanderern weiter jede religiöse Toleranz. Ein bereits 1822 entworfenes allgemeines Kolonisierungs-Gesetz, das Mexicos Grenzen öffnet, wird auf Vorschlag des Präsidenten der Republik, Guadalupe Victoria, vom Kongreß angenommen, sieht aber gewisse Beschränkungen des Erwerbs von Grund und Boden vor und fordert wieder für die Einbürgerung den katholischen Glauben; es tritt aber erst 1828 in Kraft.

1822 wird die Bergwerksagentur von Louis Sulzer und F. G. Schneider gegründet, und 1824 kommt die erste Gruppe deutscher Bergleute und Kolonisten, 1826 die nächste, deren Mehrzahl gleich

in den ersten Jahren Mexikanerinnen heiratete und im Lande so
heimisch wurde, daß sie ihre deutsche Staatsangehörigkeit aufgab.
Gerade in diesen Jahren veranlaßten die reaktionären Karlsbader
Beschlüsse viele Liberale zur Auswanderung nach Amerika: Mit-
glieder der Geheimgesellschaften oder der illegalen Burschenschaf-
ten, Teilnehmer am Wartburgfest, Anhänger des berühmten Karl
Follen. Die meisten dieser Liberalen gingen nach den Vereinigten
Staaten. Nach Mexico kommen 1827–28 jährlich nur 704 Aus-
länder.[9] Zu den deutschen Einwanderern gehören Carl Sartorius,
Gymnasiallehrer, Friedrich Wilhelm Grube, Privatlehrer, Wilhelm
Stein mit einem Bergwerksdiplom; sein Bruder Gustav Christian
und als sein Gehilfe Friedrich von Gerolt, ebenfalls diplomierter
Minenfachmann (der bei der Agentur arbeitet, dann in Deutschland
dem preußischen Ministerium seine Dienste anbietet, mit dem
ersten Generalkonsul nach Mexico zurückkehrt und als dessen
Nachfolger diplomatischer Vertreter Preußens wird), sowie der Arzt
Dr. Kassler, der bereits in Jalapa den General Guerrero behandelt.
(Kurioserweise landete bereits 1825 eine Schweizerin, Henriette
Faber, nach abenteuerlichen Fahrten über Cuba, in Männerkleidung
als erste Ärztin in Mexico, und durch Vermittlung des Militär-
kommandanten in Tampico erhält sie vom Außenminister Lucas
Alemán die Erlaubnis, in die Hauptstadt zu reisen und ihren Beruf
auszuüben.) Diese erste Gruppe kommt mit einem Plan, den sie
ursprünglich in den Vereinigten Staaten verwirklichen wollte—im
mexikanischen Veracruz eine Art Kommune zu gründen, Zuflucht
politisch Verfolgter, die deutsche Sprache und Bildung erhalten und zusammen mit der Minen-Gesellschaft eine große
Zahl von Kolonisatoren aufnehmen sollte, was allerdings, wie fast
alle Siedlungspläne, an den unüberwindlichen politischen und
finanziellen Schwierigkeiten im Lande scheitert. 1827 hatte der
Staat Veracruz den Einwanderern Grund und Boden zur Verfügung gestellt,[10] obzwar die Ansässigen aus religiösem Fanatismus
oder, wie in Puebla, aus geschäftlicher Rivalität eine feindliche
Haltung, vor allem gegen Engländer, einnehmen (1828). So wandern die meisten Neuankömmlinge in die Hauptstadt ab. Dort be-
ginnen Hehner und Jung, beide Bergleute, mit einer Tischlerei, um
die gemeinsame Wohnung zu möblieren. Carl Sartorius hat literarische und künstlerische Pläne, zeichnet Landschaften und Porträts,
um Geld zu verdienen und sammelt Material für sein Buch über

Land und Volk von Mexico, das 1848 auf englisch erscheint.[11]
Grube veröffentlicht im "Hesperus" eine Reihe von Artikeln, in
denen er zur Kolonisierung in Mexico einlädt, und Wilhelm Stein
berichtet, daß die Zahl der Ausländer täglich zunimmt und die
Hauptstadt bald einer europäischen Stadt gleichen wird. 1827 em-
pfiehlt sich bereits ein deutscher Lehrer, Juan Fiegen, in der
Zeitung. In Begleitung von Sartorius und seiner Gesellschaft
kommt, schon 1824, der Sohn des deutschen Verlegers Ackermann
aus London nach Mexico.[12] Er eröffnet dort die erste deutsche
Buchhandlung. In London war bei Ackermann, neben den Zeitungen der politischen Emigranten Lateinamerikas (wie "El Instructor
de Londres," "Correo Literario y Político de Londres," 1826) die
zweibändige "Historia antigua de Mejico" von Clavijero erschienen.
Die Zeitungen der Hauptstadt ("El Aguila Mejicana") bringen nun
Ackermanns Buchanzeigen: "La Reforma religiosa en Alemania,"
und "El curso del Rhin, con 24 láminas." Die ersten deutschen
Bücher über Mexico erscheinen: von Diplomaten, wie dem Geheimen Regierungsrat und preußischen Generalkonsul Dr. Karl
Wilhelm Koppe (1829); von Carlos Nebel, der um 1830 mexi-
kanische Typen und Landschaften zeichnet; von Geologen und
Bergwerksexperten, die Reichtümer suchen; von Reisenden und
Abenteurern, politischen Schriftstellern und Wissenschaftlern.

Die Regierung Santa Annas, die die Notwendigkeit der Einwanderung vertritt, versucht, konservative Widerstände im Lande
zu besiegen. Eine Reihe von Artikeln, S.C. unterzeichnet,[13] kämpft
gegen den herrschenden Geist der Intoleranz: "Der Haß gegen die
Ausländer und die vorherrschende irrtümliche Meinung über sie ist
eine der vielen für die Republik verhängnisvollen Folgen der eng-
herzigen und niedrigen Gesinnung des Herrn Alemán,[14] dem der
Himmel die Fähigkeiten eines Staatsmannes versagt hat... Die Aufnahme eines Ausländers, der Kapitalien, Kräfte oder Kenntnisse in
Wissenschaften und Technik mitbringt, um in irgendeinem In-
dustriezweig zu arbeiten, ist für das Land, wo er sich niederläßt,
von größtem Nutzen." Aber bis 1846 leiden alle Pläne an der
politischen Unsicherheit und dem Fehlen ständiger Maßnahmen.
Deutsche Auswanderer gingen nach wie vor fast ausschließlich nach
den Vereinigten Staaten und Brasilien, und die deutsche Regierung
widerriet der ohnehin wenig zahlreichen Auswanderung nach Mexico. Mehrere von Schweizern entworfene Projekte, etwa 200

Familien qualifizierter deutscher Arbeiter nach Mexico zu bringen, scheitern ebenso wie französische Pläne an Problemen der Finanzierung, der religiösen Intoleranz und der geringen Stabilität der wechselnden Regierungen. Im Herbst 1837 wendet sich Präsident Antonio Bustamante an den preußischen Konsul Gerolt, um die Einwanderung von Deutschen in die Nordprovinzen an der Grenze einzuleiten, was die preußische Regierung allerdings nicht unterstützt, "da die Sicherheit von Personen und Eigentum in Mexico noch nicht genügend garantiert ist." In dieser Zeit wird Texas mit amerikanischen Einwanderern besiedelt, die ungehindert in die dünnbevölkerten Gebiete strömen. Ob für Mexico zum Vor- oder Nachteil, wird zur heftigsten Streitfrage der Parteien, die durch den Krieg mit den U.S.A. für die Opposition entschieden wird. Der Plan, auch 10,000 Deutsche in Texas anzusiedeln, scheitert an dem Argument, daß die Deutschen als rassisch und religiös den Nordamerikanern Verwandte sich für die Sache der Vereinigten Staaten entscheiden könnten.

Laut Bericht des Konsuls Gerolt besteht 1836 nur der fünfte Teil aller Fremden in Mexico aus deutschen Untertanen. Und trotz allem Mißtrauen gehörten die wenigen Deutschen zu den wichtigsten und meist erfolgreichen Einwanderern. Der beste Schneider der Hauptstadt war ebenso wie der geschickteste Schuster ein Deutscher. Deutsche eröffnen die erste Gerberei nach europäischem Vorbild und eine Bierbrauerei. 1830–32 wandern Deutsche ein, die sich als Hutmacher, Möbelschreiner und Kleidermacher niederlassen und fast immer erfolgreiche Geschäfte begründen. 1833 sucht Antonio von Kleder Arbeit: "Koch von Beruf, der französisch spricht und die verschiedensten Länder Europas und Amerikas bereist hat." Enrique Hilbert, Meister für Glanzappretur, eröffnet die erste derartige Werkstatt. Und M. Schlosser, Hühneraugenoperateur, "qui a opéré sa Majesté le Roy de Bavière, S. Altesse Royale, le prince Alexandre de Wirtemberg, le Prince Richard Metternich, le Duc de Saxe-Weimar" bietet seine Dienste an. Ein deutscher Schmied, ein schwäbischer Fuhrmann, ein Bartender und verschiedene Bierbrauer—über einen von ihnen berichtet noch Ignacio M. Altamirano, der 1869 eine Bayrische Bierstube in der Avenida de los Plateros besucht—und eine Reihe deutscher Restaurants werden bekannt. 1892 erscheint sogar ein deutscher Sportler, Otto Praeger, der auf dem Veloziped, und zwar mit unglaublicher Geschwindigkeit, von San Antonio, Texas über Guadalajara nach Durango und von dort nach der Hauptstadt radelt.

Aber der sich verschärfende Konflikt zwischen Zentralismus und Föderalismus, Bürgerkrieg und Revolution von 1833, äußere und innere Verstrickungen des Landes und die ungünstigen Berichte der europäischen Presse über Fehlschläge der Kolonisation, dazu die Schwierigkeiten, die nicht-katholischen Einwanderern gemacht werden (die sich z.B. in Mexico gesetzlich nicht verheiraten können und sehr viel Feindseligkeit von seiten der Kirche und manchmal auch der Obrigkeit erfahren müssen) verhindern eine zahlenmäßig bedeutende Einwanderung. Die konservative Regierung von Alemán, dem die Presse Fremdenfeindlichkeit nachsagt, und Bustamante richten sich gegen die Ausländer, die sich der von Santa Anna dirigierten Rebellion angeschlossen haben, hinter der ausländische Einflüsse stehen sollen. Zu dieser Gruppe gehört z.B. Joseph Harkort, der [1833] als Direktor der englischen Mexican Mining Company einwanderte und Chef der Pioniere sowie persönlicher Adjutant von Santa Anna wurde. Aber als sich Santa Anna[15] zum Diktator macht, geht Harkort zur Gegenseite über, wird ins Gefängnis geworfen und zum Tode verurteilt, kann aber entfliehen. Als er mit den republikanischen Truppen nach Mexico zurückkehrt, gewährt ihm der Kongreß die Einbürgerung. Er stirbt 1834; sein Buch "Aus meinen mexikanischen Gefängnissen," das Fragmente seiner Briefe enthält, erscheint 1858 in Leipzig. C. C. Becher berichtet 1832, daß sich die Militärmachthaber der Stadt Veracruz "darin gefallen, die Fremden, welchen die Gouvernementspartei bekanntlich überhaupt abhold ist, auf alle Weise zu chicanieren und bei jeder Gelegenheit mit Grobheit und Arroganz zu behandeln."[16] Sie müssen sich im Jahre 1834 bei der Regierung melden, Vaterland, Beruf und Paß angeben, und "die Untertanen seiner Maj. des Königs von Preußen und der Staaten, die unter seinem Schutz stehen," müssen sich "Cartas de Seguridad" im Konsulat abholen.[17] Zweifellos sind an der Einstellung der Behörden und des Volkes im Konflikt von 1838/39 (Guerra de los Pasteles), ebenso wie 1862 die exorbitanten, von taktlosen ausländischen Diplomaten geltend gemachten Entschädigungsansprüche mitschuldig. Andererseits ist die ständige Klage der Ausländer über die Unsicherheit ihrer Stellung vielfach berechtigt. Latente und

offene Fremdenfeindlichkeit existiert überall. Die "anti-mexika-
nischen" Direktoren der hauptstädtischen Presse und ihre Politik
werden verdächtigt. Man verzieh den Fremden den erarbeiteten
Wohlstand nicht leicht, nannte sie "judío," und in einigen Fällen
steigerten sich Haß und Mißtrauen sogar bis zu Straßenkämpfen
zwischen Franzosen und Mexikanern (1840). Jede neue Regierung
erneuerte auch die Schwierigkeiten für Einwanderer.[18] 1842 hebt
Santa Anna zwar das Gesetz auf, das Ausländern verweigert, Eigentum in der Republik zu besitzen. Aber schon 1843, während des
Krieges gegen die Vereinigten Staaten, wird den Ausländern wieder
jeder Detailhandel verboten, durch dessen Monopolisierung die
Mexikaner in eine bedeutungslose Rolle abgedrängt würden; ausgenommen sind Naturalisierte, mit Mexikanerinnen Verheiratete und
die, deren Familien im Lande wohnen. Dennoch liegt die Aus-
beutung der Minen, die eigentliche nationale Industrie—wie der
französische Konsul in Mazatlan berichtet—fast ausschließlich
in den Händen von Ausländern: Engländern, Deutschen und
Franzosen.[19] Die übrige Industrie ist kaum in ihren Anfängen:
die Franzosen beherrschen Mode und Kleidung, die Spanier
Lebensmittel, Engländer und Deutsche Eisenwaren und Ma-
schinen,[20] und man hört Klagen darüber, daß nur wenige
Fremde ihren Gewinn im Lande selbst investieren, sondern fast alle
ihn in ihre Heimat zurücksenden. Nachdruck—auch seitens der
Presse—wird darauf gelegt, die Einwanderung landwirtschaftlicher
Kräfte zu fördern, "die neue Methoden einführt und zeigen kann,
wie der Ire, der Russe, Franzose, Deutsche und Italiener säen und
ernten."[21]

Nach dem Sturz Santa Annas (1845) kommen die Probleme
ausländischer Einwanderung erneut im mexikanischen Kongreß
zur Sprache, und 1846 wird ein Kolonisierungsgesetz erlassen,
dessen Ausführung der Krieg mit Nordamerika unterbricht. Die
neue *Dirección de Colonización e Industria* vertritt den Stand-
punkt, daß Mexico dringend Einwanderer benötigt, um die weiten
Gebiete der Republik zu besiedeln, die "heute Gegenstand ausländischer Besitzgier" sind. Aber die Regierung hat kein Geld für
die Durchführung derartiger Pläne. Das Fehlen politischer Stabilität und die Unsicherheit der Verhältnisse wirken sich weiterhin
ungünstig aus. Nach dem Krieg 1846/47 wird die Notwendigkeit,
die Einwanderungsfrage zu lösen, als vordringlich empfunden.

1848/49 liegt dem Kongreß ein neues Programm zur Regelung der Kolonisierung vor.[22] 1849 versucht eine große deutsche Einwanderungsgesellschaft vergeblich, Auskünfte und Zusicherungen von der Regierung zu erlangen. Carlos Sartorius bemüht sich 1849, ein weiteres Projekt zu verwirklichen. Während eines kurzen Aufenthalts in Deutschland sucht er die Kolonisationsbewegung nach Mexico zu fördern und gründet eine Gesellschaft für deutsche Auswanderung, die Propagandaschriften herausgibt, aber wenig Erfolg hat. Sartorius soll damals 30 000 deutsche Einwanderer für Mexico geworben haben, die aber schließlich in die Vereinigten Staaten gingen, weil ihnen Mexico keine religiöse Toleranz garantierte (1856). "La Ilustración Mexicana"[23] bringt eine Reihe von Auszügen der in Deutschland 1851 veröffentlichten kleinen Schrift des Dr. B. von Boguslawski, von der Zentralstelle für Auswanderung und deutsche Kolonisation in Berlin: "Mexico braucht Einwanderung—Vorteile, die Mexico einer deutschen Einwanderung bietet —Was hat bis heute verhindert, daß die deutschen Auswanderer nach Mexico gehen?—Die Vereinigten Staaten sind immer noch anziehend—die größere Entfernung von Europa—Das Fehlen von Wegen und Verbindungen—Antipathie vieler Mexikaner gegen die Ausländer—Fehlen religiöser Toleranz—Die häufigen politischen Unruhen—Der Zustand der Justiz—Fehlen positiver Daten über bebaubare Grundstücke—Fehlen eines Kolonisierungsgesetzes— Punkte, die in Betracht gezogen werden müssen über die Ansiedlungsorte der Kolonisten—Was für deutsche Kolonisten sollen einwandern?" "Man sieht nach dem Angeführten," erklärt "El Siglo XIX," "daß die Auswanderung nach Mexico in Deutschland Aufmerksamkeit erregt, und daß bereits Gegenden ins Auge gefaßt werden, wo die Ansiedlung am nötigsten ist. Im letzten Memorandum der erwähnten Zentralstelle wird angegeben, daß die Auswanderung aus Preußen etwa 15 000 Personen mit einem Kapital von 191 Pesos pro Kopf umfaßt—und daß die Gesamtheit der Auswanderer, ohne den geringsten Vorteil für Deutschland, in der Bevölkerung der Vereinigten Staaten aufgehen muß, weshalb die Zentralstelle beabsichtigt, die Auswanderung nach Zentralamerika, Brasilien, Südamerika, Südaustralien und Mexico zu lenken."[24] Aber als 1856 der Deutsche Gustav Schadtler (der 1858 Vertreter des Zollvereins in Mexico wird)[25] dem Präsidenten Comonfort Vorschläge zu gewissen Garantien und Vorteile für die

Kolonisten macht, scheitert auch dieses Projekt, ebenso wie ein anderes, das eine Kolonie von Deutschen und Mexikanern in Nuevo Leon and Tamaulipas vorsieht.

Die meisten dieser Projekte mißlingen durch die Verweigerung der Religionsfreiheit. Der Konflikt der Liberalen mit der Kirche wirkt sich gerade auf diesem Gebiet aus. Toleranz würde eine moderne weltaufgeschlossene Gesellschaft bedeuten und damit eine empfindliche Einbuße kirchlicher Macht. Noch 1846 hatte der preußische Gesandte um Erlaubnis gebeten, auf dem Gesandtschaftsgelände eine protestantische Kapelle zu errichten; aber die kirchliche Hierarchie reagierte darauf mit so heftiger Ablehnung, daß das Gesuch zurückgezogen werden mußte und der Gesandte sich daraufhin weigerte, die Einwanderung deutscher Kolonisten zu befürworten.[26] Die konservative katholische Presse bezog jedesmal sofort Stellung gegen die Einwanderung im allgemeinen, aber vor allem gegen die protestantische. Wer nicht katholisch ist, ist kein Christ, muß infolgedessen Jude sein und somit unmoralisch, unehrlich und verdammt: Argumente, die noch aus der Inquisitionszeit stammten und vom Klerus im Volk weiter gepflegt wurden. Danach sei das protestantische Europa auch eine Quelle von Gewalt und Atheismus, und Gott bestrafe Nationen wie Individuen für das Verbrechen der Ketzerei.[27] Religiöse Toleranz und ihre katastrophalen Folgen seien eine Invasion von Ideen aus dem Norden und die Ursache gegenwärtigen und künftigen Elends im Lande; wenn der Kongreß das einigende soziale Band der Nation, die Religion, zerreiße, müsse die Selbstzerstörung der Nation eintreten und sogar das prähispanische Heidentum würde wieder erwachen. "La Verdad" (1854) sucht, nationale Ressentiments zu wecken: "Die zivilisierten Nationen Europas haben die schlimmste Meinung von uns Mexikanern. Sie glauben, daß wir faule Wilde seien und schreiben uns alle denkbaren schlechten Eigenschaften zu. . . . Zu unseren Lastern kommt unsere Gefühllosigkeit, und die gelehrten Denker Europas rechnen uns zu den Haustieren, die keinen Trieb zur Arbeit haben. Die Ausländer, die in unser Land kommen, müßten aus Dankbarkeit, oder um der Gerechtigkeit willen, eine andere Idee vom mexikanischen Charakter gewonnen haben; denn wenn auch wahr ist, daß die Aufklärung in Mexico nicht so verbreitet ist, wie in Europa, so bedeutet das doch noch nicht, daß alle unsere Volksgenossen wegen ihrer Un-bildung den Namen Wilde verdienten. Unsere Rückschrittlichkeit ist notorisch und bedauerlich, hängt aber weniger vom Mangel an Fähigkeit ab, als von Umständen, die nur die Vorsehung verändern kann."

Es finden heftige Parlamentsdebatten über Religionsfreiheit statt (1856), deren Vertreter die bedeutendsten Intellektuellen sind: Vicente Rocafuerte, Guillermo Prieto, Melchor Ocampo. Überzeugt, daß die Lösung des Problems, die eigene Nationalität zu bewahren, in einem Bevölkerungszuwachs durch Einwanderung liegt, fordert Filomeno Mata den Kongreß auf, einer Proklamation über freie Immigration zuzustimmen, die nicht allein die zivilisierte Welt davon überzeugen müsse, daß für Mexico das dunkle Zeitalter vorüber sei, das das Land von der großen menschlichen Familie isolierte. Solche Zustimmung müsse außerdem Mexico den Vorteil bringen, daß "tausende von Arbeitern unsere glühenden Küsten, unsere verlassenen Wüsten an der Grenze besiedeln und unserem Boden unerschöpfliche Reichtümer abgewinnen werden." Aber die überwiegende Parlamentsmehrheit erreicht, daß die Frage nicht einmal zur Abstimmung gelangt. Die protestantische Einwanderung sei wegen der Verschiedenheit von Sprache und Glauben nicht assimilierbar für die Nation;[28] und die Sorge, daß künftig Protestanten die Gesetzgebung beeinflussen könnten, besiegt das Argument, daß Mexico ohne Einwanderer nicht überleben könne.

Nationalistische Abneigung oder liberale Gunst wechseln immer wieder mit den historischen Ereignissen. Die drohende ausländische Intervention (1854) bietet vielen Ausländern wieder den Vorwand für die übertriebensten Reklamationen, die verständliche Feindseligkeit gegen alle anderen wecken. Wer wegen eines polizeilichen Irrtums oder einer Intrige ins Gefängnis kam, verlangte 50–100 000 Pesos Entschädigung.[29] Man versuchte, die Intervention damit zu rechtfertigen, daß langjährige Erfahrung die ausländischen Regierungen davon überzeugt habe, daß in Mexico Verträge nichts bedeuteten;[30] daß alle Reklamationen nutzlos seien, selbst wenn sie auf dem Papier anerkannt wären; und daß die Sicherheit der Ausländer im Lande gefährdet sei, da dauernde Überfälle auf Franzosen und Deutsche die ausländischen Kolonien beunruhigten und die mexikanische Regierung mit voller Absicht alle Europäer verfolge.[31] In Wahrheit verbriefte die Konstitution den Ausländern nicht allein dieselben Garantien, die die Einwohner genossen und die vertraglich zugesicherten Rechte, sondern jeden Schutz, jede Sicherheit ihrer Person und ihres Eigentums, und seit 1860 (nach dem dreijährigen Bürgerkrieg) auch die freie Ausübung ihrer Religion.[32] Als die Hauptstadt, nach Juárez' Flucht, ohne Polizei bleibt, wird sogar eine bewaffnete Miliz der Ausländer von 500–600 Mann gebildet. Aber als Juárez 1861 auch Europäer zu Kriegsdiensten ausheben läßt,[33] den ausländischen Kaufleuten für die Verteidigung der Regierung eine Steuer von 1% auf ihre Kapitalien auferlegt, und laut Dekret alle Verbindlichkeiten gegen das Ausland für zwei Jahre ausgesetzt werden, erhebt sich ein gewaltiger Sturm der Entrüstung, und die Intervention wird eine Notwendigkeit. Strenge Maßnahmen des Präsidenten gegen waffentragende Ausländer oder Helfer der fremden Heere sowie gegen den freiwilligen Dienst von Mexikanern bei den europäischen Truppen (1862) erschweren die Lage der Ausländer zusehends. Die Abneigung gegen sie, die sich bis zum Volkshaß steigert, gewinnt an Boden je mehr die Furcht vor der französischen Invasion Gestalt annimmt. Es gibt aber auch Deutsche auf mexikanischer Seite, wie den Baron Carlos von Gagern,[34] der als begeisterter Verteidiger der nationalen Freiheit im mexikanischen Heer kämpft, bei der Belagerung von Puebla gefangen und nach Frankreich gebracht wird, später bei Querétaro Augenzeuge von Maximilians Tod wird und danach als Gegner von Juárez' Diktatur in der mexikanischen Presse eine Rolle spielt.

Das Kaiserpaar—Maximilian und Charlotte—wird 1864 in Veracruz kalt empfangen, angeblich, weil die Stadt von ausländischen Kaufleuten, Feinden des Imperiums, beherrscht war, die eine neue Ordnung fürchten mußten; in Wahrheit betrachtete die Bevölkerung die Fremden mit Mißtrauen. Maximilians Ankunft öffnet natürlich das Land für Einwanderer aus Europa. Neben den aus verschiedensten Nationen bestehenden österreichischen Expeditionstruppen kommen zahllose Beamte, Abenteurer und Spekulanten, Soldaten "die wenige Tage nach ihrer Ankunft schon Offiziere waren und das Kreuz des Guadalupe-Ordens trugen . . . alle von Adel, Prinzen, Grafen, Marquis mit phantastischen Einkünften, die einzig nach Mexico kamen, um Frieden und Wohlstand erhalten zu helfen."[35] Bis dahin waren die wenig zahlreichen Deutschen allgemein geachtet und gern gesehen, ein Kredit, den das abenteuernde Gesindel vielfach mißbrauchte. "México ist voll von

Franzosen, Engländern, Amerikanern, Deutschen und Oester-
reichern, die nur die Thronbesteigung des Kaisers abwarteten, um
große Gewinne zu machen."[36] Die deutschen Kaufleute allerdings
standen meist auf seiten der Republikaner. Sie hatten wenig Vertrauen in die Dauer des Kaiserreichs und wehrten sich gegen die
Versuche der kaiserlichen Verwaltung, den Schmuggel zu unter-
binden.[37] Dazu wuchs die Unruhe im Lande, Guerrillabanden
ermordeten fremde Reisende, vor allem Franzosen. Der heftige
Kampf gegen das—vor allem gegen die Vereinigten Staaten gerichtete—Gesetz für freie Einwanderung—verschärfte sich ständig,
die Polemik gegen die merkliche Überfremdung wurde aggressiver.
Alle Kolonisations-Projekte werden von den Mexikanern abgelehnt, vor allem von den Liberalen, da sie dem nationalistischen
Geist widersprechen, der aus der Intervention und der Anwesen-
heit einer fremden Monarchie Kräfte gewonnen hat. Ständig wird
versucht, die Einwanderungsfrage mit dem politisch-religiösen
Problem zu verknüpfen, so etwa in einer "Widerlegung der Irrtümer, die die nach Guadalajara gekommenen Protestanten verbreitet haben" (1865). Wie so oft verschanzt sich politische
Gegnerschaft hinter der Religion mit allen konventionellen Argu-
menten. "La Religión y la Sociedad"[38] polemisiert noch 1865
gegen Ausländer und liberale Zeitungen, die die Einwanderung
begünstigen: 'Die Einwanderung fordert als Vorbedingung nichts
weniger als das Opfer der religiösen Einheit unseres Landes . . . es
ist gefährlich, einem so starken und lebendigen (amerikanisch-
angelsächsischen) Element nicht eine Schranke entgegenzusetzen.
Ohne . . . Verteidigung . . . würden die Vereinigten Staaten früher
oder später Mexico annektieren. Die deutschen Emigranten sind
im allgemeinen Protestanten und gehören außerdem zu der Rasse,
die augenblicklich in den Vereinigten Staaten tonangebend ist . . .
mit ihrem Zusammenhalt und Vereinsgeist haben sie sicher nicht
gezögert, sich zu verständigen, um die Integration Mexicos zu
fördern . . . was das katholische und lateinische Europa nicht
dulden kann noch darf.' Die gleiche Zeitung veröffentlicht einen
Bericht des Barons Brackel-Welda über das "Projekt ausländischer
Kolonien in Mexico,"[39] die erste Arbeit dieses deutschen Journalisten in mexikanischen Zeitungen, die sofort eine heftige Polemik
entfesselt. Einige Konservative sehen darin Ideen der französischen
Revolution (wie die Enteignung der Großgrundbesitzer); prote-

stantische Propaganda sei der Unabhängigkeit Mexicos gefährlich, außerdem stehe in den Vereinigten Staaten, wie in der gesamten protestantischen Welt die Moral auf viel niedrigerem Niveau als in den katholischen Ländern. Die in Bremen veröffentlichte "Kolonisationszeitung" bringt einen trostlosen Artikel über Mexico, mit der deutlichen Absicht, allen Auswanderern die Lust zu nehmen, ins Land zu kommen. Danach ist Mexico ein Land ohne Zukunft, voll Anarchie und Unsicherheit, in dem die Kolonisten, die an seinen Ufern landen, nur Verlassenheit und Elend erwarten. Das "Diario del Imperio," die kaiserliche Zeitung, dementiert diese Angaben, zählt auf, was die kaiserliche Regierung schon für die Kolonisten getan hat, und zeichnet ein Bild der Zustände in Mexico, dessen Farben denen des Bremer Autors völlig entgegengesetzt sind. "L'Ère" kommentiert beide Artikel dahin, daß der zweite nur halb wahr sei, und daß die Kolonisten keine verfügbaren Grundstücke vorfinden. "Ein Beweis," sagt "La Religión y La Sociedad," "daß es nicht leicht ist, die Ausländer, so sehr man ihnen auch schmeichelt, zufriedenzustellen. Wir Mexikaner würden glücklich sein, wenn man uns Sicherheiten für unser Wohlbefinden böte, ähnlich wie die sie in unserem Lande antreffen." Ein Kolonisierungsplan in Yucatán, den der Schlesier von Hiller durchzuführen versucht, scheitert wieder.[40]

Während des Kaiserreichs spielten die Deutschen im allgemeinen keine hervorragende Rolle.[41] Sie wollten weder für kaiserlich noch für liberal gehalten werden, um es mit keiner Partei zu verderben: so sollen sie auch Geld für den Unterhalt der Juárez-Armee gegeben haben. Die meisten hatten keinerlei Vertrauen zu der kaiserlichen Regierung und hielten sich ihr soviel wie möglich fern. Gegen ihre neugekommenen Landsleute zeigten sie sich ablehnend. Nur wenige verkehrten mit den Deutschen aus dem Gefolge des Kaisers, wohl auch deshalb, weil darunter viele Abenteurer und Schuldenmacher waren.[42] Dennoch bedauerten die Deutschen das Ende des Kaiserreichs, weil dadurch das gewinnträchtige wirtschaftliche Chaos aufhörte. Mit dem Zusammenbruch (1867) steigt die Zahl der ausreisenden Ausländer, hauptsächlich der Franzosen, aber auch der Mexikaner, ganz beträchtlich. Die Maßnahmen der republikanischen Regierung, Dekrete und Konfiskationen jeder Art, der völlige Ruin zahlreicher Familien, besonders französischer, die zweijährige Haft aller gefangenen

Soldaten (die allerdings unter Regierungsaufsicht bald ihren Wohnsitz selbst wählen können), die Unsicherheit der Lage der Kaisertreuen sowie die Fremdenfeindlichkeit nach dem Scheitern der Invention verhindern neue Einwanderung, obwohl sie offiziell weiter gefördert wird und die liberale Presse sie begrüßt. Deutsche Auswanderer, schrieb "El Ferro-carril," sollten vor allem aus Preußen kommen, wo eine heftige Antipathie gegen das Militär bestehe. Bis zum Mai des Jahres hätten 63 000 Auswanderer Preußen verlassen, und die Einwanderung nach den Vereinigten Staaten würde noch zunehmen, falls Preußen sich wieder in einen Krieg verwickelt sähe. Es sei unnötig zu betonen, daß diese Einwanderung in Mexico sehr erwünscht sein würde.[43] Deutsche Familien aus Texas hätten von der Regierung Land zur Siedlung an der Grenze erbeten. "Hoffentlich nimmt die Regierung mit Freude diese Anträge an."[44] Aus den Handelsbeziehungen der Einwanderer mit dem Norddeutschen Bund müßten Mexico große Vorteile erwachsen, vermutete "El Siglo XIX."[45]

Hanseatische Kaufleute bringen Kapital und viele Angestellte, nach 1868.[46] Aber die häufigen Revolutionen und Unruhen, die dem Ende des Kaiserreichs folgen, sind solchen Beziehungen nicht günstig. Noch 1872 berichtet ein deutscher Reisender von Straßenkämpfen in Monterrey, bei denen Geschäftshäuser geplündert, Zwangsanleihen ausgeschrieben und Erschießungen vorgenommen werden.[47] Der deutsche Sieg von 1870-71 macht die meisten Mexico-Deutschen zu Nationalisten und läßt sogar Gegensätze zwischen Franzosen und Deutschen entstehen, die bis zu Tätlichkeiten gegen die verschiedenen Klubs führen.

Das Bild der Deutschen verändert sich jetzt, auch für die Mexikaner: "Biertrinker, die eine Gefahr für unsere Pulque-Industrie werden"—"militaristisch erzogen, unserer Rasse fremd, Menschen, die unsere ethnischen Charakterzüge zerstören, bis niemand mehr erraten kann, daß auf unserem Boden Tolteken, Chichimeken und Azteken wohnten."[48]

Die Regierung unter Porfirio Díaz allerdings ist ausgesprochen fremdenfreundlich, die europäische Kolonisierung wird die große Hoffnung dieser Jahre. Trotzdem sieht sich der Baron von Brackel-Welda in einer Sitzung der Sociedad de Geografía y Estadística (1877) genötigt, die deutsche Einwanderung zu verteidigen: "Mexico braucht Männer, die hier Interessen und Zuneigung schaffen, die helfen, die Nation und ihren Reichtum zu vergrößern . . . , denen man die Hand reichen muß wie einem Bruder, denn es gibt zahllose Deutsche, die Bedeutendes für das Wohl des Landes geleistet haben, stets bestrebt, durch ehrliche Arbeit und Unternehmungen ihr Vermögen zu erwerben . . . , aber diese Gefühle sind in der Masse des Volkes noch nicht allgemein geworden, in dessen Herzen Ideen von Exklusivismus und spanischer Intoleranz fortleben, die den in Ketten warf, der wagte, die mexikanischen Grenzen zu überschreiten."

"Niemand haßt oder beneidet die Ausländer . . . , im Gegenteil, man schätzt und achtet sie . . . Wenn es Mexikaner gibt, die ihnen mit oder ohne Grund Abneigung entgegenbringen, darf ihr Benehmen nicht als Regel gelten, um die Situation der Fremden in Mexico zu beurteilen," sagt die liberale Zeitung "El Monitor Republicano."[49] Und 1884 über die Einwanderungsgesetze: "Mexico kann nicht reich oder stark werden, wenn es seine Grenzen nicht mit aufrichtiger Herzlichkeit den Ausländern, seien es Amerikaner, Deutsche, Franzosen, Engländer oder Italiener, öffnet. Es muß zum nationalen Dogma werden, daß jeder, der seine Arbeit oder sein Geld nach Mexico bringt, ein guter Mexikaner ist, da er dem Fortschritt unseres reichgesegneten Landes dient."[50]

1881 kommt eine Gruppe von zwölf Deutschen, die eine Kolonie in der Nähe von Acapulco gründen sollen, und weitere werden erwartet.[51] 1883 ist die Einwanderung von 50 landwirtschaftlichen Kolonistenfamilien angekündigt, gegen die ein Artikel der "Deutschen Zeitung" polemisiert: "No vengáis a México."[52] Und die deutsche Regierung in Berlin dementiert offiziell alle Gerüchte über deutsche Kolonisation in Mexico und in Belize. Es sind nach wie vor meist Einzelne oder kleine Gruppen, die ins Land kommen. Dabei kommt die Polemik um die Einwanderung nicht zur Ruhe. "El Diario del Hogar" muß sich gegen den Vorwurf der Unduldsamkeit gegen Einwanderer verteidigen. Sie seien nur deren Gegner, wenn es sich um Leute handele, die ohne Liebe zur Arbeit, ohne Spezialkenntnisse ins Land kämen, um zu spekulieren oder Regierungsposten zu finden . . . "unternehmenden und fleißigen Ausländern, wie den Herren Zölly, Lohse und tausend anderen, die in Handel, Landwirtschaft, Fabriken, Werkstätten und allen Industriezweigen wirken, die ihre Kenntnisse weitergeben, Kapitalien ansammeln, die ihre Arbeiter mit ihnen teilen, wünschen wir Erfolg."[53]

Das 19. Jahrhundert vor allem ist die Zeit der Deutsch-
mexikaner, die ihre Kräfte, Mittel und ihren Unternehmungsgeist
dem neuen Land widmen. Eine so kurze Arbeit erlaubt nur die
Erwähnung einiger weniger Namen: den des Großkaufmanns
Esteban (Stephan) Benecke z.B., der 1808 in Berlin geboren, dem
Tugendbund beitrat und nach dem Bankrott des väterlichen Unter-
nehmens nach Mexico auswanderte. Er gehört zu den Gründern
der Freimaurerloge der Hauptstadt und der Handelskammer als
deren erster Präsident, saß in zahllosen Regierungskommissionen,
half der Presse in großzügiger Weise und war Mitglied der ältesten
wissenschaftlichen Gesellschaft Mexicos, der Sociedad Mexicana
de Geografía y Estadística, für die er geographische, statistische und
Handelsdaten sammelte. Als Konsul Preußens und des Norddeutschen Bundes war er einer der besten Vermittler zwischen
deutscher und mexikanischer Kultur.[54]

In der Reihe von bedeutenden Pädagogen ist der Philologe und
Linguist Oloardo Hassey zu nennen, Professor für alte Sprachen
sowie deutsche Sprache und Literatur am Colegio Nacional de
Minería, der als erster Germanist in Mexico eine deutsche Gram-
matik und eine Geschichte der deutschen Literatur veröffentlichte.
1843 kam er als Siebenundzwanzigjähriger nach Mexico.[55] Die
Persönlichkeit des Schweizers Enrique Rebsamen, Direktor des
Colegio Normalista (Lehrerseminar) für den Staat Veracruz, in
Jalapa, ist weitbekannt. Vizepräsident des Nationalkongresses für
Erziehung, arbeitete er für eine Erziehungsreform im nationalen
Sinn, auf Grundlage der Geschichte. Zusammen mit Dr. Fuentes y
Betancourt und Dr. Hugo Topf, einem Deutschen, gab er die Halb-
monatsschrift "México intelectual. Revista pedagógica y Científico-
Literaria" heraus.

Die wichtige Rolle der Deutschen in der Mexikanistik im
einzelnen zu schildern, würde den Rahmen dieser Arbeit sprengen.
In Betracht kommt eine große Anzahl bedeutender Namen, von
Friedrich von Waldeck, Teobert Maler (der als Soldat in Maximilians Heer nach Mexico kommt), über Eduard Seler und dessen
Frau, bis in unsere Zeit. Auch die deutsche Presse hat in Mexico
hervorragende Vertreter, seit Isidor Epstein (einem liberalen
deutschen Juden, der 1851 mit der Gruppe verfolgter deutscher
Revolutionäre einwandert, eine Reihe mexikanischer Zeitungen
gründet, dann 1872 mit dem "Vorwärts" in deutscher Sprache

aktiv an der mexikanischen Politik teilnimmt, aber von der deutschen Kolonie aggressiv abgelehnt wird).[56] Der oben erwähnte Baron Otto E. von Brackel-Welda, ein Liberaler, aber leidenschaftlicher deutscher Nationalist, setzt die Reihe derjenigen fort, die sich bemühen, zwischen Deutschland und Mexico Brücken zu schlagen.[57]

Die zweite Hälfte des 19. Jahrhunderts bis zum 1. Weltkrieg wird die große Zeit der Mexicodeutschen, meist Kaufleuten, die sich nicht integrieren wollen, sich mit nationalistischem Stolz als Deutsche fühlen, ihre Gruppen und Vereine bilden, ihre Zeitungen herausgeben, ihre Schulen einrichten, sich auf ihrem eigenen Friedhof begraben lassen, und aus deren Nachfolgern sich später die mexikanische Nazipartei rekrutierte.

Allerdings ist diese deutsche "Kolonie" niemals sehr zahlreich gewesen, 1825 zählte sie 25 Mitglieder; 1830 wanderten 52 Deutsche ein, aber 20 verließen wieder das Land. Sartorius nennt 1834 eine Kolonie von 34 Köpfen, 1857 wird die Gesamtzahl der Deutschen im Lande zwischen 8 und 9000 angegeben. Aber die rund 30 000 Ausländer kontrollierten die wichtigsten Wirtschaftsbereiche des Landes, und ihre Teilnahme an den politischen Bewegungen hatte eine gewisse Bedeutung. Von den 3000 jährlich ins Land kommenden Ausländern, gingen 1500 wieder zurück in ihre Heimat. Gaulot nennt für 1858 unter 9½ tausend Ausländern die Zahl von 615 Deutschen.[58] Von den 47 in einem Jahr geschlossenen Heiraten von Ausländern waren vier Deutsche, und nur einer von ihnen verheiratete sich mit einer Mexikanerin.[59] Der deutsche Gesandte Schlözer nennt für 1870 die Zahl von 200 Deutschen in der Stadt Mexico. 1885 leben in der Hauptstadt 200 deutsche Familien, im ganzen Lande etwa 500.[60] "Aber die meisten . . . denken nicht daran, Mexico für sich und ihre Kinder zur dauernden Heimat zu machen. Wenn sie genug Vermögen erworben haben, ziehen sie nach Europa, und die Reichsten unter den Mexikanern machen es ebenso." 1891 zählt ein Besucher 1500 Deutsche im ganzen Land, von denen 500 in der Hauptstadt leben,[61] und 1892 sollen nur 275 Deutsche als Kolonisten eingewandert sein. Um 1900 gibt es kaum 1800 Deutsche in Mexico,[62] und 1910 etwa 2500.

Weltkrieg und mexikanische Revolution wandeln Stimmung und Tendenzen grundlegend. Von der Jahrhundertwende an sind die Einwanderer überwiegend Kaufleute, eine völlige Wandlung in

Motiven und Ideologien. 1919, unmittelbar nach dem ersten Weltkrieg entstanden neue Pläne für eine deutschmexikanische Siedlungsgesellschaft in Berlin; der Verband deutscher Reichsangehöriger in Mexico gibt sogar Richtlinien heraus: "Was der Einwanderer von Mexico wissen muß"; die Niederlage 1918 bringt eine Welle deutscher Einwanderer, die die mexikanische Revolution allerdings schnell versiegen läßt. Eine Mennonitenkolonie siedelt sich um 1920 in Chihuahua an (und verläßt 1971 Mexico wieder, weil sie sich bestimmten Landesgesetzen, wie der Militärpflicht, nicht fügen will). Im Jahre 1924 leben in ganz Mexico etwa 8–9000 Deutsche, 20 000 Deutschsprechende sowie etwa 4000 deutsche Staatsangehörige in der Hauptstadt. Zwischen den Kriegen aber wächst, wie anderswo auch, in Mexico der Nationalismus, der die scheinbar drohende Überfremdung ablehnt. Dem Gastland, das eine einheitliche Nation schaffen will, müssen durch Einwanderung zusätzliche Probleme erwachsen, die seiner Politik hinderlich sind. Die Einwanderungsgesetze werden verschärft, lockern sich aber vorübergehend für die Hitlerflüchtlinge und vor allem die Teilnehmer am spanischen Bürgerkrieg. Die politischen Parteinahmen infolge des zweiten Weltkrieges verzerrten natürlich vielfach das Urteil. Nazis wurden ausgewiesen, Klubs konfisziert, Geschäfte und Schulen unter staatliche Kontrolle gestellt, aber die Deutschen im allgemeinen in großzügigster Weise behandelt. Die Mehrzahl der jüdischen und politischen Flüchtlinge kehrte nach Europa zurück, da Mexico ihnen von Anfang an nur ein zeitweiliges Zufluchtsland bedeutet hatte. Die "Kolonie" existierte nicht mehr, die Vereine verschwanden, trotz mancher wohlgemeinter Versuche, einen Zusammenhalt zu erneuern. Die Familien der alteingesessenen Mexico-Deutschen sterben langsam aus; die Verschmelzung mit dem Lande macht rasche Fortschritte. Die hier geborenen Kinder haben—trotz der weiter existierenden deutschen Schule—fast alle den Zusammenhang mit Deutschland verloren: absichtlich und kulturell beziehungslos, bemühen sie sich, den nationalistischen Landestendenzen nachzuleben und zu Mexikanern zu werden, für die der deutsche Name nur noch Hemmnis zum Aufstieg ist.

Die freie Einwanderung von einem Land zum anderen ist heute eine Sache der Vergangenheit, oder vielleicht der Zukunft. Die auch in Lateinamerika immer stärker werdenden nationalistischen Bewegungen, die nicht nur jeden europäischen Einfluß für wenig bedeutsam und unzeitgemäß halten sondern auch jede noch so wohltätige Intervention von außen ablehnen, wollen ihre Zukunft ohne Abhängigkeit kultureller, technischer oder wirtschaftlicher Art von anderen Nationen (und das große Problem sind vor allem die Vereinigten Staaten) höchstens in dem künftigen Universalismus sehen, der ihnen den gleichen Rang einräumt wie den Großmächten.

Mit voller Absicht ist hier vor allem von vier Jahrhunderten die Rede gewesen, nicht von den fünf, die seit der Eroberung vergangen sind. Die eigentliche kulturelle Pionierarbeit für Mexico und Deutschland wurde im 19. Jahrhundert von Individuen geleistet, im 20. Jahrhundert abgelöst von Institutionen, deren weltweit bekannte Industrie-Nomaden nirgendwo verwurzeln und niemals zu kulturellen Mittlern zwischen zwei Völkern werden können.

ANMERKUNGEN

1. Nach der Exkommunizierung mit der Kirche Wiederversöhnter.
2. Mütze der von der Inquisition zur öffentlichen Buße Verurteilten; hinzu kamen Anschlag des Namens und der Strafe in der Kirche. *México a través de los Siglos*, IV, 500.
3. Ibid., IV, 638.
4. Ibid., IV, 679.
5. M. Orozco y Berra, *Historia de la Ciudad de México* (México, 1973), Sepsetentas p. 73.
6. *Gacetas de México*, 1786.
7. A Cavo, *Los tres siglos de Méjico durante el gobierno español.*
8. D. G. Berninger, *La inmigración en México (1821-1857)* Sepsetentas (México, 1974), p. 29.
9. Ibid., p. 15.
10. Hans Kruse, *Deutsche Briefe aus Mexiko.* Veröffentlichungen des Archivs für Rheinisch-Westfälische Wirtschaftsgeschichte, vol. 9 (Essen, 1923).
11. Carl Sartorius, *Mexico About 1850* (Stuttgart, 1961).
12. *El Aguila Mejicana*, 1825-26. Udo Rukser, "Ein deutscher Verleger als Förderer Südamerikas," *Börsenblatt für den deutschen Buchhandel*, No. 87 (30. Oktober 1959). Marianne O. de Bopp, *Letras alemanas en México* (México, 1961), p. 217.
13. *El Fénix de la Libertad*, 1832-33.
14. Lucas Alemán, konservativer Minister, der 1832 nach der fehlgeschlagenen spanischen Wiedereroberung der Kolonien von Santa Anna gestürzt wurde.
15. Diktator und Generalissimo 1853-1855.
16. C. C. Becher, *México in den ereignißvollen Jahren 1832/3.*
17. *El Siglo XIX*, Januar 1843.
18. *México a través de los Siglos*, VIII, 506.
19. Francisco López Cámara, *Los fundamentos de la economía mexicana en la época de la Reforma y la Intervención.* Col. del Congreso Nacional de Historia, No. 7 (México, 1962-75).
20. Antonio Prado Vértiz, "Después de 5 de Mayo," in *La Batalla del 5 de Mayo.* Col. del Congreso Nacional de Historia, No. 20 (México, 1963), p. 56.
21. *El Siglo XIX*, 21. Februar 1844.
22. Kruse.
23. Vol. 3, 1852.
24. 1. Juli 1852.
25. Berninger, p. 172.
26. Ibid., p. 171.
27. *La Voz de la Religión*, Hauptorgan der kirchlichen Opposition, 1848.
28. *El Observator católico*, 1848.
29. Francisco Bulnes, *El verdadero Juárez* (Paris & Mexico, 1904), p. 817.

30. Emmanuel Domenech, *Histoire du Mexique* (Paris, 1868), p. 336.
31. *México a través de los Siglos*, IX, 474.
32. Ibid., p. 450.
33. *El Siglo XIX*, 1861.
34. Marianne O. de Bopp, "Carlos von Gagern," *HUMBOLDT*, No. 46 (1972).
35. Juan A. Mateos, *El cerro de las campanas* (México,?), p. 227.
36. E. Masseras, *Un essai d'Empire au Mexique* (Paris, 1879).
37. E. Schmit von Tavera, *Geschichte der Regierung des Kaisers Maximilian* (Wien & Leipzig, 1903).
38. Eine religiös-politische, wissenschaftliche und literarische Zeitung in Guadalajara, Jal.
39. Morelia, 1865.
40. Friedrich Ratzel: *Aus Mexiko. Reiseskizzen aus den Jahren 1874/5* (Breslau, 1878).
41. Friedrich von Hellwald, *Maximilian I. Kaiser von Mexico* (Wien, 1869), p. 557.
42. Friedrich Gerstäcker, *In Mexiko* (Berlin, 1871), p. 206.
43. *El Ferro-carril*, 4. Dez. 1867.
44. *El Ferro-carril*, 14. Oktober 1870.
45. *El Siglo XIX*, 1870.
46. Friedrich Katz: *Mexiko, Deutschland, Díaz und die mexikanische Revolution* (Berlin, 1964), p. 94.
47. H. Wilmans, *Ein kriegerischer Kaufmannszug durch Mexiko* (Leipzig, 1913).
48. *El Siglo XIX*, 1889.
49. *El Monitor Republicano*, Juni 1879.
50. *El Monitor Republicano*, 16. Januar 1884.
51. *El Monitor Republicano*, 5. März 1881.
52. *El Monitor Republicano*, 14. und 21. Januar 1883.
53. 18. März 1888.
54. Marianne O. de Bopp, *Contribución al estudio de las Letras alemanas en México* (México, 1961), p. 219.
55. Ibid., p. 249,—und: "Oloardo Hassey, primer germanista en México," *HUMBOLDT*, No. 15 — 1963.
56. Ibid., p. 229.
57. Ibid., p. 221.
58. Paul Gaulot, *L'empire de Maximilien* (Paris, 1890).
59. *El Monitor Republicano*, 1879.
60. *Deutsche Zeitung von Mexiko*, 14. Februar 1885.
61. H. Lemcke, *Mexiko. Das Land und seine Leute* (Berlin, 1900).
62. Friedrich Katz, *Mexiko, Deutschland, Díaz und die mexikanische Revolution* (Berlin, 1964).

3. The Pennsylvania-Germans: Development of Their Printing and Their Newspress in the War for American Independence
Alexander Waldenrath

ORIGINS OF THE PENNSYLVANIA GERMANS

A renewed awareness and interest exists for the role non-English speaking immigrants have played in the emergence and development of the United States. Concomitant with the growth of a cosmopolitan attitude in the country is the evolvement of a clearer understanding and significance of its pluralistic society. This pluralism, the possibility of diversity within unity, has become recognized as a major factor in comprising the greatness and the promise of America. No aspect of its multiple culture can be discounted in an evaluation of the nation's evolution.

In the eighteenth century, Germans comprised the largest non-British ethnic group in the American colonies. A mass exodus from Germany resulted from wars, religious persecution, and political tyranny, coupled with glowing reports of life in America. The southwestern area of Germany was the homeland for most of these immigrants; the majority came from the Palatinate, others from Württemberg, Baden, and Switzerland. Conditions in Germany at the outset of the eighteenth century were catastrophic. The devastation from the Thirty Years' War had depleted the population enormously and property damage was staggering. The Palatinate, as a consequence of its strategic position, probably suffered more than most other areas of central Europe in the great war of the seventeenth century and in the military conquests of Louis XIV.

Equal recognition had been granted Roman Catholics, Lutherans, and Calvinists in Germany by the Peace of Westphalia. However, religious strife continued to erupt as a result of enforcing the regulation of *cuius regio eius religio*. Each of the four princes in the Palatinate during a sixty-year period, for example, changed the official religion.

The arbitrary exercise of political power by petty princes wrought further hardships, especially upon the peasant class. Clearly then, immigration to America meant to many a new hope. Since sectarians, Tunkers, Seventh Day Baptists, Schwenkfelders, Mennonites, and Mystics were, in general, not tolerated, they became the first to seek refuge across the Atlantic in America. From 1727 onward, immigration shifted strongly in favor of the church people, i.e., Lutherans, Reformed, and also Moravians, so that by 1776 they comprised ninety percent of the German population in America.[1] The magnetic force exercised by Pennsylvania upon these German immigrants evolved from the colony's unlimited economic opportunities together with her practice of religious tolerance.[2]

German settlements grew rapidly, essentially in the rich limestone areas of the southeastern part of the Commonwealth with land ideally suited for agriculture. Estimates of the numerical strength of the German population in Pennsylvania in the eighteenth century vary. Governor Thomas reported it to be three-fifths of the total; Benjamin Franklin, speaking before the House of Commons in London, believed it closer to one-third. In 1790, at the time of the first official census of the United States, the population in Pennsylvania was comprised of one-third native born Germans or their descendants.[3]

DEVELOPMENT OF PRINTING IN PENNSYLVANIA

The value of the printing trade for the growth of colonial America is obvious since ". . . printing became one of the implements of implanting and fostering the cultural heritage of European civilization in environments that were utterly new and strange."[4]

The printer played a major role in the political and social life of the day. His trade allowed him to exercise extensive influence upon issues of public concern since he was usually not only the publisher of a newspaper but also its editor.[5] By the time of the Revolution, he had emerged as one of the prime movers in the area of political ideas and political events. British authorities often regarded him as one of the "most dangerous men" in the colonies. Benjamin Franklin employed the advantages of his trade so skillfully that he rose to become a leading spokesman and a revered statesman.

By 1776, Philadelphia, the major city in the colonies, had several important printing establishments, while other areas of Pennsylvania also supported printing offices. As early as 1685, William Bradford undertook the first printing in the city. Pennsylvania, with its liberal and open political structure, restricted editors and publishers less than most other colonies. Such a policy was conducive towards the rapid growth of the trade. Since many major political activities of the Revolutionary Era were centered in and around Philadelphia, the printer of that city played a unique role in the unfolding of the revolutionary spirit. With its large German speaking population, it was only natural that printing houses using their language also flourished in Pennsylvania.

The establishment and continuation of a printing firm in colonial America was no simple task. Most materials at first had to be imported from or through England. Only slowly after mid-century could a domestic industry begin to supply the tradesman's need for manufactured goods. The endeavors of Christoph Saur, one of Pennsylvania's important printers in the colonial era, are indicative of the difficulties encountered. In the early 1730s, this versatile craftsman was engaged in clock repairing as well as in the sale of books and medicines, both of which usually came from the city of Halle in Germany. Saur was convinced of the feasibility and desirability of producing German books in Pennsylvania rather than having to rely upon their importation from Europe. By the mid-1730s he set about this task by writing to Dr. Hermann August Francke, superintendent of the Halle Institution, from whom he requested a press and type. This institution, the center of the pietistic movement in the Lutheran Church, was the leading charitable organization in Europe and also deeply concerned about the conditions of Germans in America. Benjamin Franklin, as an astute businessman, had already attempted to enter the German language printing market, but both his German language newspaper (1732) and other printing in German were quite unsatisfactory.

Francke, however, remained skeptical towards the project and would not supply the necessary materials. He referred the matter to the Rev. Frederick Michael Ziegenhagen for further consideration. This Lutheran court pastor in London had extensive contact with the German immigrants who passed through England before their departure for the colonies. Yet, there is no indication that anything ever came of Saur's request. In 1738, Saur had the good fortune of obtaining his equipment from another source, one which has remained unknown and referred to by Saur himself merely as "N." Although lacking knowledge of the printing trade, Saur could rely upon the assistance of experienced craftsmen such as the printers from the Ephrata Cloister.

Printing presses still had to be imported. It is believed that Saur probably made his own presses as early as 1750; if correct, this early date is exceptional.[6] Domestically manufactured presses were not available until 1769. By the 1770s the utilization of presses manufactured in America was common. This was fortunate in retrospect since it meant printers were no longer dependent for essential equipment upon England.

Saur initially imported his type from a foundry in Frankfurt, Germany. In the American colonies, as well as in England, much Dutch type, apparently of a superior quality, was used before 1740. Thereafter, the Caslon type, and others similar to it, enjoyed great popularity. It had to be imported since the staggering costs for purchasing fonts from abroad could have a crippling effect upon new printing houses. Again the necessity for developing a domestic industry was evident. The first type-foundry in the colonies was begun by Adam Buell in Connecticut who made his own matrices.[7] Christoph Saur II began experiments with the production of type in Germantown early in the 1770s. This was precipitated by plans to issue a third edition of his Bible. All the letters needed were cast, however, from imported matrices and molds. Justus Fox assumed responsibility for casting a massive amount of *Fraktur,* the form of printing Saur employed in his German work. The *Geistliches Magazien* of 1772, Vol. II, No. 12, proudly announced itself to be the first printed matter employing type cast in America. This statement was, however, a slight exaggeration because imported matrices, and not domestically made ones, were used. But such work afforded Saur's journeymen, Justus Fox and Jacob Bay, both of whom played a major role in the emergence of a self-sufficient American printing trade, the incentive to develop their own. As the clouds of revolution darkened on the horizon, a provincial conference of 1775, implementing a request of the Continental Congress to support domestic industries, recommended the use of the type ". . . now being made to a considerable degree of perfection by an ingenious artist in Germantown. . . ."[8]

The production method of paper in the colonies seems primitive when compared with modern ones. Clean linen rags and clear flowing water comprised the essential components. In water troughs, rags were slowly beaten into a thin pulp which, subsequently, was poured into molds, drained, then placed upon a felt pad, and, by means of a press, water was squeezed from them or they were hung for drying.[9] The beginnings of a domestic paper making industry lie with William Bradford and Samuel Carpenter in conjunction with William Rittenhouse, a German. They built a paper mill on a tributary of the Wissahickon near Germantown in 1690. William DeWees, a son-in-law of Rittenhouse, opened the second paper mill in America, also located near Germantown, and Thomas Willcox established a third in Delaware County in 1729.

Benjamin Franklin, due to his position, exercised control over the sale and distribution of paper. Saur had to turn to him as his supplier. Franklin hesitated. He seems to have been fearful of competition and hoped to control, if not indeed to halt, commercial printing ventures which might endanger the expansion and influence of his company. He proposed to sell Saur paper only if it would be purchased with cash payments. Saur, he knew, would be unable to meet such demands. Conrad Weiser, a man held in highest esteem throughout Pennsylvania, pledged his credit to Saur and, since Franklin could not reject this offer, the infant German language printing establishment was saved.[10]

About 1744 Saur built his own paper mill on Frankford Creek near the falls of the Schylkill (today Manayunk).[11] With the Revolution, there arose an acute paper shortage because this commodity was needed in the manufacture of various military items such as cartridges. Since their trade was considered crucial to the war effort, paper manufacturers were exempted from military service. Paper was still being made by hand, and rags were in short supply during the war years. Just about every edition of most newspapers printed an advertisement offering to purchase rags. Not until after the Civil War did wood pulp become the main source of paper. Ink also was not readily available in most colonies, and before mid-century it tended to be imported. In the middle colonies, this was not as often the case because the products necessary to produce ink, linseed oil, and lampblack were attainable. Printers such as Franklin and Saur as well as Armbruster and those at Ephrata made their own and it was considered to be of high quality.[12]

Publication of printed material, taken for granted today, was, therefore, an arduous task in the eighteenth century. We can only marvel at the achievements of colonial printers.

ESTABLISHMENT OF THE PENNSYLVANIA-GERMAN NEWSPRESS

A distinct German-American social, intellectual, and religious life emerged in Pennsylvania. Essentially it was founded upon cultural forms these Germans had brought across the Atlantic from their homeland, forms which became tempered by conditions in the new world. Popularization of the Pennsylvania-German heritage has often led to misconceptions of this culture; scholars, particularly in this century, have done much to rectify this.[13] Because so much of their history is in the German language, the Pennsylvania-Germans as a group have, at times, not been accorded the attention and recognition which their significance merits.[14]

In the past, views of some Americans have now and then been unduly influenced by a slight suspicion of anything not communicated in English. Popular notions suggested these Germans of Pennsylvania to be merely uneducated peasants, who contributed little, if anything, to the building of the nation. Granted, many and probably most were engaged in agricultural pursuits; yet, among early German settlers we also encounter the names of such intellectual giants as Pastorius, the founder of Germantown, who is considered by many to have been the most educated man in Pennsylvania in his day, the mystic Kelpius, and the renowned Weiser family. Later in the century, prominent leaders such as the Saurs, the Muhlenbergs, David Rittenhouse, and J. H. Miller played an active role in the intellectual life of the colonies and the early republic. They have all left an indelible mark upon American history.

Among the first printing in the German language in America was the work done by the Ephrata sectarians under Conrad Beissel.

Their early imprints appeared in Roman type; Christoph Saur printed the first book in German type, i.e., *Fraktur,* in 1739, the *Zionitische Weyrauchs-Hügel.* The import and the accomplishments of the Saur press, active for forty years, seems unequalled for Pennsylvania-German history. The influence of this press remained essentially unchallenged until the years of overt dissention against British rule in the colonies, when, due to a change in political attitudes among Pennsylvania-Germans, the position of the Saurs became rivaled and overshadowed by J. H. Miller.

Christoph Saur, born probably in a village called Ladenburg or Lauterburg in the Palatinate close to Heidelberg, spent his early years in Laasphe in Westphalia, in the region of Wittgenstein. His views on life were influenced early by the teachings of the sectarians. When thirty-one years of age, he arrived in Pennsylvania with his wife and son.[15] Initially they settled in Lancaster County close to the Ephrata Cloister, home of the sectarian Tunkers. Although he himself had scant respect for the fanaticism exhibited by Conrad Beissel, the leader at Ephrata, his wife ultimately joined the community where she spent many years and adhered to its teachings of celibacy. Thereupon in 1731, Saur moved to Germantown where he founded his printing establishment in 1738. With thousands of German immigrants pouring into Pennsylvania, he realized they would need the Bible in their own language for spiritual edification, a newspaper to keep abreast of events, and an almanac including weather prophecies, a calendar, and notes of interest. He set about to satisfy these needs. His initial products were almanacs with articles on medicine, history, and science. A year later he commenced publication of a German language newspaper which first appeared only once a month, then weekly. Actually Benjamin Franklin's venture, the *Philadelphische Zeitung,* whose initial number is dated May 6, 1732, was the first German language newspaper to be printed in America. Its circulation was quite limited and all indications point to its demise after only two editions.[16]

Saur's *Der Hoch Deutsche Pennsylvanische Geschicht-Schreiber, Oder: Sammlung wichtiger Nachrichten aus dem Natur und Kirchenreiche* was printed from August 20, 1739 to October 1777. At various times it underwent a change of name.[17] Its highest circulation reached at least 4,000, although some estimates range to 8,000 or 10,000, an enormous number for the day.[18] It had subscribers even beyond the borders of Pennsylvania and as far distant as Georgia. After the elder Saur's death in 1758, his son, Christoph II, continued to publish this journal until 1776 when, in turn, his own sons, Christoph III and Peter, assumed management.

Saur's first printing of a German language Bible in 1743 bears witness to his faith. It was a tremendous undertaking for a colonial American craftsman. Since the Universities of Cambridge and Oxford held the prerogative for printing Bibles in the British Empire, no colonial printer had dared undertake a challenge to this right. Previously, however, in 1678, a Bible in an Indian language had been produced in Boston; Cotton Mather never was able to procure a printer for his *Biblia Americana.* Saur's work, then, is the first Bible to be printed in a European language in North America and antedates the first English language one, published by Robert Aitkens in Philadelphia, by almost forty years.[19] Saur further distinguished himself by printing the first hymn book for the Reformed Church in America in 1752 and the first Lutheran hymnal in 1757.

A pietistic Christian tone of morality dominates the Saur newspress; indeed all Saur publications exhibit a religious-educational goal. Wroth's statement, "The Pennsylvania Germans were a folk set down in a strange land in the midst of an alien race; it is no wonder that they sang longingly of Zion and turned their vision inward," would seem too exaggerated.[20] Rather, as von Skal points out, "It was only natural above all they wanted books treating the religious side of life, for the whole trend of their mind tended to keep them away from worldly things and from literature of a worldly kind. Besides, they could not have kept up a connection with the Fatherland close enough to keep them informed of the literary activity going on there. Consequently hymn and prayer books were the first which the German printers published."[21]

The elder Saur clearly established such a religious orientation in initial issues of his newspaper. He announced that his publication would be not only a reporter of events but also a medium for conveying his sectarian Christian views. His pacifism led to editorial campaigns directed against the establishment of a colonial militia, the Indian wars, and finally even against the Revolution itself. Saur often found himself in strife over religious questions with leaders of the established German churches, such as Heinrich Melchior Muhlenberg, patriarch of the Lutheran Church in America, and Count von Zinzendorf, leader of the Moravians. Yet Saur always strove arduously for the preservation of the religious and cultural diversity of the German community in Pennsylvania.

One of the major encroachments upon his belief in a cultural doctrine of equality with separation was the charity school project. Saur became convinced that this movement was, in essence, an attempt to Anglicize the Germans and to integrate them as speakers of English into an English cultural environment and, thereby, to undermine their own culture.

Another major German press in colonial days was situated at the Ephrata Cloister. Saur had been connected with printing there in its infancy. Beissel's theosophic works of mystical theology and numerous books of hymns comprised its main products. The highest achievement of the craftsmen at Ephrata was publication of a major work by the Dutch Mennonite, Tielman Van Braght, the *Blutige Schauplatz*. Peter Miller, Beissel's successor as prior, translated it into German. This 1748 edition may be considered a monumental achievement of printing in colonial America since it was the largest book produced before the Revolution.

Other printers also figured prominently in events leading to and during the Revolution. Joseph Crellius edited and published *Das Hoch-Deutsche Pennsylvanische Journal* (1743-1747?) and Godhart Armbruster the (Philadelphia) *Zeitung* (1748-1749); of both papers, however, no known copies exist.[22] The *Lancastersche Zeitung* (January 15, 1752-June 5, 1753) was the first newspaper printed in German outside of Philadelphia. This bilingual edition, with parallel columns in English and German, was issued by Samuel Holland and Heinrich Miller; the former soon became its sole editor. Lancaster did not have a completely English language newspaper until 1794.

Anton Armbruster, brother of Godhart, initially edited the *Philadelphische Zeitung* (July 12, 1755-December 31, 1957?) but was succeeded by the Lutheran pastor Johann Friedrich Handschuh. Benjamin Franklin, known as rather unfriendly towards the Germans in Pennsylvania, was also among the financial backers of this journalistic undertaking. This enterprise pursued a policy particularly aimed against the ideals of the Saur press and attempted to promote the ill-fated charity school project. The Rev. Dr. William Smith, prime backer of this movement, supported the paper strongly. When, however, he suggested these schools would be instrumental in drawing all Lutherans into the Episcopalian fold, he lost most support from the German church people. When the *Philadelphische Zeitung* printed an editorial grossly hostile to the Quakers in the Assembly, its right to publish was withdrawn.

Das Pennsylvanische Zeitungs-Blatt, a short-lived enterprise (February 4, 1778–June 24, 1778), was published by Frantz Bailey in Lancaster. Philadelphia then had two additional papers; one, *Die Pennsylvanische Gazette* of John Dunlap, seems to have been published for only several months in 1779; the other, *Philadelphisches Staatsregister* (July 21, 1779–1781), was issued by Melchior Steiner and Charles Cist. Steiner continued on his own to print the *Gemeinnützige Philadelphische Correspondenz* until 1790.

Besides the Saur press, the most influential one was that of Johann Heinrich (Henrich) Miller. Whereas Christoph Saur II, motivated by deeply felt religious values, could not support the American rebellion against Great Britain (in a more bellicose spirit, his sons openly expressed Toryism), Miller became the unmitigating champion of American independence. As a counterforce to the policies of pacifism and Toryism of the Saurs, he was instrumental in the consolidation of German-Americans behind the break with Great Britain. This was an important task since "Saur's German paper was the only newspaper circulated among the Germans for many years, and it controlled their political actions throughout."[23]

Miller was born in the principality of Waldeck on the Upper Rhine in 1702. As a youngster he was apprenticed to a printer in Basle to learn the trade he was to practice for the rest of his life, first in Leipzig, Altona, London, Amsterdam, and Paris, and finally in America. He leaned towards the beliefs of the Moravians and, accompanying Count von Zinzendorf to the American colonies in 1741, became a Moravian in Bethlehem, Pennsylvania, a year later. During this time he found employment in the printing establishment of Benjamin Franklin. After an extended stay in Europe, Miller returned again to Philadelphia and to employment with Franklin until 1754. His third visit to Philadelphia began in

1760; this time he remained permanently and soon developed into a major spokesman for German-American views.[24] His newspaper, *Der Wöchentliche Pennsylvanische Staatsbote* (1762–1779), printed a bitter attack against the ideals of the Saurs; it warned, "Lerne Hieraus, ein treuer Freund des Landes zu seyen, darin du wohnst, und wo dirs gut gehet." In comparison to other journals of the day, the *Staatsbote* demonstrated considerably more cosmopolitanism. Having attained keen insight into the political affairs of Great Britain during his stay in London, Miller had become sceptical of British policy towards America and expressed this in his own liberal and idealistic political views.

The Germans in Pennsylvania may have been pivotal for the successful conclusion of the war. Without active assistance by the inhabitants of Pennsylvania for the Revolution, its outcome would have been highly doubtful. Sentiments in the American colonies at the commencement of hostilities against Great Britain were deeply split: of the total colonial population, one-third actually supported the British; one-third viewed the struggle with indifference; only one-third actually strove for independence.[25] Miller, as a champion of American independence, recognized his task as the evocation of militant support for the war among German-Americans; without it, Pennsylvania could not have turned the tide of battle against the Empire.

When the British occupation of Philadelphia began, Miller fled the city. After his return, although much of his printing materials had been destroyed or confiscated, he continued to raise his voice and to write boldly on behalf of American freedom. His almost eighty years of age began to bear heavily upon him and finally forced his retirement in 1779. In the knowledge of having been instrumental in the fight for the freedom he was no longer to witness, Miller died on March 3, 1782 in Bethlehem, Pennsylvania.

THE PENNSYLVANIA-GERMAN NEWSPAPER IN THE REVOLUTION

During the era of the Revolution, chronologically including the decade prior to war since political issues were being crystallized then, seven newspapers printed in the German language appeared in Pennsylvania. Several existed for a short time, a few for an extended period. Only one of these seven, the Saur press under the directorship of Christoph III and Peter Saur, espoused a Tory policy, and this only in the last months of its thirty-eight-year history.

Few copies of the Saur newspaper from the 1760s have been preserved; yet a reconstruction of its views before the climactic years of war does seem possible. It was comprised of four pages. The first and second pages carried objective reports of general political events on the international scene, interspersed with practical hints for daily living. The other two pages consisted of advertisements, illustrated by wood-cuts, for devotional literature, animals, sales, or runaway servants.

The events accompanying the French and Indian War, which was concluded in 1763, had radically altered the political views the majority of the Pennsylvania-Germans held. Particularly those who inhabited frontier areas had been active on the side of the British in many campaigns. When the Germans had expressed themselves in any political affairs prior to the war, they tended to support the Quaker party and stood firm against the development of a standing army. The numerous fierce attacks by the French and by the Indians, which had ravaged many of their outlying settlements, convinced them of the necessity to maintain a colonial militia. Their pacifism, which had resulted essentially from political non-involvement, gave way rapidly to new views and new political alliances. After 1763, only the sectarians continued to uphold pacifistic doctrines while the church people threw their support behind the party of the proprietors and, strangely enough, their former foe, Benjamin Franklin. This political realignment may well be regarded as the first major step towards the Americanization of the Pennsylvania-Germans.[26]

The Saur press, representative of German sectarianism, continued to reject this new militancy. The report of King George III's proclamation ending the war with France exemplified its spirit. Saur afforded much space to the King's intentions to aid the colonies by furthering their trade, manufacturing, and commerce. The King's policy proposing benevolent treatment of the Indians was hailed as a step towards lasting peace.

Under the editorship of Christoph Saur II, journalistic objectivity was the guideline; it became modified only by his pietistic Christianity. Concern for the growing tensions between Great

Britain and her American colonies, tempered with a hope and plea for conciliation, remained paramount in his features.

Printing of letters to reflect attitudes towards major events was a common practice of the day in the German language press as well as in the English language one. The edition of April 21, 1774 indicated Saur's position. A British officer stationed in New York corresponded with a friend in London and reported that "All America is in flames because of the provocation concerning tea."[27] He further noted the determination of the people not to accept any tea shipments and to burn, if need be, any and all vessels transporting this commodity.

Was tea really the prime issue in this controversy which flared into such journalistic sensationalism? The Townsend Act of 1767 imposed a tax not only on tea, but also on paper, glass, and other manufactured goods. To assume that the tax on paper was more directly the cause for the outbreak of hostilities than that upon tea, given the importance of the printer's position, would be quite logical. Two hundred years ago, after all, the "most dangerous man" in America was the printer. A tax upon paper could seriously impair his business. And then, "Tea as the father of the Eagle has always been something of an embarrassment to the American with a sense of humor."[28] If the printer-editor emphasized the tax upon paper, he might well appear self-serving; the extensive polemic against tea could have been a convenient cover.

Consistent with his policy of conciliation, Saur stood in sharp contrast to all other German-American newspaper editors in the Boston Tea Party affair. They all demanded severe reprisals against Britain. Saur, however, pointed out that the Tea Party might have unfortunate consequences for American commerce. The fish in the Boston harbor seemed to have been so adversely affected by such large amounts of tea in the water, that the fish trade with Spain and Portugal would be seriously curtailed. Benjamin Franklin's attempts at an amelioration of the difficulties, while serving as an emissary in London, sparked renewed hopes in Saur's commentaries.

Christoph Saur's belief in pacifism, however, did not hinder him from comprehending clearly the magnitude of the issues involved in the controversy. The edition of September 22, 1774 noted that two English ships had been seized by Algeria and their crews sold into slavery. In turn, Saur illustrated the parallels to British policy in America, and that, he wrote, in "A land which gladly praises its freedom and Christian sentiment."

Saur's policy is further exemplified in commentaries on a general congress meeting in North Carolina. The members referred willingly to George III as their rightful sovereign, and simultaneously, demanded that British tradition be upheld. Thus no citizen of the British Empire might be taxed without his consent, and the blockade of the Boston harbor must be discontinued immediately for its illegality was a violation of this tradition.

Sometime between April 1775 and March 1776, Christoph Saur II took in his son Christoph III as a full partner, and not later than February 1777 the younger Christoph assumed complete control together with his brother Peter. They continued publication until the Battle of Germantown in October 1777. Thereupon, they fled to the British who were in control of Philadelphia and remained there until shortly before the British evacuation in June of 1778.

Christoph Saur II was not a Tory in the War for Independence. In strict adherence to his religious principles, he remained neutral. Under his editorship, the newspaper never expressed a pro-British attitude. Reports on the Parliamentary debates in London consistently noted both sides of the arguments. Anti-British hysteria, characteristic of much of the American press of the time, never flavored his work. His fervent attempts sought an amelioration in the developing conflagration. The report of an American's mistreatment by the British military was concilitory in tone: "We ask your Excellency that the division between Great Britain and this province, which already has grown too large, not be widened by the brutality of your troops."

Saur's opinions and actions must have been misconstrued. He was treated as a British sympathizer, even as a traitor. Virtually all his property was confiscated and he himself reduced to poverty.[29] His sons Christoph III and Peter were, however, in sympathy with the royalist cause. They printed a pamphlet for A. Emmerich in 1777 which appealed to the Germans for support of the British. With so few printers in colonial America, none found it necessary to publish anything contrary to personal views.

Emmerich seems to have been an adventurer of sorts; he had fought in the Seven Years' War against France; he allied himself with the royalist cause in America and even travelled to Germany to recruit troops against the colonists; after the Revolution, he returned to Germany and took part in the abortive attempt in Kassel to capture King Jérôme of Westphalia and was executed.

Emmerich's broadside attacked the leaders of the Revolution as a band of culprits, perpetrators of intrigues, who were destroying this country. Their purpose was "to enslave you and nothing lies closer to their hearts than to build their fortunes upon the complete ruin of the country." Further, he proclaimed, it was "one's duty to return to the best of sovereigns." A second broadside conveyed a similar message beginning: "Höre Amerikaner! Der König von England ist Dein Wohlthäter und Beschützer gewesen, durch ihn bist Du groß, reich und glücklich geworden, und nun bezahlst Du ihn in der Raserei deines Übermuths mit Undank und Ungehorsam."

Christoph Saur III, born in 1754, was only twenty-one when the war began. Born in 1759, Peter was still younger. Why the third generation of the Saur printing firm became Tory supporters is not completely clear. It could be conjectured that their adherence to the Tunker faith, a religious group often treated with animosity by the larger church community, caused them to be skeptical of an America not ruled by a King who had guaranteed their religious freedom. Further, they saw their former enemies in the vanguard of those demanding punitive measures against Great Britain. The wealth of the Saur family could also have motivated its conservative attitude automatically at odds with the revolutionary spirit.[30] The supremacy of the Saur newspress in the German community, however, had already been replaced by the ardently pro-American journal of Henrich Miller.

The last editions of Saur's paper printed in Germantown before their evacuation to Philadelphia were still characterized by a conciliatory tone, indicative of Christoph II's influence. One issue, September 11, 1776, went so far as to reproduce a speech by General Roberdeau, an American patriot, in which he condemned the "vain conduct" of the British, the cause, he maintained, for the present critical situation. Further, the actions of the Americans evoked pride, for now all would be able to contribute their full measure, and "we can leave to our children and to future generations peace and freedom, a treasure more valuable than Gold."

For the duration of their sojourn in Philadelphia, the younger Saurs printed the paper under the title *Der Pennsylvanische Staats-Courier, oder einlaufende Wöchentliche Nachrichten.* Unfortunately, few copies have been preserved; their pro-British orientation is, however, evident. Seidensticker believed it served principally the Hessian troops.[31] Objectivity, characteristic of earlier Saur journalism, was abandoned. Reporting of international events became tendentious: news from Hungary occasioned a stinging attack on Roman Catholicism; actions of France reportedly embodied inhumanity. Articles from "Rebel Newspapers," i.e., from the American press representing the colonists, were reproduced in an individual column in an attempt to create disdain for the American cause. British troops, portrayed as humane, helpful, and peace-loving, were contrasted with American leaders, "the murders of humanity," who had turned "this once happy province" into a wasteland.

After the British evacuated Philadelphia, Christoph III accompanied them to New York where he continued in their employ as an apologist for the royal cause. In April 1780, he published a sixteen-page pamphlet, *Zuschrift an die Teutschen in Pennsylvanien und benachbarten Provinzen,* an ardent plea for their return to the British fold.

Only twenty-one issues of Francis (or Frantz) Bailey's *Das Pennsylvanische Zeitungs-Blat* appeared in 1778. McCulloch relates pertinent information about Bailey's background.[32] By trade a carpenter, he became versed in printing at Ephrata. From his office in Lancaster he produced a paper for five months. Late in 1778, after the British evacuation, he established himself in Philadelphia and commenced publication of an English language periodical, the *Freeman's Journal.* In 1779 he published the *United States Magazine,* of which a mere nine numbers appeared. Since he did part of the printing for the legislature, he moved to Lancaster when it began assembling there in 1779.

Bailey was a staunch defender of the American position. However, the observation that his paper contained exclusively war news, can be affirmed only with qualification.[33] International news reporting, i.e., exclusively from Europe, formed a standard feature. A clever technique in such coverage tended to correlate European events with those in the American war. When American ships reached foreign parts, Bailey expressed joy, for this illustrated, he maintained, the prowess of American commerce. Great delight ensued upon completion of the treaty between France and America for it would surely bring France into active confrontation with Great Britain. Praise was lavished upon the King of France as the "protector of the rights of man." Indications that France, Spain, Portugal, Poland, and Prussia were on the verge of granting the colonies political recognition became widely heralded.

Bailey exposed for his readers the general disdain for the war which was rampant in the British Parliament as well as among the citizens. Speeches by the King became instruments for demonstrating royal pomposity and political ignorance. Parliamentary leaders, who exposed the American cause or who supported the political necessity of granting independence, were quoted extensively: Lord Chatham in his call for "employing the best means in order to reestablish peace and freedom"; General Conway, before the House of Commons, referring to the British deeds as worse than those of a Duke of Alva against the Netherlands.

The number of German mercenaries in British service, Bailey claimed, reached 11,500 by March of 1778. The majority, he proposed, desired to remain here and to quit British service. The American troops, he continued, were "braver than the destitute German princes, who sell their subjects as a butcher does his meat on the cutting board."

Without the support of the German farmers of Pennsylvania, Washington's army might well have been decimated by lack of food. Washington communicated with them through the columns of the *Zeitungs-Blat,* asking for a winter supply of grain and giving directions for delivery. Bailey remarked that "all who wish their country well, . . . should contribute something to support the army . . . ; and should do all that is in their power." Bailey bore witness to his fellow Germans and the cause because "we cannot hold the slightest doubt concerning the virtuous views of the inhabitants of this province since we are dealing in such a legitimate matter . . ."

In order to discredit the British and their conduct of the war, Bailey reviewed conditions American prisoners faced in English camps. The British were so slovenly, he suggested, that they even requested financial support from the Americans so that prisoners could be fed and clothed. American leaders, on the other hand, knew only benevolence since they readily supplied all necessities for captives. Protests from Congress, directed to British authorities, concerning mistreatment of American prisoners, were featured prominently.

Letters to the editor usually noted the popular support for the war and chastised the villain, Great Britain. Items from Saur's *Staats-Courier* of Philadelphia were printed under the lead "From Rebel Newspapers." Battle reports, almost always favorable to the Americans, abounded.

After the departure of the British from Philadelphia in July 1778, the rejuvenated newspress there must have drawn the readership away from Bailey's journal and caused the abandonment of his enterprise.

John (sometimes named Johann) Dunlop's newspaper also enjoyed only short duration; merely the first issue, February 3, 1779, is extant, and it is unclear if further ones actually did appear. It definitely was defunct by July 21, 1779 when the *Staatsregister* noted that no other German language newspaper was being issued in Philadelphia. Dunlop probably undertook this venture in order to win over the readership of the Saur press, which had disappeared, and of the *Staatsbote,* which began announcing its contemplated cessation. At the time, Dunlop was already an established printer in Philadelphia and did most of his work in the English language.[34] His editorial point of view was strongly pro-American. The extant issue, in a mood of elation over the treaty with France, carried a German translation of it. Confidence in American money was on the wane as a result of spiralling inflation and the great amount of counterfeit bills in circulation. Dunlop, in actions common to most other newspaper printers, implored his readers to have confidence in their country's currency.

Judging from the first issue, a definite cosmopolitan attitude in Dunlop's journalism seems to emerge. To be sure, the American War for Independence remained the focal point of all journalism of the day. Yet, Dunlop tried to develop the interest of his readership beyond the domestic scene. In a report entitled "Berlin," the precarious relationship between Austria and Prussia was discussed thoroughly. In fact, by recounting the background of their interaction over several decades, their present conflict was illuminated.

A Christian spirit, common to the German language newspress

of the eighteenth century, continued here by means of a prayer of thanks for the outcome of the Revolution because "we can never regard the progress of the war from which America attained her freedom without admiring the goodness of Divine Providence and recognizing thankfully God's contribution to it."

Melchior Steiner, originally from Switzerland, and Carl Cist, from St. Petersburg, had founded their firm in December of 1775 and planned as early as 1776 to establish a German language newspaper. At that time they were unable to attain the five hundred subscribers, the number necessary to make the undertaking solvent. Since Saur's and Miller's papers enjoyed wide popularity, the establishment of a new journal would have been difficult. However, when these two suspended publication, Steiner and Cist launched their *Philadelphisches Staatsregister* with the caption "Enhaltend Die neuesten Nachrichten von den merkwürdigsten In- und Ausländischen Kriege- und Friedens-Begebenheiten; nebst verschiedenen andern gemeinnützigen Anzeigen." Its center of interest remained one major issue, the war. Thus dedicated almost exclusively to the Revolution, this paper displayed a provincialism which hardly allowed for the coverage of foreign news, unless this had a direct link with the Revolution. Publication began on July 21, 1779 and continued into 1781.

Almost fanatical in its support for the war cause, this paper offers excellent insight into some persuasive propaganda techniques. Letters to the editor became more widely utilized than in sister journals: George Washington praised the American military victories; the moral virtues and military strength of the new nation were lauded. The fictitious correspondence of two British officers bristled with hatred toward the Americans and with threats of major destruction against their strongholds. Inhumanity and immorality, the paper maintained, highlighted all British military and personal activity. Such allegations formed part of a concerted campaign of terror. In contrast, the new nation, embodying the highest ethical values, was eulogized in a lengthy article: the American nation represents a "form of government which has been constructed according to noble principles . . . where the governors of the state are servants of the people and not their rulers . . . Despicable and unlimited power characterizes the unnatural purposes of the British King and the Parliament he has bought. He proposes to make the inhabitants of America into slaves; such contemplations place you in the necessary position of protecting your rights with weapons, otherwise you will be brought under his yoke." Most striking in this letter campaign were the words of a European to his friend in America who is told that England had not yet been humbled enough and that the hearts of all Europeans lay with the American cause of freedom.

Steiner and Cist dissolved their partnership in 1781, whereupon Steiner began his weekly the *Gemeinnützige Philadelphische Correspondenz* on May 2, 1781. In its first year the title was altered to the *Neue Philadelphische Correspondenz;* publication continued until September 1790. Its high journalistic niveau resulted in no small part from two of its editors, the Lutheran pastors, J. C. Kunze and J. H. C. Helmuth.

From the above survey, it follows that the significance of the part played by German-Americans in the war was a dominant feature which assumed two aspects. First, their life-style, shown to be reasonable and worthy of emulation, should dispel any misconceptions other Americans may have had. The second part directed itself towards the German-Americans themselves. They must stand together and retain their individual identity, for "Eintracht gibt Macht." The reason for such articles is unclear. Perhaps the Germans were becoming assimilated too rapidly into English-American culture and Steiner wished his people to retain their own individuality. There may also have been an attempt to alter pejorative views some Americans may have held about German-Americans. Their support for the Revolution was almost unanimous: thousands were serving in the ranks of the Continental Army; many held high commissions; German farmers were among the most generous suppliers of food for the troops; and even the pacifist sectarians contributed by caring for the wounded. An undercurrent of suspicion against the Germans in Pennsylvania, however, had been common throughout the century; it culminated in the fear among various leaders, including Benjamin Franklin, that the colony might become completely German. This distrust of cultural diversity reached, at times, hysterical proportions. During the French and Indian War, many were convinced that the Germans would side with the French. The thousands of German mercenaries fighting against the Americans also raised a specter of fear. Even today historical studies of the revolutionary era detail the role of the so-called Hessians but refrain almost totally from mention of the decisive contribution made by German colonists. Given the divisiveness within the colonies' attitude towards the battle and the pivotal position of Pennsylvania, it may well be conjectured that without the devoted efforts of the German-Americans the war could not have been brought to its successful conclusion.

A moralizing tone, ranging from abstinence to politics, ran through the majority of stories and anecdotes which consistently appeared after mid-1782. When the conflagration seemed destined for a successful conclusion, Steiner raised his pen on behalf of conciliation among all factions in America. His "Conversation between Wilhelm Whig and Hans Tory" explained the advantages of democracy over royal rule and absolutism, a form of government, he concluded, which represented merely a lower stage in historical development. "We must all now in America close ranks and work together as one people and not let dissensions of the past tear our nation asunder."

Anti-British sentiment ran a wide gamut of reporting. British soldiers were depicted as bandits and the King as a tyrant who believed the war would have dire consequences for the Americans and was "a civil war as bad as the one under the Stuarts." Claims of discord among the British people were widely reported, for they reputedly wished the "King to give up the war because it is madness to try to coerce our brothers in America."

The most illustrious German-American journalist-printer during the Revolutionary War was Johann Heinrich (Henrich) Miller. His extensive travels throughout Europe (he had served as a printer in many cities and even published a newspaper in London in the summer of 1756) explain his cosmopolitanism and political acumen. By nature Miller was a political man, a staunch upholder of egalitarianism, and an unmitigating idealist. His Moravian piety strengthened this latter sentiment. In quantitative production his press rivaled and finally surpassed Saur's. Miller, using his press to further revolutionary sentiments, printed in both German and English. His newspaper, *Der Wöchentliche Pennsylvanische Staatsbote,* affords insight into the intellectual development of this patriot and into the views of Americans in general.[35] Many other texts from his press also illustrate his views. For example, in 1775 he published a pamphlet "An die Einwohner Teutscher Nation in den Colonien von Neuyork und Nordcarolina" which admonished Americans to stand fast "um die unterdrückten Rechte und Frey-heiten etlicher Millionen Einwohner des Weltteiles gegen die unbe-fugte Eingriffe gewisser bösen und gewaltigen Menschen in Obacht zu nehmen." These evil people were the King and the British Parliament. Further, Parliament was indicted for making laws restricting personal freedom; the Stamp Act was called a gross violation of the rights of Americans, as were other acts which affected commerce, industry, and taxation. Miller's reputation as a tenacious fighter for freedom was firmly established in these controversies.

The Stamp Act must have been especially odious to Miller and most other German printers, for it placed an added tax upon materials printed in any other language than English; in fact, they would be taxed twice as much. From its inception, the Act was unpopular in the colonies, and also among merchants and manu-facturers in England who recognized the danger to their growing trade ties with America. Miller waged an editorial battle against the Act until its repeal in March 1767. Beyond the immediate conse-quences of the Act, Miller believed that a lack of assertiveness by Americans against Parliament would allow for "future suppres-sion." He poetically denounced the implementation of the act: ". . . Good night, good night, oh freedom! America, oh that America which has been damned by such an early judgement of slavery. . ." Miller also exhibited his disdain by printing a skull and crossbones with the words, "this is the place for the pangs of sor-row, the irritating stamp." Such action was, of course, not unique to Miller; many printers pursued similar methods. That of Isaiah Thomas' *Halifax Gazette* is well-known: Thomas turned his paper upside down, so that the stamp would be incorrectly placed and then printed alongside it a wood-cut of the devil thrusting his pitchfork into the stamp.

Jubilation erupted with the repeal of the hated Act. As a result of this controversy, the political situation in London had become critical. For the government, the problem had been clear: how could the repeal be accompanied with recognition of Parliament's supremacy in colonial affairs? The Declaration Act, passed simul-taneously with the repeal of the Stamp Act, declared Parliament to have complete authority in all matters of governance in America. Little heed was paid this Act in North America; yet, its consequences changed the British Empire only ten years later. Miller too shared in this joy, though more soberly than many. He warned of the "ecstasies of joy," and recognized this was only to be the beginning of the struggle with Great Britain. In the following years, he always mentioned the anniversary of the repeal in the *Staatsbote.*

Often the American government, the Continental Congress, and the provincial legislature called upon Miller to print official documents, propaganda broadsides, and pamphlets. Not only were these profitable for Miller, but they also represented his own political views. Indicative of such work is "The Alarm or an Address to the People of Pennsylvania" printed in English. "The long continued injuries and insults, which the Continent of America hath sustained from the cruel power of the British Court, and the disadvantages, which the several provinces in the meantime labour under from the want of a permanent form of government [allows us] to take up and establish new governments 'as the authority of the people' in lieu of those old ones which were established on the authority of the crown." The pamphlet closes "And we have no fear, that as our cause is just, our God will support us against barbarous tyrants, foreign mercenaries and American traitors."

The protest against the Stamp Act initiated Miller's campaign against British rule in America. His reputation as a journalist and propagandist became established since he could be aggressive, penetrating, and logical in his argumentation and win German-American support for the cause.

The clamor against unjust rule continued strongly and assertively during the years preceding the outbreak of open hostilities. Major efforts were directed against the British regulation of American commerce. Boycotts against British goods were often suggested, especially in reaction to the blockade of the Boston harbor, an act regarded as a violation of man's natural rights and Americans' freedom as British subjects. This issue became the principal one in the movement to unify the colonies against England. Miller was a strong advocate of unity. He never wearied in these years from using such phrases as "our natural rights," "despotic exercise of power," "British slavery," and "British vassals."

Miller listed the following grievances as: a standing Army was maintained in America without her permission; the military authorities exercised the highest political power in peacetime; customs officials arbitrarily searched private homes; judges were not responsible to the citizens; acts of Parliament concerning America were often capricious; the blockade of Boston harbor was illegal, and those responsible for the Boston massacre had never been brought to trial.

Parliamentary debates, reportedly referring to Americans as a "malcontent lot," inflamed the sentiment of Miller's readers. The Boston Massacre became the "bloodbath." Letters to the editor emphasized British culpability and premeditation. They also praised America as the land of opportunity and of the future. ". . . Ich bin so sehr überzeugt, daß Nord-America, binnen 100 jahren, der sitz der handlung, freyheit und macht seyn wird, und der zuflucht derer, die die freyheit und die Protestantische religion lieben, daß, wäre ich nicht so alt, ich mit meiner familie zu euch hinüber gehen wolte," wrote a man from London (April 30, 1771).

The first report of the Battle of Lexington and Concord was given on page two in merely a short reference to the encounter. The scantness of verifiable details must have caused such curtness, and the next issue extensively recorded the events on pages one and two; the hope was still being expressed that a state of war would not necessarily ensue. A four-page supplement to the May 16, 1775 number furnished eye-witness reports of the encounter as well as an editorial, directed to the citizens of Great Britain, which accused General Gage of having begun hostilities and implying that a state of war did indeed now exist.

In the early stages of the war, many hoped and assumed Canada would join the patriots. Miller addressed a lengthy plea for such unity to the suppressed inhabitants of Canada, ". . . Wir unterhalten noch die Hoffnung, daß ihr euch mit uns in der Verteidigung unserer gemeinschaftlichen Freyheit vereinigen werdet, und noch ist Ursache zu glauben, daß wofern wir zusammen treten, die Aufmerksamkeit unsers Oberherrn auf die unverdienten und unerhörten Unterdrückung seiner Americanischen Unterthanen anzuflehen, daß derselbe endlich die Augen eröffnen und einem ausgelassenen Staatsamt nicht länger erlauben werde mit den Rechten des menschlichen Geschlechts ihren Mutwillen zu treiben . . ."

Inflammatory poems and letters fill the columns of the *Staatsbote* as Miller strove to unify the Germans behind the patriots' cause. One letter from Germany reminded his compatriots in Pennsylvania of the reasons for which he had left Europe: ". . . der dienstbarkeit zu entgehen und die freyheit zu genießen . . ."

Miller's newspaper has the distinction of being the first to announce the adoption of the Declaration of Independence. In good part, this was due to chance. At the time, his paper appeared twice weekly, on Tuesday and Friday. July 5 fell on a Friday; on page two, curiously enough, an extremely short notice of the adoption was given; the following Tuesday, July 9, Miller offered the first translation of the Declaration to readers of German. Novel in journalistic practices for the *Staatsbote* was the utilization of headlines of varying typesize to connote the importance for America of this step, the creation of a new nation.

When the British occupied Philadelphia, Miller fled to Bethlehem and then to York where the Continental Congress had gone. There he printed the proceedings of the Congress in German.[36] Returning to Philadelphia the following year and finding most of his equipment gone, he accused in a fiery broadside the Saurs of having stolen his property. He did manage to publish the *Staatsbote* again, starting on August 5, 1778 for about a year. The shop was then sold to Steiner and Cist.

The editors of the German language newspress of Pennsylvania, with the exception of the Saurs, were in the forefront of the patriotic movement. Their mission was the consolidation of German-American strength behind the Revolutionary cause. They accomplished this by a steadfast editorial spirit which defended the American ideal of self-determination. Had they not enlisted the staunch backing of the Germans in the pivotal area of Pennsylvania, the outcome of the Revolution might have been different. The United States is deeply indebted to these men who dedicated their abilities to the creation of a new and independent nation.

NOTES

1. Glenn Weaver, "Benjamin Franklin and the Pennsylvania Germans," *The William and Mary Quarterly*, 3rd series, XIV (1957), 553.

2. See Oswald Seidensticker, "William Penn's Travels in Holland and Germany in 1677," *The Pennsylvania Magazine of History and Bibliography* (Philadelphia, 1878), vol. 2, no. 3, pp. 237-282.

3. William J. Mann, *Life and Times of Henry Melchior Mühlenberg* (Philadelphia, 1888), p. 93. Mann believes the German population of Pennsylvania at mid-century to be almost half of the total.

4. Douglas C. McMurtrie, *The Book. The Story of Printing and Bookmaking* (London, New York, Toronto, 1967), p. 435.

5. See McMurtrie, p. 445.

6. See Lawrence C. Wroth, *The Colonial Printer* (Portland, Maine, 1938), p. 82.

7. Wroth, 98 ff.

8. Edward W. Hocker, "The Sower Printing House of Colonial Times," *Pennsylvania German Society Proceedings and Addresses* (Norristown, Penna., 1948), vol. 53, part 2, p. 85.

9. See Wroth, pp. 123 ff.

10. See Paul A. W. Wallace, *Conrad Weiser 1696-1760* (Philadelphia, 1945), p. 103.

11. William McCulloch, "William McCulloch's Additions to Thomas's History of Printing," *Proceedings of the American Antiquarian Society*, New Series, XXXI (1922), 128.

12. McCulloch, p. 179.

13. See, e.g., H. M. M. Richards, "The Pennsylvania-German in the Revolutionary War 1775-1783," *Pennsylvania German Society Proceedings and Addresses* (Lancaster, Penna., 1908), pp. 1-542; F. J. F. Schantz, "The Domestic Life and Characteristics of the Pennsylvania-German Pioneer," *Pennsylvania German Society Proceedings and Addresses* (Lancaster, 1900), pp. 5-97; J. G. Rosengarten, "The German Soldier in the Wars of the United States," (Philadelphia, 1890); A. B. Faust, *The German Element in the United States* (New York, 1927); Ralph Wood et al., *The Pennsylvania German* (Princeton, N.J., 1942); Oswald Seidensticker, *The German Press in America* (Philadelphia, 1893); Oswald Seidensticker, *Bilder aus der Deutsch-pennsylvanischen Geschichte* (New York, 1885); Oswald Seidensticker, *The First Century of German Printing in America, 1728-1830* (Philadelphia, 1893); H. T. Rosenberger, *The Pennsylvania Germans 1891-1965* (Lancaster, Penna., 1966); Glenn G. Gilbert, ed., *The German Language in America. A Symposium* (Austin, Texas, 1971); Don Yoder, *Pennsylvania Spirituals* (Lancaster, Penna., 1961). These are only a few of the major works in the field.

14. It is not uncommon to find historians hardly even mentioning them and their contribution to attaining American independence from Great

Britain. George Bancroft, *History of the United States of America* (Boston, 1876), vol. 4, p. 329, honors them at least with the comment ". . . the Germans, who composed a large part of the inhabitants of the province, were all on the side of liberty . . ."

15. See Edward W. Hocker, pp. 5 ff; William McCulloch, p. 144.

16. See Julius F. Sachse, "The First German Newspaper Published in America," *Pennsylvania German Society Proceedings and Addresses* (Lancaster, Penna., 1900), vol. 10, pp. 41 ff.

17. Karl J. R. Arndt and May E. Olson, *German-American Newspapers and Periodicals* (Heidelberg, Germany, 1961), p. 523.

18. Albert B. Faust, vol. 1, pp. 144-5; Edward W. Hocker, p. 31.

19. Felix Reichmann, *Christopher Sower Sr. 1694-1758* (Philadelphia, 1943, pp. 4 ff.

20. Lawrence C. Wroth, p. 262.

21. George von Skal, *History of German Immigration in the United States* (New York, 1908), p. 16.

22. See James Owen Knauss, Jr., *Social Conditions among the Pennsylvania Germans in the Eighteenth Century as Revealed in the German Newspapers Published in America* (Lancaster, Penna., 1972), p. 8; Karl J. R. Arndt and May E. Olsen, pp. 560-578.

23. William Beidelman, *The Story of the Pennsylvania Germans* (Easton, Penna., 1898), p. 82.

24. See Charles Frederick Dapp, "The Evolution of an American Patriot. Being an Intimate Study of the Patriotic Activities of John Henry Miller," *Pennsylvania German Society Proceedings and Addresses* (Lancaster, Penna., 1924), vol. 32, part 23.

25. See Moses Coit Tyler, "The Party of the Loyalists in the American Revolution," *The American Historical Review* (New York, 1896), I, 24-25.

26. Glenn Weaver, p. 551.

27. Most newspaper quotations will be given in English. These translations are my own.

28. Wroth, p. 143.

29. See Edward W. Hocker, pp. 90 ff; Oswald Seidensticker, *The German Press in America* (Philadelphia, 1893), p. 95; Oswald Seidensticker, *Bilder aus der Deutsch-pennsylvanische Geschichte* (New York, 1885), pp. 113 ff, p. 158.

30. Cf. James Owen Knauss, Jr., "Christopher Sower The Third," *Proceedings of the American Antiquarian Society* (Worcester, Mass., 1932), New Series, vol. 41, p. 236-7.

31. Oswald Seidensticker, *The German Press in America* (Philadelphia, 1893).

32. William McCulloch, p. 103.

33. See James Owen Knauss, Jr., p. 16.

34. See William McCulloch, p. 108; James Owen Knauss, Jr., p. 16. Knauss regards this newspaper as a continuation of the Saur enterprise. It definitely did not, however, follow Saur's political orientation.

35. See Karl J. R. Arndt and May E. Olson, p. 567. Various title changes occurred.

36. John Joseph Stoudt, "The German Press in Pennsylvania and the American Revolution," *The Pennsylvania Magazine of History and Biography* (Philadelphia, 1935), vol. 59, pp. 80–90.

4. German Men of Letters in the Early United States
Harold Jantz

After a century and more of solid research in German Americana and after a series of major studies, general and special, it would hardly seem possible that a large proportion of the relevant material remains unknown, among it much of prime importance, some even of crucial importance. Yet this is indeed the case, even for the nineteenth century, as the esteemed recipient of this Festschrift has demonstrated over and over again, precisely in those fields that were believed to have been thoroughly explored. For example, after a seemingly exhaustive Sealsfield bibliography had been published, Karl Arndt discovered a number of unknown works of his, the early ones of particular interest. Beyond this, he has even opened up new fields for us, not only in the nineteenth century but also in our own, and now his research goes back into the eighteenth century.

At first sight, the period of the American Revolution, in all its German relations, would seem to have been thoroughly, indeed exhaustively explored. This phase of American-German relations has long been a subject of intense interest and through the years there have been a number of estimable studies, general and special, including a compendious recent one. Nevertheless, there have been two factors that have prevented true comprehensiveness and a full perspective on the field.

In the first place, the whole field of early German Americana, from the beginnings through 1800, has never been thoroughly investigated, not even the concluding decades, 1770–1800, although a succession of scholars remains convinced that it has been. To be sure, the obvious Americana, readily recognizable from their title or general nature, are known and recorded for the most part, as are the pertinent works of the famous men of letters, though even here, surprisingly enough, important matters have been overlooked, even in the case of Goethe and Schiller, where astonishingly superficial conclusions continue to be drawn, especially with regard to their early years. The obvious Americana, however, are only less than half of a greater whole, the scope and significance of which still remain to be probed. On previous occasions I have given examples of the hidden Americana, and it is clear that they can be among the most significant of all. For the period of the Revolution and early Republic the state of knowledge is somewhat better in the expository fields, historic, descriptive, analytic, and here perhaps as much as three quarters of the significant material is known. By contrast, in the imaginative fields, poetry, drama, novel, essay, hardly one fifth of the material is known, and among the still unknown are works not only of interest to the literary student, but also of prime importance for the student assessing the German psychological, sociological, and political climate of the time. Why, for instance, in the literature of the last fifty years has there been only one brief reference to David Christoph Seybold's two-volume novel, *Reizenstein. Die Geschichte eines deutschen Officiers* (Leipzig, 1778–1779), even though in it the situation of the German soldier arbitrarily shipped off to America is presented more dramatically, more sharply, and in closer detail than in most of the expository works of the day? Indeed, one can only marvel that such a courageously radical revolutionary work not only escaped censorship but even experienced a reprint and a sequel. Such freedom of the press is highly indicative and may be quite startling to those more familiar with the standard clichés on the Germany of those times than with the actual phenomena. *Reizenstein* was once briefly and superficially noticed fifty-one years ago; on numerous further German novels, dramas, and poems dealing with America there has been complete silence—and an almost complete one even for whole groups, such as the naive Werthers who go to America or the experienced veterans who return from there.

In the second place, not every one of the aspects of German literary relations to the American Revolution has been equally well studied. Any comprehensive account of the impact of the new republic on the German imagination would have to consider four interrelated aspects. The most familiar is the literary production of those writers who never came to America except in their imagination. A polar opposite would be those colonial German settlers who lived through the Revolution and felt impelled to give some poetic imaginative account of it. This is a far smaller group than the first, to judge from the studies of them presently available, although probably there are surprises here also, as there are in the first group. The third group, scarcest of all, would be concerned with Americans in German lands during and after the Revolution. Among the dozen or more such Americans there are a few of literary interest, not only those who left us fascinating early accounts of Germany and the Germans, but also others, such as the South Carolinian who was well known in Swiss German literary circles before he returned to America to join the Revolution; or his cousin who later participated in one of the most thrilling European prison escapes; or another American whose papers were purloined by a British envoy, whereupon the indignant German ruler quietly allowed the culprit to contrive his own retributive justice—this one of the great ironic tales of the Revolution that remains untold in our time.

My present concern is with the fourth aspect. Although it is a bit less rare than the third, it is so rare that no special study has been made of it. The present study, being the first, is bound to be imperfect. Of necessity it will also be selective, with mere allusion to the already well known, unless there are new aspects or relations to be noted. It is concerned with those German men of letters who, instead of imagining what the Revolution and the new Republic were like, came over and found out for themselves.

Among the thousands of Germans who did come over, most of them perforce on the British side (although there were larger numbers on the American side than most people realize), relatively few left written records; of these written records, as always, many were lost, and of the remaining relatively few are of literary value. From the men in the ranks a number of ballads and songs have been preserved, and busy scholars have apparently brought most (although certainly not all) of the extant ones to light. Oddly enough, one of the smallest German contingents, the one from Ansbach-Bayreuth, seems to have been literarily most active, or else most careful in preserving its verse and prose.

However, with regard to the popular verse a note of warning must be sounded: not all of the purported ballads of the common soldier of the day are authentic. One of the most frequently reprinted (and one that will probably reappear several times in these bicentennial years) is the song that Franz Wilhelm von Ditfurth entitled "Die Hessen nach Amerika. 1777" and that he claimed was recorded in 1829 from the lips of an old soldier, Mirbach, in Kassel. He included it in volume two, part two, of his collection, *Die historischen Volkslieder der Zeit von 1648 bis 1871* (Berlin, 1871-1872). It begins (9):

> Frisch auf, ihr Brüder, in's Gewehr,
> 'S geht nach Amerika!

To this day no one has publicly questioned the reliability of Ditfurth or the authenticity of the many collections of German art songs and folk songs, historical songs, and ballads (many with their melodies) that he published during the middle decades of the nineteenth century. Indeed, in our time these collections were largely reprinted without a single voice of protest being raised. The longest and most detailed biography readily available about him, in Friedrich Blume's encyclopaedic *Die Musik in Geschichte und Gegenwart*, though it dwells on his psychological problems and his frustrations at his lack of success in his own artistic endeavors, both in poetry and in music, contains not the least hint of a suspicion that his extensive publications of the words and music of others before him might in part be his own fabrications. Psychologically this whole course of events could be explained as his compensation for personal frustration and his revenge on the world for not accepting the poetry and music written under the name of Ditfurth while welcoming with open arms his other creative efforts that were masked as historical treasures of the past.

Not that all the poems and songs he published were forgeries, far from it. He was clever enough to intermingle the authentic with the fabricated. The whole affair is too complex to explain briefly at this point. Suffice it to say that I was first alerted by a group of supposedly Renaissance songs in a publication of his. Intuitively I was disturbed by them, by a feeling of "Hier stimmt etwas nicht," with regard both to the words and the music. Thereupon followed a close analysis that revealed startling anachronisms. Once one is alerted, one is left to wonder why it has taken so long for the fakery to be detected; now it all seems so obvious. And as one goes on examining volume after volume of Ditfurth's collections, the historical songs and ballads for example, one is alternately appalled and amused at the extent of his effrontery in duping the cultured public of Germany. A natural reaction would be to consign all to a general damnation. And here one must be alerted to the opposite danger: an undiscriminating, a programmatic skepticism is just as naive as an uncritical gullibility. After all, an eminent historian, Edward Gaylord Bourne, "proved" Jonathan Carver's report on his western exploration in the 1760s to have been a forgery, and yet some years later the original manuscripts were found that showed it to be authentic. The art curators have a term for a work of art that is unjustly condemned as a forgery: they call it a "fake fake." Some pieces in Ditfurth can be proved to be authentic; further ones sound authentic and need to be examined critically—and that means openmindedly. But among these "Die Hessen nach Amerika" can hardly be ranked. It is so afflicted with the anachronisms of the later period of its origins that it must be ranked among the feebler efforts of Ditfurth to achieve "authenticity." One may well question another song frequently quoted, "Die Deutschen Hülfstruppen nach Amerika. 1776" (*ibid.*, 5-7):

> Wer will mit nach Amerika?
> Die Hannoveraner sind schon da,
> Die Hessen werben mit Gewalt,
> Kommen die Braunschweiger auch alsbald.

It might perhaps seem clear on the face of it that every soldier was likely to know in the 1770's that George III's Hanoverians were not sent to America, but instead aided in the defense of Gibraltar and Minorca, replacing English troops that were sent to America. Nevertheless, at least one copy of the original print has been preserved; the mistake is a contemporary one; the poem is authentic.

To turn from the popular to the more cultivated poets among those who actually came to America, there is first of all Heinrich Julius von Lindau (1754-1776)—very young, wondrously naive, in a continuous state of ferment and exaltation, and moving in the highest literary circles of the day. He is the person who "found" Peter im Baumgarten, and so there is a biography of him in Fritz Ernst's *Aus Goethes Freundeskreis Studien um Peter im*

Baumgarten (Zürich, 1941). He was incorporated into a novel by Johann Jacob Hottinger, *Briefe von Selkof an Welmar* (Zürich, 1777), and the description of him there is a quintessential distillate of what we can put together about him from the scattered statements of Lavater, Zimmermann, Lenz, Goethe, and others (Ernst, 18):

> Dieser Baron war ein ganz besondrer Mann. Französische Lebensart im Äußern, schweizerischer Freiheitssinn, deutsche Festigkeit, englische Caprice, voreilige Güte, überspanntes Gefühl im Herzen; und im Kopf ein beständig abwechselndes Wetterleuchten und Dunkel von Trug und Wahrheit, Windmühlen, Luftschlösser, eine idealische Welt neben der wirklichen, und diese hinter einem Zauberglas, wo das unterste zu oberst erschien. . . .

When he was twenty-one, unworldly and impractical as he was, he adopted a ten-year-old Swiss boy, Peter im Baumgarten, whom he saw as the perfect child of nature, fit to be reared to become the great genius of mankind, or at least a better replacement for himself, whom he considered to be used up and moribund. Peter was turned over to the pedagogical institute at Marschlin castle and then passed on successively to Lenz and Goethe when Lindau floated off to America. Far from becoming the genius of mankind, Peter was a juvenile delinquent who became an adult delinquent, despite his competence as an engraver. He deserted his wife and children in 1793 and disappeared the following year, although no one has claimed "in Amerika verschollen."

Lindau's own course became wildly paradoxical. Though an enthusiast for liberty like all his young friends of the Storm and Stress, he became a second lieutenant in the Hessian regiment von Wutgenau that was about to embark for America. A partial explanation is that after he had seriously discussed suicide with Zimmermann and had been dissuaded from it, he decided to find death as a hero in the fray, and this was the handiest means toward that end. Lavater, incredulous, wrote to him (Ernst, 90): "Du in Amerika? Du wider die ehrlichen Kolonisten? Du so ferne, ach! ein unglücklicher Gang." Lenz, the normally irresponsible and helpless, took on a fatherly role toward Lindau, and it is a strange experience to read his letters full of sound advice and sweet reason during this period of Lindau's transition to the New World and Another World.

The ultimate in paradox was reached when Lindau sent Lenz a poem with the request to find some way and means to transmit it to Franklin or Washington. At the end of May, Lenz sent it on via Boie to Zimmermann as the man most likely to have the connections to carry out Lindau's wish (Briefe I, 264-265):

> Hier mein treflicher Freund und Gönner die gedruckte Kopey eines Gedichts das der von Seiten seines Herzens wahrhaftig liebenswürdige Lindau kurz vor seinem Abmarsch nach Amerika (der nun würklich erfolgt ist) gemacht hat. Er äußerte in seinem letzten Briefe den Wunsch oder vielmehr er beschwur uns, wenn wir mittelbar oder unmittelbar einigen Zusammenhang mit Amerika hätten, es dahin an den D. Franklin oder General Washington kommen zu lassen und ihnen zugleich einige Personalien von dem Verfasser zu melden. Wir wissen uns (Wieland, Goethe und ich) bey dieser Foderung an niemand zu wenden, als an Sie mein Theuerster und da Sie die Sache der Freiheit auch unter allen Verhältnissen lieben, so glaube ich wenn Sie es füglich thun können, werden Sie auch diesen letzten Willen des treflichsten aller Don Quischotte vollziehen helfen, da in der That wie ich glaube den Kolonieen eine Erscheinung dieser Art nicht anders als willkommen und aufmunternd seyn kann. Und man überhaupt nicht weiß was ein ausgeworfener Saamenstaub für gute Folgen haben kann.

The letter clearly indicates (1) that the poem had been printed, (2) that Zimmermann was entrusted with the transmission because he loved the cause of freedom also under all circumstances, and (3) that the poem would be welcome and encouraging to the colonies. No copy of the poem, printed or in manuscript, has been found (actually the search for it seems to have been rather cursory), and the conjectures as to what it contained differ radically. If it contained an almost offensively chivalrous message to the enemy, as Ernst believes (27) (while he omits mention of the third point entirely, 99), Lenz would hardly have written to Zimmermann in those terms. If it embraced the American cause, his friends would have recognized better than he that his position as an officer in the British forces would be seriously compromised, and one might wonder why they made no attempt to suppress it. Röderer expressed the sad paradox briefly when he wrote from Strassburg in late June (Lenz, Briefe, I, 276):

> Für Lindau will ich auch beten aber nicht für die Britten, ich kann nicht glauben, daß sie Recht haben und einem andern das nehmen wollen worüber mir's so wohl ist daß ichs auch habe! —nun ich bin nicht Politiker aber Gott erhalte und segne Lindau und geb Sieg den Gerechten!

The end came quickly. He came in sight of Block Island on October 16, 1776. Exactly one month later he took part in the bloody attack on Fort Washington, was wounded by a cannon ball, and died some time later, no one seems to know exactly when. Zimmermann heard the news of his death January 30, 1777, from an acquaintance of Major von Canitz. Goethe at first refused to believe it. When he wrote his *Briefe aus der Schweiz,* as a kind of sequel, or rather pre-history of *Werther,* he incorporated an imaginative projection of Lindau's further life in the New World. This projection occurs in a strange context, near the end of the first part of the little work, where the narrator witnesses the disrobing of a beautiful young woman. In describing the complexity of his feelings on the occasion, when the artificial gradually gave way to the natural, he uses this analogue:

> Soll ich Dir's gestehen, ich konnte mich ebensowenig in den herrlichen Körper finden, da die letzte Hülle herabfiel, als vielleicht Freund L. sich in seinen Zustand finden wird, wenn ihn der Himmel zum Anführer der Mohawks machen sollte.

So many of Lindau's circle of friends in Göttingen, Weimar, Strassburg, and Zürich had contemplated going to America to join the Americans in their fight for freedom. Fortunately for German literature, not another one actually did, so far as we know, and the same is true of those outside the circle, Schiller and Moritz for instance. Fortunate also were two men of letters who were sent over too late to join in the combat and were more or less happily stranded in Nova Scotia, namely Lieutenant Colonel Karl Ludwig August Heino von Münchhausen (1759–1836) and Corporal Johann Friedrich Seume (1763–1810). They disregarded differences in rank and station and formed a friendship that continued after their return to Europe. As a memorial to their friendship the former published an exchange of poems in 1797 entitled *Rückerinnerungen von Seume und Münchhausen,* with three charming engravings after designs of his, the second of them depicting a magic lantern projecting the ship on which they had sailed, the third a huge boulder erected upright on top of a rocky crest, one of the several prehistoric monuments he had found in the wilds of Nova Scotia, all of them a mystery even to the oldest native. The poems contain many an American reminiscence, and the notes explain the most exotic of them. It is strange that Münchhausen, despite his literary merit, remains the forgotten man, little more than a footnote to Seume.

Seume's "Der Wilde" was first published by Schiller 1793 in his *Neue Thalia,* then in Seume's collected poems, 1801, where he tells us in a note (242):

> Diese Erzählung habe ich, als ich selbst in Amerika und in der dortigen Gegend war, als eine wahre Geschichte gehört. Sie interessierte mich durch ihre ächte reine primitive Menschengüte, die so selten durch unsere höhere Kultur gewinnt. Ob man gleich ähnliche hat, so habe ich sie hier doch nicht unterdrücken wollen.

The last sentence indicates that he probably knew that the story had also been given a Virginia setting, in German for the first time, to my knowledge, in 1784 in the anonymously issued *Auswahl der nüzlichsten und unterhaltendsten Aufsäze. Aus den neuesten Brittischen Magazinen für Deutsche* (I, 349–351). There was a time when every German schoolboy had to memorize the poem, and the concluding words of the noble primitive:

Seht, ihr fremden, klugen, weissen Leute,
Seht, wir Wilden sind doch bessre Menschen,

were taken with a solemn seriousness that we can no longer summon up.

Indeed, in our time we can react far more positively and sympathetically to a poetic prose idyll by Münchhausen, "Der Wilden-Kahn. Eine amerikanische Skizze," that he published 1801 in his *Versuche* (211–220), likewise with engravings done from his designs. There is a note of authenticity about it that is not impaired

by the elevated language of the introductory pages; and the conclusion does sound like the translation of a real Indian song. The
explanatory notes at the end of the volume indicate how conversant the author was with the Indian language, customs, and
character. Altogether, Münchhausen's evocation of the American
wilderness is as much to our taste as Seume's was to the Wilhelminian. And yet, where in our time can one find even a single word
of comment on it? Possibly the book has become so rare that few
have had a chance to see it and fewer still have read it.

Von Lindau was apparently the only writer from the broader
Goethean circle who actually came to America at this time. And
yet for us he cannot represent the Storm and Stress in America
because the poem he addressed to Washington and Franklin seems
to have been irretrievably lost (*seems* to have been is all we can say
at this point). Actually, the literary circles farther to the north are
more likely to have had a poetic representative in America, for the
Göttinger Hain was planted in the hereditary Hanoverian lands of
George III, and the dynastic and intellectual relations to the adjoining Brunswick and other territories were close. Although the
Hanoverians did not come to America, a contingent of Brunswick
troops did, under the command of General Riedesel. They were
sent to Canada to become part of the army of General Burgoyne
that was to advance down the Hudson River and effect a meeting
with General Howe heading northward from New York City, thus
to split the American forces and achieve decisive victory. Too well
known to be repeated here is the story of the way in which English
plans were defeated by Burgoyne's heedless, headless overconfi-
dence, followed by his strange procrastination when retreat was
called for, and even more by Lord George Germain's lost weekend
in the English countryside that allowed Howe to refrain from the
arduous march northward and to indulge instead in a pleasant
summer voyage down to the Chesapeake and up toward Philadelphia in the company of Mrs. Loring. After Burgoyne's surrender
came the long, cold march of the Brunswick troops first to Cambridge, Massachusetts, and then in the following winter to Char-
lottesville, Virginia, and it was only General Riedesel's solicitous
care for his troops that preserved them from tragic disaster, especially during the first winter. Earlier, before the campaign, he had
trained his troops in the flexible, spread-out American style of

fighting and thus was able on two occasions early in the campaign to save British troops from defeat.

So much it is necessary to know by way of background for what follows: General Riedesel was loved by his junior officers and his troops close to the point of adoration. In battle he had exposed himself to the same dangers that faced them and in captivity he remained just as loyal to them, whereas so many of Burgoyne's officers even resorted to bribery to attain a preferential place on the list of exchanges. Naturally, this secured him the respect of the best of the British officers and, in several cases, their enduring friendship. It is not strange that such respect came to him likewise from the American officers, and in the Riedesel Papers at Wolfenbüttel there are frequent expressions of this high esteem from the American officers who corresponded with him. What is remarkable, however, is that such expressions not infrequently went beyond esteem to the point of genuine affection, and one needs only to read those wonderful letters from General Philip John Schuyler to Riedesel to come to the conclusion that here must have been a man not only of singular integrity and kindness but also of a remarkably charming and luminous personality. General Schuyler and the others likewise included Mrs. Riedesel in their expressions of high esteem and affection. From other sources also, including her own writings, we know that she must have been her husband's equal in character and personality and, beyond this, to have had a high-hearted gaity of spirit and an irrepressible wit and effervescence that lifted her whole surroundings out of the grey despair of their circumstances—all this in addition to being a good mother to three little girls and giving birth to a fourth named America von Riedesel.

It was Mrs. Riedesel's conviviality that provided the occasion for the coming of the new classical German poetry to America. Klopstock's odes in Greek measures and his dactylic verse, epic and elegiac, had a discipleship throughout Germany, but most devotedly in the Göttinger Hain. Under the circumstances it is not too surprising that the transfer to America should have come about in the Riedesel circle. A number of the young officers were university men, and ever since the heroic death of the late lamented Major Ewald von Kleist it was not considered undignified even for an aristocrat and army officer to give expression to his feelings in

German verse, even to idealistic feelings in esoteric forms. Until now there has not been the slightest hint of anything of the kind from among the Germans in Revolutionary America, and all that we have known about are the popular songs and the other verse in the older traditional forms.

Slumbering away, however, in the vast treasure of the Riedesel Papers in the state archives at Wolfenbüttel is a German hexameter poem that was written in Cambridge, Massachusetts, in the late spring of 1778. It is a long poem, one hundred and eight lines, signed with the initials of the author, H. A. L., and written to celebrate General Riedesel's third birthday in America, on June 3. Mrs. Riedesel described the birthday party, but wrote not a word about the poem or its author:

> On June 3, 1778, I gave a ball and supper in celebration of my husband's birthday. I had invited all the generals and officers. . . . There was much dancing, and my cook had prepared an excellent supper for more than eighty guests. Moreover, our court and the garden were illuminated. As the King's birthday was on the 4th, the day after, we decided not to part until we could drink to the King's health. . .

Just who H. A. L. was remained uncertain since the available army lists provide only the surnames. One could merely infer that the author might have been Lieutenant Langerjahn or Captain von Lützow or Captain von Lohneisen, even though the likeliest candidate seemed to be Riedesel's secretary Langemeier. A return to Wolfenbüttel and a comparison of handwriting showed that Langemeier was indeed the author. There was also a brilliant and witty prose writer in the Brunswick contingent who wrote some of the liveliest descriptions of the New Englanders that we have from that time; of him we do not even know the initials, although here too a concentrated search would probably reveal his identity.

In those parts of Langemeier's poem that recount Riedesel's earlier heroic exploits the writer was able to demonstrate his epic use of the classic hexameter, and here, as in the poem as a whole, he does not do badly. True, from our own anachronistic and anachoristic point of view, his characterization of the enemy would be displeasing and his description of dying soldiers literally believing the old Roman precept, "Dulce et decorum est pro patria mori," might seem a bit improbable under the circumstances. Then too there are prosy passages in the poem, places where the choice of word and phrase is not quite on the poetic level, others where the level is respectable though conventional, all this with the compensatory element of a few passages that rise well above the level of an occasional poem written by an amateur. This factor, namely its status and intent as an occasional poem, must be kept in mind, and we would do well to reread Goethe's poem, "Künstlers Fug und Recht," if we are to come to a properly balanced judgment of occasional poetry and its just place in the civilized world. One further word of caution: to a person unacquainted with Riedesel's character and personality, the poem would seem to be excessively adulatory. This is why I supplied the background information I did: Riedesel really was that good; on this his German, his British, and even his American contemporaries agree.

In sum, this is a literarily respectable and a historically important poem. It may well be the first German poem in dactyllic hexameters to be written on the North American continent. There were of course earlier Latin hexameters here in some quantity, and strangely enough a New Englander about 1650, Edward Johnson, produced excellent epic dactyls in English, nearly a century before Klopstock, nearly two centuries before Longfellow and Meredith.

Here then is the birthday poem in modern type, faithful in spelling, punctuation, and initial capitalization to the calligraphic original, although without attempt to indicate the varied use of German script, Roman script, and "Fraktur." Some of the inflectional endings will seem strange to a modern reader, but they, like the irregularities of spelling and punctuation, are those of a less pedantic age, and it seemed best to leave them thus. There seems to have been only one slip of the pen, in line 98, where both sense and meter call for the insertion of the syllable *lich* in the second-last word.

Zur Feyer
des
hohen Geburts-
Tages
Sr: Freyherrl: Gnaden,
des
Herrn Generals, Riedesel von Eisenbach.
den 3ten Juny, 1778.

Steige herab von olympischer Höhe, begeisternde Muse!
um die ganz verstimmt, ja fast zerbrochene Leyer
an dem heutigen Tage mit kräftigen Beistand zu helfen,
um den würdigsten Held ein treues Opfer zu bringen,
5 welcher im hohen Wol zur unaussprechlichen Freude
Seiner treuesten Gattin und liebenswürdigsten Kinder
diesen gesegneten Tag von Dessen Werdung erlebet.
Auch uns, die ihm hieselbst, gleich Kinder den besten der
   Väter
mit dem treuesten Herz in tiefer Ehrfurcht betrachten,
10 ist der heutige Tag ein Tag der lauteren Freude.
Tausend und tausend der heissesten Wünsche für Dessen
   Erhaltung
steigen zum Himmel empor und bitten flehend Erhörung.
Göttlicher Schuz begleite hinfort das teureste Leben,
so wie bisher zum kräftigsten Schirm in allen Gefahren
15 Ihm zur Seite gestanden auf allen Wegen begleitet,
über die brausende Fluth durch thurmend schäumende
   Wellen
sicher und ruhig geführt bis in den glorreichen Haven,
wo der schifreiche Fluß des sogenannten Laurency
ununterbrochen den felsigten Grund des ruhmvollen Quebecs
20 wäscht, und dann in friedlicher Fluth die schwimmenden
   Häuser
bald zu dem Ocean hin, und bald von daher zurückbringt.
Hier war es, wo zum ersten mal im nordlichen Welttheil
dieser geweihete Tag uns Freude und Wonne erweckte,
und die allmächtige Hand die Ihn bis daher geleitet,

25 die Seinen Othen bewahrt in stillen Seufzern danckend,   [2]
und für Sein künftiges Wol die brünstigsten Wünsche erhoben.
* Dort, wo in jedermanns Herz Sein teurer Nahme geschrieben,
wo durch so manche woltätige Handlung Sein ruhmvolles
   Denckmal
stets unvergeslich verbleibt, in Kindes Kindern gerühmet,
30 da war es wo zum andern male in grössester Freude
dieser festliche Tag in vollen Glanze erschiene.
Hier nun zum dritten mal feyren wir heute die fröliche
   Stunde
von der beglückten Geburt des menschenfreundlichsten
   Herzens.
Und gepriesen sey Gott, der in so vielen Gefahren
35 Ihn bishero geschüzt, vor allen andern bewahrt,
daß Ihn kein Unfall berührt. —
Dort, wo bey Hubertstown freche Rebellen als rasende Furien
in dem heftigsten Streit mit treuen Britten begriffen,
dies weit schwächere Corps mit vierfach stärckern Kräften
40 schon zum Weichen gebracht, und schon Victoria heulten,
brach Sein heldenmütiger Arm, gefolgt von den Seinen
plözlich herter und drang zum grössesten Schrecken der
   Feinde
mitten unter sie ein, und ward ihr kräftiger Sieger.
Haufen fielen gestürzt und Haufen suchten zu fliehen,
45 unvermögend den Arm des tapfern Siegers zu stehen
flohen zitternd zurück und fluchten Blut und Verdamniß.

† Abermals ward ein ähnliches Schiksal den Feinden des
   Königs
in den gebürgigten Höhen nicht weit von Stillwater bestimmet,
Schaaren von Feinden die sich in waldigten Bergen und
   Gründen
50 der getreuen Armée des Königs entgegengesetzet,
um den fernern March und den großen Progressen
Einhalt zu thun, und für die eingebildete Freiheit
mit vereinigter Macht rasend und tollkühn zu fechten,
drangen plözlich hervor und kamen ins heftigste Feuer
55 mit den anmarchirenden Troups der tapferen Britten,
so mit unerschrockenen Muth ihr möglichstes thaten,
um den wütenden Feind zu dessen Zurückzug zu zwingen.

Doch die überlegene Macht des Feindes, so stündlich
zu Behauptung des Orts, neue Brigaden erhielte,
60 zwang den geringern Teil, nach einem großen Verluste,
obgleich alles gathan, was man von Truppen verlanget
endlich ihr besseres Heil in deren Rückzug zu suchen.   [3]
Und hier war es wo sich der allercritischste Zeitpunckt,
und das schon auf Seiten des Feindes gewonnene Glücke,
65 durch den enerschrockenen Muth der tapferen Guelfen
so durch unübersteiglich geglaubte Verhecke und Graben
hin zur Hülfe der jezt in fliehen begriffene Brüder,
mit dem stärcksten Schritt vom tapfersten Führer geleitet,
eilten, auf einmal zu unserm Vorteil erklärte:
70 und der siegende Feind durch diesem mutigen Angrif
gleichsam betäubt, mit taumelnden Schritt erschrocken
    zurück floh,
gab das halb erfochtene Feld, ohnmächtig zu stehen,
in der schnellesten Flucht unumgesehen zurücke.
Und so endigte sich zum ewigen Ruhme der Guelfen
75 und ihres führenden Chefs zu einer unsterblichen Ehre
dieser so wichtige Tag, und Gott erhielte Sein Leben.

‡   So, wie auch da, wo zulezt das alles entscheidende
        Schicksal,
an dem traurigen Tage das Glück der Waffen verkehrte,
Gottes allmächtige Hand Ihm stets zur Seite begleitet.
80 Hier in der stärcksten Gefahr, und dorten mitten im Feuer
überall, wo Er hinsah, daß Seine Gegenwart nötig,
um den streitenden Volck die nötigen ordres zu geben,
Hier den wütenden Feind den fernern Angrif zu wehren,
dorten die fluchtigen Trups in Ordnung wieder zu bringen,
85 Hundert fielen zur Rechten und Hundert fielen zur Lincken,
lagen blutend in Staub und flehten winselnd um Hülfe,
andere hauchten gestreckt den lezten Othen zum Himmel,
starben vergnügt weil sie im Dienst des Königs ihr Leben
auf dem Bette der Ehren so tapfer und ruhmvoll beschloßen,
90 und beseufzten nur dies, daß ihre streitende Brüder
an den heutigem Tag nicht Sieger der Feinde geworden.
Doch Gott beschüzte auch hier, dem, der uns bishero geführet,
dessen wachendes Aug uns jederzeit väterlich schüzzet,
und dessen liebreiches Herz stets unser Beste besorget.

95 Und so steige denn brünstiger Wunsch zum Trone des Ewigen
für das fernere Wol des menschenfreundlichsten Herzens,
Segen und Heil begleite die Tage des teuresten Helden,
so als Gemal zur Seite der unvergleich[lich]sten Gattin,   [4]
welche alles in Ihm und Er nur alles in Ihr ist;
100 und als Vater zugleich von drey geliebtesten Töchtern,
die voll Anmuth, so wie der treffende Pinsel des Rubens
uns die Grazien mahlt, von holder Anmuth beseelet,
heitere Stunden geneußt, und alles widrige Schicksal
philosophisch verbannt, der Seele Ruhe zu schaffen.
105 Lasse allmächtiger Gott die heutige Stunde der Freude
in entzückender Pracht noch oftmal wieder erscheinen:
Ehre und Ruhm bekröne Sein Leben zum spätesten Ziele
menschlichen Alters. —

unt[er]t[äni]g[st].
H A L:

*. Trois Rivieres.
†. d. 19.^{tn} Septbr: 1777.
‡. d. 7.^{tn} octobr: 1777.

After the conclusion of the war two German playwrights came
to Philadelphia, one in 1787, the other in 1794. This transit, about
which there has been an utter silence, is actually not too surprising. Just at this time, at the height of the *Theaterfieber* in Germany, there were about three-hundred persons writing for the
stage, and, by the law of averages, one or two of them are likely
to have crossed the ocean to what was then the American metrop-
olis. It adds to the interest that one was an actor who became a
serious physician and that the other was a theologian who became
a strolling actor, involved in such a succession of difficulties that
just about the only thing left for him to do was to decamp for
America. One of the nice things about the decades around 1800
was that when a character in a drama or novel got into an impossible situation, his author did not have to kill him off, he could
send him to America. This, however, is not the reason why this

period is called "das Zeitalter der Humanität." Since life is an imitation of literature, it is to be expected that an occasional author would himself be moved to come to America.

Gottlob Timotheus Michael Kühl, alas, was not protected by the formidable sanctity of his baptismal names. His first literary effort, at sixteen, in 1772, while he was a scholar at the Hamburg Johanneum, was unfortunately a satire against the powerful Pastor Goeze, and he was promptly suspended. The next year, after further delinquencies, he was definitively expelled. A few years later the older and more stable Lessing was to have better success against the same formidable opponent. Kühl wanted to study medicine but was destined by the vow of his mother for theology. He was a most effective preacher but had no taste or reverence for theology and so became a strolling actor temporarily, thus furnishing the example for Faust's remark (528-9):

Ja, wenn der Pfarrer ein Komödiant ist;
Wie das wohl zu Zeiten kommen mag.

So he seesawed back and forth, earning his living by his facile pen, issuing sermons, novels, stories, essays, periodicals, dramas, occasional poems, a space voyage, and a novellistic autobiography, *Geschichte der Verirrungen des menschlichen Herzens,* 1785, the second, unwritten part of which apparently transpired in America. Meusel (IV, 291) reports: "gieng aber im Jul. 1787 nach Philadelphia (was er dort treibt, und ob er noch lebt, ist unbekannt)." And Hans Schröder can only add: "wo er dem Gerüchte nach 1802 noch lebte." Over here there seems to be as little trace of his further writings as of the man himself.

Anton Christian Hunnius, born 1764 near Jena, early had ambitions to be a writer, studied medicine at Jena, and apparently under the influence of his elder brother, was briefly an actor in Weimar. This elder brother, Friedrich Wilhelm Hunnius, was later singled out by Goethe for special praise for his performances in *Wallensteins Lager* and *Die Piccolomini.* Anton published two youthful works anonymously at Weissenfels in 1788: *Junker Anton. Ein komischer Roman in acht Gesängen,* with a fine though drastic frontispiece by J. Pentzel, and *Natur, Lieb' und Abentheuer. Eine drollichte Geschichte,* with the fictitious imprint "Abdera, gedruckt auf Kosten der jungen Witwe des Verfassers," this imprint possibly a protective comic device to preclude investigation and prosecution of the author. Nicolai's review of the latter in his *Allgemeine deutsche Bibliothek* (C, 123-124) is brief and unsparing:

> Dieser Roman enthält einige witzige Einfälle, die ihm aber gar keinen Werth geben. Der Verfasser erzeigt den beyden Hauptpersonen, Franz dem Sohne eines Amtsschreibers und Lotte der Tochter eines Amtmanns im ersten Abschnitt die Ehre, ihr Daseyn, aus dem unehelichen Beyschlaf eines jungen Juristen und eines Husarenwachtmeisters herzuleiten. Scenen dieser Art kommen in dem Buche sehr viele vor, und werden immer recht handgreiflich vorgestellt.
>
> Jeder Abschnitt fängt mit einem Knittelvers an, und endigt sich damit.
>
> Der Schluß zeigt sehr deutlich, daß der Verf. die letzten 16 Seiten wohl nicht geschrieben habe, und es ist daher wahrscheinlich, daß er darüber gestorben sey.

This means that Hunnius was able to fabricate an ending so successfully simulating a quite different author's style that such a sharp critic as Nicolai was taken in by it, but this seems to have been the author's only triumph. The verse novel *Junker Anton* had been demolished more lengthily and totally in an earlier number of the same periodical (IIC, 2, 460-463), although even here the author's basic talent is not denied. Hunnius then turned to drama, and a three-act comedy of his, *Der Taubstumme,* had the honor of being published in 1791 in volume two of Friedrich Ludwig Schröder's *Sammlung von Schauspielen für's Hamburgsche Theater.* In the year of his departure for America two numbers of a periodical of his appeared, ostensibly in Amsterdam, actually in Gotha: *Momus und Apollo.* By this time Hunnius apparently decided that a career in medicine and in America would be more likely to bring success. We have the accurate record that he arrived in Philadelphia, November 6, 1794, on the ship *Peggy* from Amsterdam, John Elliott, Master. But we have no record of any further ventures of his into the field of imaginative literature.

When we turn from the poets, novelists, and dramatists to the writers of expository prose, there are three especially who have some reputation for literary quality. Of them General Riedesel and especially his remarkable wife need no further appraisal since their records of their American years are esteemed in English translation as well as in the original German. Another person is also mentioned with unanimous respect for his literary as well as his observational talents; it is Johann David Schoepf, chief surgeon to the Ansbach troops, eminent naturalist, who came over primarily for scientific reasons and, after the cessation of hostilities and before the conclusion of the peace, crossed over from the British lines in New York to the American lines in New Jersey and from there proceeded westward to the Ohio and thence through the southern states of the new confederation.

The two volumes of his *Reise durch einige der mittlern und südlichen vereinigten nordamerikanischen Staaten . . .* (Erlangen, 1788), are filled with detailed, often minutely detailed accounts of all he observed underway. By every inference or conclusion that one might logically reach, this should be a tiresome account that one bears with only because of the valuable data it contains. Actually, it is an interesting, at times enthralling account that draws one on and on beyond one's normal bedtime. One is left wondering what it is about Schoepf that enables him to write a detailed account, of value still to the most sober natural and social scientist, and at the same time to make a literary masterpiece out of it. One factor certainly is the marvelous human touch. Human beings and actions arise before us in all their nobility and fallibility; stories are told in a way that haunts the memory; observations are made that still arouse our sense of wonder.

One of the strange, unexplained, and as yet unexplainable features about the English translation is its stylistic contemporaneity with the Schoepf original. The English title page tells us that it was translated and edited by Alfred J. Morrison (1876–1923) and published at Philadelphia in 1911. And yet long passages of it sound as though they had been put into English in the eighteenth century. What is the solution? Was Morrison so well trained literarily and so sensitive to long-lost eighteenth century diction and rhythm that he could successfully evoke its prose harmonies for pages on end? Or did he have an eighteenth century English translation in manuscript of which he kept the style and cadence for the most part, while discreetly improving its accuracy and reliability? I do not know. But from the scanty records of Alfred J.

Morrison at present available to me, I should guess the former. If that is the case, he would be a literary personality as remarkable as Schoepf himself.

In sum, in brief, the phenomenon America holds surprises for us at every turn. It is one continuous "unerhörte Begebenheit" that makes mockery of any generalization or ideological analysis that pretends to encompass it. There is an ancient Mohawk proverb that tells us: "It is unwise to try to put salt on the tail of the bald eagle." And only the unwise will ask why.

5. The Reception of
C. M. Wieland in America
Lieselotte E. Kurth-Voigt

It is no longer a well-guarded secret of the initiates that in his own time and for decades after his death in 1813 Christoph Martin Wieland—to borrow some of the epithets by which American critics have characterized him—was considered one of the most illustrious writers, a genius of great versatility, one of the literary giants who revolutionized the German language, and personally a man of great charm, congeniality and tolerance.

The avenues by which the knowledge of his life and work was transmitted were remarkably diverse.[1] American travellers who went to Europe often received their information first-hand if they lived in Germany or spent some time at Weimar, and they often shared their experiences with those at home. At the end of the eighteenth century John Quincy Adams resided in Berlin and made occasional excursions into other parts of Germany. Thirty years later he recalled these visits, remembering vividly the impression Wieland had made on him: "At that time, Wieland was *there* I think decidedly the most popular of the German poets, . . . there was something in the playfulness of his imagination, in the tenderness of his sensibility, in the sunny cheerfulness of his philosophy, and in the harmony of his versification, which, to me, were inexpressibly delightful."[2] Another American statesman, Aaron Burr, reported on his sojourn in Weimar in greater detail.[3] Wieland's collaborator in editing the *Teutscher Merkur,* Friedrich J. Bertuch, a man "in *liaison* with all the *literati* of Germany," acquainted Burr with the leading figures of the town and introduced him to Wieland, who immediately won his affection. It is amusingly ironic that Burr left the city in great haste and for the very same reason Wieland's hero Agathon fled Smyrna. Both men feared the consequences of an unwise involvement with a beautiful woman and felt that only a precipitate flight would save them. Burr regretted that he was thus unable to honor his engagements in Weimar, and was deeply concerned that he could not offer an acceptable apology "to the great and amiable Wieland" whom he had promised to visit that evening.

Later travellers who arrived at Weimar after Wieland's death remembered him as one of the great men who still contributed to the fame of the city. When in 1815 George Ticknor passed through Weimar, he and his friends "breakfasted with the names and poetry of Schiller, Wieland, and Goethe often on our lips, and oftener in our recollections."[4] A decade later he corresponded with Thomas Jefferson about the acquisition of German books for the University of Virginia, and it was no doubt on Ticknor's advice that among the books purchased abroad was a complete set of Wieland's *Werke*.[5] Many others remembered the importance of Wieland during their sojourn in Weimar, and in the winter of 1873-1874 Bayard Taylor, visiting the town, was delighted to become acquainted with the descendants of the great poets, particularly Wieland's granddaughter, who invited him to deliver a lecture on American literature. In one of his letters Taylor recalls the event with great joy and assures his friend: ". . . it gave me a thrill of pride to stand in Weimar, with the grandchildren of Carl August, Goethe, Schiller, Herder, and Wieland among my auditors, and vindicate the literary achievement of America."[6] Naturally not only male visitors wrote of the splendor of Weimar or recalled the influential participation of Wieland in its literary life. In her *Impressions of Germany by an American Lady* Mary Sands Griffin, for example, celebrates this "consecrated ground," where during the years of turmoil the "great geniuses of Germany" lived in "peaceful meditation," where Goethe reigned with "the despotism of genius, where Wieland and Herder wrote in calm serenity."[7]

Such personal observations were supplemented by a variety of works, German, English, and French, that first appeared in Europe but very soon found a receptive audience in the states. One of the most popular accounts was that of Johann Kaspar Riesbeck. Translated as *Travels through Germany, in a Series of Letters,* it was well known among Americans interested in German affairs. In his 45th letter[8] Riesbeck draws an informative portrait of Wieland, "the first of all the German writers," whose genius is matched only by that of Lessing. Compared to the "rhapsodies of the modern German poetasters" his writings are genuine art. Before Goethe appeared on the scene, Wieland was "at the top of the German Parnassus," and, Riesbeck predicts, will be one of the few German writers to "go down to posterity as a classical writer." This generous praise is balanced by perceptive censure. Although Riesbeck admires Wieland's thorough acquaintance with the ancients and his profound knowledge of French, Italian, and English literature, he feels that the poet "exposes his immense reading" too much, an ostentatious display of erudition that he cannot sanction. Furthermore, Riesbeck admits that Wieland has favorite ideas which he seems to repeat insistently; yet since he constantly refashions them "in order to set them before the reader in every point of view," one should perhaps not consider such reworkings a serious flaw. Some of the more personal characteristics did not at all please Riesbeck. Wieland, it seems to him, lacked "self-sufficiency"; he displayed "frequent variations in his way of thinking," and did not seem to be willing to adhere to his principles or to defend them ardently. This kind of criticism was often repeated by those who did not notice that these traits could also be seen as strengths: they express a courteous tolerance toward the views of others and indicate the realization that most matters permit multiple interpretations if they are considered from different vantage points. Another personal aspect that delighted Riesbeck was the poet's conduct as *pater-familiaris:* "Wieland is, what few poets are, a good domestic man. He lives, in fact, more for his family than for the public." Such exemplary virtue pleased the nineteenth-century reader, and Riesbeck's praise was frequently reiterated in the biographical sketches of Wieland that were to appear in American journals.

Several decades later an important contribution to a favorable image of Wieland was made by Goethe, whose conversations on the day of Wieland's funeral were recorded by Daniel Falk; translated into English by Sarah Austin it became a reliable source of information for American readers.[9] Through Goethe (and Austin) they became acquainted with the admirable traits that had endeared Wieland to his friends in Weimar: "the moral greatness" with which he had conducted his affairs, his life of "unblemished dignity and honour," and the refined wit and elegant thought that he had cultivated to perfection. The best of his works reflected his "matchless humour," the beauty, grace, and inimitable charm of his nature, and his verse tales, among them the renowned *Oberon,* remained unsurpassed: "The natural genius that breathes through them is matchless—all flow, all spirit, all taste!" Goethe also affirms the lasting effect of Wieland's works on the public and corrects those who misunderstood his flexibility. In contrast to Riesbeck, he approves of Wieland's mental habits and his tendencies toward perspectivism: "When he gave himself up to the variety of his sensations, to the mobility of his thoughts, and permitted no single impression to obtain dominion over him, he showed by that very process the firmness and certainty of his mind. He loved to play with his conceptions, but never . . . with his opinions."

More impersonal, formal treatments of Wieland were included in German histories of literature, among them the influential surveys of Horn and Bouterwek that were extensively discussed by George Bancroft in the *American Quarterly Review.*[10] The most accessible to the American reader, however, was Wolfgang Menzel's controversial history of German literature, translated into English by Cornelius C. Felton, the Harvard classical scholar, and published in George Ripley's *Specimens of Foreign Standard Literature.*[11] Menzel's portrait of Wieland was even more favorable than Goethe's. Reaching beyond the warm and affectionate tone of his predecessor, he delivers an enthusiastic encomium of the poet whom he—"the first among the younger literary men"—had proudly "vindicated" against the "German cockneys whose skulls are thicker than Boeotia ever produced."

After the vigorous reforms of Klopstock and Lessing the return to gracefulness seemed inevitable, and it was ushered in by "Wieland—the cheerful, amiable, delicate Wieland—a genius overflowing, inexhaustible in agreeableness, ease, raillery, and wit." He "restored to German poetry the unrestrained spirit, the free look of the child of the world, the natural grace, the love and desire of cheerful pleasantry, and the power of supplying it." Menzel seems particularly sensitive to the charges that Wieland was excessively interested in ancient Greece and overly receptive to French influence. To be sure, Wieland's genius was strongly attracted by all things Greek; yet he did not merely imitate the Greeks, he "made the harmony and grace with which the whole life of the Greeks was pervaded, a part of his own mind," and his formative influence was undeniable: "He did for poetry what Winckelmann did for plastic art. He taught us to recognize and embody natural beauty again, after the model of the Greeks." Menzel admits that French writers had been Wieland's models; yet again he did not simply imitate them but used what was functional and set aside with "unerring tact and skill" the "real obscenity and the moral poison" of their works.

Menzel's *German Literature* received considerable attention in America. During the first few months after its publication, at least six reviews appeared,[12] among them a most searching one by Barnas Sears in the *Christian Review* and a sharply perceptive one by Theodore Parker in the *Dial*. Both critics object to the personal polemics that characterize parts of Menzel's history and, rather ironically, defend the defamed German intellectuals against their compatriot. Since Menzel had not assailed, but rather praised Wieland, there was no need to single him out. Parker mentions him briefly, but then only to affirm Menzel's judgment that there are very few poets who match the original quality and freshness of Wieland's writings.[13]

French literature was another medium of transmission. Whether or not American readers were acquainted with the laudatory descriptions of Wieland's works in the August and September numbers of the *Bibliothèque universelle des romans* of 1778, virtually "Wieland issues," must for the moment remain a matter of speculation.[14] That a later periodical, the *Journal des savants,* was known in America can be demonstrated more readily. The *Journal* was the source for an extensive review of his selected letters that appeared as a translation from the French in *The Port Folio* of 1818.[15] Although the reviewer regrets the absence of local anecdotes, references to contemporary intrigues, and the discussion of historical events, he nevertheless finds the letters interesting because of the knowledge they convey about the character and opinions of Wieland. The contribution, however, is not actually a review of the *Ausgewählte Briefe;* it is essentially a biographical essay which acquaints the reader with important events in Wieland's life and judges—in detail and favorably—the major works of the poet. Those who might object to the seemingly inordinate length of the essay are reminded that Wieland's achievements justify this much attention, for he was "one of the most illustrious writers of his age and country" and distinguished himself in many genres; readers who, on the contrary, might object to the brevity of the treatment and desire a more comprehensive article are conciliated by a concluding outline of various aspects that the reviewer indicates would indeed deserve a more thorough analysis.

The most important French intermediary was no doubt Madame de Staël, author of *De l'Allemagne* (Paris, 1810), whose influence on American views of Germany is well known. She arrived at Weimar when Wieland was still alive, and in his conversations with her he revealed himself to be a charming and animated man.[16] She recognizes some similarities between Wieland and Voltaire, but considers the German much more attached to the truth and not inclined to imitate Voltaire's sarcastic irony or "the brilliant freedom" of his "pleasantry." Although many other Germans had written in the French manner, Wieland is the only one "whose works have genius," and despite a seeming lack of originality he has rendered great service to his nation by improving the German language and its poetic versification. It is Wieland, she maintains, "whose works, even in translation, have excited the interest of all Europe: it is he who has rendered the science of antiquity subservient to the charms of literature; it is he also who, in verse, has given a musical and graceful flexibility to his fertile but rough language." She selects *Oberon* for a warm commendation, praising its exceptional poetic quality, its charm and grace, the originality of its design, and the ingenious artistry of "uniting fantastic fictions with true sentiment" which was uniquely characteristic of Wieland.

An even more abundant source of information about Wieland was provided by England, where in the second half of the eighteenth century no German writer except Gessner was as popular. By 1800 twenty-five of his works had appeared in English translation, about fifteen more were added by 1830,[17] and most of them were accompanied by searching reviews in the *Monthly Magazine,* the *Critical Review,* the *Monthly Review,* and other periodicals which Edward Everett, writing for the *North American Review* in 1822, acknowledged as the "popular vehicles of information" that spread much "useful knowledge" among the American reading community. Many of the English translations found their way to America and numerous articles were reprinted in American periodicals, particularly in the *Museum of Foreign*

Literature and Science which in 1828 brought out a long and laudatory review of Wieland's *Sämmtliche Werke* (1824-1827) that had previously been published in the *Foreign Quarterly Review*.

An early nineteenth-century survey, John Dunlop's *History of Fiction,* assigns a unique position to Wieland. By that time countless German novels had appeared, among them the works of Goethe, but he does not mention any German novelist except Wieland. In the chapter "Romances of Chivalry" he simply abbreviates the summary of Huon de Bordeaux' adventures, for all the important incidents are conveniently contained in Wieland's *Oberon* and "are universally known through the beautiful translation of Mr. Sotheby."[18] In his chapter on "Comic Romances" Dunlop assigns relatively much space to Wieland's first novel, *The Adventures of Don Sylvio,* which he believes to be one of the most "agreeable imitations of Don Quixote."[19] Every one of the later editions of Dunlop's *History* maintains Wieland in this exclusive position, somewhat unrealistically, to be sure; neither the American edition of 1842, nor the German version of 1851, nor the fourth English edition of 1876, attempts to shift the emphasis.

The most ardent English advocate, translator, and reviewer of Wieland was William Taylor of Norwich. His *Historic Survey of German Poetry* contains a sketch of Wieland's life which in its factual information closely follows the biography of Gruber; a comprehensive review of his collected works and an extensive selection of translations from his writings follow.[20] The introductory paragraph of the *Survey* functions as an explanation for the unusual length of this part: Taylor sees Wieland as a man representative of his time and country whose life is "peculiarly instructive," as his development paralleled that of the "public mind itself" and conversely influenced the culture of his community and the literature to which he contributed for sixty years as a writer of "eminence, fertility, and beauty." Taylor is generous in his praise of Wieland, in whose permanent influence on the "refined portion of the whole European public" he firmly believes. He lauds his author for elegant erudition and philosophic penetration and applauds his avoidance of unnatural bombast and "vulgar insipidity." He approves of Wieland's wit which aims at exciting a continual smile but does not ape the bitter grin of Voltaire or provoke in the manner of Swift to "open-mouthed laughter." *Agathon* is a work of excellence and perfection; *Musarion,* an "exquisitely finished" poem of "inexpressible ease and grace," playful and delicate; and Wieland's style "probably possesses the highest degree of elegance and polish to which the German language has attained." Taylor allots much space to the *Oberon,* "the master-piece of Wieland—the child of his genius in moments of its purest converse with the all-beauteous forms of ideal excellence; . . . an epic poem, popular beyond example, yet as dear to the philosopher as to the multitude." Together with his interpretation he reproduces forty stanzas of the *Oberon* from Sotheby's translation which had appeared in 1798 and was unusually well received in England and America. Taylor is not completely uncritical of Wieland, yet his strictures are modest and do not at all question the merits of "the greatest poet among the geniuses of Germany." Judging by striking similarities in interpretation and formulation, Taylor's favorable picture of Wieland had an impact on American critics; his at times eulogistic laudations, however, were challenged by George Bancroft who in 1830 evaluated the *Survey* for the *American Quarterly Review.*

It was not, of course, only through translations from the German and French or through the reprinting of English studies that American readers became acquainted with Wieland. Quite a few of their own critics contributed to the interpretation of his writings. Those who wished to be informed in rather succinct fashion could consult the *Encyclopedia Americana,* which in 1833 published an objective and well-balanced account of the life and work of Wieland. The description of the best of his works as particularly pleasing because of the author's "lively imagination, knowledge of languages, sound judgment and benevolent spirit," the characterization of the *History of the Abderites* as a delightful work, and the mention of *Oberon* "as the most successful of his larger works" may have encouraged some readers to broaden their knowledge of Wieland's writings.

American histories of German literature contain at least informative references to Wieland and often substantial sections. One of the earliest surveys to include a discussion of German authors, the *Brief Retrospect of the Eighteenth Century* by Samuel Miller,[21] praises Wieland for his lasting enrichment of German style and vocabulary and counts him among the four "earliest and most succesful labourers in attuning the German language to poetry." Wieland and Gessner are justifiably "celebrated throughout Europe" because they have most eminently distinguished themselves in epic poetry. For a more specific characterization Miller singles out the *Agathon* and acquaints his readers with the opinion of Lessing, who believed the novel "to be one of the finest efforts of genius in the eighteenth century; nay, he called it the *first* and *only* novel of the Germans, written for the thinking men of classical taste." In Miller's own judgment Wieland occupies the very first place among the "extremely numerous" writers of romance and novels in Germany, and he believes that the *Oberon* clearly demonstrates "the bold and vigorous imagination, and the felicity of description for which the author has been long celebrated."

A later survey, the *Handbook of Universal Literature* by Anne C. Lynch Botta, counts Wieland among the four most eminent writers of the generation that preceded Goethe and Schiller. As with Klopstock, Lessing, and Herder, his predominant characteristics are described in a brief paragraph[22] which in rather puritanical fashion censures his "epicurean romances." Botta objects to what she considers their purpose: "to represent pleasure or utility as the only criterion of truth." Yet she admits that Wieland "maintains his place in the literature of his native country as one of its most gay, witty, and graceful poets," whose *Oberon* is "one of the most charming and attractive poems of modern times."

An American edition of *Outlines of German Literature* (New York, 1873) by Joseph Gostwick and Robert Harrison, more comprehensive than the slim volume of the earlier English version (Edinburgh, 1849) edited by Gostwick alone, is rather explicit in its discussion of Wieland's life and works. The authors contrast him with Klopstock—a point of departure often taken in the eighteenth and nineteenth centuries; they discuss his attitude toward the reading public, describe several of his larger works, and summarize their content in such a manner that the reader is stimulated to pursue his acquaintance with Wieland. They also analyze the judgment of German critics attempting to explain the unusual influence of Wieland who "received, during his life, such praises as were hardly bestowed on Klopstock and never on Lessing." The chapter concludes with their prediction that "Wieland's important contributions to the culture of the German language will not be forgotten."[23]

A similar comparison with Klopstock is an essential feature of Kuno Francke's *Social Forces in German Literature* which appeared at the end of the nineteenth century.[24] Francke first delineates significant differences between the two poets and then indicates that their writings have greater than merely historical value. It is "an injustice to both Klopstock and Wieland to speak of their works in a manner which is now only too common, as though they had no message to deliver to our own time, as though the spiritual ardour of the former, the serene sensuousness of the latter had lost their meaning for us moderns." From the works of Wieland he selects for a first detailed discussion the *Agathon,* because "in the whole period between the *Simplicissimus* and *Wilhelm Meister* there is no German novel dealing with as broad phases of life in as successful a manner as Wieland's *Agathon.*" The verse narrative *Musarion* receives attention because it is "undoubtedly one of the most graceful and delicate impersonations of his imperturbable serenity and optimism, and of the 'charming philosophy' of enlightenment and toleration." The *Oberon* must, of course, also be mentioned: ". . . in all later Romanticism, there is no work which in brilliancy of imagination, in lightness of movement, in crystalline clearness of action, and in golden worth of sentiment [Francke quotes Goethe] surpasses the ever youthful romance of *Oberon.*" The universality of Wieland's works is convincingly shown in Francke's discussion of the novel *Die Abderiten,* which "will forever be the classic representation of German provincial town life in the eighteenth century." The third book seems particularly charming: "There are few happier inventions in all comic literature than the lawsuit about the donkey's shadow," a judgment which modern writers who have adapted this episode (most recently, Friedrich Dürrenmatt) would no doubt echo.

Earlier generations of Americans who studied German in school were particularly familiar with this novel, for the most frequently used anthology, Charles Follen's *Deutsches Lesebuch für Anfänger,* which from 1826 to 1847 appeared in eleven editions, contains long sections from the *Abderiten.* The selection was a real challenge to those who wished to translate it, as Charles Francis Adams discovered.[25]

Americans who did not read German could easily become acquainted with Wieland through the translations of his works that existed in many private and public libraries. Another source of information were the American magazines that included Wieland's shorter works in their entirety, or sections from his longer works in English translation. Perhaps the earliest example of such inclusion was the publication of "Zohar:—An Eastern Tale," which appeared in 1791 in the *Massachusetts Magazine or Monthly Museum.*[26] Although it is correctly considered to be the very first English version of Wieland's verse narrative "Der Unzufriedene," it is not actually a proper translation but rather a condensed, yet well executed prose adaptation of one of the early *Erzählungen* (1752). Another fragment, "The Emir," which appeared in the Boston *Ladies Magazine* (1829), has until now passed as the first and only English translation from Wieland's *Schach Lolo.* The identification was probably based on the similarity of the titles and not on an actual comparison of text and translation, for the excerpt is not at all from *Schach Lolo* but from the *Golden Mirror.* It had previously appeared in several English periodicals and is the very same section Charles Follen included in the first edition (1826) of his *Deutsches Lesebuch.* It would have been amazing if a Boston periodical intended for the entertainment of New England ladies had printed a section from the wantonly frivolous *Schach Lolo,* but it is, of course, quite understandable that the *Magazine* might reprint Danischmend's fable of the emir who was taught that "without *labor* no *health* of the soul and the life, without *this*, no *felicity* is possible."[27]

American anthologies of German prose and poetry in English translation invariably included selections from Wieland, most of them different from the ones contained in periodicals. In his collection *Prose Writers of Germany*, Frederic H. Hedge prefaced the section on Wieland with a biographical sketch and a brief characterization of some of his best works; he also attempted to establish the features that distinguish him from others: "Wieland's excellence lies rather in the manner than in the matter. He is more graceful than energetic, more agreeable than impressive, more sportive than profound. 'Words that burn' are not found on his page, nor thoughts that make one close the book and ponder, and rise up intellectually new-born from the reading. But then he has charms of manner that lure the reader on and hold him fast."[28] For most of his description Hedge depends on two authorities: he quotes at length from Bouterwek's *History of German Poetry and Eloquence* and from Goethe's Eulogy in Mrs. Austin's translation. From Wieland's writings Hedge selected several of the later pieces, among them three *Dialogues of the Gods* that are concerned with politics and revolutions; they require a most careful reading, for the views presented in them are so subtly balanced that the interpreter will do well to remember Goethe's explanation of Wieland's method (quoted by Hedge): ". . . in all he did he cared less for a firm footing than for a clever debate."

Two later collections introduce the American reader to three different pieces. Alfred Baskerville's *The Poetry of Germany,* presenting "selections . . . of the most celebrated poets," includes "The Pain of Separation," part of the fourth scene of the *Singspiel Rosamund,* and the cantata *Serafina.*[29] The collection *Songs and Poems from the German* by Ellen Heath (New York, 1881), which does not include any other poems of the eighteenth century, and none by Goethe and Schiller, contains a fairly long section from Wieland's *The Graces,* rendered into English verse.

Two other anthologies, both of them more comprehensive in scope, Longfellow's *Poets and Poetry of Europe* (Philadelphia, 1845) and Warner's *Library of the World's Best Literature* (New York, 1897), include Wieland among the German writers who even in this broader context demand attention. Longfellow's introduction is a fair appraisal of Wieland and contains a defense of his personal conduct against those who considered the questionable morality of his works to be a mirror of his life: "Notwithstanding the objections that have been justly urged against many of his writings, the personal character of Wieland was free from moral blemish."[30] In his private life he was "amiable, upright, friendly and hospitable," and as a poet he was a great master of style, of a lively fancy, prolific invention, and a peaceful manner. The primary source for Longfellow's descriptive evaluation is Wolfgang Menzel's *German Literature.* Despite his insight that Menzel's depiction is a "high-wrought eulogy" and marked by the partiality of an admirer,

Longfellow does not hesitate to acquaint his readers with Menzel's views through extensive quotations. In his own opinion, Wieland's principal poetic work is the "romantic epic of 'Oberon'," and he therefore reproduces thirty-eight stanzas of it in Sotheby's translation.

The editors of the *Library* reiterate some of the favorable comments previously made about Wieland.[31] Although they realize that writers of the past who exercised a fruitful influence in their day and formed an important part of the contemporary literary development of their country have lost "much of their claim on our interest," Wieland nevertheless deserves attention, for he helped to make the German language "an artistic instrument of expression, lending it grace, definiteness, elegance," and "by his keen, sane criticism did much for German culture." The editors, however, do not share Longfellow's enthusiasm for *Oberon*. Although the work had "an immense vogue in his own and other languages" and was "received with a favor rarely extended to any literary work," in 1897 it commands "little more than a formal regard." The editors therefore include in their *Library of the World's Best Literature* two different works of Wieland that have a more modern appeal. These are segments of two *Göttergespräche,* the fourth, here entitled "Managing Husbands," in which Juno and Livia discuss their marital difficulties and arrive at unusual solutions to their problems; and the sixth dialogue, "The Deities Deposed," in which the Gods deplore the disrespectful treatment they have received from Theodosius the Great and are consoled by Jupiter who, with clearly political overtones, optimistically minimizes the importance of this Roman revolution and predicts the God's return to power.

In addition to these inclusions of Wieland's writings in anthologies and magazines, there are revealing observations in works primarily concerned with other writers. Two characteristic examples must suffice here. In her *Life of Jean Paul Frederic Richter* (New York, 1850), Eliza Buckminster Lee mentions Wieland several times and quotes some of the favorable opinions that were expressed in the correspondence of Jean Paul and his friends who thought of Wieland as one of the "three watchtowers of our literature" (Goethe and Herder were the other two). They were grateful for his support of Richter and were delighted to know that Wieland would rejoice at having him in Weimar. Yet more important than these brief remarks is the appendix of the book, for it contains a biographical essay on Wieland, not very original—it depends to a large extent on the work of Austin and Schindel[32]—but intriguingly selective in the emphasis on details that would no doubt charm her female readers and admirers of Jean Paul.

George Calvert in his essay on Goethe refers to Wieland in a similar way: he acknowledges his influence in Weimar, indicating the importance of Wieland's warm reception of the young Goethe and the impact of his views on others in their reaction to the writers and critics associated with the literary circles at Weimar.[33] Also relying on Mrs. Austin's translation, Calvert reproduces sections of Goethe's conversation with Falk on the day of Wieland's funeral, with particular attention to their discourse on the fate of Wieland's soul and its present "occupation," which according to Goethe will be "nothing petty, nothing unworthy, nothing out of keeping with that moral greatness which he all his life sustained." Nature could not possibly be "such a spendthrift of her capital" as to eternally destroy Wieland's soul, one of her "treasures, a perfect jewel." Significantly, the discussion echoes Wieland's own thoughts on the continuation of man's existence after death, ideas which he sometimes presented in a humorous manner and on other occasions treated more seriously. During his sojourn in Weimar, Calvert was greatly stimulated by the intellectual heritage that was perceptible everywhere, and he limited his participation in the mundane activities of the town, for had he not done so he would have felt "an unworthy participant" of a society refined by the influence of her great poets, among them naturally Wieland.

Beyond this kind of mention there are numerous incidental references to Wieland in American periodicals.[34] Virtually all of them have one aspect in common: they refer to him by his last name only and do not add any identifying remarks, a clear indication that the authors were aware of a general familiarity with Wieland and did not find it necessary to give specific information which would be indispensable with a writer of lesser fame. Through casually introduced observations the American reader is reminded of Wieland's stature as one of the most distinguished men Germany has produced, a literary giant of immortal fame. The reader is informed of the "universal approbations" with which his translations of other authors were received; his universally beneficial influence on the German language is praised again and again; and his importance for the development of German literature and culture is repeatedly emphasized. Not all of the authors are concerned principally with Wieland's writing; they also acknowledge him as an important figure of Weimar and an authority whose views of his contemporaries and of current events are a standard against which the opinions of others can be measured.

There are even poems that include laudatory references to Wieland. Joseph Story of Salem, stimulated by Johann Georg Zimmermann, a friend of Wieland and the author of *On Solitude,* contrasts in his poem *The Power of Solitude* the spiritless writings of some pessimists with the enchanting poetry of Wieland:

> For them no spirits walk the dusky cave,
> No murmuring Naiads drink the lucid wave,
> No fine enchantments, raised at W I E L A N D ' S call,
> Convene her shadowy train to fancy's hall;

And his identification of the German poet is raptly enthusiastic: "Wieland, the darling of the German muse, by turns sweet, affecting, magnificent, sublime, commanding, terrible: the favorite of fancy, to whom she unveiled her most beautiful forms, drest in the voluptuousness of the loves, and the translucent snow of graces."[35]

More than half a century later, E. G. Holland, publishing in the *Knickerbocker,* celebrates in his poem "To Weimar" its most famous men:

> Ye Athens of the German realm,
> Where GOETHE, WIELAND, SCHILLER dwelt
> Where KARL AUGUST, in generous pride,
> To high-born genius favors dealt,

and thus alludes once more to Wieland's part in establishing the fame of Weimar.[36]

More significant than these incidental references are several comprehensive essays primarily concerned with Wieland. An important early one was published as the "Preface to the First American Edition" of *Oberon.* Since its appearance in 1780 the poem had been the most popular work of Wieland, and it became known to the English speaking world in 1798 when it appeared in London in the translation of William Sotheby. Had this version not appeared that year, it is quite possible that John Quincy Adams would have introduced the work to the American reader, for his own verse translation was finished not much later.[37] The *Oberon* was as enthusiastically received in America as in Europe;[38] it was frequently included among the very few German works the booksellers would stock and advertise;[39] and a dramatic adaptation of several episodes was successfully performed in New York and Philadelphia.[40]

The author of the "Preface" was William Hunter, at the time a member of the General Assembly of Rhode Island and a Trustee of the College (later Brown University).[41] The biographical information contained in the "Preface," of which the more personal details are borrowed from Riesbeck, reflects Hunter's thorough knowledge of the important writings about Wieland and reveals his admiration for the poet, with whose merits "few scholars are unacquainted" and who in Germany is "the envy of his rivals, the idol of the multitude, and the pride of his country." A brief survey of Wieland's major contributions demonstrates Hunter's familiarity with them and with their reviews in French and English periodicals, and particularly the *Monthly Review,* where William Taylor had published his articles on Wieland before they were incorporated into the *Historic Survey of German Poetry.* From the works of Wieland, Hunter selects the *Agathon* for a detailed discussion. What impressed him most is the convincing depiction of the Greek milieu and at the same time the universality of the portrayals; he finds it "perfectly natural" that such works "have endeared the name of Wieland to classical scholars." Hunter's enthusiasm for the *Oberon* is expressed in rather subjective terms. It is an "exquisitely beautiful poem" and its reader "revels at a literary banquet, where every poetick luxury that can allure or gratify a refined taste, is profusely lavished." He agrees with Taylor's praise of the poem and although he realizes that his predecessor was inspired by the subject itself to a poetic encomium he quotes the relevant description of this "elegant critick" in its entirety. In a most sensitive analysis Hunter then attempts to capture the beauty of the poem and compares it with English poetry from which it distinguishes itself by a perfectly balanced structure, an evenly distributed poetic quality, and a "polished diffusiveness over the whole surface"; it thus resembles "a column of un-blemished marble, where all is finished, faultless, and beautiful, touched by the exactest chissel, and smoothed by the hand of grace." This passionate appraisal influenced many of the later judgments of the *Oberon*.

The American edition of the work received two important reviews in the year of its publication, one by George Ticknor writing for the *Monthly Anthology and Boston Review*,[42] the other by John Dennie published in *The Port Folio*.[43] Both reviewers discuss Hunter's preface, Wieland's poem, and the quality of the translation. Yet in their judgment they do not always agree. Whereas Ticknor believes that Hunter (who remained anonymous) writes with considerable spirit but is sometimes "pedantick and bombastical," Dennie praises the skill and elegance with which Hunter "has served up his literary viands." Both reviewers borrow some of their biographical information from Hunter. Whereas Dennie seems satisfied with Hunter's selection of details, Ticknor objects to the omission of the "atrocious opinions, which have been entertained by Wieland ever since he arrived at years of dis-crction," and feels that his notorious development from fanaticism to scepticism, indeed even jacobinism, should not have been hid-den from the reader. Although Ticknor discovers some "occasional defects," and, contrary to modern views, believes that Wieland is more successful in description than in dialogue, he nevertheless thinks the *Oberon* to be a poem in which the author concentrated all his "mental energies" and united the "prominent beauties of the different kinds of writing in which he excels." It is a delightful work, he believes; "the poetry shines forth with surpassing splen-dour, and the Oberon, considered as a whole, exhibits an exub-erance of imagination, unparalleled in modern poetry."

Dennie's review is much more spirited than Ticknor's dry, occasionally even pedantic description. He welcomes the poem and contrasts it with the literature that had previously come from Germany, beginning his review with a diatribe against Kotzebue, the "disseminator of poison," and ending it with an attack on M. G. Lewis who had "ferried over the Thames" armies of foreign ghosts and monsters, which he hopes will now be expelled by Wieland's delightful creatures of fantasy, Oberon and Titania. In his appraisal of the poem Dennie charmingly plays with Hunter's imagery: The *Oberon* is not really a marble column, but "resembles a smooth ball of ivory complete and entire; turn it this way or that it rolls with equal facility, and it would be a vain endeavour to find the spot where the artist began to polish the surface." Finally, both reviewers agree that the translation is excellent; yet they doubt that the selection of "Spencer's measure" was the wisest choice. Dennie objects to its "ponderous gravity" and gives a convincing example: As a result of the heavy measure that seems to restrain flight, "Oberon appears to escape with the lovers, not in his tight and graceful chariot, but in a ponderous Dutch wagon." Yet such are minor flaws, and the reader will "rise from the entertainment light of heart, and his mind replete with delightful images."

Wieland's *Oberon* was not universally admired. A scathing yet amusingly biased evaluation appeared in Baltimore's *Portico*.[44] The article on the "State of Polite Learning" begins its section on the Germans with a questionable generalization: They are "renowned for elaborate criticism and profound science," but "elegant literature is not agreeable to their natural taste or genius." Gessner is their most eminent poet and—the grouping is revealing— far better than Schiller, Goethe, Kotzebue, and Bagessen. Among these, "Kotzebue is superiour to Schiller, and undisputably the first of the German dramatick poets." Bürger's *Leonore,* then a favorite ballad here and abroad, is "replete with absurdities and blemishes," and, turning to Wieland, the *Oberon* "is not less objectionable"; it is a tale of "dull charms," "contemptible effeminacy, and whining puerility"—altogether a righteous but erring judgment.

An entirely different work of Wieland is discussed in an 1822 article by Edward Everett, professor of classics at Harvard, which is in part a searching review of *The Comedies* of Aristophanes, introduced and translated by T. Mitchell.[45] Author and reviewer reveal a thorough familiarity with Wieland's translations of the plays and a close acquaintance with his essays on the attic comedy. In his "Preliminary Discourse" Mitchell mentions his German predecessor several times: he acknowledges Wieland's accuracy in establishing the age of Aristophanes, credits him with a perceptive analysis of an "immortal dialogue" of the Greek comedy, and praises the excellent taste of his judgment. The notes accompanying Mitchell's translations of the comedies—particularly *The Clouds*—are equally laudatory. In general, Wieland's "extensive erudition and extreme impartiality make him a most valuable assistant to a person engaged in a similar labor." Mitchell therefore frequently relies on Wieland's solutions to puzzling problems in the Greek text, quotes the German lines to demonstrate the felicity of the translation, and weighs the wording of earlier translations against the usually more accurate decisions of Wieland. In one instance, however, Mitchell departs from Wieland and questions an interpretation he had suggested in the "Versuch über die Frage: ob und wie fern Aristofanes gegen den Vorwurf, den Sokrates in den Wolken persönlich mißhandelt zu haben, gerechtfertigt, oder entschuldigt werden könne?"[46] Mitchell's criticism of Wieland, although polite and understated, is passionately contested by the American critic. Everett fears that the English scholar has misinformed his readers, and he therefore presents his own thorough analysis of Wieland's essay. He initially states the precise nature of the question in his own translation from Wieland and suggests that one should gratefully accept his solution; he then refutes contrasting interpretations and supports his confutation with documentation borrowed from Wieland and quotations extracted from the *Versuch*. Intermittently he reminds his readers of the excellence of Wieland's scholarly and reliable argumentation and recommends the essay as a successful "attempt philosophically and historically to explain the literary enigma." Wieland could not have found a more ardent advocate, and considering Everett's position, he may well indirectly have influenced classical scholarship in America.

In striking contrast to Everett, another Harvard scholar, George Bancroft, was unsparingly critical of Wieland, whose writings he condemned in the *American Quarterly Review*.[47] His intense dislike for the works of Wieland reveals a strong personal bias and reflects rigidly orthodox views on the function of literature. Bancroft believed that the literature of a Christian nation should advance religious values, indeed, even the critic should devote attention to such qualities. These principles are evident in his review of William Taylor's *Historic Survey*. After an introduction full of criticism, he raises one major objection: "But the greatest fault which can be charged to Mr. Taylor is a wanton and officious exhibition of his indifference to religion." His speaking "with extreme sang-froid" of the " 'intrusion of Christianity' among the Scandinavian nations," his "clumsy attempts at representing Christianity in an odious light," and the "wholly unnecessary gratuitous displays of hostility to Christianity" are utterly offensive to Bancroft. Literature and its critic should express "a reasonable regard for the moral institutions of the Christian world," and he reserves his admiration for those writers who show a profound esteem for religion.

Among the German poets it is Klopstock who possesses his respect, because he had "genuine dignity of character" and "his muse never had cause to blush for him." He "led the way to nobler creations" and "introduced into letters, patriotism, with a generous love of religion." Since Bancroft also praises Klopstock's poetry for moral beauty and Platonic love which "knows no earthly passion," it is not surprising that he feels no "veneration" for Wieland. There are too many detestable features in Wieland's works: his "licentious" philosophy, the "perversion" of moral principles, the "fiendish scoffing and trampling on human virtue," his passion for "vehement irony and scornful insolence," and "the indecent descriptions passing the limits of delicacy, and bordering on coarseness." Wieland's lack of concern for the beyond is equally offensive to Bancroft; there is too much emphasis on worldly matters: "Of hopes beyond he is silent. Of aspirations, which rise above the world, he takes little heed." A final comparison with Klopstock candidly explains Bancroft's partiality: "Wieland and Klopstock are of opposite polarities; those whom the one attracts, the other as surely repels. Wieland treats of actual life, Klopstock of sentiment; Klopstock is heavenly minded, Wieland is earthly to excess; Klopstock is elegiac, Wieland is gay; Klopstock is an eagle, soaring through the clouds to the sun; Wieland a starling, that insults all the passers by."

A condensed version of Bancroft's articles appeared in his *Literary and Historical Miscellanies.*[48] It is more conciliatory in tone and many of the invectives are deleted, yet the comparison between Klopstock and Wieland is retained. Ironically, Wieland might well have agreed with the essential aspects of this judgment. At the beginning of his career he had shared Klopstock's enthusiasm for religion and expressed it in his poetry, but he gradually "descended" from "the clouds to the earth," "reinstating" his soul "in its natural position."[49] Bancroft's idealism would probably have amused him; to be sure, he would not have pecked at him like a starling, yet he would most certainly have gently ridiculed the lofty expectations of his critic and included him among the unrealistic enthusiasts, the *Schwärmer,* that populate his fiction.

Fortunately for Wieland's reputation, Bancroft's was not the last American voice to be heard. Seven years later the *National Quarterly Review* published an article by Edward I. Sears (for many years professor of languages at Manhattan College), in which he reviewed Gruber's biography and the *Sämmtliche Werke* of Wieland, "one of the most fertile and most profound of modern thinkers," unique as a poet, for "no one mind has exhibited such wonderful versatility as that of the author of *Oberon.*"[50] Sears' discussion is less abstract than Bancroft's, it is more fairly balanced, detailed, personal, occasionally even anecdotal. The biographical section of the article highlights Wieland's relationship with Sophie Gutermann and his meeting with Napoleon. Both events are compared to similar experiences in Goethe's life and it is Wieland who gains in the comparison. Whereas he remained "nobly and honorably" silent about his love affairs, or at the most so thoroughly disguised them that the identity of the women was not revealed, Goethe in his *Werther* recklessly and selfishly caused his friends no little embarrassment. Whereas Goethe, Sears believes, humbled himself before Napoleon, Wieland had the courage to question the emperor's reputation among the philosophers and mildly rebuke him for speaking lightly of Christianity in the presence of a devout woman, the Duchess of Weimar. The literary quarrels which involved Wieland Sears attributes in part to the "boldness and freedom" of his criticism that "excited the enmity of many." Quite a few of the attacks directed against Wieland were "stupid, coarse and illiterate," and the more perceptive of his adversaries, particularly Goethe and Herder, did not persist in their hostile attitude. To a far greater extent than Bancroft, Sears discusses the individual works of Wieland and in doing so exonerates him from the accusations of immorality and licentiousness. Unlike Bancroft he does not object to the absence of religious ideas in Wieland's later works. Although they do not extoll the virtues of

Christianity, they are nevertheless lofty and noble in tone and are "replete" with "food for thought," for they embody the best ideas of the Romans and are richly imbued with the spirit of ancient Greece. Sears also understands much better than Bancroft Wieland's favorite method: the poetic adaptation of literary materials and the reshaping of traditional motifs for the creation of a new work. He recognized the aesthetic purpose behind Wieland's many allusions to literature and approved the skillful blending of diverse elements, particularly in the *Oberon,* that resulted in its admirable structure and contributed to the merits of a work that was "undoubtedly the most beautiful modern poem since the *Gerusalemme* of Tasso."

These examples of Wieland criticism indicate a broader trend: He captured the attention of many, but a small circle of orthodox and conservative critics rejected his writings because they lacked the qualities that in their views were essential attributes of acceptable literature—the propagation of virtue, religion, earnestness, a moral lesson and absolute independence of other writers. A larger group of critics, however, expressed a cordial, often even enthusiastic admiration for his lasting contributions to language and literature. The full effect of this favorable reception is hard to measure, for many of the critics mentioned here had wide personal contacts and conducted an extensive correspondence with friends and acquaintances; others were teachers of aspiring writers or mentors of young poets; and all of them may well have mediated their affection for Wieland in a fashion less obvious than public pronouncements.

One final aspect needs to be considered—that is Wieland's possible influence on American writers, or, to phrase it more cautiously, the stimulus some of his writings may have had in suggesting to them structures or technical details, motifs, configurations or patterns of thought. Charles Brockden Brown, who is generally judged the best American novelist before Poe and Hawthorne, was intimately acquainted with German literature. His second work carries the title *Wieland* and establishes intriguing connections between the hero's family and the "modern poet of this name," who "is sprung from the same family."[51] The novel tells a tale of religious fanaticism and superstition, of deception and horrible murder. Since the events may seem impossible to some readers, the author must appeal to "men conversant with the latent springs and occasional perversions of the human mind" to affirm their verisimilitude.

The crucial incident, a religious fanatic murdering his wife and children, was modeled after an actual crime, and its artistic adaptation testifies to Brown's essential originality. The story is cast in the form of an epistolary memoir and constitutes the personal perspective of Clara Wieland, sister of the murderer, who has the firm intention of giving in retrospect a rational account of the tragedy. The poetic embellishment of reality reveals the stimulation Brown received from literature, and since *Wieland* supposedly reflects "the influence which formed Brown's bookish mind,"[52] scholars have diligently hunted for "sources," and depending on their nationality, have credited English and French writers for their impact on Brown's fiction. German overtones have of course also been discovered: Schiller's *Geisterseher* has been identified, but also discredited, as a source, and a strong case has been made for the influence of Kajetan Tschink's novel *Geschichte eines Geistersehers*.[53] Connections with C. M. Wieland have also been suggested: a few lines from the *Don Sylvio* are quoted to indicate a modest measure of influence, and his early religious epic *Der geprüfte Abraham* is thought to contain the ideas Brown's hero expressed in his religious outbursts.[54] However, there are much more obvious similarities to Wieland's works and striking parallels to his novel *Geheime Geschichte des Philosophen Peregrinus Proteus* (1789; trans. London, 1796).

For the characters of Wieland and Brown, literature is a medium of vicarious living and an influence that may decisively affect the course of their lives. For example, C. M. Wieland's Don Sylvio, whose aunt encourages him to model his life after the heroes of baroque romances, accidentally discovers behind these heavy books a volume of fairy tales, and under their influence begins to chart a new course of adventures. Peregrinus Proteus, acting as reader for his grandfather, becomes acquainted with the estate's immense library of books about gods, ghosts, and the supernatural. More important, however, is another book he accidentally discovers under dust and spiderwebs. It is Plato's *Symposium,* whose thoughts on love inspire Peregrinus to begin the search for other idealists who might share his new enthusiasm for divine love and perfection. One of Brown's figures, the elder Wieland, has a similar experience. Although he did not know the pleasures of reading because a stern uncle kept him occupied with commercial matters, he too discovers rather accidentally the book, "half hidden in dust and rubbish," that is to change his life. The pattern of his development is almost the same as that of Peregrinus: possessed by their ideals they leave their homes in search of like-minded men and attempt to make converts to their causes. Both have mystical experiences, dreams, visions, and believe they hear strange voices; both are disappointed by the indifference of others to their ideals; both become lonely men and die in similar fashion, one of mysteriously contracted burns, the other through self-destruction by fire.

Theodore, the hero of Brown's *Wieland*, is in his youth more rational than his father. Like the German poet he studies Cicero for whom he has great admiration; he further collects and investigates the facts that "relate to that mysterious personnage, the Deamon of Socrates," a task which the German Wieland had already accomplished. Like the aunt of Don Sylvio, Theodore's aunt had not been a completely successful educator. By design or neglect, neither youth was carefully guided into the sphere that began to dominate his life: Don Sylvio into the world of fairy tales and Theodore Wieland into the realm of religion. Both became (like Peregrinus Proteus) irrational enthusiasts because they misinterpreted the impressions their senses received and constructed what C. M. Wieland called a second reality, in which fact and fancy form the unit of the hero's world. Whereas Don Sylvio is gently led back into reality, Peregrinus and Theodore Wieland move toward disaster, the one exploited by a clever manipulator, the other deceived by a ventriloquist whose orders to kill wife and children Theodore mistakes as a command from God. The personality pattern is readily recognizable: Theodore is "in some respects an enthusiast" of the very same type C. M. Wieland portrayed so frequently in his fiction; he is an ardent *Schwärmer*, fanatically religious, superstitious and idealistic, who—in the definition of the eighteenth century—bases his judgment and actions on unclear notions and confused conceptions, and considers his impressions, indeed even his fantasies, to be the truth.[55] The complex intertwining of specific themes so prominent in Wieland's works is paralleled in Brown's fiction: the impact of impressions on the senses invariably activates the secret springs (*die geheimen Triebfedern*) of man's action. Yet the senses are easily deceived and a powerful imagination as well as a blinding enthusiasm augment the misconceptions. Man's reason, at least in the realm of the particular illusion, becomes inoperative so that the hero is unable to solve the dilemma and thus becomes a victim of his delusions.

The structure of Brown's novel also recalls that of Wieland's fiction, for it reflects his favorite method, the employment of first-person narrators and the perspectivistic presentation of events. Clara Wieland is the primary narrator, but there are incidents she has not witnessed, emotions she does not comprehend, and her brother's deed is shrouded in a mystery she cannot penetrate. Theodore, the murderer, and Carwin, the ventriloquist, are therefore permitted to present their thoughts and explain their deeds. The court record of Theodore's testimony is reproduced, and Carwin defends his role during a conversation with Clara in an extended speech that is essentially the kind of soliloquy C. M. Wieland used so frequently as a device for psychological self-analysis.

A younger contemporary of Brown, Washington Irving, was equally well informed on German literature and its criticism in English and American periodicals.[56] He first mentioned Wieland in a biographical sketch of Thomas Campbell that accompanied the *Poetical Works* of the English author.[57] Initially interested in German philosophy, above all in the writings of Kant, Campbell soon changed direction and turned away from "metaphysics," for he found nothing to "reward his labours." His pursuit of literature seemed to promise greater benefits, because in "belles-lettres the German language opens a richer field than their philosophy." And there was one among their authors who impressed him profoundly: "I cannot conceive a more perfect poet than their favorite Wieland," a judgment which Irving not only quoted in this sketch but also entered in 1810 in his personal notebooks.[58] In 1813, when Irving was editor of the *Analectic Magazine,* the periodical published a brief anonymous "Account of C. M. Wieland."[59] Although the article tells of his personal relationships, his death and the carefully planned arrangements for his burial, the introductory paragraph lauds his achievements as a poet: There is no other writer to whom Germany owes a greater debt for the refinement of her literature, language and public taste; he possessed "uncommon versatility of genius" and was "equally eminent as poet and prose writer, as a moralist and a philosopher, as a translator and an author of the most brilliant originality and invention." Again, the *Oberon* is singled out for specific praise, and the "spirited and elegant translation" by Sotheby is approvingly mentioned.

Irving's acquaintance with German literature was broadened when in 1817 he stayed with Walter Scott in Abbotsford, where he had access to an extensive collection of German books, among them the works of Wieland. There are indications that in the following year he read Riesbeck's *Travels through Germany,* and it was again a remark about Wieland that impressed him enough to be copied in his notebooks: "Wieland is, without doubt, the first of all German writers."[60] Years later Irving still seemed fascinated by him, for in 1822 he purchased eighteen volumes of his works in Aachen,[61] and among the books he kept in the library at Sunnyside were at least three of Wieland's novels in the original German: *Die Abenteuer des Don Sylvio von Rosalva, Der goldne Spiegel,* and *Die Geschichte der Abderiten.*[62]

This more than casual awareness of Wieland's fiction should permit some speculation about the stimulus Irving might have received from the German writer. One particular entry in his 1818 notebooks invites even stronger conjecture: "Light tales in the manner of Wieland,"[63] a note that seems to indicate his plan to select some of Wieland's tales as his models. The *Don Sylvio* has already been suggested because of its contrast to the Gothic novel of Walpole and Reeve, its wit, spirit of enlightenment, the satiric note and the kind of "rational explanation of *diablerie,*" for which Irving developed a strong predilection.[64] Yet a convincing case could also be made for the *Oberon.* Although in verse, the tale foreshadows characteristic aspects of Irving's fiction, particularly *The Sketch Book* (1819–1820), *Bracebridge Hall* (1822), and *Tales of a Traveller* (1824). A description of major features immediately calls to mind the "manner" of Wieland's narrative. Like his predecessor, Irving was not unusually original, and his inventive power was modest. He preferred to borrow his materials from literature, to act as a poetic interpreter of legend, and his search for suitable motifs and configurations led to a romantic rediscovery of the past. Technical perfection was of greater importance to him than invention, and his style—light, natural, graceful, urbane, and carefully wrought—was the product of the same care and concern with which Wieland reworked his tales for later editions. Another characteristic Irving shares with the German poet is the debt he owes to the arts. The pictorial quality of his prose, the metaphors of painting, the intricately detailed visual images, and the allusions to works of graphic and plastic art direct the reader to a reliable frame of reference.

In his portrayal of man Irving, like Wieland, developed a greater tolerance for human frailties as he matured. The *History of New York* (1809) is at times merciless in its satire in which the city fathers are as grotesquely ridiculed as in Wieland's *Abderites*. In later tales the satire becomes less biting and is replaced by a kind humor, comic wit, and genuine compassion. In the fiction of Irving, invented narrators play important, diversified roles, and the perspective of many a tale is meaningfully broadened by the interpolation of first-person narratives. The resulting ironic detachment is no doubt intended: neither Irving nor Wieland tried to involve their readers emotionally. Such similarities do not necessarily or undeniably demonstrate Wieland's influence; they could be explained by other factors: a common heritage, inherent affinities for the same artistic techniques and literary methods, or a natural resemblance in talent, inclination, and temper. Yet one should not overlook the fact that the parallels become more pronounced after Irving's self-motivating reference to Wieland in 1818.

Charles Brockden Brown and Washington Irving belonged to a generation of American writers who, like their European contemporaries, still considered the creative use of past literary works acceptable practice: the adaptation of poetic artifacts was a respectable method, allusions to the writings of others were an intellectual challenge to the reader, and the conscious emulation of literary models did not seem to impugn the integrity of the poet. The generation that followed, however, developed a distinctly different attitude. During the second quarter of the nineteenth century writers and critics began to demand creative originality in American letters, and declarations of intellectual independence were repeatedly issued. When Emerson, for example, delivered his lecture "The American Scholar" before the Phi Beta Kappa Society at Cambridge and predicted that "our day of dependence, our long apprenticeship to the learning of other lands, draws to a close," and that American poetry was entering a new age, he merely affirmed what others had expressed previously, perhaps less formally.[65] Traditional literary methods, adaptation, imitation, and the emulation of models were rejected, and rash accusations of plagiarism were levelled at the most reputable poets, at times with little justification.[66] Foreign criticism made them even more fearful of being considered derivative. An unusually sarcastic review of Rufus W. Griswold's *The Poets and Poetry of America* (1842) which appeared in the *Foreign Quarterly Review* (London, 1844)[67] increased the self-consciousness of American poets, whose writings were rejected as imitative of the poorest examples, unoriginal, and an inferior, artificial substitute for "genuine" English poetry. It is not surprising, then, that under these circumstances the formative influence of literature on the creative process was seriously challenged. To be sure, the works of American writers do exhibit parallels to other literatures, but Poe, for one, maintained that such similarities are often purely accidental and not at all intentional. Or, to rely on an authority cited by Emerson, if there are semblances in thought and ideas, the demonstration of a source is not essential: "Little matters it to the simple lover of truth to whom he owes such or such a reasoning."[68]

The pursuit of originality did not make these writers insensitive to values and qualities of other literatures. But their attitude was intentionally different from that of earlier generations. Again, Emerson seems to express it most eloquently: "Books are the best of things, well used; abused, among the worst. What is the right use? What is the one end which all means go to effect? They are for nothing but to inspire."[69] If inspiration is a desirable effect of literature, confirmation of one's ideas and conceptions is another acceptable result of reading. Although in modest measure, Wieland seems to have fulfilled both these functions for at least three writers of the younger generation, Emerson, Longfellow, and Poe.

Emerson's familiarity with the works of Wieland is easily documented. Over a period of thirty-four years, from April 1834 to May 1868, he borrowed twenty-three volumes of Wieland's *Sämmtliche Werke* (1824–1826) from the library of the Boston Athenaeum, the *Don Sylvio* three times, and two volumes of the later verse tales four times.[70] Although this seems to indicate an extensive occupation with Wieland's writings, it must not be overlooked that there were almost a thousand other books which Emerson borrowed from public and private libraries, and beyond that, additional ones from his friends. His journals do not indicate the purpose of his reading Wieland; they contain only one remark that contrasts him with those among the German authors who are "introversive to a [vice] fault & pick every rose to pieces," as for example Tieck and Richter. Quite differently, "Wieland writes of real Man," as do Herder and Goethe.[71] A cursory reading of Emerson's own works does not reveal obvious parallels. It may well be that he, like other contemporaries, read these works, above all the charming verse tales, purely for his own enjoyment, or perhaps as inspiring specimens of perfect form in prose and verse. There is, however, one work Emerson specifically mentioned in his correspondence with Margaret Fuller, from whom he borrowed the book, that is the *Briefe an Johann Heinrich Merck von Göthe, Herder, Wieland und anderen Zeitgenossen* (Darmstadt, 1835) that constituted a valuable source of information which he consulted in preparation for the Goethe lecture of his series *Representative Men.* "The Merk book I have nearly finished," he wrote. "It is inestimable to the biography of Goethe & not less for the picture it gives of the inside of Germany. Wieland is the charm of the book."[72] Again, there are no obvious parallels between Wieland's reports of Goethe's early life in Weimar and Emerson's depiction; but a similarity in mood and tone, the same affectionate admiration for "the young man of genius," and a comparable conception of his personality do suggest that Emerson's memory retained some of the color Wieland applied in his portrait of the young Goethe.

Longfellow, not yet as critical of creative imitation and emulation as Poe, wrote his novel *Hyperion* (1839) in the tradition of the German *Bildungsroman,* the genre of which Wieland's *Agathon* was the celebrated eighteenth-century landmark and Goethe's *Wilhelm Meister* the deliberately chosen model, both works as overtly semi-autobiographical as Longfellow's romance. The *Hyperion* includes countless references to German authors and contains many allusions to fictive figures and literary situations.

One of its chapters is entitled "Goethe" and is designed to introduce the German poet to Paul Flemming, the hero of the novel.
The image of Goethe as it is fashioned by Flemming's companion,
Baron von Hohenfels, is a mosaic of partly subjective views, one
of which reflects a judgment of Wieland. As the two travellers
stroll through the Goethe House in Frankfurt, they see a picture
of the eighty-year-old poet, and at this moment Hohenfels recalls
a contrasting image of the young Goethe that was conveyed in an
episode Gleim used to tell. When in 1777 Gleim was in Weimar, he
spent an evening at the court where a mysterious and somewhat
mischievous young man dressed like a hunter helped him entertain
the duchess and her circle with readings from the *Musen-Almanach*.
At first puzzled by the identity of the stranger, Gleim finally
guessed who he was: " 'that is either Goethe or the Devil,' said the
good old father Gleim to Wieland, who sat near him. To which the
'Great I of Osmannstadt' replied,—'It is both, for he has the Devil
in him to-night; and at such times he is like a wanton colt, that
flings out before and behind, and you will do well not to go too
near him!' "[73] Wieland's characterization delights the hero of the
novel as much as it had pleased Gleim, and the anecdote informs
him well of these traits in young Goethe's personality.

Two further references to Wieland reflect a favorite technique
of the German novelist, whose own allusions to literature were
often intended as a symbolic extension in which a fictive being was
subtly characterized by the implied identification with another
literary figure. Longfellow's allusions are to *Oberon*. Paul Flemming and a later companion, the Englishman Berkley, are compared
to "Huon of Bordeaux and Scherasmin on their way to Babylon"
(279). Berkley does indeed play the same role for Flemming that
Scherasmin had taken in the life of Huon. As an older, more
mature and broadly experienced mentor he introduces the young
idealist to the realities of life, corrects his vision of Providence,
guides him out of a place of disappointments, and leads him toward new adventures in his search for fulfillment. And in Inns-
bruck Flemming himself identifies for a fleeting moment with
Huon. The statues "which stand leaning on their swords between
the columns of the church" remind him of Huon's struggle against
the "flail-armed monsters that guarded the gateway of Angulaffer's
castle in Oberon" (300). They are thus interpreted as symbols of

the formidable obstacles that impede, though only temporarily, the progress of the young quester.

Edgar Allen Poe knew at least two works of Wieland, which he mentions in the *Marginalia* (1844-1849). He uses the *Abderites* as a frame of reference, specifically the episode of the third book that portrays the townspeople in their irrational enthusiasm for the theater. They are providing the answer to a question the Bishop of Durham had raised, "whether ... communities went mad *en masse,* now and then." "This thing," Poe believes, "need not have been questioned. Were not the Abderites seized, all at once, with the Euripides lunacy, during which they ran about the streets declaiming the plays of the poet.?"[74] Not only does the fictional event provide a fitting reply to the Bishop's question, it also prefigures the reaction of the people to the "uproar about Pusey," that according to Poe caused the English and Americans to become as lunatic as the Abderites.

A more general view of humanity, man as an imperfect being who strives in vain for perfection, Poe found confirmed in another work of Wieland: " 'He that is born to be a man,' says Wieland in his 'Peregrinus Proteus,' 'should nor can be anything nobler, greater, or better than a man.' The fact is, that in efforts to soar above our nature, we invariably fall below it" (161). The effects of this insight are evident in the tales of Wieland and Poe, both of whom created a corresponding image of man in their fiction and thus artistically exemplify and confirm a realistic conception of man's nature. There are other thoughts expressed in the *Marginalia* that could be understood as echoes of Wieland, for example Poe's deliberations on "fancy" (88-90), his definition and application of the German term *Schwärmerei* (166), a maxim on the dignity of man (161), and the contemplation of a future existence in which the present life appears as a dream (161). These and perhaps other parallels may, of course, be entirely unintentional, yet they could also be indications of certain stimuli Poe received from reading Wieland.

Whether there are further echoes in other writings of these men or in the works of younger poets must for the moment and for the practical reasons of space and time remain a matter of speculation. Standard bibliographies do not indicate the continuation of a significant interest in Wieland, and a cursory sampling of later nineteenth-century literature does not reveal more than a casual awareness of his works.[75] This lack of interest in a German writer of the past century reflects the general development of American literature which involved a turning away from European models, a strong emphasis on originality, the selection of American subjects, and a greater attention to American history and indigenous folklore.

The importance of German literature for American letters cannot be seriously challenged. The reception of many authors has been carefully studied and the significance of their work for American writers has in many cases been sufficiently treated. Wieland, however, experienced a similar fate here and abroad. Widely read by his contemporaries and into the nineteenth century, enthusiastically praised by many of the early critics and universally recognized for his formative influence on the language and literature of Germany, he was treated with ambivalence by some of the later critics, who vascillated in their attitude toward him, ignored the important role he had played in the development of German literature and even disparaged his works for reasons of patriotism and morality.

When in 1949 Friedrich Sengle published a new literary biography of Wieland, he initiated a conscientious re-evaluation of his writings that is still in progress. One of the topics that until now needed closer investigation was the reception of Wieland in America. The present study is meant as a contribution to this area,[76] and beyond that to the broader field of German-American relations to which Professor Karl Arndt, in whose honor this *Festschrift* is published, has so generously and expertly given of his time and scholarly efforts.

NOTES

1. Henry A. Pochmann's *German Culture in America* (Madison, Wisc., 1957), the most useful survey of "philosophical and literary influences 1600–1900," establishes many patterns of mediation and treats a great variety of authors. Wieland, however, is only briefly discussed or mentioned in passing.

2. Adams' letter of October 24, 1831, to Charles Follen, in *The Life of Charles Follen* (Boston, 1844), p. 202. In his "Inaugural Discourse" delivered before the University of Harvard, September 3, 1831, Follen had not mentioned Wieland, but he did so in the published version of the address at the advice of John Quincy Adams.

3. *The Private Journals of Aaron Burr* (Rochester, 1903), I, 346-358.

4. Quoted by Orie William Long, *Literary Pioneers—Early American Explorers of European Culture* (Cambridge, Mass., 1935), p. 26.

5. The list of books Ticknor was to purchase has not been published. The Library of the University of Virginia kindly supplied a copy of the invoice for books that were shipped in 1825 from Hamburg to Richmond on the *Mazzinghi*. Wieland's "sämmtliche Werke von Gruber—49 vols., 8°," were billed at £4,18.

6. *Life and Letters of Bayard Taylor*, ed. Marie Hansen-Taylor and Horace E. Scudder (Boston, 1884), I, 643.

7. (Dresden, 1866), p. 346.

8. (London, 1787), II, 207-213. The first German edition, *Briefe eines reisenden Franzosen durch Deutschland*, appeared in 1783.

9. *Characteristics of Goethe, From the German of Falk, von Müller & c.* (London, 1833), particularly I, 67; II, 49; II, 50, II, 218.

10. *American Quarterly Review*, II (1827), 171-186; III (1828), 150-173; IV (1828), 157-191.

11. (Boston, 1840), VIII, 379-385.

12. Scott Holland Goodnight, *German Literature in American Magazines Prior to 1846* (Madison, Wisc., 1807), pp. 202, 206, 210.

13. "German Literature," in *The Dial*, I (Boston, 1841), 326.

14. William Hunter, whom I shall discuss in more detail later, mentions the *Bibliothèque* in his "Preface to the first American edition" of *Oberon*, p. xviii; and William Taylor refers to the French periodical in his *Historic Survey* (see note 20), II, 322.

15. *The Port Folio*, VI (1818), 184-193.

16. The American edition, called *Germany*, from which I am quoting, appeared in New York in 1814. Vol. I, part 2, Chapter IV, pp. 141-143, treats Wieland.

17. See V. Stockley, *German Literature as Known in England 1750-1830* (London, 1929), pp. 77-106; Julius Steinberger, *Bibliographie der Wieland-Übersetzungen* (Göttingen, 1930), pp. 11-54. Bayard Quincy Morgan and A.

R. Hohlfeld, eds., *German Literature in British Magazines 1750–1860* (Madison, Wisc., 1949).

18. (London, 1814), I, 336.

19. *Ibid.*, III, 93–96.

20. (London, 1828), II, 243–495. The following quotations are taken from pp. 276, 287, 290, 311, 312, 403, 494.

21. (New York, 1803), Vol. II, part 1, pp. 170, 182, 188.

22. (New York, 1860), p. 426.

23. (New York, 1873), pp. 213–220.

24. (New York, 1896), pp. 251–265.

25. He was the son of John Quincy Adams. His *Diary*, ed. Marc Friedlaender and L. H. Butterfield (Cambridge, Mass., 1968), Vol. IV, contains several entries concerning his translations from Wieland's work: pp. 417, 418, 419, 423, 427.

26. III (1791), 235–237 and 273–275. Steinberger, p. 24, lists it as a translation.

27. *Ladies Magazine*, II (1829), 419. Steinberger, p. 34, lists it as a translation from *Schach Lolo*. The German text reads: "Ohne Arbeit ist keine Gesundheit der Seele noch des Leibes, ohne diese keine Glückseligkeit möglich." *Wielands Werke*, IX (Berlin, 1931), 59.

28. (Philadelphia, 1849), p. 128.

29. I have consulted the fourth edition that appeared in 1858 in Philadelphia.

30. *Poets and Poetry of Europe* (Philadelphia, 1845); introduction to Wieland: pp. 261–263. Another collection, Charles Knight's *Half-Hours with the Best Authors*, includes in every one of its English and American editions Wieland's "The Beautiful and the Useful," a translation of the essay "Über das Verhältniß des Angenehmen und Schönen zum Nützlichen," first published in 1775 in the *Teutscher Merkur*. The inclusion is the more remarkable since only three other German authors are represented: in addition to Goethe, only A. v. Humboldt, in the editions of 1859 and 1931, and Ranke, in the editions of 1880 and 1931. Knight's anthology is not listed in B. Q. Morgan's bibliography *German Literature in English Translation 1481–1927* (London and Oxford, 1938).

31. *Library of the World's Best Literature*, XXXIX (New York, 1897); introduction to Wieland: pp. 15954–15956.

32. For Sarah Austin, see note 9. The second source of Eliza Buckminster Lee is Carl Wilhelm O. A. von Schindel, *Die deutschen Schriftstellerinnen des neunzehnten Jahrhunderts*, part 2 (Leipzig, 1825), entry "Marie Sophie la Roche," pp. 180–209.

33. *Goethe. His Life and Works. An Essay* (Boston and New York, 1886), p. 119.

34. Scott Holland Goodnight, *German Literature in American Magazines Prior to 1846*, and Martin Henry Haertel, *German Literature in American Magazines 1846 to 1880* (Madison, Wisc., 1908), have presented a bibliography of articles contained in the library of the Wisconsin Historical Society

which lists approximately half of the American magazines that are now available on microfilm. See also Goodnight's article "Lessing and Wieland in American Magazines Prior to 1846," *German American Annals*, NS (Philadelphia, 1908), VI, 243–247.

35. (Salem, 1804), pp. 14 and 133–134, note iv.

36. *Knickerbocker*, LV (1860), 492.

37. Adams finished his translation on May 22, 1800, and on December 4, 1800, he "saw for the first time Sotheby's translation of Oberon." Although he continued revising his version, it remained in manuscript until 1940, when A. B. Faust prepared a scholarly edition with an informative introduction relating the important details, correspondence, and diary entries connected with Adam's translation (New York, 1940), pp. xcii and 340; see particularly pp. lxvi and lxviii.

38. It would be possible to write a richly documented, extensive study on the international reception of *Oberon*, which was translated into French, Polish, Portuguese, Russian, Swedish, and Hungarian, in each case several times (see Steinberger, pp. 40–43); it was also frequently reviewed, often discussed, and mentioned countless times, usually with warm praise.

39. Around 1828, for example, Haskell's Circulation Library in Vermont published a list of 350 books available to their readers. Among these were only two German works (in translation), the *Memoirs of Goethe* and Wieland's *Oberon*. (A copy of the list is bound with the *Memoirs of Andrew Jackson* [Hartford, 1818] in the library of Harold Jantz, Baltimore.)

40. Louis Charles Baker, *The German Drama in English on the New York Stage to 1830* (Philadelphia, 1917), pp. 129–130; Charles F. Brede, *The German Drama in English on the Philadelphia Stage from 1794–1830* (Philadelphia, 1918), pp. 257–267.

41. The Providence Athenaeum Library Catalogue, 1853, p. 433, indicates that Hunter was the author of the "Preface"; see Frederick H. Wilkens, *Early Influence of German Literature in America* (New York/London/Berlin, 1899), p. 45. Wilkens' monograph contains further useful information on Wieland, pp. 39–53. The excerpts that follow here are quoted from Hunter's "Preface to the First American Edition" of *Oberon* (Newport, R. I., 1810), pp. v–xlviii.

42. IX (1810), 191–194.

43. IV (1810), 592–603.

44. II (1816), 18–21.

45. Mitchell's work appeared in London in 1820; Everett published his article in the *North American Review*, NS X (1822), 272–296; for the discussion of Wieland see pp. 281–296.

46. The essay was published in Wieland's *Attisches Museum* III (1799), 57–100.

47. The first article, III (1828), contains a review of "Wieland's Life" by J. G. Gruber, vols. 50 and 51 of Wieland's *Sämmtliche Werke*, pp. 168–171. The second, VII (1830), is a review of William Taylor's *Historic Survey of German Poetry*, pp. 436–449, of which pp. 445–449 are an analysis of Taylor's treatment of Wieland.

48. (New York, 1855), pp. 146-150.

49. Wieland, *Ausgewählte Briefe* (Zurich, 1815), II, 195.

50. IV (1862), 286-304.

51. (Port Washington, 1963), p. 27, the first edition appeared in 1798.

52. Richard Chase, *The American Novel and Its Tradition* (Garden City, N.Y., 1957), p. 61.

53. Harry R. Warfel, "Charles Brockden Brown's German Sources," *Modern Language Quarterly*, I (1940), 357-365.

54. For *Don Sylvio*, see Lulu Rumsey Wiley, *The Sources and Influences of the Novels of Charles Brockden Brown* (New York, 1950), pp. 42 and 84; for the connections with Wieland's *Der geprüfte Abraham*, see John G. Frank, "The Wieland Family in Charles Brockden Brown's 'Wieland'," *Monatshefte*, 62 (1950), 351-353.

55. Johann Christoph Adelung, *Versuch eines vollständigen grammatisch-kritischen Wörterbuches der Hochdeutschen Mundart* (Leipzig, 1780), 4th part, colms. 333-334.

56. Walter A. Reichart, *Washington Irving and Germany* (Ann Arbor, Mich., 1957).

57. (Philadelphia, 1810), p. 22.

58. Stanley T. Williams, *The Life of Washington Irving* (New York, 1935), p. 215.

59. II (1813), 419-421.

60. Reichart, *Washington Irving and Germany*, p. 22.

61. Washington Irving, *Journals and Notebooks*, III (1819-1827), ed. Walter A. Reichart (Madison, Wisc., 1970), p. 4.

62. Reichart, *Washington Irving and Germany*, p. 202.

63. *Ibid.*, p. 16.

64. *Ibid.*, p. 21. Two earlier articles by Henry A. Pochmann do not take Wieland into consideration; his name is only mentioned in a list of several authors. See Pochmann, "Irving's German Sources in *The Sketch Book*," *Studies in Philology*, XXVII (1930), 477-507; "Irving's German Tour and Its Influence on His Tales," *PMLA*, XLV (1930), 1150-1187.

65. "The American Scholar," in *The Works of Ralph Waldo Emerson* (Boston and New York, 1883), I, 83-84.

66. Sidney P. Moss, *Poe's Literary Battles* (Carbondale and Edwardsville, Ill., 1969), is an informative study on this subject.

67. I have consulted the American edition of the *Foreign Quarterly Review*, XXXII (New York, 1844), 159-176.

68. Amusingly, Emerson seems to recall the wrong source of this quotation. He identifies Mendelsohn [sic] as its author, yet scholars have been unable to trace the maxim in his writings. See *The Journals and Miscellaneous Notebooks of Ralph Waldo Emerson*, III, eds. William G. Gilman and Alfred R. Ferguson (Cambridge, Mass., 1963), 317.

69. "The American Scholar," op. cit., I, 91.

70. Kenneth Walter Cameron, *Ralph Waldo Emerson's Reading* (Raleigh, N.C., 1941). The Library of the Boston Athenaeum kindly informed me of the contents of vols. 21 and 22 of the *Werke*.

71. *The Journals and Miscellaneous Notebooks*, V, ed. Merton M. Sealts, Jr. (Cambridge, Mass., 1965), 202.

72. *The Letters of Ralph Waldo Emerson*, I, ed. Ralph L. Rusk (New York, 1939), 70–71.

73. *Hyperion* (Cambridge, Mass., 1845), pp. 162–163. Further page references are given in parentheses in the text. See also *Goethes Gespräche*, part 1, *Gedenkausgabe der Werke, Briefe und Gespräche*, ed. Wolfgang Pfeiffer-Belli, XXII (Zürich, 1949), 111.

74. *The Complete Works*, ed. James A. Harrison (New York, 1902), XVI, 5. Further page references are given in parentheses in the text.

75. For a more general study with occasional references to Wieland, see Stanley M. Vogel, *German Literary Influences on the American Transcendentalist* (New Haven, 1955).

76. At the outset I had hoped to write for this occasion the definitive study on the subject. But as happens so often in Wieland scholarship, I underestimated the wealth of material new research would uncover and therefore had to be selective in the presentation of evidence and analysis.

6. The American Expedition of Emperor Joseph II and Bernhard Moll's Silhouettes
John Andre and
Hartmut Froeschle

Shortly after his arrival in Philadelphia on September 9, 1783, a member of the Austrian expedition which Emperor Joseph II had sent out to explore North America sent his report to his sponsor, Ignaz von Born:

> How wonderful it is here, in this free city. We have already been here eight days and nobody bothers us—we are as free as born Americans. I like it so much that, if permitted, I would immediately settle down here. Since there are but a few artists, and not one in my field, I am not going to suffer want. It is true that the authorities of the United States permit scientists to travel to the remotest parts of the country. Thus, I need not worry about my needs because local gentlemen pay well. Until I am familiar with the situation in all the states, I could earn good money with my silhouettes. I have already cut a collection of American personalities . . .[1]

These enthusiastic but somewhat disloyal lines came from Bernhard Albrecht Moll, a bachelor 39 years of age and a resident of Vienna. His candid words may have embarrassed Ignaz von Born[2] because such correspondence was censored and copied for the Imperial secret service. The expedition was partly the fruit of Born's enlightened mind, and he had recommended Moll to the Emperor as the most competent painter of natural objects.

For the time being, though, Bernhard Moll was drawing rare animals for His Majesty's director of the expedition, Professor Franz Joseph Märter. Moll described the mood of his four fellow explorers on board the ship:

> I am honoured to report to you in all haste that we arrived

safely in Philadelphia on the 9th, after a sea voyage of 40 days. During the voyage we had almost constantly stormy weather. Mr. Märter was sick throughout the trip, Mr. Stupitz[3] wished to die, and the gardeners [i.e., Boos and Bredemeyer] almost perished because of hunger. I felt fine except for the first four days, and I might have enjoyed a somewhat pleasant voyage in the company of a healthier group. All this time Mr. Märter did not speak a word, Stupitz whined and prayed, and I could not do much with the gardeners. I found but a few objects to occupy my time by drawing. Other than a flying fish, a medusa, and a little . . . [illegible], there was nothing. Those three items I drew in the cabin during quiet weather. Here, in Philadelphia, I have already finished this *exococtus volans* [?] which, in his publication, Catesby has drawn and coloured completely incorrectly. On the first return trip, I will be able to deliver many of my works.[4]

Bernhard does not mention his Excellency, Baron de Beelen-Bertholff, the first Austrian agent sent to the new republic of the United States. Beelen's duty was to explore the political climate and the potential of the United States with a view to concluding an economic treaty between the two countries, and also to facilitate Professor Märter's work. Together with the others on board the formerly British, now American frigate *General Washington,* Beelen may have felt as miserable as most members of the scientific expedition, or he may have deliberately avoided their company due to his rank. Later on, Beelen assisted the group constantly by expediting their correspondence and shipments, and by collecting some botanical and ethnographic items himself. Apparently through John Bartram, the pioneer botanist of America,[5] this diplomat was able to supply the Imperial gardens with many rare plants.

Although Joseph II's American expedition lasted five years, and the first reports of Director Märter were published in Vienna almost immediately,[6] this interesting enterprise has never been dealt with extensively in American historiography. Besides various printed summaries, there exist thick files in the Austrian State Archives which cover in great detail the early stages of this undertaking but contain only a few letters sent from America. Professor Märter's journal and other manuscript material from Latin America as well as from Boos' subsequent African expedition have been either lost or misplaced. This is probably due to tragic events, such as the sickness and death of Joseph II in 1790 and of Born in 1791, and because of certain changes in the administration.

In Ware, Massachusetts, John Andre recently found Moll's album of silhouettes mentioned in the quoted letter to Born. This pictorial diary, further evidence of the expedition and Moll's contacts with various European and American individuals, is a little book, 6 X 4 inches in size, and contains 148 black silhouettes from 1783 to 1785. Fortunately, the name, place, and year of creation are written under most portraits, and an index can be found at the end of the collection.[7] Emperor Joseph II, and Bernhard's mother along with his three sisters, appear therein, as well as Professor Märter with his gardeners Boos and Bredemeyer. Bernhard Moll cut only part of these silhouettes "for good money." His mother, his sisters, friends, and colleagues were depicted out of love and respect.

Maria Theresia, the widow of the Emperor of the Holy Roman Empire, Franz I, died on November 29, 1780. During the long and fairly conservative reign of his mother, the actual Emperor, Joseph II, had to swallow many rejections of his enlightened ideas. But the Empress was progressive enough to respect and further build up her late husband's institutions of learning, particularly the study of natural sciences, so that in 1775 all universities within her domain possessed faculties of science. The originally private collections of the Hapsburg dynasty had already been transferred to the state in 1765. Some peculiar contracts, however, such as the hereditary rights of the Baron von Baillou's family to the director's position of the Imperial *Naturalien-Cabinet,* slowed down the progress. The quite remarkable little museum contained all sorts of "curious" minerals and petrified objects which were placed in huge oak cupboards with glass windows and drawers. Since 1761, a devoted volunteer, Johann Baptist Megerle, and since 1766, the old painter, Franz Joseph Wiedon, had assisted the passive and ignorant director, Ludwig Freiherr von Baillou. Count Rosenberg started the badly needed modernization shortly after his appointment to the portfolio responsible for the natural sciences collection in 1775. Rosenberg also brought the great scholar Ignaz von Born in 1777 from Prague to Vienna, in order to enlarge, systematize, and scientifically describe the state collections of natural history. Nicolaus von Jacquin[8] and Van der Schot had already improved the botanical and zoological gardens with material from tropical America. In accordance with his altruistic principle of helping mankind first and himself last, Born donated many important items to the section of minerals, and persuaded his friends to do the same. This new collection was set up between 1778 and 1780, with the enthusiastic help of the young mineralogists Karl Haidinger, and Karl Moll, Bernhard's nephew, as well as old Megerle, and many other volunteers. Born published a partial catalogue as early as 1778, and at the beginning of 1780, he sponsored Haidinger for the position of a deputy director. About this time the painter Wiedon retired, and very probably Born's recommendation was the basis for Count Rosenberg's request to Joseph II to hire the painter Moll, "who is without any doubt the most competent in his profession."[9] The Emperor approved, and the new "Kayserlicher Cabinets-Mahler," Bernhard Moll, received a yearly salary of 800 florins as of April 1, 1780.

An accident which caused the overnight ruin of most tropical plants in the Imperial hothouse influenced Joseph II considerably, but it is questionable whether this was the only reason for an expedition to America. There is sufficient evidence, such as the Emperor's political interest in overseas colonies and commerce, the presence of East Indian leader Haider Ali's[10] agents in Vienna, and his dealings with the adventurous British East Indian captain Willem Bolts, to suspect other Imperial plans as well, such as the Far East trade. Haider Ali's emissary, "Mr. Munschi," and an Englishman "Mr. Watts" appear in Moll's album. Thus, in spite of all the economic measures to cut "frills" out of governmental spending, Joseph II accepted Born's idea to equip a whole ship for a voyage around the world.

With the personal participation of Ignaz von Born, and with the Dutchman in British services, Willem Bolts, as the captain of the Imperial ship *Cobenzl,* this scientific expedition was shortly to leave from the harbor of Trieste in the hope of surpassing the explorations of Captain Cook. Since particular interest was directed to India and China, the projected endeavor was called the India Expedition, although Africa and America were also included. Once under way, the explorers were supposed to split into two groups, led by the botanist-zoologist Märter and the mineralogist Haidinger, and to meet again at the Cape of Good Hope. On account of ill health, Born had meanwhile been persuaded to give up his ideas of personal participation. Together with von Jacquin, the Imperial botanist of international reputation, he continued to advise the government about the selection of personnel and necessary equipment. Born also found an ingenious solution to the problem of high costs: Austrian mines should supply the ship *Cobenzl* with tons of locally cheap mercury to be sold abroad for high prices. Contrary to the narrow approach of ordinary specialists, mineralogist Born urged the explorers to study all aspects of the social life of the native population, too, and to collect and describe in detail specimens of their industry and arts.

For reasons no longer clear (probably including costs as well as difficulties with the now Austrian Colonel "von" Bolts), Joseph II delayed his final approval for some time. He travelled extensively and was preoccupied with his important reform work, including the abolition of religious intolerance and the liberation of the peasants from servitude. Moreover, there was a prospect of getting a good load of tropical plants much cheaper through the kind offices of Director Cerre, the Royal gardener of France. Meanwhile, the already appointed members of the expedition waited in suspense. Born's long letters to Count Cobenzl, the Minister in charge, illustrate well the general situation and his growing frustration. Haidinger finally resigned, and there seems to have been an intrigue which, through the appointment of Dr. Mathias Leopold Stupich (a recent graduate of medicine and a part-time botanist with Jacquin), changed the expedition into a preponderantly botanical undertaking.

We learn the following about Bernhard Moll from Born's memorandum to Count Cobenzl, dated June 23, 1782:

> Since I now know that his Majesty is not against the idea that the two scientific explorers split and meet again only at the Cape, I would wish that a person educated in drawing and painting be allowed to take part in the voyage in order to support the one of the two who received no education in drawing. Bernhard Moll, a painter of natural objects, formerly employed in the Imperial *Naturaliencabinet,* who is incomparable in this specialty and who is a single, healthy man of about 30 years desires

nothing more eagerly than to be permitted to participate, without asking for more than the minimum upkeep during the voyage. I leave it to your Excellency's generous opinion if your Excellency would kindly consider the merits of the addition of this painter, the further advantage being that even during the trip he could sketch and professionally finish such objects which would require copper plate engraving for the future publication of these travel descriptions . . . According to the opinion of Lieutenant-Colonel von Bolts, the yearly cost of the two scholars would be about 400 florins, the cost of the painter about 200 florins, whereas their present salary which they have been receiving from you amounts to 800 florins each. Perhaps it would, therefore, be advisable to grant 1200 florins yearly to both explorers, 600 florins to the gardener, and as much also to the proposed painter, which sums would cover their expenses on board the ship as well as on land, besides meeting their private needs.[11]

In his calligraphic application to the Emperor, Moll also stressed his experience in drawing prospects and landscapes, and mentioned that his greatest desire since his youth had been to explore distant lands. Obviously his steady job in the museum had lasted only one year, probably due to the Emperor's drive for economy, for he signed his letter as "the former" painter of his Majesty. Moll's pay was subsequently raised to 800 florins, and this annoyed the gardener Boos who felt himself entitled to the same amount.

At the beginning of December 1782, Born urged Cobenzl to come to a decision because of the growing financial difficulties of the waiting members of the expedition: "The same embarrassing situation applies also to the painter Moll who at first could not accept any new jobs and also dismissed his pupils because of the weekly expectations of the order for his departure; now he has already been unemployed for almost five months and is in miserable circumstances."[12]

The decision came soon thereafter, but contrary to the expectations, Joseph II reduced Born's ambitious plan of a world cruise, on board a specially equipped exploration ship, to a more primitive expedition to the two Americas. The explorers were to travel as passengers on suitable foreign ships, whereas the heavy baggage would go separately on more modest vessels. Professor Franz

Joseph Märter, Dr. Mathias Leopold Stupich, Bernhard Albrecht Moll, Franz Boos, and Franz Bredemeyer left Vienna towards the end of April, 1783. Instead of sailing from Trieste, they travelled across Germany to Brussels, then to Paris and to Le Havre, to wait for a ship bound for North America. The heavy baggage, books, and instruments were shipped ahead from Ostende.

PHILADELPHIA

Director Märter's substantial reports[13] contain long and, for the non-specialist, tedious descriptions of various local plants, animals, and minerals together with brief glances at the climate, the landscape, and the people. He begins with the ocean voyage on board the American frigate, *George Washington,* which was under the command of the American war hero Joshua Barney. During the trip Märter made daily observations about the prevailing winds, the temperature, currents, etc.:

> The first of August, 1783, was the long desired day when we at last were able to leave Europe, after five days of waiting for a suitable wind . . . It was 11 o'clock before noon when the sails were hoisted in the port of Havre de Grace, with an advantageous but quite weak breeze from the east . . . After one hour the wind became a little stronger, and all passengers who had never been at sea and therefore were not accustomed to the unstable movement began to become seasick one after the other; with the exception of an English lady, I was the first and most violently attacked person, so badly that towards the evening I was without feelings and completely unconscious, and it was necessary to carry me to bed.[14]

Märter goes on to describe the following days, sometimes cheerfully, sometimes full of horror, when lightning and heavy storms came close to sinking the ship, leaving only two tea cups intact. Then the color of the water began to change again, and on September 7 the professor saw a butterfly of the sphinx variety, a sure sign of nearby land. The ship was approaching Philadelphia on September 8, and Märter writes about the great occasion:

> Shortly before 6 o'clock in the morning, we entered Delaware Bay between Cape Hinlopen and Cape May; here one again sees

the difference in the colour of the water which does not appear dark blue any more but totally greenish. Because of numerous and dangerous sandbanks which are located in this bay, the sailors took turns measuring the water's depth which averaged between 12 and 4 fathoms. From time to time various landbirds greeted us, while the flying fish and the seagrass had vanished. The porpoises which we had already noticed more frequently during the past few days appeared to be more numerous. This proves that this type of sea animal prefers to stay in shallow waters instead of the boundless ocean, for they had also been seen more often on the first days after our departure from Europe. Nevertheless, during the whole voyage we were never lucky enough to catch one, which would have allowed me to observe it more precisely.

Shortly before noon the two coastlines began to come closer and closer, and about 1 o'clock we entered the Delaware. It is impossible to think of scenery more romantic than that which we saw before us during the whole afternoon: the white beach of the river which, farther inland, disappeared into the dark forest; the softly undulating hills, and between them the natural simplicity of the scattered farms of the first European inhabitants of America; little canoes criss-crossing everywhere gave us the happiest idea of the new world lying before us, where nature has succeeded in displaying so much beauty with so little human help.

Towards the evening we passed Newcastle, and a little farther Wilmington appeared quite distantly. Finally, we arrived before Chester at about 9 o'clock, where we cast anchor because, during night time, our pilot did not dare to take us over those dangerous spots where during the war the new States of America had erected wooden and iron-bound piles as a protection against English ships. Meanwhile, the Captain went ashore with a boat, and returned soon with various expensive local fruit: watermelons, apples, peaches, etc. which refreshed us excellently after the long time we had to put up with the English cuisine consisting of almost nothing else but meat.[15]

On the 9th Dr. Märter found particularly noticeable

the very numerous islands covered with reeds from which many wild ducks flew up and frequent flocks of those birds which the inhabitants call black birds (*ordus phoenicus L.*). They blackened the sky and gave us the most convincing proof of the natural opulence of this country. At last, far to the north, we noted some towers of Philadelphia, and before noon, after having fired a thirteen-cannon salute, we arrived to everybody's greatest satisfaction, happy and congratulating one another, in the capital of Pennsylvania, having been under way for forty days.[16]

On the 12th, Märter paid a visit to the governor of the state who provided him with several contacts of possible usefulness regarding the purpose of the expedition. Märter realized soon, however, that he could not rely too much on local experts. He was not able to find persons "who had a solid knowledge of natural sciences or who had compiled collections of any of the various categories of natural curiosities according to expert criteria; thus, what one is able to learn from the inhabitants of this part of the world so abundantly rich in data relevant to natural sciences, is mostly based upon mere empirical knowledge."[17]

Märter therefore decided to start immediately collecting specimens of plants unknown to the members of the expedition. The route of their field trips was to start around the capital of this state; next, the expedition was supposed to split, one party visiting the upper coastal strip, the other group penetrating some distance into the west. Then they planned to continue their search into the southern states, particularly Virginia and the two Carolinas.

In his second letter to Ignaz von Born (obviously dated by error September 25, instead of October), Märter complains about their bad luck concerning the baggage of the expedition. After staying in the Philadelphia area for six weeks, the ship from Ostende with all their instruments, books, and clothing had still not arrived, and in Philadelphia there existed not one copy of Linné's *System of Nature,* the reference work so vital for their research. They had been very busy, however, mainly collecting and classifying seeds of various plants, and Moll was engaged in drawing "cryptogamous plants"[18] and novel tortoises and birds. Märter himself had studied the western part of New Jersey, and the adjoining land of Pennsylvania including at least Lancaster, Trenton, and New Brunswick, and, to please Born, described briefly the country and the predominant minerals of the area. Moll's silhouettes of 1783 prove his early visits to Lancaster, Bethlehem, New Jersey, and New York, whereas the exact route of Dr. Stupich and the gardeners Boos and Bredemeyer remains unknown.

Märter's very thorough third report from Philadelphia, dated November 1783, deals with the climate, the physical characteristics of the land and the soil, the animals, the plants, the agriculture, the principal cities, the population, the economy, and the government. His comments are often fairly dull, but he always strives to be objective. The following passage reveals both his philosphical convictions and his objectivity:

> The inner part of Pennsylvania is inhabited mainly by Germans who still speak their mother tongue. Due to the low-class origin of these people, who for several years had to serve as slaves to earn their ship transportation, one cannot expect from them anything else but the rudest habits and the greatest ignorance in all matters concerning the values of the present enlightenment. In spite of that, they are looked upon as the safest source of the daily increasing wealth of the country, due to their moderation, thrift, knowledge in land cultivation, and stock farming, and particularly because of their untiring assiduity. As a result of having acquired the biggest wealth without possessing any special monopoly of trade, Pennsylvania has aroused the jealousy of all other states.[19]

Märter's description of Philadelphia also reveals details of his own character and timely preferences:

> Philadelphia, the capital of this state, and at the same time one of the most beautiful and largest cities of this part of the world, is situated on a very pleasant site between the confluence of the two rivers, namely the Skuylkill and the Delaware, and while the first one is navigable only with canoes because of numerous hidden rocks, it is possible in the second river for ships of 500 tons to reach the wharves of the lowest street of the city. It is built with the greatest regularity, according to the exemplary plan of its founder, as an oblong quadrangle which lengthwise

measures 2 miles. In this direction there are 8 completely parallel streets throughout the whole length, which streets are in right angles crossed by 16 streets of the same width, again completely parallel and one mile long. Through daily expansion the city will soon cover the whole ground between the rivers. The majority of houses, which amount to about 6,000, is very beautiful, one to two, seldom three stories high, and built of bricks. Until now there is nothing remarkable regarding the public buildings, except the numerous churches, the city hall, the newly erected jail, and the library building. The very spacious streets are, without exception, paved with granite stones, and along both sides a space is situated for pedestrians covered with bricks and protected by poles. The two main roads are the so-called Front and Market Streets which are both 100 feet wide; it is just too bad that the latter is very much spoiled by the ugliness of the market building in the middle of the street . . .[20]

Since its recent founding, the capital has already gained 40,000 inhabitants of all nationalities and religions, as a result of its most advantageous situation for trade, but especially because of its complete tolerance, and no European misses his own countrymen or fellow-believers. There, one finds Jews, Presbyterians, Sondemanians, Lutherans, Baptists, Anabaptists, Methodists, Separatists, Herrnhuters who are also called Moravians or Zinzendorfians, and Quakers who make up a great part of the population.[21]

The professor mentions nothing about the many interesting individuals he met in this busy city, and its neighborhood. The times, in the year 1783, were still full of excitement from the recent War of Independence. The courageous and adventurous merchants from overseas, the Dutch, Germans, and Danes, were still present, trying to continue their profitable war-time trade, and many newcomers had entered the scene after the signing of the peace treaty.

The silhouettes of many of those merchants appear in Bernhard Moll's pictorial diary, besides various local figures. Because of the language barrier, Moll and his companions seem to have first contacted people who were able to converse in German. French was helpful, too, and Märter and Moll, as well as the Dutchman Boos, at least spoke broken English. Dr. Stupich, a Croat, mastered eight languages, but these were only Slavic tongues, apart from German, Latin, and Hungarian.

Among Moll's silhouettes we find the profiles of the energetic and jovial Major Führer, the commander of several military units, of Captain Oesterly of the militia, and of Colonel Adam Hubley, a war hero. Besides the Danes—Messrs. Götze, Köhler, and Captain Madsen—and the Dutch—Mr. Sayer and Mrs. van Doren—there appear in the album twelve Germans, mainly merchants from Hamburg, including the interesting Mr. Delius. In Philadelphia, Moll also portrayed a Jewish lady, Mrs. Levy, and in New York three other Germans, in addition to Miss Schall of Bethlehem, a total of 33 silhouettes from this area, counting also the portraits of Bredemeyer and Boos.

Moll travelled with Bredemeyer, Stupich with Boos, whereas Professor Märter seems to have operated alone, using Philadelphia as the base for his numerous short trips. While waiting for the equipment to arrive from Ostende, Märter probably used material of the public library for some parts of his reports. This period in and around Philadelphia lasted about two months, and at the beginning of November, Stupich and Boos sailed to Charleston, S.C., where they arrived on the 17th day of that month.

THE JOURNEY SOUTH

Director Märter continued his studies in Pennsylvania and parts of Maryland and Virginia during November, and sent another mineralogical report to Born from Philadelphia which also describes the landscape and towns along his routes. During December and part of the new year, the professor moved farther south, towards Charleston, which he reached on January 16, 1784.

Moll and Bredemeyer had joined Stupich and Boos there exactly one month earlier, apparently by ship, and with part of the baggage. Contrary to Märter's usual precision when dealing with his plants and animals, there are no exact dates from his two, or probably three, somewhat overlapping routes into Maryland, Virginia, and the two Carolinas.

On December 20, 1783, he was in Williamsburg, Virginia, and reported to Born that during his last journey he had travelled the following routes: starting from Philadelphia in a northwestern direction, 17 miles along the west bank of the Skuylkill River; afterwards to "Schwedesfort"; then northwesterly 18 miles to some iron mines; then in a southwestern direction along the "Welsh" mountains as far as the other side of the Susquehanna River; from there to the Allegheny mountains, a total of 80 miles; then to the western end of Maryland. Later he crossed the Potomac River into Virginia where he visited the cities of Fredericksburg, Richmond, and Williamsburg. Subsequently he appeared in Edenton and Wilmington, N.C., intending to continue to Charleston, S.C.

On this journey Märter took note of many interesting phenomena, such as mastodon bones near Yorktown, some recently found Indian spearheads at "Schwedesfort," an old shoreline of the ocean near Yorktown, etc. But he must have completely forgotten Born's wish to study the native Indians. Two years later, however, Baron de Beelen-Bertholff sent a portrait to Vienna of the Chief Philipulla, together with a copy of the following report:

This American hero was a chief in the Creek nation who call themselves Muscoges or Muscogulges. Ulge in the Creek tongue signifies people or nation. Creek is a name given to them by the white people, who trade among them. He was not only Mico or King in his own town or district, but was acknowledged to be worthy of the title of Mico-Chlucco (Chlucco in the Creek tongue signifies great or supreme) or the representative of that sovereign power which presides over the empire. The man was, when I saw him, of a middle age, tall, erect, and in every way a most perfect human form; rather above the common stature of men, near seven feet in height, but above eight feet to the top of his crest or plume. There appeared a very eminent dignity and gracefulness in his countenance and deportment. Mico-Chlucco is equivalent to our title of Emperor, Supreme Governor, or most perfect sovereign power on earth. He is elected their King, but yet his progress and establishment in the throne is somewhat mysterious and altogether different from that in the old world; he does not meanly supplicate or bribe his fellow citizens to place him in a situation to rule over them, no! he appears their father or guardian; as the sun rises to bless their land, but they tell you no one knows how or when.

You ask them why Philipulla became their Mico? because he is the best and wisest man. And who placed him on the throne? the great spirit gave him to us, to preside over and influence the councils with wisdom and virtue and to vindicate our rights against our enemy.

This portrait was taken at a trading house in East Florida (he was then leading a party of warriors against their valiant and formidable enemy, the Chactaws) at the instant he was acting the war face at the head of this party.[22]

Joseph II may have seen this portrait and read the description of another worthy Emperor. Meanwhile Märter had a few words to say about the life style of the people and the workings of democratic government in Virginia:

After crossing the Potowmac River towards the end of November, I arrived in the largest of all of the independent states: Virginia; the changed physical appearance seemed to indicate that natural borders were set between this state and the previous ones. The thermometer started to rise above average, butterflies and mosquitoes were to be seen even in daylight, bats in the evenings, and all over in ponds and swamps one could hear the croaking of frogs. The doors and windows of the inhabitants stood open, while they themselves wore summer clothing, and they assured me that only a short while ago the swallows (martins) had departed. Altogether it was very remarkable that during the continuation of this journey I again met all those migrant birds which I had previously seen leave Pennsylvania, but in such an order that those which had left last, I met again in Virginia, whereas those which I had not seen any more since the early fall, I met again in Carolina. The country is much less inhabited than the northern states, and one can travel half a day without seeing a single house. The reasons for this is that this state is divided up among aristocrats into overly large parcels, most of them owning a few thousand acres, being unwilling to sell anything to smaller people and entertaining the flattering hope of seeing their present deserts sometime transformed into rich, lordly estates. One can easily visualize the state of the industry of this area if one takes into account that all household duties as well as the labours in the fields are carried out only by black slaves, and that it would be considered a disgrace to a white person to be discovered doing the smallest job. The land, therefore, is cultivated only by such people who groan under the hardest yoke which suppresses all desire for assiduity. Here, the beautiful wheat fields of Pennsylvania are completely replaced by tobacco plantations, partly because one deems tobacco cultivation more profitable, and partly because one finds here a certain type of insect, called a weevil, which causes too much damage to wheat . . .[23] From Fredericksburg I journeyed in a south-easterly direction to Richmond on the James River which has a considerable slope amounting to a difference in altitude of 72 feet within six miles. Although situated 150 miles from the sea, the city can be approached up to a few miles by sizeable ships with cargo. Moreover, the large rivers that are navigable far into the country, such as the Potomac, the Rapahanok, the James, and the York, all of which flow into Chesapeakbay, assist Virginia's trade considerably. Nevertheless, because of the taxes on European imports which are much higher than in Pennsylvania, I saw only a few ships of any significance. I noticed that there was a fairly strong demand for, among other European industrial products, rough cloth, hats, and stockings of the lowest quality, for use by slaves.

Richmond is at present the seat of the Governor, and of the Assembly of this state. On a few occasions I was fortunate to be present at the meeting of the houses, but I must confess that I never expected to experience such an indecorum from men participating in a public meeting. To me, it seemed extremely peculiar and remarkable to find the greatest carelessness at the place where laws are made and where one should ensure the wellbeing of the whole nation. Among 200 members present, about one-twentieth listened to the report by the speaker; the remainder either conversed among themselves about their private affairs or were called outside of the meeting by persons who wished to pay them a visit or to speak to them. Regarding a brief outline of the habits of born Americans of British origin, who live here together and quite apart from others, I must say that their manner might be best characterized by crudeness and harshness, and that their lack of education and philosophy seems to have exiled all good taste from them. The usually, though partly necessary, cruel handling of the slaves may have contributed considerably to their base attitude. In view of the sloppy and often even dirty suits even of wealthy males, one might not believe that the fancy dress of local females, considering the circumstances of the country, surpasses its European counterpart.

Recently, while on my journey, I arrived a bit too early at a lonely tavern in the wilderness, devoid of human beings within a radius of at least twenty miles, and I was not permitted to enter the room for breakfast before the daughters of the house were so completely dressed up and decorated with such a feather hairdressing that, when entering, I felt as though I were in the company of the gentlest European ladies.[24]

Moll's silhouettes supplement Märter's observations on this point.

CHARLESTON

Dr. Stupich, as mentioned earlier, arrived with the gardener Boos in Charleston on November 17, 1783. According to Professor Märter's plan, the two men had been sent ahead of the others to prepare new headquarters for the expedition and to start collecting seasonal plants and seeds there, while Märter himself covered the territory between Pennsylvania and the south. Moll and Bredemeyer meanwhile continued their operations north of Philadelphia and around New York.

The brief and quite barren diary of Stupich,[25] covering the period from the start of his sea voyage at Philadelphia, on November 4, until the arrival of Märter, on January 16, 1784, is written in a curiously faulty German. He may have been a Hungarian, as stated by Jacquin, or, more likely, of Croatian origin, as indicated by his name, some peculiarities in his grammar, and a remark by Märter. He was a dry and humorless individualist who could gain respect neither from his companions nor from others. Due to his impractical nature he was called "Dr. Stupid" by the sailors on board the *General Washington,* and Märter became very concerned about the ridicule which the expedition was beginning to arouse in Charleston.

According to his diary, Stupich had more endurance than

others, although he complained much about cold weather and rain. Moll's remarks about Stupich's constant "whining and praying" on board the ship applied to him on land as well. Sometimes the gardeners refused to follow him deep into the damp and marshy bushes of South Carolina, so that the botanist quite often went out alone. Being a deeply religious man, he in turn visited all the churches of the city. He also inspected the marketplace for interesting items, and made many short and some longer trips into the neighboring areas. Although subsequently becoming an American, like Moll, and a resident-physician in Charleston, his silhouette does not appear in Moll's album, constituting a significant omission.

Furnished with imperially guaranteed money orders for 800 Thalers, for weeks Stupich was unable to exchange them into local currency, thereby irritating his partner Boos. Stupich was stubbornly unwilling to pay the usual 5 percent discount rate, offering only 2 percent, until finally a captain who received some medical treatment from Stupich, obligingly agreed to a deal. Meanwhile, much time had been wasted, and the explorers were forced to operate with very primitive equipment and under quite humiliating circumstances. Sweating under heavy loads on their backs, they were asked by passing travellers if they had lost their horses. When sorting out and drying their botanical findings, they had to gather odd pieces of wood from all over the fields and nail them together themselves. Sometimes they slept on damp ground under the stars, sometimes they shared the floor of a tavern with snoring drunkards, and sometimes they found accommodation in negro huts or in old boats infested with rats. They also lost some of their material to thieves.

Stupich operated mainly on the road to "Monscorner," and around the so-called "6-mile-house," the "13-mile-tavern," and the "18-mile-house," occasionally using an old boat for the return passage of his equipment and botanical material. Two long journeys, undertaken during the first couple of weeks in December 1783 and in January 1784 were particularly profitable, and in spite of rain, the obstacles of creeks and swamps, and dangerous alligators, the explorers collected, sorted out, and dried many seeds of unknown plants. With Moll's and Bredemeyer's arrival, on December 16, the situation improved a little, probably as a result of Moll's good common sense and because of the arrival of much needed equipment. While they visited the Governor, the gardeners went out in search of entertainment and indulged in other social activities. Boos had meanwhile received useful bits of advice from the Dutch consul and his fellow freemasons. Moll's silhouettes prove his early contacts with the local society.

Stupich, this solitary introvert, did not notice anything remarkable in Charleston, and remained indifferent to everything, including the charming ladies with all their fancy hairdos, dresses, and what not. Here are some examples from his diary:

23rd (of Dec. 1783). Twice again I went with Moll on board the ship. The merchant went with us to his acquaintance who did not accept our cheques, though. From there we went to the Governor, where I apologized and explained why I could not pay him my respects sooner, and we spoke with him regarding the money. From there we went to a Jew, without success. The afternoon was filled with the same occupation.

10th (of January 1784). Having already taken care of the seeds yesterday, seeing that one cannot do anything here on account of endless and high waters, and in order not to lose time, I said that we should take the now dry seeds with us. We headed for the city on this very cold day, after everyone had paid 16 shillings. I carried all my books and other things with me, and before we had covered half the distance it started to rain heavily. We made a small fire in the forest, and I cooked the chocolate which I had brought with me from Philadelphia. We ate a little bread, and, completely frozen from the persistent rainfall, arrived in Pusgrick, a distance of 14 miles. We recovered a little near the fire, had a small supper, and were forced to sleep in a small bed which the four of us had to share.[26]

Six days later, the number of Austrian explorers in Charleston increased to five: Märter now resumed his direction of the somewhat disintegrating group. At first, he intended to send Stupich together with a gardener to the Bahama Islands, while Märter would study the Bay of Mexico. Because of Stupich's poor English, Märter decided to visit the Bahamas himself, accompanied by Boos, and ordered Stupich to collect worthwhile items among the few German settlers of North Carolina. Moll and Bredemeyer continued in and around Charleston, arranging the material for the first shipment to Europe.

Returning from the Bahama Islands with tropical plants, birds, and "sea products" towards the end of May, 1784, thereby concluding a difficult journey which also included the St. Augustin area of Florida, Märter added those "sun birds," and plants to the shipment. Bredemeyer, carrying a long letter of Director Märter addressed to Count Cobenzl, was assigned to look after the Imperial collections on board the brigantine *Friendship* which sailed to London. This letter contains rather interesting complaints of the professor about the behavior of his staff:

> Regarding the sun birds, I must humbly report to your Excellency that I had already bought four times the present amount of them, but they melted down through the carelessness of Moll and Bredemeyer to whose care I had left them during my absence. I also had two racoons and two opossums who either ran away or perished due to lack of supervision. Moreover, and reluctantly, I must report most humbly to your Excellency about the unpleasant situation in which I find myself with regard to my companions. The two gardeners begin to claim more and more their imaginary and already declared right to choose their own items, and by daily increasing attempts at every suitable opportunity to hinder or frustrate me, according to a deliberate intrigue having already originated in a dirty source in Vienna. The one I am now sending back was a particularly outstanding schemer . . . Notwithstanding his numerous assurances to be careful, I am rather worried about the proper care of the transported items.
>
> Moll whom I, after all, could best use so far, has totally changed since the time when he began to promise himself golden mountains in America on the basis of his profession. During my absence, when I was in the Bahamas, he did not apply one brush stroke for the duty assigned to him, regardless of the backlog of many items. On my return, he answered most impolitely that this was due to my refusal to grant him an immediate monthly raise of 16 Thalers, and he is now altogether so sloppy that he has barely finished for the engraver those few drawings he delivered. Regardless of my intention to pay his requested raise to obviate all excuses, I must, nevertheless, infer

from everything that his refusal to do his duty is calculated only to achieve his dismissal, a very ungrateful scheme.

Dr. Stupitz also shows his intentions and his character more clearly from day to day; disregarding the fact that I get no help from him, which the returning gardener may also witness, he not seldom makes our whole expedition appear ridiculous by his clumsiness and strange behaviour at every opportunity; he has also complained at various places as if I had cheated him out of a part of his salary. He is not willing to accept the Spanish Thalers at their true value corresponding to the bank rate here for which I got them from the bank, but rather according to the value in Vienna; I would have preferred to send him back with the first transport had I not been afraid of the total loss of these important rarities through his well-known carelessness with such objects. Your Excellency must not assume that I did not use enough kindness and friendly warnings, because it was, at any rate, impossible to take other measures in a country where excessive freedom not seldom becomes a protection of vice.[27]

Professor Märter does not particularly condemn Franz Boos, whom he had left behind in the Bahamas in May to continue the work throughout the summer and early fall of 1784. Dr. Johann David Schöpf, a former physician of the Ansbach German troops, and a recognized scholar himself, had accompanied Märter on parts of the journey. Boos, in spite of all sorts of difficulties which included hurricanes and the lack of drinking water, persevered on New Providence and various other islands for about five months until September, and also visited Guanahani, the landing place of Christopher Columbus. He gathered a very rich collection of tropical material which delighted Joseph II so much that he twice personally watched the unpacking of these rarities in Vienna, after Boos had returned on September 8, 1785, via London and Brussels with this second shipment of the expedition.

In his above letter to Cobenzl, Märter went on to paint a rather grim picture of the future of the expedition, and he explained his plan to stay in Charleston during the hurricane season, and then explore Georgia. Three months later, on September 28, 1784, Märter reported again to Count Cobenzl:

The matter of the painter Moll was brightly illuminated a few days ago; his habit of totally neglecting his duty, and his

constant grumbling about his small salary despite a monthly
increase of 8 Thalers, which is relatively a much larger sum
than my own, brought me to this decision: to order him, as a
dissatisfied and completely useless member of our company, to
be ready for a journey to Europe with the first available ship;
but from this moment on, the secret of his probably prompted
complaints and his dissatisfaction was revealed. A short time
ago, he replied to me that he was not a subject of the Emperor,
and therefore not at all obliged to return, that from now on he
did not need his assigned job any more, and that neither my
master nor I were at present in a position to send him away
from here, nor did he wish to see his fatherland again.[28]

To verify this serious accusation, Märter attached a signed statement by Boos and Stupich which reads: "The undersigned hereby
witness that Mr. Moll has refused to comply to the order of Director Märter who wanted to send him back on the ground of being a
useless and dissatisfied member of the company."

Moll officially abandoned the expeditionary group and his nationality sometime towards the end of September 1784. He became a *de facto* American, residing in Charleston, S.C., at least
until December 1786. As correctly presumed by Märter, Moll had
certainly informed his family and friends in Vienna about his
intention which is mentioned in Ignaz von Born's letter to Count
Cobenzl, dated November 15, 1784: "Painter Moll and Mr. Stupitz
intend to settle down here, certainly at least the former, both on
account of finding sufficient employment in North America, and
particularly because of your orders that they cannot expect any
job from the state after their return."[29]

Obviously, Born was trying to excuse the men, thereby shifting
part of the blame upon the recent economizing policy of the government. Witness Stupich did not know, of course, what Märter
wrote about him in the same letter (quoted above) to Cobenzl:
"Dr. Stupitz would have deserved a similar order because his
constant grumbling against his job, against your Excellency and
against the Emperor himself does not end, and because this behaviour, occuring at foreign places, damages the reputation of our
mission."

It was in Märter's mind, anyway, to have Stupich return next
so that no further harm would be done to His Majesty's interests.

THE LAST JOURNEYS

Märter's next two letters to Ignaz von Born came from St. Augustin, East Florida, on March 17, and from New Providence, Bahamas, on May 15, 1784. These quite lively descriptions show the professor's enthusiasm for southern areas, and we must therefore lament the loss or displacement of his subsequent reports from St. Domingo, the Antilles, and from the South American continent. Märter may also have penetrated deep into North America, according to some unclear notes in Beelen's correspondence about Kaskaskia, and Märter's contacts with the Jesuits in Ohio and on the Mississippi, but these possibilities require further verification. Born's instructions to Märter contained a request that two copies of an official journal of the expedition be prepared, and Märter intended to publish a thorough book about his travels, probably with Moll's copper plate illustrations. The search for these important manuscripts should continue, in spite of the sad possibility that they were burned during the nineteenth-century upheavals in Vienna. Obviously, they were not available to Fitzinger,[30] the historian of the Imperial collections, a fact which explains the numerous inaccuracies in his narrative. Fitzinger is the main source of the following outline about the last phases of the expedition.

We do not know the exact dates and places of Märter's journeys to the Antilles and South America. We know, however, that Moll was replaced by the gardener Joseph Schücht towards the end of 1784. In spite of Märter's criticism, Franz Bredemeyer, who seems to have been a dedicated amateur botanist, was again sent out with Schücht to meet the professor in the Antilles. After first visiting Martinique, they joined Märter in St. Domingo sometime in the early summer of 1785. Boos departed from Charleston with the second shipment in May, after Stupich, following Moll's example, had refused the director's order to return home. In desperation, Märter had intended, at this time, to take the rarities to Europe himself, as shown in his letter to Baron Beelen from Charleston, May 10, 1785:

J'ai donc l'honneur de vous informer, Monsieur, que parceque le docteur Stupitz se refuse à son devoir d'accompagner en

Europe mon présent transport, et qu'il a suivi en tout l'exemple ingrat de Moll, je me trouve pour cette fois dans la nécessité d'aller moi-même jusqu'en Angleterre; c'est pourquoi je vous supplie de renvoyer en Europe les lettres qui pourraient vous parvenir à Philadelphia à mon adresse.[31]

Beelen's letters to his superior, in turn, prove that Märter was present in Charleston in February 1785 and that his main activity consisted at that time in sorting out and classifying the various plants and seeds. John Bartram helped Beelen with similar material, whereas the Lutheran pastor of Lancaster, Peter Mühlenberg, seems to have assisted Märter previously. It is probable that the news from Vienna about the coming of Bredemeyer and Schücht made Märter change his mind. For Stupich, it meant a new career in America, as a practising physician in the old city of Charleston.

Bredemeyer, Schücht, and Märter himself continued the expedition in Puerto Rico, on the South American continent mainly in and around Carácas, and on the island of Curaçao. Their explorations lasted about two years. They returned to Vienna in 1788, with a substantial collection of living and dried tropical plants, insects and small animals. Bredemeyer continued his "haughty" and independent botanical research during these voyages. Evidently, he was capable of classifying and describing the exotic specimens himself, as is reflected by his collaboration with the well-known botanist C. L. Willdenow of Berlin, who in 1801 published three studies based on Bredemeyer's objects and notes. The living plants continued to grow in the Schönbrunn Botanical Gardens, and in turn were depicted, between 1797 and 1804, in Nikolaus von Jacquin's monumental *Plantarum Rariorum Horti Caesarei Schoenbrunnensis Descriptiones et Icones*. Johann David Schöpf had meanwhile written a book about his travels together with Märter.[32] After all his troubles and devoted efforts in America, Märter, therefore, may have been left to hold the proverbial bag, together with Born whose expectations had already been crushed earlier. Born's invention of the amalgamation method for the separation of gold from rocks benefited the Imperial treasury greatly, but the poor scholar who had lost his health by accidents and poisonous fumes in the mines, died in 1791, penniless and deeply in debt.

Franz Boos, accompanied by another gardener, Georg Scholl, was sent out again by Joseph II in October 1785 in order to gather more exotic material, this time from Africa. The explorers worked mainly in the neighborhood of the Cape of Good Hope. Boos also travelled to Isle de France and Bourbon, and on the island of Madagascar he gathered 52 boxes full of native clothing, tools, and weapons. He then went back to the Cape, and finally, in 1788, returned to Vienna while Scholl continued researching and collecting for several years on the Cape peninsula.

Although the stir of "sun birds" was now heard in Vienna, exotic masks were amusing the people, and tropical plants were again briskly growing in the Imperial hothouse, Joseph II could not enjoy the fruits of his expedition for a long time, as was the case with his other enlightened, often revolutionary, and sometimes over-ambitious ideas. The man who had freed the peasants and sent the monks to work, who had wanted to beat the Turks decisively and had wished to create a strong, prosperous, and unified empire in the heart of Europe, died in 1790, a bitter and disillusioned man.

BERNHARD ALBRECHT MOLL'S EUROPEAN SILHOUETTES

The freedom and the "golden mountains" of America have always lured people to this continent. Artistic opportunities, however, were scarce in 1783, and even more so in Moll's special field. While it is true that a few prominent people required large-scale portraits of themselves and their families, and that others asked for little miniatures, profile drawings, and silhouettes, the masses remained uninterested for a long time to come. Travelling painters and silhouettists, among them quite substantial artists, attempted to tap the market by advertising their services at very low prices.

Moll's remark that "the gentlemen pay well" for his silhouettes, is a relative statement. His superb silhouette-portraits are psychological studies carefully designed and cut. To achieve a lively effect with this delicately summarizing method of characterization required previous thorough analysis. In spite of the amazing intensity and high quality of most of Moll's silhouettes, the naturally low market price for these profiles, by an almost unknown artist, must have forced the newcomer to produce other types of portraits as well. If so, there should exist somewhere at least a dozen of his oil, pastel, or watercolor portraits, considering the length of his residence in Charleston. Unsigned, they have either been attributed to other artists or have remained "anonymous," in the case of obvious stylistic differences from the work of identified artists. Did Bernhard Moll develop a style of his own, and from which sources? Will we be able one day to say something of his landscapes, and his "natural" objects?

The term "silhouette" originated shortly after the middle of the eighteenth century. Louis XV of France had a Finance Minister, Étienne de Silhouette (1709–1767), whose hobby was cutting shade pictures. Because of his parsimony, a mock term "à la silhouette" was coined, meaning any cheap article including the cheapest type of portraits. The silhouettes became very popular in Europe in the second half of the eighteenth century. The term was then used mainly for little profile portraits which were cut with scissors from very thin black paper and then pasted on light sheets of paper or cardboard.

The theory of the influential Swiss poet and religious mystic, Johann Kaspar Lavater (1741–1801), claiming that there is a clear correlation between an individual's physical appearance and his character, found widespread acceptance in Germany and elsewhere in Europe. A multitude of amateur psychologist-silhouettists found this technique of silhouettes particularly suitable and fruitful, when engaging in "side by side" outline profile comparisons. To man's creative curiosity which apart from the study of minerals, plants, and animals had now begun to observe and categorize human beings, too, the silhouettes provided very convenient and cheap assistance. If bound into little books or albums, these portable collections of portraits could also keep the owner in constant company with his dearest relatives and friends, even on travels. Such albums are scarce, nonetheless, because this possibility was generally overlooked.

Bernhard Moll's album is one of those rare collections: a unique personal diary of an early silhouettist. Recalling a sentence from his letter to Born, "until I know the situation in all the states, I could earn good money with my silhouettes," and measuring the quality of the work, we may conclude that Moll's high opinion of his work was justified, and that he rightly considered himself a professional artist. On the other hand, the word "until" means that the silhouettes were to help him only temporarily, that is, until he had discovered more lucrative commissions. At the same time he must have been pleasantly surprised about the generosity of his American customers, as compared to European patrons.

Before leaving Vienna in April 1783, the artist had cut 24 silhouettes in memory of his family and friends. The first pages in the album naturally belonged to royalty, to Emperor Joseph II and his brother Maximilian. Next, there are several empty pages, probably reserved for other members of the royal family whom Moll had hoped to portray. Ignaz von Born, Madame "de" Moll, his sisters Jeanette, Susette, Eleonore, and his friends, colleagues, and acquaintances complete the hometown group.[33]

Underway to Le Havre, the explorers spent some time during June and July in Brussels, where Bernhard portrayed ten persons consisting mainly of members of the Deslandes family, their servants, and friends. All ten silhouettes are of outstanding quality, particularly the profile of the rough and outspoken Caroline, a maidservant, which deserves close study as to the effectiveness of Moll's methods. Caroline's robust natural wit must have delighted Bernhard, as did the gentle Madame Reine with her well-mannered young son.

Arriving in Philadelphia on September 9, 1783, our album of silhouettes contained a total of 34 silhouettes from Europe, including Boos and Bredemeyer whose portraits were probably done in Philadelphia shortly thereafter.

MOLL'S AMERICAN SILHOUETTES

An aura of tranquility or deep contemplation characterizes the silhouette of Arnold Delius, as if belonging to a philosopher or a preacher rather than to an energetic merchant of Bremen. This fine man went through worse misfortunes than beset other, much harder wartime entrepreneurs whom Moll also portrayed in Philadelphia.

When Delius enquired about the war, he saw surprised faces. During the long voyage the peace treaty had been signed and sealed, and the cannon were quiet—an awful situation for someone who had especially arrived from across the sea to make his fortune in wartime trade. Worse still, he had on board goods worth 97,566 Thalers, including tea and wine, tar and asphalt, ham and salted meat, cloth, and Osnabrück linen. Much of it was second rate, brought under the assumption that the wartime scarcity would provide customers anyway. During the stormy voyage many barrels had broken open with the tar spreading over the Ammerland hams, and the raisins were spoilt as well. Once again there was a surplus of tea in America, and fresh meat was cheaper than in Bremen. The linen was too fine for local people, and the tin unsuitable because they were accustomed to obtaining it in small bars from England. Nobody wanted to pay with ready cash. For exchange he was offered wastelands, or he received uncovered money orders.[34]

By contrast, other merchants, like Captain Madsen, Mr. Bemke, Mr. Boden, or Colonel Hubley did not faint like Delius, even when meeting harsher situations, such as the subsequent confiscation of the latter's ship by a French governor.

There is a great variety among the fourteen ladies from the Philadelphia area with regard to their personalities and costumes. Probably as a result of the Quaker influence, many of them wear simple bonnets or have only moderately fancy coiffures. Even Mrs. Thully's high tower and Mrs. Levy's neat little mountain on top of their heads do not contain any feathers or flowers. Among the silhouettes from Pennsylvania and New York, we miss children, a fact which signifies that Moll's contacts were casual acquaintances. At the same time, these people form, more or less, a middle class group when compared with the wealthy Hall and Fraser sisters in Charleston, Moll's later customers. Moll cut these 33 silhouettes between September and December of 1783, and they are, on the average, smaller than those from Europe. He almost certainly did not use mechanical equipment, such as screens to catch candle-light projections of his clients. Emperor Joseph II and his brother could not be bothered that way, for example, and Moll was in any case a very good observer-draftsman of "natural" objects.

Charleston, founded in 1670, was at the time of the visit of the Austrian expedition not only a large city but also a center of much cultural activity. It is therefore surprising that Märter's published reports do not contain anything about the city, nor about the physical characteristics of its neighborhood with the huge rice plantations. The explanation for this information gap is that Märter's letter from Charleston did not reach Ignaz von Born. Between the reports from Williamsburg, Virginia, and from St. Augustin, there is an obvious vacuum. Dr. Stupich, on the other hand, was completely closed to such impressions, noticing only the weather. Charleston could boast numerous beautiful churches and houses, various clubs and associations, musical performances, a newspaper, and even a theatre, as well as the first scientific museum of America. The work of Dr. Alexander Garden who was a good amateur botanist must have attracted the attention of Professor Märter, as had the scientific studies of Dr. John Lining. Moll's silhouettes of the newlyweds, Alexander Garden Junior, a major and writer, and Mrs. Anna Garden, née Gibbes, make it likely that professional contacts were established in early 1784.

The homes of rich rice plantation owners and merchants were well known for their hospitality and refined culture. The beauty of the Charleston ladies captured the eyes of most visitors, except Dr. Stupich, but including our expert of "natural objects," Bernhard Moll. Johann David Schöpf, who also visited Charleston in 1784, remarks in his book, *Travels in the Confederation,* that "throughout, there prevails here a fine manner of life, and on the whole there are more evidences of courtesy than in the northern cities."[35]

In Moll's Charleston silhouettes, there is a special charm very difficult to define. It is as if the artist had felt a particular pleasure cutting his silhouettes there. He probably liked Charleston even more than Philadelphia, the place of his first enthusiasm, in spite of the wet climate and the dangerous fevers. According to his profiles, the last of which are dated in 1785 when the album was full, and he was possibly starting a new one, Moll continued to live in this charming city. This conjecture is corroborated by a statement of his sisters that his last letter to Vienna came from Charleston, postmarked December, 1786.

Instead of merely envisaging "the golden mountains of America" which, according to Märter, blurred Moll's clear vision when finishing scientific drawings for his Majesty, Moll's mind, and quite probably his heart, too, were fascinated by all those pert and beautiful girls of Charleston, and the witty gentlemen of the city. The famous wine cellar of Reverend Henry Purcell was an interesting object, too, and so our artistic turncoat, a cosmopolitan (new) democrat, may have uttered to himself the same congratulatory words which his brother Albrecht, i.e., William Berczy, used in 1780 in a letter to a girlfriend: "I am free! Wherever I may be today or tomorrow, there is my fatherland. Kingdoms may fall, and landscapes get ravaged, but I shall find my property anywhere."[36]

We do not know if Bernhard Moll found any property somewhere in America, but he certainly enjoyed his freedom.

The 81 silhouettes give ample evidence of his new career in Charleston. Some of these exquisite profiles are very small, particularly the silhouettes for the Rev. Henry Purcell's family, as if Moll had wished to demonstrate his dexterity as an artist of miniature portraits. The tense and nervously vibrating outline of George Tunno is employed to express the dynamic personality of this prominent member of the St. Andrew's Society. How delicately drawn are the proud daughters of George Hall, and of Alexander Fraser, the elder sisters of the future artist Charles Fraser who was just a baby in 1785.

There are ten Frasers and ten Halls in the album, six Purcells, three Rutledges, pairs of the Heyward, Beresford, Garden, and various other families, all excellent characterizations. The Dutch, German, and Danish citizens of Charleston are represented, too, but only in 17 silhouettes, which constitute less than a quarter of the total number. Perhaps Moll had already gained recognition in the early part of 1784 from local prominent persons, including the first intendant of Charleston, Richard Hudson. Only 13 silhouettes were cut at the beginning of 1785. Among them, the well-fed Doctor Irving, the lively Major Edwards, and an elderly Mrs. Newman, who may have been his landlady.

Besides the above few analytical details which may be of some help to less experienced observers of Moll's technique and style, the 148 silhouettes[37] contain much useful information for students of this period and constitute a valuable contribution to American historiography and history of art. Bernhard Moll served Joseph II and Ignaz von Born very well by paying attention also to human subjects during this remarkable scientific expedition.

GOLDEN MOUNTAINS?

In spite of the frequent rains he disliked so much, Mathias Leopold Stupich continued to live in Charleston until his death in 1794.[38] He attended some people there as a physician, and his botanical studies were known at least to his friend John Jacob Kalckoffen, who erected a tombstone upon his grave in the St. Mary's Cemetery. The Latin inscription mentions briefly Stupich's origin as a "Transilvanus," and his accomplishments. It denotes his age as 62, which means that he must have received his diploma, in 1782 or 1783, as an elderly student of medicine. The estate of this old bachelor was advertised on November 15, 1794.

Remarkably, Baron de Beelen-Bertholff also became a resident of the United States.

Did Bernhard Moll change his name, like his brother Albrecht, and is that why, besides his unique album of silhouettes, we have failed to find any other trace of his activities in America? Why did his album turn up in the Boston area? But even in case of Moll's early death, in 1787 or thereabouts, those three years of his life in Charleston should have left some marks upon the local scene. Did Moll travel on to other countries, possibly to Latin America? Why did his letters to Vienna stop so suddenly? Who can shed more light on the life and work of this gifted but forgotten German-American artist?

NOTES

1. Vienna, Nationalbibliothek, Manuscripts Dept., *Expedition Märter*, Ser. Nr. 3517, Fol. 19. All translations are from German to English.

2. Ignaz von Born (1742–1791), mineralogist and scientific inventor, was an intellectual leader and prominent freemason in Vienna, and has been immortalized by Mozart as the high priest of humanity in his opera "The magic flute."

3. Most frequent spelling is Stupich. In some documents his name appears as Stupicz or Stupitz.

4. *Expedition Märter.*

5. John Bartram (1699–1777) was the first native American botanist. Cf. *Encyclopaedia Britannica*, vol. 3, London, 1964, pp. 209–10.

6. See ft. 15.

7. Thanks to Miss Helen McCormack, Director of the Gibbes Art Gallery, Charleston, S.C., we know a little about the former fate of this album. According to Mr. Howe, the antique dealer in Ware, Mass., this album previously belonged to Mr. Coffin, a dealer of old books and antiques, who in turn had bought it "a long time ago" in Boston from another antiquarian. Mr. Howe rebound the disintegrating book, which had meanwhile lost a few pages containing at least 6 silhouettes from Charleston.

8. Nicolaus von Jacquin is author of the work *Plantarum Rariorum Horti Caesarei Schoenbrunnensis Descriptiones et Icones*, Vienna, 1797–1804.

9. Dated March 13, 1780. Haus-, Hof-, und Staatsarchiv, Vienna, Oberkämmereramt, Karton 6, 2 L. 99/1780.

10. Haider Ali was an Indian ruler and military commander (1722–1782) who played a considerable part in the wars in southern India in the 18th century. See *Encyclopaedia Britannica*, vol. 10, London 1964, pp. 1114–15.

11. Vienna, Haus-, Hof-, und Staatsarchiv, Obersthofmeisteramt, Sonderreihe 176, *Expedition Dr. Märters*, Fol. 6.

12. *Ibid.*, dated December 4, 1782.

13. The reports are found in: *Physikalische Arbeiten der einträchtigen Freunde in Wien*, ed. by Ignaz von Born, vol. 1, 1784 and vol. 2, 1786. The different reports bear the following headings: Herrn Professor Märters erstes Schreiben an Herrn Hofrath von Born, über seine Reise von Europa bis nach Philadelphia in Nordamerika (dated Sept. 15, 1783); Herrn Professor Märters zweytes Schreiben aus Philadelphia an Herrn Hofrath von Born (dated Philadelphia, Sept. 25, 1783); Herrn Professor Märters Nachrichten über die natürliche Geschichte Pennsylvaniens, an Herrn Hofrath von Born (dated Philadelphia, Nov. 24, 1783); Herrn Professor Märters mineralogische Bemerkungen auf einer Reise von Philadelphia in Pensilvanien nach Charleston in Karolina (no date); Herrn Professor Märters Nachrichten aus Virginien an Herrn Hofrath von Born (dated Williamsburg, Dec. 20, 1783); Ebendesselben Nachrichten aus Ostflorida (dated St. Augustin, March 17, 1784); Herrn Professor

Märters Nachrichten aus den bahamischen Inseln, an Herrn Hofrath von Born (dated New Providence, May 15, 1784).

14. *Ibid.*, vol. 1, pp. 53–54.

15. *Ibid.*, pp. 63–64.

16. *Ibid.*, p. 65.

17. *Ibid.*

18. These are spore plants, like fern, moss, seaweed, mushroom.

19. *Physikalische Arbeiten* . . . , op. cit., vol. 2, p. 37.

20. *Ibid.*, pp. 36–37.

21. *Ibid.*, p. 37.

22. Hanns Schlitter (ed.), "Die Berichte des ersten Agenten Österreichs in den Vereinigten Staaten von Amerika Baron de Beelen-Bertholff an die Regierung der österreichischen Niederlande in Brüssel 1784–1789," in *Fontes Rerum Austriacarum*, 2. section, *Diplomataria et Acta*, vol. 45, 2nd half, pp. 289 ff. Quotation is on page 553.

23. *Physikalische Arbeiten* . . . , op. cit., vol. 2, pp. 94–95.

24. *Ibid.*, pp. 97–98.

25. Stupich's journal is located in Vienna, Nationalbibliothek, Manuscripts, *Expedition Märter*, Ser. Nr. 3794, Part II, Fol. 82–86. (Concerning Stupich, compare also E. M. Kronfeld, *Park und Garten von Schönbrunn*. Zürich, Wien, Leipzig, 1922.)

26. *Ibid.*, Fol. 84–86.

27. Dated Charleston, June 15, 1784. In: *Expedition Märter*, op. cit., Ser. Nr. 3794, part I, Fol. 30.

28. Dated Charleston, Sept. 28, 1784. *Ibid.*, Folio 31.

29. *Expedition Dr. Märters*, op. cit., Fol. 40.

30. Leopold Joseph Fitzinger, "Geschichte des K. K. Hof-Naturalien-Cabinetes zu Wien," in *Sitzungsberichte der Mathematisch-Naturwissenschaftlichen Classe der K. Akademie der Wissenschaften zu Wien*. Vol. XXI, 1856. (Fitzinger's "Adam Moll" is actually our Bernhard Albrecht Moll; he also errs by stating that painter Wiedon was not replaced. Moll occupied Wiedon's position from 1780–1781.)

31. Hanns Schlitter (ed.), *Die Berichte* . . . , op. cit., p. 428. That this is Beelen's translation is uncertain. He corresponded with Belgioioso, his superior in Brussels, in French.

32. It has been translated into English: *Travels in the Confederation* (1783–1784), 2 vols., Philadelphia, 1911.

33. In Johann Albrecht Ulrich Moll's birth certificate of Dec. 10, 1744, his father's name appears as Albrecht Theodor de Moll. (We owe this knowledge to Pastor Max Dünsser of the St. Alban parish in Wallerstein; he kindly provided us with a copy of this birth certificate.) Apparently he had been raised into the class of nobility due to his diplomatic positions, and his scientific accomplishments. Although it is not sure that this title was hereditary, Albrecht Theodor's daughters were addressed as "Mlles. de Moll," quite in line with the Viennese habit. Johann Albrecht Ulrich, and Bernhard Albrecht never used this title of nobility.

The portrait of his younger brother, Johann Albrecht Ulrich, is missing in Bernhard's album. This restless man who travelled much in Europe changed his name to Berczy under adventurous circumstances in Hungary. He kept his adopted name when he emigrated to North America in 1792. Nowadays he is referred to as William Berczy or William Moll Berczy. The rediscovery of this colorful personality, who was forgotten for about 170 years, is credited to two books of John Andre: *William Berczy, Co-founder of Toronto*, Toronto, 1967; and *Infant Toronto as Simcoe's Folly*, Toronto, 1971. This very talented man, as the leader of German peasant immigrants to the Pulteney lands in the Genesee region of New York, dreamed of surpassing William Penn, and subsequently became the co-founder of Toronto in Canada. After being forced into bankruptcy as a land developer, Berczy returned to painting, and his fine portraits may serve us now as comparisons, when attempting to discover his brother's works in Charleston. (Dennis Reid, *A concise history of Canadian painting*, Oxford University Press, 1973, p. 37, writes on Moll Berczy's best known family portrait: "The Woolsey Family (National Gallery of Canada) is one of the few exceptional Canadian paintings of the first half of the century. The complex interrelation of the figures, the masterly treatment of the patterned floor covering, the purely pleasurable attention to the landscape seen through the open window, to the door-jamb and ceiling detail reflected in the mirror to the left, all go far beyond anything accomplished in the country before, or for some time after. It is one of the masterpieces of Canadian painting.")

Although the handwriting, and the character of these two Moll brothers differ considerably, their lives, for a long time, followed parallel tracks. Some features of their personal histories have deep roots in the genealogical background of the Moll family which also accounts for their manifold talents. (For details about the many prominent members of the Moll family, see Andre's first book.) In surveying this Moll heritage, we see that the feeling of independence of his Lutheran ancestors, the restrictive society he was born into, the talent to observe fine detail inherited from the ancestral goldsmith, as well as the famous minerals of his father, and the prospects and vedutes of his uncle, all together influenced Bernhard's path of life.

Besides royalty and relatives, Moll's silhouettes of the Vienna period include the five members of the befriended Föhrmann family, the humorist Martin Perfetta, the coffee house owner Franziska Kunzmann, the artists Mr. and Mrs. Karl Schütz, and Johann Ziegler, the scientists Karl Haidinger, and Ignaz von Born, among others. For lack of space we must dispense with the individual characterization of these silhouettes. May it suffice to say that Moll succeeds in illustrating the main characteristics of both jovial, fat fellows like Föhrmann and Perfetta, and serious thinkers, thoughtful scholars like Born and Haidinger. The more we look at the little details Moll uses for characterization, the clearer becomes Moll's mastery capturing the essential features of a character by means of raising, balancing, or dropping the eye, opening or closing the lips, and relatively increasing or decreasing the intensity of the general outline of the profile.

Moll's album also contains the silhouettes of three members of the expedition. Märter's energetic but somewhat harsh and cold face was portrayed prior to the trip. The gardeners Boos and Bredemeyer are shown as young fellows with round and undistinguished faces. Boos' soft and plebeian profile seems even less marked than that of Bredemeyer. The latter's "haughtiness" claimed by Märter is confirmed by Moll's illustration: Bredemeyer's nose and chin are slightly lifted.

34. A. Schmidtmayer, Arnold Delius, "Die Geschichte eines Pechvogels," in *Bremer Nachrichten,* Feb. 21, 1929.

35. Philadelphia 1911, Vol. II, p. 167.

36. Quoted from a letter by Berczy from Turin, Italy, December 1780, in Box 104, S-Series, Collection Bâby, Reference Library, University of Montreal (not catalogued).

37. Listed at the end of this article.

38. The Charleston *City Gazette* registered his death on the 20th: Inst. M. L. Stupich, Doctor of Physics; being perfectly sensible of his approaching dissolution, he resigned to his Creator's will with that fortitude becoming a Christian. His remains were deposited according to the Roman Catholic rights of which denomination he was a worthy member, in the Roman Catholic churchyard, Saturday, August 23, 1794.

SILHOUETTES (WITH MOLL'S CAPTIONS)

1. Josephus II. J.R. The present Emperor. 1783
2. Maximilian of Austria. 1783
3. de Born. 1783
4. Madame de Moll. 1783
5. Jeanette de Moll. 1783
6. Mr. Heydinger. 1783
7. Susette de Moll. 1783
8. Eleonore de Moll. 1783
9. Mr. Munschi, a Vienne des Etats d'Hyderaly. 1783
10. Mr. Rugker. 1783
11. Madame Föhrmann. 1783
12. Madelle (sic) Föhrmann. 1783
13. Mr. Vats a Vienne d'Engleterre (sic). 1783
14. Mr. Föhrmann. 1783
15. P. Prosper Seivert. 1783
16. Mr. Schütz. 1783
17. Madme (sic) Schütz. 1783
18. Madme Kunzmann. 1783
19. Mr. Perfetta. 1783
20. Mr. Bruchar. 1783
21. Mr. Ziegler. 1783
22. Mr. Ferd. Föhrmann. 1783
23. Mr. Franc. Föhrmann. 1783
24. Mr. Maerter. 1783
25. Mr. Deslandes, de Bruxelle. 1783
26. Madelle Deslandes. 1783
27. Mr. Deslandes, jun. 1783
28. Madelle Vuillam. 1783
29. Made (sic) Reine, chez Mr. Deslandes. 1783
30. Mr. Reine. 1783
31. Caroline, chez Mr. Deslandes. 1783
32. Madelle Joassens, d'Anvers. 1783
33. Mad. Schiquie. 1783
34. Mr. Deslandes juvin. 1783
35. Major Führer von den amerikans. Trouppen in Phyladelphia. 1783
36. Madame Thully de Philadelphie. 1783
37. Madame Sanders de Phyladelphie. 1783
38. Mr. Sanders de Hambourg a Neujou en Amerique. 1783
39. Mis (sic) Moly Tully de Philadelphie. 1783
40. Mr. Götze Danoi en Phyladelphie. 1783
41. Mr. Ruge de Hambourg en Phyladelphie. 1783

42. Mr. Köhler, Danois, en Philadelphie. 1783
43. Catharine Schmid de Phyladelphie. 1783
44. Mis Petzi Hes de Phyladelphie. 1783
45. Mr. Delius. 1783
46. Mr. Bredemeyer. 1783
47. Mr. Oesterly Capitain de la Milice en Phyladelphie. 1783
48. Mistris Oesterly. 1783
49. Miss Schall N. de Bethlehem en Pensilvanie. 1783
50. Mr. Boos. 1783
51. Mistris Levi. Juive en Phyladelphie. 1783
52. Mis Petzi Parcker en Phyladelphie. 1783
53. Mr. Bencke de Hambourg, en Phyladelphie. 1783.
54. Mr. Matzen. Capitain du Neptun, Danois en Phyladelphie. 1783
55. Mis Cath. Hoolden des Quakers en Phyladelphie. 1783
56. Mr. Boden de Hambourg en Phyladelphie. 1783
57. (?) de Philadelphie. 1783
58. Mad. van Doren de Philadelphie. 1783
59. Mr. Herlitz de Neujork. 1783
60. Mr. Meyer de Neujork. 1783
61. Mde. Kapli de Philadelphie. 1783
62. Mistris Gross de Philadelphie. 1783
63. Mr. Emeroth de Hambourg en Philadelphie. 1783
64. Mr. Hasenkleber de Philadelphie. 1783
65. Mr. Sayer de Hollande en Philadelphie. 1783
66. Mr. Hubley Collonel Americain en Philadelphie. 1783
67. Mr. Maetsch de Hambourg en Philadelphie. 1783
68. Mr. Gaer from Landkaster in Charleston. 1784
69. Mr. Hessling de Hollande a Charleston. 1784
70. Mr. Hubert from Holland in Charleston. 1784
71. Mistris Hubert from Kuracao in the West Indies in Charleston. 1784
72. Mr. Henning de Frankfort sur le Mayn a Charleston. 1784
73. Mr. George Hall of Charleston. 1784
74. Miss Betsy Hall of Charleston. 1784
75. Miss Sarah Hall of Charleston. 1784
76. Miss Maria Hall of Charleston. 1784
77. Miss Louisa Hall of Charleston. 1784
78. Miss Juliett Hall of Charleston. 1784
79. Miss Henrietta Hall of Charleston. 1784
80. Miss Carolina Hall from Charleston. 1784
81. Master George Hall of Charleston. 1784
82. Master John Hall from Charleston. 1784
83. Judge Heyward. 1784
84. Mr. Readhead from Soud Carolina in Charleston. 1784
85. Mr. Lecke from Hamburg in Charleston. 1784
86. Mr. Berkmeyer from Hamburg in Charleston, 1784
87. Mr. Daniel Heyward from Charleston. 1784

88. Mr. Purcell, Minister from Charleston. 1784
89. Mrs. Purcell from Charleston. 1784
90. Ms. Nancy Purcell from Charleston. 1784
91. Ms. Jeny Purcell from Charleston. 1784
92. Ms. Petsi Purcell from Charleston. 1784
93. Mr. Henry Purcell from Charleston. 1784
94. Ms. Stark from Charleston. 1784
95. Mrs. Garden from Charleston. 1784
96. Mr. Garden from Charleston. 1784
97. Mr. Inglis from Charleston. 1784
98. Mr. P. . . from Coppenhagen in Charleston. 1784
99. Mr. Behagen from Coppenhagen in Charleston. 1784
100. Ms. van Rhein from Amsterdam in Charleston. 1784
101. Ms. van Braun from Amsterdam in Charleston. 1784
102. Mr. Chion from Amsterdam in Charleston. 1784
103. Mr. Chion Jun. from Amsterdam in Charleston. 1784
104. Mr. Stuermann from Holland in Charleston. 1784
105. Mr. Beresford of Charleston. 1784
106. Mrs. Birisford from Charleston. 1784
107. Mis Rumiz from Charleston. 1784
108. Mrs. Rumiz from Charleston. 1784
109. Ms. Fraser from Charleston. 1784
110. Mr. Richard Hutson Intendant of Charleston. 1784
111. Mr. Charles Brown of Charleston. 1784
112. Mr. Salser from Frankfort in Charleston. 1784
113. Mrs. Salser from Charleston. 1784
114. Ms. Muckenfus from Charleston. 1784
115. Mr. Schmidt from Stutgard in Charleston. 1784
116. Mr. Seibel from Elberfeld in Charleston. 1784
117. Mr. Fraser at Charleston. 1784
118. Mrs. Fraser at Charleston. 1784
119. Mr. Alex, Fraser at Charleston. 1784
120. Ms. Poly Fraser at Charleston. 1784
121. Ms. Betsi Fraser at Charleston. 1784
122. Ms. Judy Fraser at Charleston. 1784
123. Ms. Nancy Fraser at Charleston. 1784
124. Ms. Suky Fraser at Charleston. 1784
125. Mr. James Fraser at Charleston. 1784
126. Ms. Hayn at Charleston. 1784
127. Mr. Frederick Rutledges at Charleston. 1784
128. Mr. Edward Rutledges at Charleston. 1784
129. Mr. William Rutledges at Charleston. 1784
130. Mr. Middleton at Charleston. 1784
131. Mr. Jacob Dreyton at Charleston. 1784
132. Mr. Motte at Charleston. 1784
133. Mrs. Marschall at Charleston. 1784

134. Ms. Mary Huger at Charleston. 1784
135. Mr. Irwing at Charleston. 1785
136. Mr. Joseph Brown at Charleston. 1785
137. Mr. Wm N Davis at Charleston. 1785
138. Mr. Edwards Major at Charleston. 1785
139. Mr. Irwing Doct. at Charleston. 1785
140. Mr. Daniel Wilson at Charleston. 1785
141. Mrs. Krause at Charleston. 1785
142. Mr. Charles Beckmann at Charleston. 1785
143. Mr. Harrelbrinck from Prussia at Charleston. 1785
144. Mr. George Tunno at Charleston. 1785
145. Mists. Newman of Charleston. 1785
146. I Somarsall. 1785
147. Mr. Beach. 1785
148. (?) Bernhard Moll (?)

Missing silhouettes: Mr. Armstrong, Mr. Braun, Mr. Krause, Miss Purcell, Mr. Smyth, Mrs. Terons.

7. Charles Sealsfield and Weimar
John T. Krumpelmann

Students of German-American relations are often at a loss to account for the dearth of information concerning contact between
Goethe's Weimar and Karl Postl of Znaim and Prague, Austria,
who, having deserted his monastery, escaped to the United States
there to become a writer of prose in both English and German
(1827, under the *nom de plume* of "C. Sidons, Bürger der Vereinigten Staaten von Nordamerika"), and later (1829–1843) of
prose fiction, in both English and German, under the pseudonym
of Charles Sealsfield.

The facts that Goethe's initial interest in the United States was
quickened by some of our most outstanding young scholars and
government officials-to-be,[1] that the court circles, including
Goethe, in the Duchy of Saxe-Weimar, were interested in mineralogical activities and investments in Mexican mining ventures and
that Sealsfield in five volumes of fiction, viz. *Der Virey und die
Republikaner oder Mexiko im Jahre 1812* (3 vols.) and *Süden und
Norden* (2 vols.) treats of those regions, should have created in the
Weimar circles some interest in that author. That Bernhard, brother
of the reigning Duke Karl August of Saxe-Weimar, undertook a
long and expensive voyage to America to ascertain the conditions
and prospects of German progress in Mexico, where the Duke and
the Ducal family had made costly investments in such enterprises,
should have accelerated that interest. But, most specifically, one
fact is seemingly most significant: that Charles Sealsfield, who had
previously spent much time in New Orleans, was there again, while
the Duke was, for five weeks, visiting the social elite of that city,
after the author had on November 7, 1826, directed the publishers
of his *Die Vereinigten Staaten von Nordamerika* (2 vols., 1827),[2]
to send a copy of these volumes to Prinz Bernhard. One seeks in
vain for a token of acknowledgement of the receipt of these
tomes!

When the Duke's *Reise Sr. Hoheit des Herzogs zu Sachsen= Weimar=Eisenach durch Nordamerika in den Jahren 1825-1826*[3] appeared, Goethe rejoiced and honored the publication with the composition of a poem later recited by his son, August.[4] But no-where does one find a record, or even so much as a mention, that a copy of the Duke's volumes was ever sent to Sealsfield. Nor does one discover even a mention of those volumes which Sealsfield directed his publishers to send to his fellow-traveller and co-visitor in New Orleans, Duke Bernhard.

Nevertheless, it would hardly be proper to suggest that the German Duke was being guilty of disrespect to the Austrian ex-priest, who had meanwhile become a brother-Mason and co-resident of New Orleans, even though Sealsfield, whose 1827 work is in some respects quite similar to the Duke's, is nowhere ever mentioned by Bernhard. Such lack of interest is hardly to be expected from a gentleman, who, during his American sojourn, did not fail to pay a visit to Aaron Burr, whose earlier visit to Weimar received merely the scantest mention in the published works of Goethe.[5]

As a matter of fact the Duke must be commended for his pleasing factual account of his visit to Burr in New York, wherein he concedes that he might have been amiss in not visiting Burr on his first visit to that city.[6] He concludes by stating "von dessen Seite (Burr's) ich mich eines sehr guten Empfanges erfreute."

To understand Duke Bernhard's position concerning Aaron Burr it is essential that the scholar know the basic facts about Burr and those factions in American politics which opposed Burr.

In his *Reise,* Bernhard writes:

Dieser Ort [settlement] ist dem verstorbenen Herrn Claiborne—dem ersten Mann der Mrs. Grymes zu Ehren so genannt. Er war Gouverneur des ehemaligen Mississippi territory . . . und starb vor 8 Jahren als Gouverneur des Staats Louisiana in New Orleans . . . Herr Claiborne war ein besonderer protégé und Landsmann des Präsidenten Jefferson. Er hatte durch seine Stimme die Präsidentenwahl zu Jeffersons Gunsten gegen seinen Concurrenten Aaron Burr entschieden; dafür blieb Jefferson lebenslang erkenntlich.[7]

Duke Bernhard had, as early as August 23, 1825, met Mr. Grymes and his wife, "die Wittwe des verstorbenen Gouverneurs

Claiborne, eine sehr reiche und schöne Creolin,"[8] in the vicinity of Niagara Falls. He had greatly enjoyed their company and rejoiced that she, as he, spoke French. He writes: "Den ganzen Abend erfreute uns Mrs. Grymes durch ihr schönes Guitarrenspiel und ihren herrlichen Gesang französischer und spanischer Lieder."[9]

On the estate of Mr. J. R. Livingstone, Massena on the Hudson River, above Red Hook, New York, the Duke and the Grymes couple were guests at a house-party and a ball. Here Bernhard met Edward Livingstone, M.C., who had settled in Louisiana and was engaged in completing a New Criminal Code for that state.[10]

Having arrived in New Orleans on January 21, 1826 the Duke reports:[11] "Meine erste Ausflucht war zu Herrn Grymes . . . Ich traf anfangs nur Mrs. Grymes zu Hause, welche . . . am 10. Dezember hier angekommen war, und vor 14 Tagen einem wohlgebildeten Sohne das Dasein gegeben hatte."

Almost immediately thereafter the Duke writes: "den Plan nach Mexico zu gehen mußte ich aufgeben, weil in diesem Lande keine Fremden zugelassen werden sollten, die nicht aus Ländern wären, welche den neuen Staat anerkannt hätten."[12]

The editors of the *Jubiläumsausgabe* of Goethe's *Sämtliche Werke* assert:

In drei Perioden seines Lebens hat Goethe ein besonders lebhaftes Interesse für die Entwicklung Amerikas bekundet: zuerst während der dortigen Freiheitskriege, dann in Juni 1818, wo eine neue Karte der Freistaaten ihn auf die geologischen Verhältnisse Amerikas führte (vgl. Tagebuch; auch 10.-14. Mai 1819), endlich in den letzten Lebensjahren, wofür die Bd. 2, S.348f. erwähnte Reise eines weimarischen Prinzen anregend war . . .[13]

Evidence of enthusiastic interest in America, especially in its politics, geology, and its academic affairs, is attested to by the frequent visits of prominent academicians who were welcomed at the Ducal residence between 1810 and 1830.[14]

Mention of the year of 1810 suggests an additional point of contact between America and Weimar, for it was on January 2 of that year that Colonel Aaron Burr (1756-1836), the third Vice President of the United States, arrived, evidently as a guest of Herr Bertuch (1749-1822), who was imbued "mit der Absicht, Teil-

nehmer für seine mexikanischen Bergbauprojekte zu gewinnen."[15]
On January 4, 1810 Burr's *Private Journal*[16] records: "At 10 *père
et fils* (Bertuch?) called. Went first to Wieland's, 77, To Goethe 58
(sic!) Y [i.e. = present] Humboldt." A rather uninspiring account
of the first, and only, private meeting of Germany's greatest poet
and scholar and America's highest-ranking official ever to visit in
Weimar! The diary of each of the principals is eloquent in its terse-
ness! *Dum tacit clamant!* Of course Burr did not go to Weimar to
visit Goethe, but rather because he knew that there were those in
the court circle there who were directly interested in the mining
ventures in Mexico.[17]

Since he had recently been acquitted by the courts of his own
country of plotting to set up an American empire in Mexico (of
which he was to be "Emperor," and to be succeeded as "Empress"
by his only, and dearly beloved, daughter Theodosia, then married
to Joseph Alston, Governor of South Carolina), he evidently hoped
to make a deal with the Weimar courtiers who by then had large
sums invested in Mexican mineral explorations.

Why was Goethe likewise so very laconic about the visit by this
American in Weimar (cf. *Tagebuch* January 4: "Herr von Humboldt, Obrist Burr aus Nord-Amerika.")?

It is interesting to note that Jesse Burton Harrison of Virginia,
and later of New Orleans, the twentieth and last of Goethe's
American student-visitors (who, in his youth, had been virtually a
member of President Jefferson's household), visited, in New York,
when he was *en route* to Weimar in June, 1829, Aaron Burr and
was informed by the former Vice President that the "hostility of
Mr. Jefferson and the government . . . made his travelling in Europe
quite uncomfortable . . . He was watched in every coach, hotel &
street, where he went; this he did not discover 'til at Weimar . . .
where the late Grand-Duchess told him that everything he said &
did that evening would be communicated to Paris next morning.
And so it turned out as the Duke of Bassano afterwards told
him."[18]

Of course Goethe must have known that every moment of
Burr's presence in Weimar was under secret surveillance of Jefferson's agents. The very presence of "Herr Humboldt" (whose brother, Alexander, had already in 1804 become the visitor, friend and

correspondent of President Jefferson), might have contributed to Burr's taciturnity.[19]

On the other hand, the fact that Burr was an American colonel might have embarrassed the Sage of Weimar, if one may judge by the alarm evoked in Goethe by the presence of another American Colonel, Pearce, in Weimar in 1793.[20]

Wadephul suggests "Something in Burr's personality must have affronted Goethe; otherwise he would not have disregarded Knebel's request to tell him something about 'this man Burr'."[21] What might be considered an incentive to this request is found in a letter from Knebel's sister in *Aus Karl Ludwig Knebels Briefwechsel mit seiner Schwester Henriette:*[22]

> Den Amerikaner[23] habe ich nach seinem ersten Besuch noch vorgestern nebst Emilie Gore Abens zum Thee bei mir gehabt.[24] Da er Briefe und Nachrichten von Imhoffs mitbrachte, so wollte ich ihm doch etwas Ehre anthun. Emilie wollte, ich sollte Dich gleich holen lassen, und wie gerne hätte ich es gethan! Es wäre Dir doch immer interessant gewesen, da er aus einem andern Welttheil kommt und in seinem halbenglishen Französisch gerne und viel erzählt. Er mag in [sic] Fünfzigen sein und sieht sehr gescheit aus, lebhaft und unternehmend. Von Figur ist er klein und mager, und sieht einem amerikanischen Napoleon nicht unähnlich. Die Stirn ist groß und die Augen lebhaft. Mein Schicksal möchte ich ihm aber nicht anvertrauen, ob er gleich große Achtung vor unserm Geschlecht hat, und sagt, die Treue der Männer hielt' einen Tag, die aber der Frauen wäre für's ganze Leben. Das Gauche und Halbwilde in seinem Betragen machte mir Spaß; denn, da ich die Büste von Franklin hereinbringen ließ, so stand er ehrerbietig auf und sein Gesicht war so von Freuden bewegt und von Liebe, wie man es bei einem Europäer selten sieht. Er fand die Büste sehr wohl getroffen.

Had the gentlemen in Weimar only been able to perceive the veteran soldier and retired politician as this lady instinctively esteemed him!

Although Burr was a shrewd, clever, and fearless leader, able to outmaneuver those American politicians who had brought against him charges of conspiracy, Goethe seemingly made no effort to elicit from him much information which might have enlightened the Wizard of Weimar in his longing for American lore. Had the gentlemen of Weimar been able to appreciate Colonel Burr as well as did its ladies, e.g., "the late Duchess," Henriette Knebel and Tinette von Reizenstein,[25] he might have been able to interest them, and to inform them better about American and Mexican mining operations, and thus have prepared them for the new literature and the new politics then taking shape in Latin America, and thus have set the stage for the advent of the new works of C. Sidons (1827), Herzog Bernhard (1827–1828), and Charles Sealsfield (1833).

Despite the fact that Goethe was growing old, it is recorded: "Sein [Bernhard's] ausführliches Reisejournal . . . hatte Goethe mit großem Interesse gelesen,"[26] and that his son, August von Goethe, read his father's poem, "Dem Herzog Bernhard" containing the verses:

Gesellig auch im Tanze froh,

Willkommen schönen Frauen,

when the masonic lodge celebrated the Duke's July 1826 return from America.

This couplet recalls not only an earlier one, referring to the poet himself,

Urahnherr war der Schönsten hold,

Das spukt so hin und wieder.[27]

but it also impinges on a phase of Aaron Burr's nature, which led to his sudden departure from Weimar in "Nacht und Nebel."

Since C. Sidons' (Sealsfield's) volumes on his American travels were in print before the travel-volumes of Herzog Bernhard were written, and, since both authors visited some places and persons visited by the other, it seems strange that there is no mention by Goethe or Bernhard, or by any other contemporary German author, of the Austrian's volumes. Nor is there any mention in Wadephul's monograph, *Goethe's Interest in the New World* (Jena, 1934), in the "list of titles of works on America and by Americans with which Goethe had come in contact,"[28] of the names of Sidons (1827) or of Sealsfield's (1829) *Tokeah or the White Rose,* which appeared in German (3 vols.) in 1833 in modified form. But *Tokeah* (1829) would have presented to Goethe the native, or Indian, element which he seemed to appreciate greatly in Fenimore Cooper's novels,[29] despite the fact Cooper personally demonstrated no appreciation of Goethe or Weimar,[30] which town he passed through, with jocular comment, on August 15, 1830.

Heinz Bluhm's publication of Ottilie von Goethe's diaries[31] (seemingly made possible by the acquisitiveness of some Allied personality active in German territory and engaged in non-professional activities in the War Zone of World War II) enabled me to include in *Southern Scholars in Goethe's Germany*[32] much of the material concerning contacts between Thomas C. Reynolds of South Carolina and Ottilie, Goethe's daughter-in-law, in Weimar. These contacts which began on June 2 and 3, 1839, manifest the resulting effects of interest in American visitors, American literature and fine arts, as set forth in hundreds of pages in the succeeding volumes.[33]

In the first volume of the Bluhm edition of Ottilie's diary one finds under June 2 and 3, 1839: "Den Morgen brachten mir zwei Amerikaner, Mr. Reynolds and Mr. Guerar (*sic!* for Guerard) einen Brief von Mrs. Robinson."[34] In the same entry is found: "das Werk der Miss Martineau über Amerika für mich. Es ist aus Versehen der 2te Theil zweimal."[35] These volumes might well have been a present from Thomas Caute Reynolds to his newly found friend and Weimar sponsor, Ottilie.

On June 5th the diary discloses: "Billet von Mr. Reynolds das [sic] er wünsche an Hof vorgestellt zu werden, an Spiegel deshalb geschrieben . . . Die beiden Amerikaner an Froriep gebracht. Beide Chevalier (?), Lawrence[36] und Emma Froriep den Abend hier."

Although Reynolds is recorded to have attended social functions with Ottilie, at her home and elsewhere, on June 8, 13, 14, 17, 22, 27, and on July 4 (to take leave of Weimar), the editor of the diary offers no explanation as to who this American really is.

On July 3 Ottilie wrote for her two American visitors an "Empfehlungsbrief" to the distinguished Professor Karl Friedrich Phillip von Martius at the University of Munich, where they both were to matriculate.

On the following day, July 4, came "die zwei Amerikaner um Abschied zu nehmen."

On August 2, the diary records: "Miss Martineaus Buch über Amerika bekommen"; August 29: "Miss Martineaus Buch über Amerika weitergelesen"; August 30: "1ten Theil beendigt."

The reading of "Miss Sedgwicks Buch begonnen" on November 3, was completed on November 8.[37] Here again one suspects that this book was a gift from Mr. Reynolds, since his friend and patron, Simms, has recorded: "I took a trip to Stockbridge and called on Miss Sedgwick."[38]

On January 11, 1840: "Rainolds[39] schickte mir eine Broschure von Channing" ["Channing, William, amer. Schriftsteller, Geistlicher"]. On January 18 Ottilie records: "Channing über die Sclaverei gelesen," evidently the same book sent by "Rainolds" [Reynolds].

Finally on January 16, 1840 Ottilie in Chemnitz records: "Abends den Legitimen angefangen." Thus was a mention of Sealsfield recorded for the first time in the Goethe family. Evidently the reading was relished, for the January 17 entry reports: "Den Legitimen beendigt." On January 20: "Mittag 12 Uhr in Prag angekommen." A most intriguing situation! Ottilie von Goethe in Prague, the site of Karl Postl's 1810 reception into the Kreuzherrenorden and into the Roman Catholic priesthood (1816),[40] within two days after she had completed the reading of Postl's first American novel written in German!

When, on March 10, 1840, Ottilie asserts: "Ich las . . . das indianische Märchen vor" one recalls that she had, on December 6 (1839) recorded: "Ich schrieb gleich das indianische Feuermädchen" and wonders whether she had dipped into Sealsfield's *Der Legitime und die Republikaner* before January 16, 1840. The promptness with which she completed the reading of her American volumes indicates a lively interest in the subject matter and suggests the query whether the diary-entry of March 10 is not a result of her contact with Sealsfield's *Der Legitime und die Republikaner.*

The diary-entries of December 21, 1840: "las über die Indianer," and of January 14, 1841, where she indicates that she was shown "mehrere recht interessante indianische Gegenstände" at the home of Mr. and Mrs. J. A. Schurz, the American Consul in Vienna,[41] emphasize that her interest must have been incited, or stimulated, by the reading of Sealsfield's novels, for she had, on April 10, 1840, recorded: ". . . ich las Virey."[42]

Interest in the Indians continues, viz. 20 January 1841: "Zwei Pamphlets der Aborigen Protection Society gelesen." Note also: "d. 13 März": "Indianisches Buch von Heckwelder ausgelesen."[43]

d. 16. März: "Selig kam . . . wir lasen erst was ich angemerkt über die Indianer."

d. 1. Juni: "lass [sic!] ein bischen in den indianischen Biographien."

On August 24 (1841) Ottilie records: "Howitt beendigt." This is undoubtedly a reflection of Reynolds who became acquainted with, and quite fond of, William and Mary Howitt, who were residing in the vicinity of Heidelberg while he was a student at that university (1839).[44] We are also informed: "He once sent to his friend, Baroness Goethe, daughter-in-law of the poet, a copy of Yemassee."[45]

When Ottilie's diary records (p. 76) that in Weimar during July 1841 she read "Das Cajütenbuch vom Autor des Legitimen 2ter Theil" and "Visits to Remarkable Places" by William Howitt, 1840, we are again reminded that Reynolds may have been the source of her acquaintance of both these authors.[46]

On September 20, 1853:[47] "by Hook or by Crook"; "Lass Scarlett Letter"[48] [by Hawthorne, 1850].

On January 12, 1854 begins a series of reports on Ottilie's contacts with Mr. and Mrs. [?] Washington Irving. Although Irving spent much time in Dresden and its vicinity, no record exists to indicate that he ever expressed any desire to visit Goethe, who had been hostile, or, at best, indifferent to Aaron Burr, during the latter's visit in Weimar in 1810.

In this connection it must be recalled that, at the time of Burr's trial and acquittal in 1804, Irving not only was present as a Burr partisan, but was reputedly in love with Burr's daughter, Theodosia, her father's deepest and most enduring love.[49] She later became the wife of Joseph Alston, a fervid Burrite, who later became Governor of South Carolina. No dearer was Ottilie to Goethe than was Theodosia to Aaron Burr, whom Goethe had allowed to pass through Weimar with a minimum of respect and attention.[50]

The initial Irving entry (January 12, 1854) merely reports: "Lady St. Germains mit Mr. and Mrs. Irving wollte visite machen. Ulrike u. Walter waren aus und ich konnte noch Niemand sehen."[51] The series of references continues: 25. April: "Nach Tisch Mr. Irving" with a friendly comment by Ottilie.

Although there are numerous references in the succeeding pages of Ottilie's diary, extending from January 2 to May 20, 1854, concerning the Irving couple and several further identifications of this couple as our American author and his "spouse," it seems quite evident that the man referred to in this volume could not have been our Washington Irving, a bachelor.[52]

The American incidences in Ottilie's diary close with the mention of that German author who, after Sealsfield, is probably best-known as an American traveller, as well as an author of American lore, when Ottilie records: "d. 3. Juli, 1856": "Ich schenkte an Ricco u. Anna das Kinderbuch von Gerstäcker." This indicates her continuing interest in American literary material to which Thomas C. Reynolds seems to have directed her attention shortly after his arrival in Weimar on June 3, 1839. It is significant that Ottilie should have become so extensively interested in not only the writings of Karl Postl (Charles Sealsfield), a name avoided by the devoted father-in-law and by His Highness Bernhard, Duke of Saxe-Weimar-Eisenach.[53] It is also evident that the influence of Thomas C. Reynolds of South Carolina had caused Ottilie to become interested, as is witnessed in her diary, in other American authors and other English-language writers.

Although no direct evidence has been adduced to explain the failure of Goethe's generation to even mention the name of Karl Postl (Charles Sealsfield), it seems that here, as in the case of Aaron Burr,[54] Goethe and his inner circle, believing that familiarity breeds contempt, and that "Le silence seul est le souverain mépris," eluded contacts with those whom they did not relish. Similarly, Burr was in Weimar as a guest, not of Goethe, nor of the Ducal Court, but merely as a "Geschäftsverbindung mit Bertuch."[55]

NOTES

1. Cf. John T. Krumpelmann, *Southern Scholars in Goethe's Germany,* Chapel Hill, 1965.

2. See Eduard Castle, *Der große Unbekannte. Das Leben von Charles Sealsfield, Briefe und Aktenstücke,* Vienna (Karl Werner Verlag), 1955, p. 119.

3. Hersg. Heinrich Luden, Weimar, 1828, by Wilhelm Hoffman. Also in English translation: *Travels Through North America during the Years 1825 and 1826* (Philadelphia, 1828).

4. Cf. Goethe's *Sämtliche Werke,* Jubiläums-Ausgabe, II, 237; II, 348 f.

5. Note the curt record of Burr's visit in Goethe's *Tagebuch* (Jan. 4, 1810): "Herr Wilhelm von Humboldt, Obrist Burr aus Nord Amerika." Cf. *Aaron Burr, The Private Journal,* ed. William K. Bixby, 1852, vol. I, p. 352, Jan. 4, 1810: "Went first to Wieland's 77. To Goethe's 58. Y. Humboldt" [Y = "There"].

6. *Cf.* Bernhard, *Reise,* II, 252: "Er [Burr] hatte sich gegen Jemand von meiner Bekanntschaft geäußert, daß ich ihn bei meinem ersten Aufenthalt in New York nicht besucht hätte; desshalb holte ich das Versäumte so schnell als möglich nach . . . und von dessen Seite ich mich eines sehr guten Empfanges erfreute." N.B. These passages are omitted in the American edition of Bernhard's *Travels,* II, 196!

7. *Reise,* II, 46 f.

8. *Reise,* I, 135.

9. *Reise,* I, 140. *Cf.* also I, 143, 159, 165.

10. *Reise,* I, 210 f.

11. *Reise,* II, 70.

12. *Reise,* II, 71. "Du sollst nicht . . .", but, nevertheless, one often does! As did Charles Sealsfield and, later, John J. Pershing. It does not seem plausible that a Duke of Saxe-Weimar-Eisenach, whose brother, Duke Carl Friedrich, was wedded to Maria Paulowna, daughter of the Czar of Russia (at whose wedding the American diplomat, Joel Roberts Poinsett, of South Carolina, was present, because he was a favorite guest of the family of Czar Paul, and who was later [1825–1829] the United States Minister to Mexico, at the time Duke Bernhard desired to visit that country) should not have been able to obtain permission for a brother-in-law of the Imperial Russian family to visit Poinsett, as a personal guest, and thus to enable the young nobleman to acquaint himself with the status of the Weimarian investments in the mining industry of that country.

13. IV, 308.

14. See Orie Long, *Literary Pioneers, Early American Explorers of European Culture* (Harvard University Press, 1935) and my book *Southern Scholars in Goethe's Germany* (University of North Carolina Press, 1965).

15. Eduard Castle, *Der große Unbekannte. Das Leben von Charles Sealsfield* (Vienna & Munich, 1952), p. 185.

16. Reprinted in full from the *Original Manuscript*. In two volumes, Wm. K. Bixby, Rochester, N.Y., 1903. I, 352. (See fn. 5 above.)

17. During his brief stay in Weimar Burr was a house-guest of Bertuch. *Cf.* Walter Wadephul, *Goethe's Interest in the New World* (Jena, 1934), p. 21.

18. See *Southern Scholars*, p. 52, and *Aris Sonis Focis, being a Memoir of an American Family. The Harrisons of Skimoko* (1910), p. 107.

19. The suspicion that Burr had purloined a copy of Humboldt's map of Latin America while the German scientist was visiting Jefferson in Washington in 1804 has been stated. *Cf.* H. R. Friis, "Alexander von Humboldt's Besuch in den Vereinigten Staaten von 20 Mai bis 30. Juni 1804" in *Alexander von Humboldt Studien zu seiner universalen Geisteshaltung*, Berlin, 1959, 177 pp. (Hrsg. Joachim H. Schulze.)

20. See Goethe's letter to Minister J. F. v. Fritch, 12, III, 1793. Also, at the time he was visiting, Burr was fond of calling attention to his own German heritage and even of boasting that his daughter, Theodosia, was probably the only Burr in America who could communicate in German. See *Private Journal of Aaron Burr during his Four Years in Europe* (1858) edited by Matthew L. Davis, II, 28; "To J. G. Burr, Aug. 1, 1810" "My daughter . . . the only person of the name [Burr], who speaks and understands it [the German language]. See also *op. cit.*, I, 412 (Jan. 30, 1810) and II, 19.

21. *Op. cit.*, p. 22, "Knebel to Goethe," Jan. 11, 1810.

22. Ed. Heinrich Düntzer (Jena; Mauke, 1858), p. 400, 438: "An Karl. (Weimar) Mittwoch, den 6. Januar 1810."

23. Düntzer's note (ibid.): "Oberst Burr, den Knebel nach seinem in Amerika gezeigten Betragen für 'intrigant und unsichern Charakters' hielt."

24. *Cf.* Burr's *Diary*, 1858 (p. 386): "La Baronne de Knebel asked me to tea tomorrow" (Jan. 3, 1810).

25. See Erwin G. Gudde, "Aaron Burr in Weimar," *South Atlantic Quarterly*, XL (1941), 360–367.

26. "*Zahmen Xenien*," IX, 742. Cf. Jubiläums Ausgabe, II, 348 f. and S. 237, "Dem Herzog Bernhard." "Am 15. September, 1826."

27. "*Zahmen Xenien*," VI, 1828 f., Jubiläums Ausgabe, IV, 99.

28. See Wadephul, p. 77 ff.

29. See Wadephul, p. 60 ff. N.B. e.g., "He devoured The Last of the Mohicans in the briefest time, and one week after began *The Spy* (October, 1826).

30. *Op. cit.*, p. 67.

31. Bergland Verlag, GmbH., Wien, 1962–1966.

32. University of North Carolina Press, Chapel Hill, 1965.

33. Bergland Press, Bd. II, 1963; Bd. IV, 1966. *Ottilie von Goethe Tagebücher und Briefe an und von Ottilie von Goethe.*

34. No editor's note to identify "Reynolds, Guerar, Mrs. Robinson," but see note 1839, S.3, and "Namensregister," S.XXI: "Robinson, Mr., aus Amerika" [sic!]! See *Southern Scholars*, pp. 2, 19, 77 for Guerard.

35. *Society in America* (1837) or *Retrospect of Western Travel* (1838)? Probably the former which is in two volumes and was critically reviewed by

Reynolds' friend, William Gilmore Simms (*Southern Literary Messenger*, III (Nov. 1837), 641-657). See also *The Letters of William Gilmore Simms* (University of South Carolina Press, 1952), I, 114: "I have written a long article on slavery in reply to Miss Martineau." (i.e., *Slavery in America, Being a Brief Review of Miss Martineau on that Subject*, Richmond, 1835, I, 144, note 39. The entry in Ottilie's Diary on August 2 (p. 19): "Miss Martineaus Buch über Amerika bekommen" evidently indicates that the "Versehen" reported above has been corrected, i.e., part *One* has been received from the bookseller.

36. "James Lawrence [1773-1840], engl. Schriftsteller, zeitweilig in Weimar, lebend." An acquaintance of Aaron Burr.

37. Catherine Maria Sedgwick (1789-1861), the novelist.

38. *Letters*, etc. vol. I, p. 114 f, Aug. 30, 1837.

39. One finds various spellings: "Ranalds," "Rainolds" in Ottilie's text. For Channing see "Namenregister," I, xx.

40. Eduard Castle, *Der große Unbekannte*, pp. 35, 38, 51.

41. *Tagebücher u. Briefe*, I, XXII.

42. *Der Virey und die Aristokraten*. 3 vols., 1835.

43. Johann Gottlieb Heckewaelder, "*Nachrichten von der Geschichte, den Sitten und Gebräuchen der Indianischen Völkerschaften . . .*" Göttingen, 1821.

44. See *Southern Scholars*, pp. 79; 77, 82, 89.

45. *Cf. The Letters of William Gilmore Simms*, I, cxxxiii, in five volume set (1830-1844). See I, 61, 63, 71 for indications of possible connection between Simms' *Yemassee* and Sealsfield's *Der Legitime* (1833).

46. *Ibid.*, p. 397. Simms urged Reynolds to write a review of Howitt's *Student-Life in Germany* for the *Southern Quarterly Review*.

47. III, 276. *Cf.* Sealsfield's *Ralph Doughbys Brautfahrt* (*Werke*, X, 41): "And gaining by what they call Hook and Crook."

48. Cf. also, Bd. IV, 315, April 30, 1855.

49. Cf. Charles Felton Pidgin, *Theodosia, The First Gentlewoman of her Time*, Boston, 1907, p. 223: "the statement has been made that Washington Irving was, at one time, in love with Theodosia Burr − − − He was also a great friend of Judge van Ness, who was Burr's second in his duell with Alexander Hamilton and her father's most intimate friend." This information may help to explain why Irving avoided Weimar and Goethe, who had failed to display any evidence of interest in, or any civility for, the ex-Vice President of the United States when he visited him in Weimar.

50. Heinz Bluhm asserts of Ottilie: "Sie vermählte sich eigentlich mit dem Vater nicht mit dem Sohn" (I, xiii).

51. See S.401, 412, 463, 464, 468, 480, 485, 492, 493, 501.

52. A personal letter from the editor of the voluminous diary has privately informed me that the enormity of the task undertaken and the tremendous pressure are responsible for the misidentification.

53. Castle, *Der große Unbekannte*, S.119.

54. Of course Bernhard did visit Aaron Burr in New York (*cf.* note 6, p. 4, *supra*) and did, as Burr, believe that "St. Louis will some time be a metrop-

olis of a large empire." "Duke Bernhard had in mind a separation of the western states, such as Burr has contemplated." Cf. B. A. Uhlendorf, *Charles Sealsfield, Ethnic Elements and National Problems in his Works.* Reprinted from *Jahrbuch der Deutsch-Amerikanischen Historischen Gesellschaft von Illinois* (Chicago, 1920–21), p. 60, quoting Bernhard's *Reise,* Bd. II, 121: "Vielleicht kann es [St. Louis] noch einst die Hauptstadt eines großen Reiches werden."

55. Castle, *Der große Unbekannte,* S. 185. Also Wadephul, p. 21: "According to Burr, only two Americans were then known in the Weimar circle, namely Smith and Pinsett [*sic* for Poinsett], both natives of South Carolina." *Cf.* Castle, *Der große Unbekannte,* S. 367.

8. Sealsfields Erzählformel Seiner Amerika-Romane: Raum und Zeit als Welt und Geschichte. Anmerkungen zur Erzähltheorie am Beispiel des Romans Kajütenbuch

Alexander Ritter

Durch die zahlreichen direkten und fingierten Anmerkungen zu seiner schriftstellerischen Arbeit will Sealsfield offensichtlich auf zwei ihm wichtige Anliegen hinweisen. Er möchte auf jeden Fall allgemein verstanden werden und über die Verwirklichung des angestrebten nicht-elitären, sondern sozialen Anspruchs belehren, also durch Information aufklären. Auch die einleitenden erzähltheoretischen Hinweise zum *Kajütenbuch* haben sich, einfach in der Diktion und bestechend schlüssig in der poetologischen Aussage, als griffbereites Reservoir literarkritischer Argumentation erwiesen.[1] Diese bündig gesprochenen Formeln von der schriftstellerischen Aufgabe können zukünftig nur dem Überdruß der unentwegt wiederholten Zitierung entgehen, wenn diese Mitteilungen verstärkt in ihrem theoretischen Ansatz hinterfragt und auf ihre Beziehungen zur praktischen Umsetzung in den epischen Vorgängen analysiert werden.[2] Welche Konsequenzen für den Erzählprozeß, weniger für den geistes- und literargeschichtlichen Zusammenhang, hat die Übertragung der Heldenfunktion auf die bislang zugeordneten Begleitfiguren? Was bedeutet dies für das erzählte Geschehen, will es nicht handlungsarme Personenbeschreibung oder langatmige autobiographische Monologkette sein? Die häufige Bearbeitung von Sealsfields Romanen zu Jugendbuchlektüre beweist den Aktionsreichtum der Handlung. Sind dann aus dieser Sicht Sealsfields Behauptungen, Vergangenheit und Zukunft seien für den Erzählvorgang "historische Gewänder," Handlungsinhalte lediglich "Folie," poetologische Fehlaussagen, gemessen an der nachweisbaren Bedeutung von Raum und Zeit?[3] Liegt die Lösung dieses Widerspruchs von Dichtungstheorie und praktischer Ausführung in der Erklärung der Mitteilungslücke, mit der die Zeitebene der Gegenwart und das Raumverständnis der praktischen Arbeit in der Landschaft ausgespart bleibt? Ist demnach für

Sealsfield seine Literatur schriftstellerische Vorarbeit, gerichtet auf eine weltanschauliche Zielvorstellung, erzähltheoretisch formuliert, aber transliterarisch als gesellschaftspraktischer Zustand gemeint?

Walter Weiss hat bei der Interpretation des *Kajütenbuchs* auf die "exemplarische Bedeutung" dieses Romans für das Gesamtwerk hingewiesen, denn "es entspricht . . . wohl am besten den theoretischen Überlegungen Sealsfields."[4] Wir konnten die immer noch nicht befriedigend geklärte besondere Position und Funktion des Romans im Gesamtwerk registrieren, als sich das *Kajütenbuch* bei dem Nachweis einer geschlossenen Raumkonzeption in seiner Extraposition bestätigt.[5] Diese Erfahrungen und auch die auffällige Dauerhaftigkeit, mit der dieser Roman als des Dichters populärstes Werk die Leser fasziniert und die Literaturwissenschaft zu fortgesetzten Deutungsversuchen herausfordert, sind noch nicht genügend geklärte Signale für die erzählerische Besonderheit des Romans. So wollen wir im folgenden versuchen, durch weitere Beobachtungen die bislang vorliegenden Ergebnisse der Forschung zu ergänzen und über gewandelte Fragestellungen zu weiteren Überlegungen anregen. Dabei geht es uns vor allem um die Struktur des Erzählprozesses, die von der Erzählerhierarchie und der Gesprächsfunktion, dem korrelativ gebrochenen Handlungsverlauf und den eingearbeiteten erzählten Realien bestimmt wird. Weiterhin können auf diesem Wege die Einsicht in das kompositorische Symmetriedenken des Dichters erweitert und die im Einzelwerk zyklische Konzeption als symptomatisch für die planmäßige Anlage des Gesamtwerks gewertet werden.

I

Fragen wir uns als erstes, wer eigentlich im *Kajütenbuch* erzählt und für wen erzählt wird. Die Erzählsituation erweist sich in doppelter Hinsicht als außergewöhnlich. In eine geschehnisarme Grundhandlung, berichtet vom insgesamt verantwortlichen Erzähler, sind mehrere aktionskräftige Einzelerzählungen eingebettet, von beauftragten Rollenerzählern vorgetragen. Das ist literargeschichtlich an sich nichts Neues, wenn wir z.B. an Goethes *Unterhaltungen deutscher Ausgewanderter* (1795) oder E. T. A. Hoffmanns *Serapionsbrüder* (1819–1821) denken. Bei näherem Zusehen jedoch zeigt sich die erzählerische Konstruktion des *Kajütenbuchs* als eine für Sealsfields erzähltheoretische Auffassung charakteristische Variante mit eigenwillig gesetzten Akzenten. Der 24-köpfige Zuhörerkreis—die Zahl 12 gewinnt im Verlauf der Handlung auffällig an sinnbildlicher Bedeutung, auf die wir aber nicht weiter eingehen können—hat sich nicht zufällig getroffen, befindet sich auch nicht im Sinne der erzählerischen Tradition in einer erzwungenen Wartesituation, bis bestimmte unangenehme Termine oder Geschehnisse vorbei sind. Dieser Zuhörerkreis ist gezielt eingeladen worden, in seiner personalen Besetzung und in der gemeinsamen Tätigkeit eines scheinbar belanglosen, gesellschaftlich nicht unbedingt außergewöhnlichen gesellingen Beisammenseins bei gutem Essen, Trinken und Räsonieren festgelegt. Die Personenrunde ist erzählerisch zweckmäßig ausgesucht: eine gesellschaftlich, sozial und politische Gesinnung nach fast homogene Männergruppe von lautstarker und fast arroganter Selbstzufriedenheit. Für den epischen Zusammenhang stellt sie die typischen personalen Varianten des neureichen Mississippi-Establishments, das seine gefällige, aber leicht verletzbare Eitelkeit, die allgemeine Wohlhabenheit und den verblassenden Schneid ehemaliger Kämpfer für die Union in exklusiver Clubatmosphäre meist unbekümmert, nicht immer dezent demonstriert.

Diese fiktive Zuhörergruppe steht hier repräsentativ für die etablierte gehobene Schicht weißer Amerikaner in Natchez, in Louisiana. Doch darüber hinaus gilt sie stellvertretend für die stabilisierte, aber weltanschaulich-moralisch für Sealsfield problematisch gewordene Gesellschaft der damaligen Vereinigten Staaten, ja letztlich des damaligen Europa oder generell einer jeden, Sealsfields Vorstellungen nicht mehr entsprechenden Ordnung. Ihre erzählerische Funktion liegt im übertragenen negativen Stellenwert. Darum werden auch die entscheidenden Erzählungen nicht von Vertretern ihrer Runde berichtet, sondern sie verbleibt eine belehrenswerte Versammlung von Männern, die sich mit ihren Gesprächsbeiträgen über Geld, Wirtschaftsprobleme und gesellschaftliche Ereignisse selbst als oberflächlich und materiell kennzeichnet. Ihre Funktion ist es, weltanschauliches und gesellschaftliches Kontrastbild zu liefern. Die Zuhörergruppe bleibt dabei schwach konturierte Skizze, mehr personale Staffage, akustischer Reaktionsrahmen des Widerspruches, Spottes und der Provokation. Statt einer umständlichen Beschreibung von Personen und Schauplatz gestaltet der

Erzähler stellvertretende Aktion einer überschaubaren Personen-
zahl in überschaubarem Raum, an geographisch-symbolischem Ort
(Natchez), Fluß (Mississippi) und Grenze (Vereinigten Staaten/
Texas [Mexiko]). Die in dem engen Innenraum der sogenannten
"Kajüte" wie auf einer Bühne referierten und kommentierten
aktuellen brisanten politischen und wirtschaftlichen Themen (Verhältnis USA/Mexiko, Frontier-Recht, Baumwollpreise usw.) wirken durch die in der Erzählerhierarchie geschickt in verschiedene
Handlungen gegossenen Erlebnisberichte unmittelbar und über-
zeugend.

Die beiden wichtigen Rollenerzähler, Nathaniel Edward Morse,
General aus Texas, und Daniel Duncan, Bankpräsident aus Natchez,
zwei Männer in gesellschaftlichen Spitzenpositionen, werden von
außen herangeführt. Beide sprechen aus Gründen der persönlichen
Rechtfertigung gegenüber persönlich gemeinten Provokationen, die
als temperamentvoll gesteigerte Vorurteile gegenüber dem unge-
betenen und unbekannten Gast Morse und dem abwesenden, dem
Leser als Person unbekannten Gastgeber Kapitän Murky, alias
Ready, in zunehmend aggressivem Tonfall hervorgebracht werden.
Vergewissern wir uns an dieser Stelle noch einmal der erzähltheoretischen Bedeutung des Rollenerzählers. Rollenerzähler sind
in der Erzählerhierarchie Berichterstatter, die vom Erzähler scheinbar losgelöst doch nur seinen weitergegebenen Auftrag durchführen, exemplarisch gültige Erfahrungen aus individueller Sicht
vorzutragen. Sie sind die fingierten Zeugen, die durch ihr personal
gegenwärtiges Verbürgen die Gewißheit des Erzählten besiegeln
und beim Leser höchste Glaubwürdigkeit hinterlassen. Sie produ-
zieren aus der Erinnerung Vorzeithandlung, an der sie als Akteure
selbst beteiligt gewesen sind, indem sie durch die ambivalente
Handhabung der Perspektive, des begrenzten Standpunkts eines
naiv Erlebenden und des olympischen Standpunkts des erfahren
Beurteilenden, an Geschehenes erinnern und Zukünftiges anlegen.

Schauen wir uns zuerst Morse an, der die Reihe der Erzählungen
mit dem qualitativ und quantitativ wichtigsten Beitrag eröffnet.
Mit seinen autobiographischen Ausführungen demonstriert er
selbstbewußt die Beispielhaftigkeit seiner Vita für einen gesellschaftspolitischen und wirtschaftlichen Pionierraum. Seine Rede
richtet sich gegen die Existenzformen einer verbürgerlichten Gesellschaft wie die seines Heimatstaates Maryland, gegen die kriminell

mißbrauchte Vogelfreiheit im gesellschaftspolitischen Vakuum der Frontier-Zone (Bob), gegen die Sattheit einer Pflanzergesellschaft, die den echten Pioniergeist nur noch aus sentimentalisierter Erinnerung kennt (seine Zuhörer). Für das unabhängig gewordene Texas verkörpert Morse die unabhängig gewordene Persönlichkeit und damit die Chance einer ihm gleichen freibürgerlichen und gottesfürchtigen Agrargesellschaft, die in der täglichen unmittelbaren Auseinandersetzung mit der noch wenig erschlossenen Landschaft ausdauernde Mühe und rastlose Mobilität, bürgerliche Solidarität und politisches Selbstbewußtsein bezeugen muß.

Diese Überzeugung trägt Morse in zwei Berichten vor. In der "Jacinto-Prärie" bekennt er, wie er als der junge selbstbewußte Nordstaatler im Frontiergebiet gedemütigt und durch die beiden Elementarerfahrungen von Raum (Landschaft der Prärie) und Geschichte (Belehrung durch den Alkalden und Bob) erzogen und für ein Leben in diesem gesellschaftspolitisch unterentwickelten Land vorbereitet wird. Der annehmbar vom Haupterzähler beauftragte Rollenerzähler Morse delegiert die Sprecherfunktion in seinem Bericht an den älteren und damit lebenserfahreneren Alkalden weiter: eine Geste der Toleranz gegenüber dem mehr Wissenden und damit dessen Befugnis, Grundsätzliches sagen zu dürfen, das außerhalb der eigenen Erfahrung liegt. Dieser zugebilligten Autorität, glaubwürdige Lebensphilosophie mitteilen zu können, entspricht der Alkalde nur zum kleinen Teil aus eigener Einsicht. Auch weiß er sich nur in einer übertragenen Rolle des Berichtenden, des Delegierten in dem weltweiten historischen Prozeß der politischen Traditionen, somit den Einzelnen, den Gruppen und Völkern verpflichtet, die den Sprecherauftrag an ihn weiterreichen, zu halten. Die überragende Bedeutung seiner Lehrer-Funktion wird zusätzlich dadurch unterstrichen, daß Bob, der moralischen Anti-Figur, als Rollenerzähler nur eine knappe Selbstdarstellung zugebilligt wird. Im zweiten Teil von Morses Bericht über den Texanischen Befreiungskrieg schildert er die Lebensphase seiner Bewährung. In dem flüchtig skizzierten historischen Abriß der militärischen und politischen Ereignisse wird die lebensphilosophische Theorie durch das Exemplum belegt, wie der Lehrer-Alkalde und der Schüler-Morse diese Lebenslehre leben und dabei siegreich überleben; wie die Anti-Gesellschaft der Mexikaner zerstört, auf der Flucht aber toleriert wird, und wie die Anti-Figur

Bob, Krimineller als sozialer Katalysator für eine neue Welt, mit dem Anbruch dieser neuen Welt in der Apotheose des reuigen Sünders stirbt. Mit dem biblisch-symbolischen Schlußbild des nach-gruppierten Marienschmerzes weisen der Erzähler und somit der Autor auf die Einordnung dieser irdischen Begebenheiten in den makrokosmischen Zusammenhang, aus dem die göttliche Recht-fertigung den Menschen die Taten und die Worte delegiert: Das Rollenspiel des Erzählers ist nicht nur literarische Sprecherbe-rechtigung, sondern säkularisierte Mission, Raum und Geschichte nach einem aufklärerisch stabilisierten Harmoniedenken zu ordnen und notfalls zu korrigieren.[6]

Die beiden Berichte Daniel Duncans, des zweiten Rollener-zählers, sind von auffallend ähnlicher Anlage. Er selbst kommt auch von außerhalb erst im Laufe des Abends hinzu, wiewohl er zur einheimischen Gesellschaft gehört, sie aber—wie es z.B. seine Einstellung zum Duellieren deutlich macht—aus kritischer Distanz einzuschätzen vermag. Morse kennzeichnet sich als den Vertreter einer neuen Gesellschaftsordnung und den Alkalden als einen seiner geistigen Väter. So sieht sich Duncan auch, allerdings weniger prononciert, gemessen am gesellschaftlich relativ stabilen Zustand. Er ist eher der Wahrer gesellschaftlicher Gerechtigkeit und Ordnung in der Nachfolge einer der geistigen Väter, des Kapitäns Murky. Dessen integre Persönlichkeit wird durch Duncans Erzählungen gerechtfertigt, und es wird gleichzeitig der Geist beschrieben, aus dem diese Gesellschaft von Louisiana einstmals erwachsen ist. Wie der Alkalde, so wird Murky zum moralischen und politischen Vor-bild des amerikanischen Ehrenmannes hochstilisiert, der die Toleranzprinzipien von gesellschaftlicher Selbstbestimmung und grundsätzlich politischer Freiheit bis zur persönlichen Ächtung verficht. Wir wollen auf die leicht erschließbare Bedeutung des Inhaltlichen und seinen Beispielwert nicht weiter eingehen, aber doch noch auf die Erzählerrolle Duncans aufmerksam machen. Wie Morse schildert er den Kriegsbericht über die Belagerung von Cal-lao selbst. Die Vorgeschichte dazu, das moralische Versagen der amerikanischen Bürger von Philadelphia und der Nordstaaten im allgemeinen gegenüber dem nach vergessenen moralischen Prin-zipien handelnden Kapitän Ready, später Murky, wird quasi in-direkt an drei Rollenerzähler delegiert, nämlich an den Kapitän, dessen Frau und den vormals vor den Spaniern geretteten, später

prominenten südamerikanischen General. Alle drei benannten
Zeugen des zu schildernden Geschehens aber läßt Duncan nicht
selbst sprechen, sondern weist über ihre Nennung lediglich auf den
Wahrheitsgehalt seines Berichtes hin und integriert ihre möglichen
Sprecherrollen in seinem eigenen kommentarlos-neutralen Erzähler-
verhalten, das an ihn nicht mehr gemahnt und einen weiteren, aber
von Duncan beauftragten Erzähler annehmen läßt. Sealsfield schien
eine Wiederholung des abgestuften Erzähler-Delegationssystems
vermeiden zu wollen. Vielleicht scheute er auch vor einer die
Lektüre beeinträchtigenden Überlänge des Romans zurück. Mög-
licherweise aber sollte auch die Gewichtigkeit der Jacinto-
Erzählung nicht gemindert werden. Wir können nur Vermutungen
äußern. Auf jeden Fall sind aber nach 4/5 Erzählzeit die beiden im
letzten Fünftel sich begegnenden und über den familiären Zusammenschluß sich vereinigenden Exponenten der Romanhandlung,
Morse und Murky, vorgestellt. Die doppelte Erzählfunktion der
Berichte von Morse und Duncan scheint erfüllt, nämlich zum
einen die vorbildliche Bedeutung von Einzelschicksalen herauszu-
stellen und zum anderen deren singulare Bedeutung als Voraussetzung im Sinne des integrierten Bestandteils einer pluralistischen
Gesellschaft für deren Fortbestehen zu kennzeichnen.

Man hat sich immer ein wenig gemüht, die Erzählerrolle Phelims
zu deuten. Wir wollen uns trotzdem nur auf wenige Anmerkungen
beschränken, die sich auf unsere Fragestellung beziehen. Phelims
Erzählung über Kishogues Flucht ist vom Dichter in der Mitte des
Symmetriegefüges von Thema und Funktion der anderen Berichte
plaziert. Der lustig-lautstarke Ire, Typus einer karikierten etwas
naßforschen Bedientenseele, verkörpert treffend jene kurzfristig
erheiternde, aber langfristig suspekt opportune Haltung aus sub-
alterner Verbindlichkeit und gewohnheitsrechtlich angemaßter Ver-
traulichkeit, also keine personale Vorbildlichkeit, eher die Kom-
parsenrolle in einem unterhaltsam auflockernden erzählerischen
Zwischenspiel. Und so demonstriert er in seiner Irland-Burleske,
in der die Bob-Handlung und, damit verbunden, bestimmte amerikanische Tugenden und Untugenden andeutungsweise persifliert
werden, wie mit geistiger Anspruchslosigkeit, Lautstärke und
derber Schwank-Handlung prächtige Unterhaltung produziert werden kann. Über die scheinbar arabeske Funktion hinaus bleibt
diese Kishogues-Handlung von Sealsfield eingefügte Sozialkritik,

indirekt durch die erzählte Handlung, direkt durch den Vortrag dieser Handlung in diesem Gesellschaftskreis mit einem bezeichnenden Hörererfolg verbunden—vom Erzähler gut gewählt, geschickt verpackt, aber dabei nicht minder deutlich, vor allem im Zusammenhang mit den kontrastierenden Inhalten der flankierenden Berichte.

Der weltanschaulich bestimmte, pädagogisch-aufklärend zu verfolgende Auftrag des Dichters, an den Sealsfield glaubt, kennen wir aus zahlreichen Hinweisen des Dichters. Die planvolle literarische Umsetzung im Werk und die damit verbundene unbedingte Erfordernis weitgehender Glaubwürdigkeit romanhaft gestalteter Weltanschauung bedingen notwendig bestimmte erzähltheoretische Konsequenzen, zu denen die Diversifikation des Einzelhelden zur Heldengruppe und die Delegation der souveränen Erzählerfunktion von Er- bzw. Ich-Erzähler auf die vervielfachte Erzählergruppe gehören, die als Rollenerzähler nacheinander oder parallel auftreten, bei Sealsfield aber vor allem als erlebende Erzähler im epischen Geschehen des Nebeneinander, dann aber auch als mehrfach erinnerte Erzähler des Vorher berichten. Die dann entstehende Erzählerhierarchie als ein handlungsinternes Sprechersystem, in dem sich die verschiedenen Helden gegenseitig erinnern, begründen und letztlich bestätigen, beweist gerade im *Kajütenbuch* die beabsichtigte Illusion einer literarisch fiktiven Wirklichkeit:

		[Autor]		
I		[Er-] Erzähler		
II	Morse	Phelim		Duncan
Prärie am Jacinto	Der Krieg	Kishogues	Callao 1825	Havanna 1816
Vorge-schichte (Morse)	Unabhängig-keitskrieg (Texas) N-Amerika	Politische Abhängigkeit	Unabhängig-keitskrieg (Peru) S-Amerika	Vorge-schichte (Murky/ Ready)
III Alkalde/Bob				[Murky/ Ehefrau/ General]

Die im Verhältnis zum Erzählereinsatz symmetrisch angelegte Erzählerhierarchie und Thematik der Rollenerzählungen ist für Sealsfield das abgestufte Figurensystem, mit dessen aufeinander abgestimmtem Einsatz er aus scheinbar individueller Perspektive

Weltbeschreibung und Weltbeurteilung vortragen läßt. Autobiographisch gesicherte Berichte der fiktiven Personen und deren Einbindung in einen nachprüfbaren historischen, räumlichen und auch personalen Zusammenhang lassen, als wesentliches erzählerisches Ziel, die Grenzen zwischen berichteter fiktiver und realer Wirklichkeit verschwimmen. Mit diesem gestaffelten Zeugensystem der zueinander komponierten Vorzeithandlungen läßt der Dichter Männer als teilnehmende, also erfahrene Akteure von historisch-politisch folgenreichen Vorgängen berichten, nicht darüber diskutieren, wie Weiss angenommen hat.[7] Hier gibt es nur den belehrenden Monolog nicht antastbaren Inhalts, weil erfahrungsgemäß verbürgt, dessen Verbindlichkeit durch die Autorität einer maskulinen, streng patriarchalisch regierten Welt bestimmt wird, in der man unnachgiebig belehrt und Recht spricht (Alkalde), kämpft (Bob, Austin und seine Armeen), Geld verdient (Duncan, die anwesenden Pflanzer) und liebt (Morse/Alexandrine). Die Rollenerzähler sind als Positiv-Gestalten patriarchalische Vorbilder, die ihre "notions" erläutern. "Patriarch" und "notion" erweisen sich durch die häufige Verwendung, ihre Bindung an unterschiedlichen Kontext (Gesellschaft, Natur=Baum) und die lexikalisch ambivalente Bedeutung als Schlüsselwörter. Die "patriarchalischen" Führerpersönlichkeiten sind herrisch *und* väterlich, wie der Alkalde gegenüber Bob und Morse, Murky gegenüber Morse und im Kriegseinsatz vor Callao. Mit ihren "notions" besitzen sie die "capability" für "the general concept under which particular things may be classed" und die "intention" der Durchsetzung dieses Konzepts.[8]

Die Integration der zahlreichen Rollenerzähler und ihrer Berichte gelingt Sealsfield durch eine korrelative und konsekutive Bindung an die Rahmenhandlung. Die erzählten Handlungen münden als Vorzeitgeschehnisse in die Gegenwartshandlung (Morse) oder entwicklen sich umgekehrt als zeitlich rückläufiger Bericht von der Gegenwartshandlung aus (Duncan). Ein weiteres Integrationsmoment ergibt sich aus der Absicht, die beiden wichtigsten Personen (Morse, Murky) für die sie zusammenführende Schlußhandlung vorbereitend zu profilieren. Die erzählerische Einbettung gelingt weiterhin durch ein schon früher in Sealsfields Werken nachgewiesenes planmäßiges Anlegen eines epischen Vorgangs in symmetrisch entworfene Bezüge, die als übergeordnete Klammer wirken. Diese personalen und, wie in der obigen Skizze erläutert, thematischen Symmetrieverhältnisse sind für die beiden herausragenden Figuren Morse und Murky die handlungsinternen Konvergenzbedingungen, unter denen ihr Zusammentreffen im Schlußteil angelegt wird.

Das am *Kajütenbuch* beobachtete differenzierte System der Erzählerhierarchie mit den für Sealsfields Erzählweise typischen Integrationsmerkmalen kann als ein wesentliches erzähltheoretisches Merkmal seiner Dichtung angesehen werden. Die schriftstellerische Absicht, die vor allem europäische Lesererwartung und der zeitgenössisch schwierige transatlantische Informationsfluß bedingen die Wahl der wechselnden Rollenerzähler und ihrer beglaubigenden Autorität. Der in der Ich-Erzählung des einzelnen Rollenberichtes implizierte Perspektivenwechsel von berichtetem erlebendem Ich und berichtendem Ich aktualisiert und distanziert die Mitteilungen, was ganz entscheidend den Leserreiz des Buches ausmacht. Darüberhinaus gelingt es dem Haupterzähler durch die Erzählerdelegation, dem Leser über die fingierte Sprechervielfalt zusätzlich auch Perspektivenvielfalt und damit ein scheinbar umfassendes Bild der Vereinigten Staaten zu vermitteln. Diese Perspektivenvielfalt erbringt aber keine individuell differenzierte Sicht der Welt, sondern lediglich Standpunktvariationen, in die der Erzähler sein gesellschaftspolitisch aufklärerisches Weltbild aufgelöst hat, um den Leser vermutlich nicht durch langatmiges Theoretisieren zu ermüden—Konzeptionsbruch bei der Rede des Alkalden! —, ihn vielmehr durch einen "erzählerischen Kostümwechsel" beständig neu zu motivieren.

Sealsfields Anliegen ist die gesellschaftspolitische Aufklärung in schriftstellerischer Form. Ausschlaggebend sind ihm die Personen und ihre Rede, weniger ihre Aktionen. So jedenfalls hat er es selbst festgelegt, wenn er die dichterischen Bedingungen von "Vergangenheit" und "Zukunft" als "historische Gewänder" versteht, "Liebesszenen und Abentheuer gelegentlich als Folie." Der Belehrungsauftrag wird also vor allem von den beauftragten Rollenerzählern vollzogen, die durch Monologe belehren (Morse/Phelim/Duncan: Zuhörerrunde; Alkalde: Bob/Morse; Bob: Johnny/Soldaten; Ready: spanischer Offizier usw.). Es sind Personen, die aufklärerisch-missionierend wirken wollen, eben "demokratische Aristokraten" mit geistig-politischem Führungsanspruch in einer patriarchalisch geordneten Gesellschaft, republikanisch im staatlichen Grundver-

ständnis und autoritär im wohlverstandenen Sinne einer delegierten
Autorität in Anerkennung besonderer Fähigkeiten. Löst man diese
herausgehobenen Personen aus dem Erzählgeschehen und vereinigt
sie zur Gruppe, dann ergibt sich über ihre beruflichen Spitzen-
stellungen bzw. sonstigen führenden Tätigkeiten eine allen gemeinsam eigene Inkognito-Sphäre: der General (Armee: erst spät
bekennt Morse seine Beförderung); der Bankpräsident (Finanz-
wirtschaft: die Verwandtschaftsbeziehung zu Morse wird erst spät
offen gelegt); der Richter (Justiz: der eigentliche Name des Alkalden bleibt unbekannt); der Kriminelle (Subkultur: Bobs richtiger
Name bleibt unbekannt); der Siedler (Pflanzer: der Namenwechsel
von Ready zu Murky bleibt ungeklärt). Die individualisierende
Benennung dieser Personen, entweder verzögert, verschleiert oder
gar nicht durchgeführt, und ihre Funktion der personalen Ver-
einzelung vermeidet der Erzähler zugunsten einer nunmehr eher
möglichen stellvertretenden gesellschaftlichen Rolle, unterstützt
durch die diesen Personen bewußt übertragenen Repräsentativ-
funktionen. Diese Zusammenhänge erinnern an Sealsfields eigene
pseudonyme Existenz, die ihn erst hat frei werden lassen für ein,
nach seiner Auffassung, repräsentatives politisch-schriftstellerisches
Sprechen. Diese Befugnis scheint symbolisch auch den vier wichtigen Rollensprechern des Romans übertragen worden zu sein,
denn sie vertreten die vier elementaren Staatsbereiche und erinnern so in ihrer herausgehobenen politisch-gesellschaftlichen Funktion an den "Rat der Geprüften," an jenes staatszentrale Führungs-
gremium in Bolzanos Staatsutopie, das durch ein autoritär-
patriarchalisches Regiment die demokratische Grundordnung
bewahrt.[9]

II

Der Einzelne, so haben wir festgestellt, impliziert in der Erzählerhierarchie den anderen, den Vorgänger, Stellvertreter, Mit-
kämpfer, den Lehrer, den Freund und den Feind, letztlich das
personale Kontinuum der Gesellschaft der Menschheit. Diesem
erzählerischen Prozeß der personalen Ausweitung entspricht die
Behandlung von Raum und Zeit als Raumausweitung und Zeitaustiefung. Für Landschaft und Raum bedeutet der beobachtete
Perspektivenwechsel auf Grund der erzählenden Doppelexistenz

des Rollensprechers, als erzählendes Ich erzählte Landschaft und als erzähltes Ich erlebende Landschaft mitzuteilen. Die für den in der Lektüre fortgeschrittenen Leser immer unmerklicheren Übergänge im kontinuierlichen Wechsel der Erzählhaltung suggerieren den aus verschiedenen Gründen bedingten landschaftlichen Wandel, indem erinnerter Landschaftszustand und erinnertes Landschaftserlebnis mit dem Kommentar aus der Erzählergegenwart bruchlos verknüpft werden. Vergegenwärtigen wir uns das an einem Textbeispiel: 1. "Ich kam an mehreren wunderschönen Inseln . . . vorbei. 2. Es haben aber diese Inseln so wie überhaupt die Wälder in Texas das Eigentümliche, daß ihre Baumarten nicht gemischt . . . sind . . . 1. Mehrere dieser herrlichen Inseln betrat ich."[10] Erlebniserinnerung und Gegenwartskommentar aktualisieren Vergangenes, verknüpfen es mit der Gegenwart und kennzeichnen so das Kontinuierliche an dem kulturgeschichtlichen Prozeß einer politischen und wirtschaftlichen, also moralisch berechtigten Landnahme. Die Raumillusion ist also weniger ein Ergebnis der raumschaffenden Aktion des Helden und seiner Begleitpersonen, sondern die erzählende Personengruppe, die über sich als agierende Helden berichtet, deren Aktionen von der Zielformel eines aufgeklärten konservativen Amerikanismus bestimmt sind, entwirft über die Reihe der Einzellandschaften das stimmige Raumgefüge: Keine Raumkette, wie sie der reisende Held in Eichendorffs Romanen aufbaut, vielmehr Rauminseln unterschiedlicher geographischer und kultureller Zuständlichkeiten, verbunden durch den erzählerischen "Brückenschlag" der Geschichte.

Wenden wir uns nach diesen Vorüberlegungen dem Raumverständnis im einzelnen zu. Weil wir an anderer Stelle schon ausführlich darüber berichtet haben, sehen wir hier davon ab, auf den erzählerischen Landschaftsaufbau noch einmal einzugehen.[11] Genau so wie die Informationsabsicht des Erzählers repräsentativ funktionierenden Rollenerzähler sind die von ihnen berichteten Räume exemplarisch bedeutungsvoll zu verstehen. Jost Hermands Stichwort vom "Raumroman" ist in diesem Zusammenhang so zutreffend wie irreführend.[12] Der vor allem landschaftliche Raum stellt sich zwar als roman-übergreifendes Raumgefüge dar, als eine Bühne kontinentalen Ausmaßes für die Darbietung der Szenen amerikanischer Kulturgeschichte des frühen 19. Jahrhunderts, aber der Raum in seiner horizontalen wie vertikalen Erstreckung, als

Außenraum und Innenraum ist ein funktional von der Aktion der zahlreichen Personen und Gruppierungen bestimmtes Mosaik der Schauplatzfelder, bar jeder Zufälligkeit, in symmetrischer Komposition kunstvoll angelegt. Der Funktionswert, den die jeweiligen Erzähler zu erkennen geben, liegt in dem gedanklichen Zusammenhang begründet, denn Landschaft ist bei aufklärerisch-pragmatischer Perspektive vor allem nützlicher Raum. Raum ist: 1. augenfällig erlebbares säkularisiertes Sinnbild immerwährender göttlicher Schöpfer- und Erhaltungskraft, von hoher pädagogischer Wirksamkeit (vgl. Morses Jacinto-Erlebnis, u.a. sein Hinweis: Landschaft als "die Vorhalle des Tempels des Herrn."[13] 2. Beispielhaft gemeintes wirtschaftliches und kulturelles Entwicklungsobjekt (z. B. Wildnislandschaft der Texas-Prärien), Zeichen wirtschaftlicher, kultureller, moralischer Fehlentwicklung (z.B. Philadelphia und die Verurteilung Kapitän Readys), bei Sealsfield degradiert zu Herkunftsräumen zukünftiger Bürger des Westens, die schon moralisch gefestigt sind (Ready) oder erst umerzogen werden müssen (Morse). 3. Bevor sich die demokratisch-patriarchalische Agrargesellschaft etablieren kann, muß der Raum militärisch gesichert werden. Motiviert durch eine nicht ganz unproblematische Missionsidee, einer z.t. diffusen Mischung von natürlichem, politischem und religiösem Anrecht (vgl. Staatstheorie des Alkalden), das mit Gewalt durchgesetzt wird, hat Landschaft bis in die menschlich noch verwaltbare Raumtiefe in Besitz genommen zu werden, um dann als natürliche (Prärie), politische (mexikanische Herrschaft) und kulturelle "Wildnislandschaft" (katholische Kirche) verändert zu werden. 4. Landschaft ist in letzter Funktion als Aktionsfeld des von einer aufklärerischen Staatsidee geführten Menschen politischer Raum, in dem Gesellschafts- und Herrschaftsstrukturen entstanden sind und entstehen, die dem Raum seine historische Dimension geben, indem geschichtliche Prozesse in ihrem weltverändernden Ablauf verräumlicht und Raumbedingungen, die die gesellschaftliche Entwicklung bestimmen, verzeitlicht werden.

Bei diesen typenhaft geordneten Raumfunktionen sind zusätzlich des Erzählers klar erkennbare Dimensionsstaffelungen und Bedeutungsrelationen der unterschiedlichen Raumweiten zu berücksichtigen. Die Menschen bewegen sich in Innenräumen und Außenräumen, die in der Ausgestaltung personengebundene Bezugsräume sind mit der Ergänzungsfunktion, dieses "environment"

über die romaninterne Aufgabe von Stimmungsbild und Charakter-
kennzeichnung hinaus als exotisch interessante, geographisch-
volkskundlich und kulturgeschichtlich-politisch lehrreiche Raum-
kulisse zu verstehen. So begrenzt wie Sealsfields sprachliches und
kompositorisches Repertoire bei der Beschreibung von Raum trotz
scheinbar gegensätzlicher Lektüreerfahrung tatsächlich ist, genauso
konsequent eng und damit leicht überschaubar erweisen sich die
Grundformen erlebter Raumtypen. Haus und Natur als Innen-
raummöglichkeiten sind in der einen Form modisch-behagliche
Wohnkultur (Farmhaus des Alkalden/Cottage, Kajüte des Kapitäns)
und in der anderen dekorativ-behagliche Florakomposition (Wein-
laubhöhle als militärische Deckung im texanischen Unabhängig-
keitskrieg/"Paradies"—Garten des Kapitäns), in beiden Fällen also
Innenräume in der Tradition des Idyllen-Genre aus der Literatur
des 18. Jahrhunderts wie z.B. Wielands *Agathon*. In diesem Zusammenhang des Personen/Raum-Bezugs gelten solche Milieube-
dingungen nur für die im Sinne Sealsfields vorbildlichen Persönlich-
keiten, während den gesellschaftlichen und politischen Kontrast-
figuren (Johnny/Kapitän Cotton, Kommandant von Galveston)
Blockhäuser primitiver Bauart mit unkultiviertem, vernachlässigtem
Inneren zugeordnet werden. Interessant ist, wie also diese Personen
durch den Raum, den sie prägen und der sie kennzeichnet, definitiv
als gut oder böse gekennzeichnet sind, der "unbehauste" Bob
dagegen, zwischen Johnnys Blockhaus und des Alkalden Cottage
pendelnd, die moralisch noch rettbare Existenz verkörpert, die der
Alkalde wortreich ankündigt, tatkräftig unterstützt und während
seines Sterbens mit der symbolischen Geste der "Schmerzensmut-
ter" erfüllt. Entsprechend ambivalent ist die Innenraumqualität
unter dem "Patriarchen" als Raum rechtlich-moralischer und
sakaraler Geborgenheit (Alkalde als Richter/Grabstätte des Ermordeten), aber auch unheimlich als Stätte der Mordtat, des
Todesurteils und der Hinrichtung.

Diese Innenraumbedingungen werden ergänzt durch die zwei
Formen des erlebten Außenraums, den Überblick vom festen
Standort und die panoramisch-kursorische Beschreibung vom be-
weglichen Standort. Analog funktional erweist sich die Außen-
raumqualität, orientiert an der vom Erzähler als optimal bestimmten Form des Einklangs von agrarwirtschaftlich tätigen Menschen
mit entsprechend kultivierter Landschaft und politisch-sozial

patriarchalisch gefügter Agrargesellschaft der Großgrundbesitzer. Kompositorisch daher keineswegs zufällig läßt der Erzähler den General Morse einmal vom Alkalden, dem Lehrer in gesellschafts-politischer Theorie und dann vom Kapitän Murky, dem Lehrer in gesellschaftlich-praktischem Leben, jeweils vor deren auf einer Anhöhe liegenden Häuser führen und von dort im Überblick die natürlich gewordene Idylle der vom Menschen gestalteten Agrarlandschaft demonstrieren.[14] In beiden Szenen, eingeschlossen die Schauplatzidylle des sogenannten "Paradieses" (sic!), schränken überzeichnete Harmonie und eigentümlich statische Zuständlichkeit den unterlegten missionarischen Ernst einer Meldung von einem im biblischen Sinne urtypisch angelegten Leben ein. Die letzte kategorisierbare Form erzählter Landschaft ist die panoramische Beschreibung durch den Erzähler oder selbst den unmittelbar erlebenden Helden, der sich durch den Raum bewegt und ihn so erschließt. Landschaft ist dabei Durchgangsraum, im regionalen wie vor allem pädagogisch-moralischen Sinne, dessen Erscheinungsform zwischen paradiesischer Idylle und höllischem Chaos schwanken kann, je nach Erzählerperspektive als tatsächliche Naturbedingung oder innerpersönlich seelisches Erlebnis. Der Irritt von Morse kann hier für beispielhaft gelten.

Als Zwischenergebnis kann also gesagt werden, daß der Raum vor allem als Zielobjekt menschlicher Tätigkeit verstanden wird, formbar und damit menschlichen Ideen von Gesellschaft und Welt anpaßbar. Raum ist damit auch Demonstrationsobjekt in der Weise von Vorbildlichkeit und Abwegigkeit. So erfolgt im Innenraum die Aufklärung durch die menschliche Rede, im Außenraum besonders durch die Erscheinung der Natur und den ihr immanenten religiösen Urkräften. Jede Aufklärung bei Sealsfield ist positiv verheißend, führt beispielhaft ungeordnete und geordnete Räume vor, deren letzte Form in der literarischen Gestaltung nach den Kriterien der überlieferten Idyllentradition von Sealsfield unkritisch gestaltet wird: ein deutliches Zeichen für des Dichters aufklärerisch-konventionelles Denken.

Die vom Helden erlebte Landschaft wird zur geographisch markierten Stationskette bis zu teilweise weltweiter Ausdehnung, wenn es nicht mehr um die Beispielhaftigkeit des Einzelschicksals geht, sondern um die Beispielhaftigkeit eines historischen Vorgangs, zwar getragen von Einzelpersönlichkeiten, aber historisch und damit auch räumlich anders dimensioniert. Der texanische Unabhängigkeitskrieg gegen Mexico stellt eine solche Aktionsfolge dar, die in diesem Falle fast als Berichterstattung eines Krieges durch die Mitteilung geographisch verbindlicher Fixpunkte in der Erzählung auch als das raumweite Unternehmen erscheinen kann, das es tatsächlich gewesen ist. Entsprechend der Weltsicht Sealsfields, daß sich nämlich im Einzelnen die Weltgeschichte wiederholt bzw. von ihm mitgetragen wird, gestaltet der Erzähler dieses Einzelschicksal in individuell bezogenen Räumen (Morse), das Gruppenschicksal in historisch-geographisch verbindlich, aber in den Details nur kursorisch skizzierten Großräumen (Morse/Alkalde/Austin und die texanische Armee), das Menschheitsschicksal (Normannen, Spanier usw.) in kontinentalen Raumbezügen. Das exemplarisch gesellschaftlich-philosophische Rollenspiel des Alkalden gewinnt seine Autorität aus den kenntnisreichen Verweisen des Sprechers, mit dem er die Weltgeschichte der Politik und Philosophie und deren geistige Herkunftsräume durch weltumspannende Markierungen kennzeichnet. Sealsfields epische Räume sind nur scheinbar begrenzt, denn so wie sich in der baulich bestimmten Raummenge des Alkalden-Hauses nur zwei Personen gegenübersitzen, genau so sprengt der Vortrag des Alkalden diese Enge und überträgt beiden Personen nahezu die Stellvertreterfunktion der Menschheit, ein vielleicht anmaßendes, aber zumindest deutliches Zeichen für den politischen Anspruch Sealsfields. In diesem Raumverständnis spiegelt sich die biographische Erfahrung des Dichters, zumeist räumlich beengt und zurückgezogen zu wohnen aber geistig weiträumig zu denken.

Der nachgewiesene wechselweise Bezug von Raum und Mensch ist erzähltheoretisches Merkmal, das aber nicht unbedingt als erzählpraktische Folge einer originellen poetologischen Konzeption zu werten ist. Dieser Bezug und seine besonderen Merkmale sind des Dichters erzählspezifische Konsequenzen aus seiner Einsicht in den kulturgeschichtlichen Prozess, in dem sich das Leben in Amerika des frühen 19. Jahrhunderts befand. Reale Strukturen überträgt Sealsfield auf fiktive Vorgänge literarischer Gestaltung. Die historische Wirklichkeit prägt den dichterischen Nachvollzug als "faktische Poesie." So entspricht die Erzählerhierarchie der Kommunikationsstruktur der Zeit, die von den Informationsprinzipien der Erinnerung an Erlebtes und deren vorwiegend mündlicher Weitergabe bestimmt war. Glaubwürdigkeit konnte nur über den namentlich zitierten Augenzeugen erlangt werden, den man zur näheren Charakterisierung mit Namen und geographischer Herkunft vorstellte. Die Fluktuation der amerikanischen Bevölkerung mit den Grundformen der nachrückenden Einwanderer aus Europa, der binnenkolonisatorischen Wanderungsbewegung aus den Neuenglandstaaten in die periodisch angegliederten Staaten des Westens und Südens, das Überwechseln in die Kampfzone des Frontiergebietes schafft bei den daran Beteiligten Herkunfts-, Transit- und Zielräume, deren Namen sie als Vertreter einer mobilen Gesellschaft zur Eigenkennzeichnung mit sich führen und deren Mitteilung raumweitende Funktion besitzt. Für Sealsfields literarische Arbeit bedeuten diese selbst erlebten Bedingungen äußerst wirksame Kriterien, wie erinnerter Raum oder erlebender Raum der Gegenwartshandlung, geographische Herkunftsattribute bei Personen (Morse/Maryland, Ready/Philadelphia, Oberst Bentley/Virginia, Baron M./Louisiana usw.), Sachen im weitesten Sinne (Kentucky-Rifle, Louisiana-Kirschholz, englische Sessel und Sofas, türkische Ottomane, österreichische Musikschränke usw.) und Ideen (vgl. den Vortrag des Alkalden mit den Verweisen auf Norwegen, England, Ägypten, Algerien usw.).

Raum ist also besonders Aktions- und Zielraum des politisch, militärisch, wirtschaftlich und kulturell tätigen Menschen. Er muß daher zum einen Raum der Konfrontation von Einzelnen (Bob/Morse, einsamer Reiter, Johnny, Alkalde; Ready/spanischer Offizier; Morse/Alkalde) und von Gruppen bzw. Völkern (Texas: Mexico/USA; Peru: Spanier/Peruaner usw.) werden. Die räumliche Begrenzung des Aufeinandertreffens wird wiederum dadurch ausgeweitet, daß beide Parteien nach den Bedingungen ihrer räumlichen und ideellen Herkunft geschildert werden: Alkalde/europäische Philosophie—Morse/Nordstaatlerdenken—Bob/Frontiergesetz von Sodoma—Peruaner vor Callao/Unabhängigkeitsphilosophie Bolivars usw. Sealsfields Gesellschafts- und Weltbild ist aber auf Harmonie hin angelegt. Ist eine Verständigung oder auch Versöhnung eingetreten, so verlieren die diesbezüglich zugeordneten und entsprechend beschriebenen Räume ihre einengende Raumgrenze und den ihr u.U. zugeteilten Negativwert: Alkalde/Bob—neuer Staat/Problem Frontierzone; Ready/Philadelphiaeinwohner—Süd-Staaten und Nord-Staaten; Morse/Kajütengesellschaft—Texas/

Louisiana bzw. Union. Der Raum ist ein wesentlicher Teil der agrargesellschaftlichen Verfassungsvorstellung des Dichters. Darum kann man von kontrastiven Räumen sprechen, die seiner Idee von Raumgestalt und Gesellschaftsstruktur entgegenstehen (Stadtlandschaft, Neuenglandstaaten), von affirmativen Räumen, die vorbildliche Funktion bestätigen (natürliche, agrarwirtschaftlich bestimmte oder häuslich-gärtnerisch gestaltete Idylle) und von antizipatorisch wirksamen Räumen, die kommende Entwicklung möglich erscheinen lassen (Texas, Peru). Sealsfields amerikanische Landschaften und die durch sie gestaltete Raumauffassung sind exemplarische Teilräume eines Kontinents, spezifisch beschrieben und beispielhaft für die Entwicklung amerikanischen Lebens im Sinne seiner Weltanschauung von weltweit gültiger symbolischer Bedeutung zu verstehen.

III

Der Autor Sealsfield schätzt die vorausdeutenden Leistungen von direkten und fiktiven Einleitungen und Vorworten, in denen er bestimmte Zusammenhänge ankündigt, mögliche Lesererwartung im voraus korrigiert und vorzugsweise die nachfolgenden Ausführungen auf eventuell unzutreffende Interpretation hin kommentiert und rechtfertigt. Die meist allgemein geschichtlich und poetologisch belehrenden Proömien sind unübersehbares Merkmal seines insgesamt aufklärerisch angelegten Werkes, im besonderen Maße auch des *Kajütenbuchs*. Das Understatement, mit dem der fiktive Herausgeber die unter Umständen an das Buch herangetragene "Prätension auf eigentlichen geschichtlichen Wert" bescheiden abwehrt, wird aber gleich anschließend durch einen rhetorischen 'Trick' wieder aufgehoben, indem der anonyme Leser, als "der tiefer Blickende" geschmeichelt, zu einer aufs Historische zu achtenden Lektüre ermuntert wird.[15] Fragen wir nun nach der Funktion der 'Geschichte,' verstanden als entstehendes und entstandenes Aktionsmuster, vollzogen von vielen Personen in bestimmten Räumen und Zeitspannen, erlebt und vor allem erinnert und berichtet.

Zeit ist vorzüglich erinnerte Zeit, d.h. Geschichte. Das beweisen schon die Relationen von erzählter Zeit und Erzählzeit sowie von Gegenwarts- und Vorzeithandlung. Der Umfang der eingefügten

Vorzeithandlungen, also die Berichte der Rollenerzähler, belegen mit der historisch dimensionierten Zeitaustiefung des Erzählten von der dreitägigen Gegenwartshandlung um 1837 bis in die Anfänge der Menschheitsgeschichte die dominante Rolle von Erinnerung und Geschichte. Diese Zeitaustiefung steht in erzählerischer Spannung zu der annähernden Übereinstimmung von Erzählzeit und objektivem Zeitverlauf, zumindest gültig für den Erzählabend des 1. Tages in der "Kajüte," der bis zum nächsten Morgen um 4 Uhr andauert. Die dann folgende Gegenwartshandlung umfaßt weitere 1½ Tage, die in zeitraffender Kürze mit Handlung gefüllt wird und lediglich ein Fünftel der Erzählzeit ausmacht. Wenden wir uns daher besonders der Frage der erzählerischen Funktion von Erinnerung und Geschichte als berichteter Vorzeithandlung zu.

Alle Personen sind auffällig an der Vergangenheit interessiert. Alle erinnern sich an Personen, an Handlungen, an Räume: Morse erinnert sich des Farmers Neal, des Alkalden und Bobs, Johnnys, der Kriegskameraden usw.; er erinnert sich an den Jacinto-Irritt, die Pflege in Johnnys Blockhaus, das Gespräch mit dem Alkalden, an Bobs Verurteilung und Hinrichtung und an die Landschaft der Golfküste, Johnnys Blockhaus, des Alkalden Cottage, die Prärie von Texas usw. Der erinnerte Alkalde erinnert sich an lokale und weltweite Ereignisse seiner Erzählergegenwart und der Vergangenheit. So erinnern sich der erinnerte Bob, Onkel Duncan, Alexandrine usw. Wir brauchen das im einzelnen nicht mehr auszuführen. Erinnertes Geschehen dient nicht nur der Unterhaltung, sondern —gemäß der aufklärerischen Erzählabsicht des Dichters—das Erinnerte wird zum Erfahrungsstoff, zum Material für die anschauliche Belehrung anderer. Über das Erinnerte belehrt jeder jeden: der Alkalde und Bob den jungen Morse, dieser die Mississippi-Gents und Alexandrine, der Alkalde Bob und die Texas-Soldaten, Duncan belehrt Morse und umgekehrt, Bob den Johnny, Ready den spanischen Offizier usw. Alle betreiben untereinander wohlgemeinte Aufklärung aus der sicheren Überzeugung der eigenen erinnerten Erfahrung und darauf begründeten Weltanschauung. Aber dieses vielfältige Sprechen ist als poetologisches Konzeptionsmerkmal lediglich erzählte Sprechervielfalt, gesteuert und kontrolliert vom Autor, für den die Sprechervielfalt als dichterisch interessantes 'Stimmengewirr' chorische Wiedergabe eines Leitthemas ist. Hierin liegt ein weiteres Integrationsmoment dieses durch ein lockeres Erzählgerüst scheinbar so wenig geschlossenen Romans. Die erinnerten Zusammenhänge laufen als Teilaspekte in der Geschichte von den Vereinigten Staaten und ihrem großen Demokratie-Experiment zusammen, finden sich letztlich als Erfahrungssumme eines unentwegten Geschichtsprozesses verstanden, wie ihn der Alkalde aufzeigt: Die Erinnerung an die Vergangenheit, das Ausfiltern des gesellschaftspolitisch sowie moralisch Behaltenswerten und dessen Weitergabe in der Belehrung antizipieren gleichzeitig Zukunft. Diese Zukunft ist ausschließlich auf die agrargesellschaftliche Erschließung des Westens und Südwestens der Vereinigten Staaten gerichtet, vorbildlich gelebt von dem Alkalden, von Murky und, mit Einschränkungen, von allen anderen in Natchez, die ihren ursprünglichen Beruf aufgegeben haben, um als Mitglieder einer patriarchalisch geordneten Pflanzergesellschaft Raum im Kulturraum zu formen. Morses Verbindung mit Alexandrine ist die symbolisch wegweisende menschliche und politische Union, die Demonstration des Glaubens an die Familie als intakten Mikrokosmos, der die zukünftige Entwicklung trägt, die— so verheißt es ja der Romanschluß—mit Sicherheit stattfinden wird. Daß diese Verheißung aber schon Züge des Utopischen aufweist, ahnte Sealsfield wohl schon, denn die von ihm geschilderte Idylle der Liebenden charakterisiert das ätherisch Unwirkliche des zu Wünschenden, aber nicht mehr Realisierbaren. Was hier noch verbindlich erscheint, bleibt in dem nachfolgenden Roman *Süden und Norden* offen: das junge Paar im handlungsparallelen Romanschluß kommt als Kajüten-Passagiere des Auswandererschiffs "Hornet" in der für sie "neuen Welt" nicht an. Die Zukunft der eigenen Weltanschauung ist für Sealsfield später fragwürdig geworden. Eine erzählerische Zeitdimension fällt weg, das politische und poetologische Konzept ist gestört. Sealsfields persönliche und fiktive Welt ist zur Stagnation verurteilt.

Die so in Geschichten erzählte Geschichte kann nur durch die Mittel von Zeitraffung und Zeitsprung gestaltet werden. Aber mit dem Gebrauch dieser Möglichkeiten gelingt es, wie in keinem anderen Buch Sealsfields, die Zeitaustiefung der schmalen Frist der Gegenwartshandlung vom Kulturbeginn der Menschheit und über den immanenten Vorausdeutungswert des zitierten idealen Weltzustandes bis zu einem nicht unproblematischen statischen Zustand

zukünftigen Daseins zu vollziehen. Die Rückerinnerung läßt also
die Romanhandlung nicht zur distanzierenden Geschichtsschreibung werden, sondern weist als ausschließlich aufbauende Vorzeithandlung in die schon begonnene Zukunft. Es ist faszinierend, wie
der Erzähler z.B. über Morse und den Alkalden aus der Erzählergegenwart und dem Schauplatz des engen Kajüteninnenraums
durch drei Erinnerungsebenen die Gegenwartshandlung und den
Gegenwartsraum ausweitet und austieft: 1. Morse: Alkalde/Bob;
Jacinto-Prärie. 2. Alkalde/Bob: Geschichte der Vereinigten Staaten;
Frontier-Zone. 3. Alkalde: Zeitgeschichte bis zur ägyptischen Früh-
geschichte; Welt-Raum. Im Schnittpunkt dieses Koordinatensys-
tems von Raum und Zeit, in der erzählten Auswertung von Welt
und Geschichte stehen die symbolisch gemeinten Helden Morse
und Alexandrine. Über die berichtete welthistorische und global-
geographische Entwicklung der Menschheit führen die Wege zu
diesen beiden Menschen, die in ihrem gegenwärtigen und zukünftigen Schicksal gebündelt erscheinen. Die Welt wird in die Raum-
enge einer individuellen Schauplatzhandlung hereingeholt und
spiegelt sich im *exemplum,* wie umgekehrt das Beispiel auf die
Welt verweist. So vollzieht sich in drei Tagen erzählter Zeit der
Gegenwartshandlung ein Stück Geschichte, aus dessen Kontinuum
die flüchtige Phase des Gegenwartsmoments, das Ineinander-
übergehen von Vergangenheit in Zukunft dem Leser vorgeführt
wird. Die dreitägige dialektisch angelegte Ereignisfolge bringt am 1.
Tag die von zahlreichen Erzählern vorgetragenen Voraussetzungen
der bindenden Gesellschaftsordnung, die in der personalen, politischen und moralischen Vorbildlichkeit als Ergebnis historischer
Entwicklung autorisiert ist, eine ideologische Basis zu sein. Morse
wird dabei zum Exponenten dieser Gesellschaftsordnung. Der 2.
Tag ist der Tag Alexandrinens und ihrer gesellschaftlichen Bedingungen, in die Morse eingeführt wird. Am 3. Tag vollzieht sich die
Vereinigung, die Union, gesegnet von der amerikanischen Partner-
figur des texanischen Helden, für immer im sinnbildlichen Sakra-
ment der Ehe den Frontier-Mann Morse aus Texas, aus dem Westen
westlich des Mississippi, mit Alexandrine, der kultivierten Frau aus
Louisiana, östlich des Mississippi, zu verbinden. Auf ihre Frage
nach einer möglichen Trennung Morses d.h. Texas' von der Union
antwortet der Angesprochene mit einer nur rhetorisch gemeinten
Gegenfrage, in der Sealsfields Philosophie diffuses *mixtum compo-*

situm von Nationalismus und heiligem Naturrecht arg simplifiziert wird: "Kann sich trennen, was Natur und Blut und Erziehung vereinen?" Als "heimisch vaterländisch Trauliches" ist der persönliche Akt ein politischer Akt.[16]

Raum und Zeit sind für Sealsfield wesentliche Erzählelemente. Während Zeit als historisches Kontinuum von individuell-biographischen und national-geschichtlichen Aktionen vorgestellt wird, ist der Raum als Schauplatz die korrelative Komponente. Historisch fixierte Zeit und geographisch festgelegter Raum sind sicher nicht nur erzählerische "Gewänder"; es sind die Grundbedingungen des Erzählens, die sich wechselweise als Verräumlichung der Zeit und Verzeitlichung des Raumes bestimmen und dies als Funktionsfolge einer subtil gehandhabten erzählerdelegation, sowie der auf Vorausdeutung angelegten erinnerten Vorzeithandlungen. Aus diesem Zusammenhang ergibt sich die fast pulsierende Expansion und Reduktion von Raum zu Welt und Zeit zu Geschichte.

IV

Wir greifen die anfangs schon zitierte Annahme von Weiss noch einmal auf und sind auch mit ihm der Meinung, daß das *Kajütenbuch* im Gesamtwerk Sealsfields ein Text von herausragender erzähltheoretischer und weltanschaulicher Bedeutung ist. Keiner der anderen Romane ist von seiner Konzeption einer aufwendig komplexen Rollenerzählerhierarchie und der damit verbundenen Komposition ineinander gefügter Einzelerzählungen so auf den delegierten Erzählervortrag ausgerichtet wie gerade dieses Buch. In keinem anderen wird so ausgiebig theoretisiert, werden so bekenntnisfreudig Erfahrungen mitgeteilt, wird so viel doziert und belehrt. Kein anderes Buch enthält bereits den Addressaten in so ausgeprägter Form wie es die fiktive Männergesellschaft ist, die als eine Art zwischengeschaltetes Rezeptionsmedium das Mitgeteilte für den Leser durch ein vom Erzähler steuerbares Reaktionsverhalten verständnisgerecht präpariert, natürlich im Sinne des Autors. Auch die besondere Titelformulierung unterstreicht die Extraposition dieses Buches. Von ihr wollen wir für unsere Schlußüberlegungen ausgehen.

Sehen wir von den frühen journalistisch-dokumentarischen Schriften und dem letzten Roman *Süden und Norden* ab, so fällt bei den übrigen Titeln auf, daß sie in der einfachen Konjunktional-konstruktion inhaltsreiche Doppeltitel nach barockem und auf-klärerischem Vorbild sind, die regelhaft aus einem Personalteil und einem Raumteil bestehen: Allein beim *Kajütenbuch* ist es anders, und als zusätzliche Besonderheit erscheinen die sonst national-staatlichen oder kontinentalen Raumangaben auf einen engen Innenraum reduziert, dessen Benennung im Kompositum an das Substantiv "-buch" gebunden ist.

Das Vorderglied dieser für die deutsche Sprache außergewöhn-lichen Bezeichnung bezieht sich auf ein schiffskajütenähnliches Gebäude, das einer der Mississippi-Gents etwas spöttisch-unbehag-lich als "wahres Ungeheuer von Balken und Brettern" bezeichnet.[17] Für den verliebten Morse ist es das "Paradies," für den Erzähler—er sieht sich zur Korrektur der erwähnten Vorstellungen genötigt—"glich" es eher "der alttestamentarischen Arche oder auch einem schwedischen oder holländischen Vierundziebziger," aber auch "wieder mehr einem enormen vegetablischen Auswuchs denn Arche, Vierundsiebziger oder Herrenhaus."[18] In seiner Unbe-schreibbarkeit steht die "Kajüte" in der literarischen Tradition fiktiver und unbeschreibbarer Gebäude wie Goethes Turm in den *Wanderjahren,* Hoffmanns Haus des "Rat Krespel" oder Kafkas "Schloß," Gebäude, in denen wesentliche Entscheidungen getrof-fen, Erfahrungen Unerfahrenen mitgeteilt werden und Zukünftiges vorbereitet wird. Das "Dings," wie es einer der Mississippimänner ganz im Sinne des Erzählers neutralisierend nennt, ist in seinem spezifischen Äußeren nach nicht beschreibbar, in seiner Konstruk-tion phantastisch und insgesamt mit einem Zug des Märchenhaft-irrealen versehen.[19] Es gemahnt teilweise an marine Herkunft, aber auch an die Blockhaus- und Cottagekonstruktionen des ameri-kanischen Westens. Dieses undefinierbare, zwischen zwei Vor-stellungen nicht fixierbare Äußere korrespondiert auffällig mit der gleichfalls ambivalenten Bedeutung und etymologischen Herkunft der angloamerikanischen Vokabel "cabin."[20] Die diesem Wort implizierte Bedeutungsambivalenz von Blockhaus/Kajüte ist Seals-field, dem die englische Sprache vertraut ist, vermutlich so geläufig, daß er sie zu dieser symbolischen Titelgebung nutzt. So erweist sich die "Kajüte" in der Funktion des Blockhauses des Kapitäns Murky als Zeichen für die beständige Eroberung der Welt und Etablierung einer bestimmten Gesellschaft in Gegenwart und Zukunft. Als

imitierter Schiffsteil ist die "Kajüte" ein Zeichen für die Vor-
phase der kulturellen und politischen Tätigkeit, in der diese neuen
Räume mit dem Schiff erst erreicht werden müssen. Darüberhinaus
verweist das Symbol aber auch auf das dauernde Unterwegssein des
Menschen und seine notwendige Bereitschaft zum immer möglichen neuen Aufbruch. Die zentrale Funktion dieser Symbolik
archetypischen Zuschnitts wird vom Erzähler ausdrücklich mit dem
Verweis auf die biblische Arche unterstrichen, und diese biblische
Ursituation der Rettung, des Aufbruchs und des Neubeginns ist
mit der "Kajüte" und den Menschen in ihr gemeint. Die schicksal-
hafte Verbundenheit der patriarchalischen Farmergesellschaft ge-
rät schon fast zum resignativen Notsignal gegenüber der dem Dichter fremden wirtschaftlichen, technologischen und gesellschaftlichen Entwicklung im Norden der Vereinigten Staaten und in
Europa. Die "Kajüte" wird zum Reduktionsraum eines ideologisch
und damit existentiellen Mikrokosmos, zum sinnbildlichen Schutz-
raum angesichts einer möglichen "sintflutartigen" Veränderung der
Welt, zum Versammlungsraum für ideologische Fortbildung und
Solidaritätsbeweise. Die Zukunft aber bleibt trotz der symbolischen
Verbindung von Morse und Alexandrine undeutlich und verstärkt
den Eindruck, daß durch den Rückzug in die räumliche Enge, die
betont feste Bindung an die Vergangenheit durch Erinnerung und
die verklärte Schlußhandlung Sealsfields Resignation wirksam wird.
Die spürbare persönliche Betroffenheit des Dichters bestätigen zusätzlich die bekannten biographischen Umstände, denn in Louisiana
betrat Sealsfield zum erstenmal amerikanischen Boden, hier erwarb
er die amerikanische Staatsbürgerschaft, hier distanzierte er sich
auch namentlich von Europa und identifizierte sich im Pseudonym
mit einem bestimmten Teil des amerikanischen Lebens, das er als
Grundbesitzer in der Nähe von Natchez selbst zu verwirklichen
versuchte. Mit dem zitatweisen Gebrauch von Chateaubriands Erzählung *Atala* (1802) und einer ähnlich idyllischen Ausgestaltung
des Romanschlusses gelingt fast das Bekenntnis, daß die mit der
literarischen Fiktion angestrebte Realität Fiktion geblieben ist und
sich unaufhaltsam als antiquierte Utopie zu erkennen gibt.

Für Sealsfield scheint sich mit diesem Buch weltgeschichtlich
wie literarisch der Kreis der dichterischen Wirksamkeit zu schlies-
sen: im Doppelsymbol Kajüte/Blockhaus als Sinnbild des Auf-

bruchs und als Sinnbild des Rückzugs. Die Bitterkeit, mit der Sealsfield einen von ihm nicht mehr nachvollziehbaren Wandel der Welt, die zunehmende Unfähigkeit literarischer Reaktion und seinen parallel dazu erlebten physischen Verfall kommentiert, dieselbe Bitterkeit zeichnet auch Kapitän Murky aus, der wie Sealsfield seinen biographischen Fluchtraum der Pseudonymität zu Lebzeiten nicht mehr erklärt. Wie Sealsfield gewinnt auch er seine geistige und allgemein existentielle Identität und damit persönliche Freiheit erst durch die Veränderung der namentlichen Identität, die nicht nur dadurch Sealsfield und Murky, den Dichter und die von ihm geschaffene Person verwandt erscheinen lassen.

Bei der Ausdeutung des Romantitels darf der zweite Teil des Kompositums nicht unterschlagen werden. Es lassen sich in der deutschen Literaturgeschichte eine Fülle von Buchüberschriften nachweisen, in denen das Substantiv "Buch" enthalten ist, wie z.B. das *Marterbuch* (1320–1340), Wickrams *Rollwagenbüchlein* (1555) oder Heines *Buch der Lieder* (1827). Es soll ganz sicher damit auf die buchgewordene Besonderheit des Inhalts verwiesen werden, so u.a. auf die autobiographische Funktion (z.B. Tagebuch), die moralische oder fachwissenschaftliche Aufgabe (z.B. Regelbuch) oder den Sammlungsauftrag von Chroniken oder zyklisch geordneten Arbeiten. Sealsfields *Kajütenbuch* ist in diese Bezeichnungstradition einzuordnen und das damit besondere Buchverständnis bei seiner Beurteilung zu berücksichtigen. Die erwähnten Funktionen erscheinen hier gemischt, sind aber nachweisbar, und der Buch-Hinweis im Titel läßt somit diesen Roman auch als Buch grundsätzlicher Aussage erkennen. Vielleicht ist es als eine Art literarischen "Logbuches" anzusprechen, wenn man noch einmal an die marine Bedeutung von "cabin=Kajüte" denkt, an die Bezeichnung "log-cabin" und Carringtons Übersetzung von "Kajütenbuch" als "Log-cabin book."[21] Eingedenk der Neigung Sealsfields, angloamerikanische Formulierungen direkt ins Deutsche zu übertragen, kann eine solche Fehlübertragung von "Logbuch" als "Kajütenbuch" nicht ausgeschlossen werden. Alexandrines neckender Ausspruch, mit dem sie den Bankpräsidenten als "personifiziertes Hauptbuch" bezeichnet, läßt sich unter Vernachlässigung der eigentlichen Bedeutung des Wortes auf Sealsfields *Kajütenbuch* anwenden: sein literarisches Hauptbuch.

V

Wir haben versucht, die kompositionelle Struktur des *Kajüten-buchs* und die eingesetzten erzähltechnischen Mittel zu erläutern. Unsere Beobachtungen stützen die energischen Hinweise auf "die exemplarische Bedeutung dieses Buches" und seine "geschlossene Konzeption," wie sie Weiss gegenüber den oberflächlich urteilenden Ausführungen von Baumgart gibt.[22] In Ergänzung der schon früher mitgeteilten Kriterien einer bislang nicht genügend beachteten Werkhermetik, für das Gesamtwerk bestätigt durch die von Friesen am *Virey* beispielhaft nachgewiesenen Funktion des "panoramic scope" und einer von Weiss für das *Kajütenbuch* erläuterten "thematischen Gestaltenkonstellation," haben wir die von Morse selbst gebrauchte Formel der "Welt und Geschichte" als Perspektivbedingungen des Alkaldenvortrags zum Ausgangspunkt unserer Überlegungen genommen. Und in der Tat stellt diese Formel das erzählerische Zentrum dar, wenn man die damit verbundenen Erzählbedingungen von Raum und Zeit, die übergeordneten und eingearbeiteten Komplexe von Idee und Erfahrung sowie die damit gekoppelte Erzählerabsicht von Aufklärung als Belehrung und Korrektur genügend beachtet. Die Geschlossenheit der Konzeption ergibt sich also durch mehrere Bedingungen des Romans, über den ideengeschichtlich aufklärerischen Plan entsprechend der gesellschaftspolitischen Vorstellung, ferner die realistisch geschriebene Handlung mit den Beispielbedingungen der amerikanischen Demokratie in der amerikanischen Landschaft, weiter durch die romaninternen Symmetrieverhältnisse von gesellschaftspolitischer Theorie und deren praktischer Umsetzung. Ihre symbolisch gemeinte Bestätigung findet die Einheit des Romans in der personalen Union von Morse und Alexandrine als einer glücklichen Verbindung von praktisch bestimmter amerikanischer Welthaltung und politischer Erfahrung (Morse) mit theoretischer europäischer Welthaltung und kultureller Erfahrung (Alexandrine/Frankreich). Diese Zusammenhänge werden von Sealsfield im Titel des Romans zusätzlich thematisiert, wie wir es oben erläutert haben.

Nicht nur die Überwindung des zeitgenössisch poetologisch aktuellen "Antagonismus von Realismus und Tendenz" gelingt,[23] sondern mehr noch die Integration der verschiedenen Darstellungsweisen von journalistischem Realismus mit literarisch romantisch-frührealistischer Dichtung bei thematisch festgelegter politischer Tendenz. Entsprechend vielfältig sind die eingesetzten erzähltheoretischen Mittel. Um das Ziel der Erzählerabsicht zu erreichen, am speziellen Beispiel der Vereinigten Staaten möglichst allgemeingültige Ideenzusammenhänge demonstrieren zu können, weitet Sealsfield herkömmlich einfache Erzählstrukturen zu komplexer Strukturkomposition aus. Die Einzelperson des Helden wird zur Gestaltengruppe, die Einzelperspektive eines übergeordneten Erzählers oder erlebenden Helden zum Perspektivenfächer variiert. Die damit verbundene Erzählerdelegation führt über abgestufte Rückerinnerungsebenen von der Gegenwartshandlung zu Zeitaustiefung und Raumausweitung der gestaffelten Vorzeithandlungen, die wiederum verschränkt zueinander als Haupt- und Nebenhandlungen das subtile Erzählgeflecht des Romans bestimmen. Die zahlreich geschilderten individuellen "Lebensläufe nach aufsteigender Linie," ein interessantes Parallelmerkmal zu Hippels gleichnamigem Roman und zu den Romanen der deutschen Aufklärung,[24] und alle begleitend mitgegebenen Fakten lassen als erzählerisches Mosaik das gemeinte überpersönliche Lebensgesetz der gesellschaftspolitischen Vorstellungen des Dichters erkennen. Die so erzählerisch gebrochene Sukzession von Handlung und Mitteilungsfolge schließt sich wieder wie im Kaleidoskop zur beabsichtigten Kunstwirklichkeit zusammen, die als symbolisches Bild amerikanische Welt und Geschichte vermittelt, dabei aufklärerisch-ideale Welt und Geschichte meint.

Das *Kajütenbuch* läßt sich nicht in den thematisch und formal bestimmten Symmetriezusammenhang des erzählerischen Gesamtwerkes einordnen. Der fiktive Herausgeber selbst spricht von "Abwechslung und Zwangslosigkeit," von "Laune und Caprice" und betont über diese scheinbar mehr persönlich zufälligen Entstehungsbedingungen die besondere Rolle dieses vorliegenden Buches, indem er bestätigend auf den außergewöhnlichen politischen Anlaß der Niederschrift hinweist, den "Geschichtsmoment . . . der Gründung eines neuen anglo-amerikanischen Staates." Sealsfields auffällig betonte Verschleierung seines sonst schriftstellerisch planmäßigen Vorgehens, was ja auch durchaus seiner fixierten gesellschaftspolitischen Vorstellung und dem festgelegten Erzählerauftrag entspricht, und die Wahrnehmung eines aktuellen

politischen Ereignisses als Anlaß für die Erstellung dieses Buches
unterstreichen in dreifacher Hinsicht die Bedeutung dieses Romans:
biographisch—die wache Aufmerksamkeit, mit der er weiterhin die
transatlantische Geschichte verfolgt; ideengeschichtlich—die jour-
nalistisch schnelle Reaktion auf ein aktuelles, literarisch auswert-
bares politisches Geschehen als markantes Beispiel für die weitere
Mitteilung seines Weltbildes, dessen Glaubwürdigkeit er mehr und
mehr schwinden sieht; literarisch—die gleichzeitig gegebene Gelegenheit, mit diesem politischen Grundsatzbuch auch die erzähltheoretischen Einsichten in besonders prägnanter Form noch einmal vorzuführen.

Wir haben schon früher auf die sogenannte "Sleepy-Hollow"
Episode bei Hawthorne hingewiesen, auf den dort literarisch gestalteten Einbruch der gesellschaftlich und wirtschaftlich-technisch
orientierten "Neuzeit" in die ländliche Idylle.[25] Es bleibt Zufall,
ist aber Symptom, wenn auch Sealsfield seine "Sleepy-Hollow"-
Episode hat. Alexandrine und Morse befinden sich sinnbildlich
beide im Sleepy Hollow, wenn sie in diesem behaglichen Möbel
sitzt, und er davor kniet.[26] In diesem idyllischen Winkel warten sie
auf die Erfüllung einer "gütigen Vorsehung," die sie in "eine noch
unverkünstelte Natur und Zustände geleitet."[27] Sealsfield schirmt
seine Personen und sich gegen die Signale der "Neuzeit" ab und
führt sie in die Reduktion einer utopisch gewordenen Lebens-
konzeption.

NOTES

1. Textgrundlage: Charles Sealsfield, *Das Kajütenbuch*, München, 1963. (= dtv 118).

2. Hartmut Steineckes kritische Bemerkungen zum Stand der Sealsfield-Forschung, die erst in den letzten Jahren "ihren desolaten Zustand" überwunden habe und auch in jüngsten Beiträgen wenig "über das Romanverständnis" aussage, werden allzu pauschal vorgetragen und beachten nicht gründlich genug die vorliegenden Resultate. Dennoch ist Kritik weiterhin gerechtfertigt, hat man sich bislang doch zu sehr um die biographisch und inhaltlich erläuternde Bestandsaufnahme bemüht, zu wenig um Fragen der Romankonzeption und der Struktur des epischen Vorgangs. (Vgl. Hartmut Steinecke, *Romantheorie und Romankritik in Deutschland*, Band 1, Stuttgart 1975, S. 275, Anmerkung 20; Alexander Ritter, "Forschungsbericht: Charles Sealsfield (Karl Postl), Die Deutung seines Werkes zwischen Positivismus und Funktionalität, europäischer Geistesgeschichte und amerikanischer Literaturgeschichte." In: *Literatur in Wissenschaft und Unterricht*, 4, 1971, S. 270–288).

3. Eduard Castle, *Der große Unbekannte, Das Leben von Charles Sealsfield (Karl Postl), Briefe und Aktenstücke*, Wien 1955, S. 291 f.

4. Walter Weiss, "Der Zusammenhang zwischen Amerikathematik und Erzählkunst bei Charles Sealsfield." In: *Litwiss. Jb. d. Görres-Ges.*, 8, 1967, S. 113 f.

5. Alexander Ritter, *Darstellung und Funktion der Landschaft in den Amerika-Romanen von Charles Sealsfield (Karl Postl). Eine Studie zum Amerika-Roman der deutschen und amerikanischen Literatur in der ersten Hälfte des 19. Jahrhunderts*, Diss. Kiel 1969, S. 237, Anm. 1.

6. Auf Sealsfields geistige Bindung an die politische, kulturelle und katholisch-religiöse Aufklärung des zeitgenössischen Österreichs und seines Prager Lehrers Bernard Bolzano haben wir an anderer Stelle aufmerksam gemacht: Alexander Ritter, "Charles Sealsfields gesellschaftspolitische Vorstellungen und ihre dichterische Gestaltung als Romanzyklus." In: *Jb. d. Schiller-Ges.*, 8, 1973, S. 395–414.

7. Vgl. Weiss, "Amerikathematik," S. 109.

8. *The Shorter Oxford English Dictionary*, 3. Aufl., Oxford 1970.

9. Vgl. Ritter, "Vorstellungen," S. 400.

10. *Kajütenbuch*, S. 36.

11. Vgl. Ritter, *Landschaft*, S. 138–190.

12. Jost Hermand, *Die literarische Formenwelt des Biedermeier*, Giessen 1958, S. 144 f. (= Beiträge zur deutschen Philologie Bd. 27).

13. *Kajütenbuch*, S. 19.

14. *Ebd.*, S. 8.

15. *Ebd.*

16. *Ebd.*, S. 291.

17. *Ebd.*, S. 214.

18. *Ebd.*, S. 306 f.

19. *Ebd.*, S. 214.

20. *The Shorter Oxford English Dictionary*, 3. Aufl., Oxford 1970, S. 244, vgl. auch S. 1161.

21. Ulrich S. Carrington, *The Making of an American, An Adaptation of Memorable Tales by Charles Sealsfield*, Dallas 1974, S. 13. (=Bicentennial Series in American Studies, II).

22. Wolfgang Baumgart, Nachwort zu: *Charles Sealsfield, Das Kajütenbuch*, München 1963, S. 322 ff.

23. Steinecke, *Romantheorie*, S. 108.

24. Theodor Gottlieb von Hippel, *Lebensläufe nach aufsteigender Linie*, Berlin 1778/81.

25. Vgl. Ritter, "Vorstellungen," S. 412.

26. *Kajütenbuch*, S. 292.

27. *Ebd.*, S. 293.

9. Johann Georg Wesselhöft and the German Book Trade in America
Robert E. Cazden

During the 1830s no one more singlemindedly championed the
cause of German culture in America than Johann Georg Wesselhöft (1805-1859), publisher of the *Alte und neue Welt* in Philadelphia and for a short while the premier German bookseller in
the land. Aside from his friend Gustav Körner's affectionate biography, Wesselhöft's career has been undervalued, perhaps because
the conventional indices of worldly success were lacking. He was
not a politician like Körner or Franz Joseph Grund,[1] never attended a German university, and his Philadelphia affairs ended in
bankruptcy. For whatever reason, Wesselhöft does not even rate
passing mention in Albert B. Faust's *German Element in the
United States* (1927). His reputation also suffered from a lack of
available primary sources, all the more regrettable since he faithfully kept a diary, wrote or at least began an account of his
American travels, composed an autobiography that was consulted
by Körner and carried on an extensive correspondence. Of all this,
only two letters to his old friend Heinrich Zschokke have been
recovered.[2]

The Wesselhöfts were a large and prosperous clan with branches
in North Germany and Thuringia. Johann Georg Wesselhöft was
born in Meyendorf, Hannover, not far from Bremen, and grew up
in poorer circumstances than most of his kinsmen for his father
was not a success in business and had to call on his young son for
help. A good collection of books at home made some amends for
an erratic formal education; but there was no money for a university degree. Instead, at the age of fifteen young Wesselhöft was
sent to Jena to learn the book trade with his uncles Friedrich
Frommann and Carl Wesselhöft. The years spent in Jena were a
hard apprenticeship from which Johann Georg later traced the
seeds of chronic ill health. There were compensations—the society

of his relations and the stimulation of living in a university town.[3]

Frommann's drawing room was a center of cultural life in Jena, with the septuagenarian Goethe, who had formed an attachment to Frommann's adopted daughter Wilhelmine Herzlieb, a frequent guest. Goethe warmly recommended the Frommann household to Eckermann: "Es wird Ihnen in diesem Kreise gefallen, sagte er, ich habe dort schöne Abende verlebt. Auch Jean Paul, Tieck, die Schlegel und was in Deutschland sonst Namen hat ist dort gewesen und hat dort gerne verkehrt und noch jetzt ist es der Vereinigungs-Punkt vieler Gelehrter und Künstler und sonst angesehener Personen."[4] Other habitués included the popular novelist Johanna Schopenhauer, and from the university, Heinrich Luden, Lorenz Oken and Jakob Fries. The young apprentice was a silent witness to their conversation.

In 1824, Johann Georg Wesselhöft grasped the *Wanderstab* of the journeyman printer and set out across Europe working intermittently in Brussels, London, and Paris, touring Switzerland and South Germany. He settled temporarily in Magdeburg as foreman and factor of the busy Hänel'sche Buch- und Noten-Druckerei, typefoundry and stereotyping establishment. The stress of his new job affected his health, and after seventeen months Wesselhöft resigned and went again on the road searching for a chance to establish his own business. During these travels he made a number of friends, none more important to him than the Swiss author and educational reformer Heinrich Zschokke, thirty-four years his senior.[5] The oppressive political atmosphere and the tight government regulation of the book trade made it difficult for a newcomer to get started and persuaded Wesselhöft to consider emigration. Accompanied by his bride, the former Johanna Monses, and his brother Carl Friedrich, Wesselhöft endured a stormy fifty-two-day crossing to arrive in New York harbor on the 31st of October, 1832.

After a visit to his cousin Wilhelm Wesselhöft, who had preceded them and was living in Bath, Pennsylvania, the couple settled temporarily in Nazareth where their only son, also named Wilhelm, was born. The new father took this opportunity to learn about America and traveled to Boston where he met Franz Lieber, Carl Follen, George Ticknor, and Franz Grund. Some months later Wesselhöft moved permanently to Philadelphia, purchased a printing press from Johann Georg Ritter,[6] and started a directory and intelligence service for German emigrants. With this as a base, he built a retail book business that grew larger with each passing year. On January 1, 1834, Wesselhöft introduced his newspaper, the *Alte und neue Welt*, an epochmaking event in German-American journalism.

Since the demise of Johann Carl Gossler's *Philadelphischer Correspondent und allgemeiner Deutscher Anzeiger* in August, 1830, the German press in Philadelphia was almost devoid of interest. True, there was a paper called the *Philadelphier Telegraph*, edited and published by Augustus Gräter during 1833, and continued briefly through most of 1834 as the *Zeitlauf*,[7] but it was not a very formidable rival. Thus the *Alte und neue Welt* came as a breath of fresh air, and with its second issue had amassed 350 subscribers.[8] It soon contained more reading matter in its weekly number, as Körner remarked, than any daily newspaper in Germany, the *Augsburger Allgemeine Zeitung* excepted.[9] Local news, fiction, much German-American poetry, essays, and biographical notices were accompanied by news of European affairs supplied in part by the paper's own Frankfurt correspondent. The policy of the *Alte und neue Welt* was to promote unity among the Germans living in America and to avoid partisan politics as far as possible— no mean feat! For a time the paper achieved a distribution unrivalled during the period, with agents in fifteen states, the Territory of Iowa, the Republic of Texas, and Montreal, Canada.[10] On one topic, during these early years, Wesselhöft held staunchly to a minority position. He was a believer in German exclusiveness at a time when much of the German press in the east and west opposed in principle the creation of any all-German settlements. This commitment was not merely rhetorical, for Wesselhöft as an officer of the Philadelphia Colonization Society was instrumental in the founding of Hermann, Missouri, of which he was quite proud.

The pressroom of the *Alte und neue Welt* served as a nursery to the local German book trade. Wesselhöft's first assistant, Wilhelm Radde, was soon encouraged to open an agency in New York, and August Ludwig Wollenweber, who came to work in 1834 as a compositor and subscription collector, later carved out a fine career as editor and publisher of *Der Demokrat* (Philadelphia). Concerning the time after he was hired, Wollenweber recalled: "In unserer Buchdruckerei wurde es jetzt immer lebendiger, denn neben Herrn Radde und mir waren nun noch Herr [sic] Schüllermann, Birk, Gronau angestellt, und später noch Herr Heinrich Schwacke, Herr Franz Schreiber und Herr Fabian."[11] These men, with Wesselhöft's blessing, formed a *Bildungsverein* which soon attracted young men from outside the shop. In 1835, this group was largely responsible for organizing the *Philadelphia Männerchor,* the first German *Sängerverein* in America.[12]

The retail book business was also a success. By the summer of 1834 the shop at No. 9 Bread Street had on its shelves the works of Carl Franz van der Velde, Johanna Schopenhauer, Moritz August von Thümmel, Zschokke, Christian Contessa, Heine's *Reisebilder* und *Salon,* Börne's *Briefe aus Paris,* Oken's *Naturgeschichte,* and the gamut of German classical literature. Later that year Wesselhöft sent Wilhelm Radde to New York to open a branch store. Radde, an experienced printer and friend of Wesselhöft's from Europe, built up a remunerative book business and even attempted some publishing of his own during the 1830s. Eventually, Radde became a fixture of the New York booktrade and a wealthy purveyor of popular German-language literature. Körner mentions other branches opened by Wesselhöft, presumably involving more than just agencies for the *Alte und neue Welt* and the intelligence service. These were, *ca.* 1834–1843: Gustav Herder, Main between Eighth and Ninth Streets in Cincinnati; G. H. Mittnacht, succeeded in 1838 by Henry L. Reitz, who was located on the corner of Camden and Eutaw Streets in Baltimore; Karl Panknin, corner of Church and Tradd Streets in Charleston; Karl Rosenthal in Washington, D.C.; and Johann Hahn on Poydras Street, New Orleans.[13]

For most if not all of these agents (Radde excepted) bookselling was just another source of income, a *Nebensache.* Gustav Herder (1810–1884) ran a successful hardware store in Cincinnati while H. L. Reitz in Baltimore owned a grocery and feed store. A Reitz advertisement that coupled German books with herring[14] would have sent a chill up the spine of any respectable German bookseller in Europe, but the merchandising of books as any other commodity—in combination with stationery, notions, toys, drugs, groceries, *et al.*—was an old American custom to which German-Americans soon adjusted.

Wesselhöft's first sales catalogue was a printed broadsheet, *Verzeichniss von Büchern* . . . , inserted in the *Alte und neue Welt* for August 23, 1834. In the introduction, the proprietor promised a regular catalogue as soon as the size of his book stock warranted one,[15] but unfortunately no later sales lists have yet been discovered. Of exceptional interest, however, is a catalogue Wesselhöft printed on commission in 1834 (hitherto unrecorded) listing an extensive private library for sale. This was the library brought to America in the entourage of the enigmatic Count Leon, the "Lion of Judah," gathered together by his secretary Johann Georg Goentgen.[16] The title page reads: *Verzeichniss der Bücher, welche Dr. S. [sic] G. Goentgen, erster Bibliothekar in Frankfurt a.M. gesammelt und nun von den Gebrüdern Dr. J. C. Müller und Johann Müller zum Verkauf angeboten werden. . .* Ausgegeben im Monat July 1834.[17]

Homoeopathic books and *materia medica* were the most profitable specialities pioneered and cultivated by Wesselhöft and his associates. Wilhelm Wesselhöft was an early convert to this new system of healing originated by Samuel Hahnemann, and influenced his bookseller cousin in the same direction. Dr. Constantin Hering from Dresden, "a homoeopath of impeccable credentials,"[18] came to Philadelphia in 1833 by way of Surinam. In Hering, the homoeopaths found an energetic leader. J. G. Wesselhöft printed the German version of Hering's *Concise View of the Rise and Progress of Homoeopathic Medicine,* a speech given before the Hahnemannian Society of Philadelphia. Hering and Wesselhöft also offered on subscription a *Homöopathische Bibliothek* in both German and English editions, a condensation of more than thirty original works by Hahnemann and his disciples into six royal octavo volumes (small type and double columns). Neither edition, however, was published.[19] That failure was more than offset by the founding of a homoeopathic academy in Allentown in 1835, the first college of homoeopathy in the world. Hering's *Homöopathischer Hausarzt für die deutschen Bürger der Vereinigten Staaten* . . . , printed by J. G. Wesselhöft in 1837, proved immensely popular here and in Germany, where it was greeted as a "Rückwanderer aus Amerika," and imported by Friedrich Johann Frommann, Wesselhöft's cousin, who also published several European editions.[20] The demand for homoeopathic books and preparations during the 1830s was met by Wesselhöft in Philadelphia, Heinrich Ebner in Allentown, Jacob Behlert in Allentown and Philadelphia, and Wilhelm Radde in New York.[21] For most of the nineteenth century German-American firms dominated this market.[22]

As a publisher of German books, Wesselhöft struck a nice balance between speculation and the common weal of the German element, at a time when the meager output of the German book press in America was limited to religious texts, school books written under the aegis of different confessions, or popular literature such as the ubiquitous *Ritter- und Räuber Geschichten, Egyptische Geheimnisse,* and similar colportage.[23] Wesselhöft developed a small list of publications, apart from his homoeopathic *Verlag,* with which he hoped to raise the educational and cultural standards of German-Americans everywhere. These books were to be distributed through his branches and newspaper agencies. First off the presses, probably in 1834, was an *Elementarbuch der englischen Sprache . . . ,* by Ernst Ludwig Walz, then editor of the *Alte und neue Welt.* In 1837 appeared Friedrich Stohlmann's *Gebetbuch für die deutsche Jugend in den Vereinigten Staaten . . .* and the same author's *Bettkämmerlein zur Einkehr für gläubige Christen.*[24] Another sort of venture was a Caspar Hauser *Schriftchen* advertised in 1834 as *Hausers kurzgefasste Lebensgeschichte und Tod . . .*[25] In the same year a proposed American edition of Carl Neyfeld's memoir of the Polish Revolution of 1831, at $1.50 per copy on subscription, failed to attract sufficient support.[26]

To accomplish his self-imposed *Bildungsarbeit,* Wesselhöft brought out special American editions of three noteworthy German books. One of these was Johann Heinrich Wilhelm Witschel's *Morgen- und Abendopfer in Gesängen . . . Für die deutschen Bewohner Nord-Amerika's* (1838), a departure from the traditional books of piety that ruled the German-American market. Witschel's volume of religious poetry was, according to his biographer, "neben Zschokke's *Stunden der Andacht* ohne Frage das verbreitetste *Andachtsbuch* unter uns in der Zeit des Rationalismus . . ."[27]

Wesselhöft might well have chosen the Zschokke book to reprint, as did later German-American publishers, but out of friendship preferred to further sales of the original Swiss edition. Textbooks by Heinrich Stephani[28] and Friedrich Philipp Wilmsen[29] rounded out Wesselhöft's list. Soon after the Wilmsen book was published, Wesselhöft wrote to Zschokke:

> . . . Soll aber das Glück unserer hiesigen deutschen Bevölkerung wahrhaft gehoben werden, so muß man von unten herauf anfangen und dazu gehören gute Schulen, womit [zu] beginnen ist u. immer mehr u. mehr gethan wird. Ein zweckmäßiges Lesebuch fehlte hier ganz u. ich glaube durch eine den hiesigen Verhältnissen angemessene Verarbeitung von Wilmsens deutschem Kinderfreund diese Lücke ersetzt zu haben, dem noch ein Anhang, eine kurze Geographie der neuen Welt wie eine Geschichte der Ver. Staaten enthaltend, beigefügt wurde. Ich habe den Preis so billig gestellt, daß mir bei der ersten Auflage gar kein Nutzen bleibt; doch habe ich die Freude, daß schon 500 Exemplare davon bestellt wurden u. wird dieses Buch in seiner jetzigen Gestalt großen Nutzen schaffen. Später sollen noch zweckmäßige und zeitgemäße Unternehmungen folgen und so wird hier nach und nach auch eine neue Aera in der Erziehung u. Bildung der deutschen Jugend hier aufgehn.[30]

The nationwide financial crisis that began in 1837 did not spare Wesselhöft although he managed to keep solvent for some years. A more severe shock was the death of his wife in 1839 leaving him alone to care for two young children. His son went to stay with Dr. Wilhelm Wesselhöft in Allentown, while his four year old daughter Johanna remained with friends in Philadelphia. The letter to Zschokke opened on a note of deep sorrow as the writer described the break-up of his family, but soon moved to more mundane subjects like Zschokke's contributions to the *Alte und neue Welt,* and Wesselhöft's difficulties with Heinrich Remigius Sauerländer in Aarau, Zschokke's Swiss publisher.

> . . . Für Ihre interessanten Nachrichten über Europa's Verhältnisse sage ich Ihnen herzlichen Dank; ich war so frei, sie in meinem Blatte aufzunehmen, was ich mir glaubte erlauben zu dürfen, da ich natürlich den Einsender nicht nannte u. den

Artikel zu interessant fand, um ihn den Lesern der „alten und neuen Welt" vorenthalten zu dürfen. Erfreuen Sie mich recht oft durch solche trefflichen Aufsätze, wodurch Sie nicht nur mir, sondern manchem Deutschen und Schweizer einen hohen Genuß bereiten.

. . . Wie kommt es, daß ich die bestellten Portraits wie auch die Exemplare der Brannteweinpest[31] nicht bekommen habe? Bitte, vergessen Sie mich nicht.—Sollte es Sauerländer nicht seinem Interesse angemessen finden, wenn er mir eine Parthie von den Stunden der Andacht zukommen ließe, verschiedene Ausgaben, wie auch Ihre "Novellen u. Erzählungen in einem Bande," auch einige Exempl. in 8 Bänden? Ich kann mehr für die Verbreitung seiner Verlagswerke thun, wie irgendeine andere Handlung in den Ver. Staaten, da meine Verbindungen durch meine Zeitung u. deren Agenten sehr ausgebreitet sind. Hat er Lust dazu, mag er von Leipzig eine Kiste an meinen Spediteur J. C. Peterssen, Addr. C. Traute, Bremen, abgehen lassen mit möglichst gutem Rabatt, so daß ich meinen Agenten wieder einen Nutzen zugestehen kann. . . Grüßen Sie S. freundlich von mir, so auch Ihre liebe Frau u. ihre Kinder, vorzüglich den Doctor. Mögte er seine Patienten gnädiger als mich behandeln, wo er auf einem Spaziergange, ich glaube nach Montmorenci, am liebsten den Braten selbst aß, damit ich nicht wieder er-kranke—Glückliche Zeit; sie kehrt nicht leicht zurück.

Nun leben Sie wohl, werther Herr und Freund! Entschuldi-gen Sie mein flüchtiges u. schlechtes Schreiben; ein anderes Mal mehr u. besseres. Vergessen Sie nicht u. schreiben Sie bald an Ihren aufrichtigen und dankbaren

.
J. G. Wesselhöft,
124 N. 2^d St., Philad^a

Wesselhöft kept his business afloat and even enhanced his dis-play with some imported "Old Masters." Körner reported seeing for sale in 1841 paintings attributed to "Hannibal Carrachi, Palamedes, Gerhard Dow, Van der Velde, Berghem, Wouverman, Adrian von Ostade, Peters, Tischbein und Brower."[32] Poor health forced the bookseller to take on C. L. Rademacher as an associate in April, 1842, and the latter was soon entrusted with the day-to-day management of the business. From about August, 1842, to

June, 1843, Wesselhöft was away from Philadelphia, traveling through Baltimore, Washington, New York State to Canada, then south to Cleveland, Cincinnati, Louisville, and St. Louis[33] (where he fell ill again for several months), on to New Orleans for recuperation and back home via Vicksburg and Pittsburgh. A lending library with 1,679 books was opened by Wesselhöft and Co. on the first of November, 1842,[34] but this must have been handled by Rademacher alone. A few months later, Rademacher was caught short with debts he could not pay, and almost immediately the assets of the firm were confiscated and sold at auction. This disaster took place in February or March, 1843, while Wesselhöft was in St. Louis.[35] He returned to Philadelphia a ruined man. Later he described these dismal events for his friend Zschokke:

. . . Meine Abwesenheit, meine Krankheit in weiter Ferne benutzend, ließ man, da mein Associée gleichgültig handelte, Alles gut hieß u. Nichts verlieren konnte, weil er kein Capital ins Geschäft gegeben, um einiger hundert dollars halber, für welche er keine Deckung schaffte, mein sämmtliches Habe u. Gut, was ich seit 10 Jahren mit Opfern, Sparsamkeit u. unerschütterlichem Fleiß aufgebaut hatte, so heimlich als möglich durch Sheriff's Hand verkaufen. Meine Freunde erfuhren die Sache erst als Alles zu spät war. Und ein Geschäft, 8 bis 10,000 Dollars werth, wurde unter dem Hammer bei einigen anwesenden Käufern für circa 800 Dollars veräußert, waren sich einige Creditoren, die die Sache angriffen, bezahlt meistens u. andere einstweilen Nichts bekommen konnten.—Sie können denken, mit welchen Gefühlen ich diese Trümmer anschaute.
. . . .
In Philadelphia mochte ich nicht bleiben. In New Orleans u. N. York kam man mir liebevoll entgegen und wollte mir die Hände zu einem neuen Etablissement bieten. In letzterem Ort wäre ich wol geblieben, hätte ich nicht bei meinen Geschwistern für meine Kinder eine sichere Heimath gewünscht, wenn meine Pflicht mich vielleicht wieder von ihnen rufen sollte. Ich zog daher einstweilen St. Louis vor, wo ich glücklich mit den Meinigen Ende Septbr. v. J. ankam. Da hier wie im ganzen großen Westen noch keine deutsche Buchhandlung sich befand,[36] so entschloß ich mich, ein Anerbieten meines Schwagers

u. meines Bruders anzunehmen, um bald wieder in Thätigkeit zu
kommen u. für die Deutschen nach Möglichkeit zu wirken, hier
für der Bruder Rechnung eine kleine Buch- u. Schreibmateri-
alien-Handlung etabliren, die wir den Anförderungen u. dem
Zeitgeist gemäß immer nach u. nach vervollständigen werden.
Seit Mitte Oktober sind wir mit dem Geschäft im Gange u. für
den Anfang geht es ziemlich. Nebenbei benutze ich meine Zeit
zur Bearbeitung eines Werkes: Meine Reisen in den Ver. Staaten,
was ich gerne von Dr. K. Rotteck[37] revidiren u. dann in Deutschland drucken lassen möchte. Doch dies einstweilen noch unter
uns. Ich schreibe es Ihnen nur, weil ich weiß, daß Sie gerne aus-
führlicher über meine Reisen unterrichtet sein möchten. Einen
Verleger wählte ich noch nicht. Ich hoffe, das Buch wird Absatz
finden, da ich es so bearbeite, daß es dem Auswanderer von
praktischem Nutzen ist, woran es noch den meisten über Amerika erschienenen Schriften fehlt.
· ·

Meine beiden Kinder, ein Knabe von 11 u. ein Mädchen von
8½ Jahren, blühen fröhlich heran und scheinen unter dem westlichen Himmel zu gedeihen. Meine Geschwister wohnen in Camp
Spring, eine engl. Meile von der Stadt u. verhielt meine Schwester, die kinderlos ist, Mutterstelle bei meinen Kleinen. Mein Wilhelm geht nach St. Louis zur Schule. Damit er abgehärtet wird,
muß er jeden Abend nach Camp Spring u. jeden Morgen wieder
zur Stadt. Er hat sich jetzt schon an Regen, Schnee u. Frost ge-
wöhnt—Meine Johanna erhält noch Unterricht von der Tante u.
wird nebenbei als eine tüchtige Wirthschafterin erzogen. Ich
konnte meine Tochter, ganz das Ebenbild ihrer sel. Mutter,
unter keine bessere Obhut gestellt haben. Wenigstens alle Sonn-
abend gehe auch ich nach Camp Spring u. bleibe des Sonntags
im Kreise meiner Lieben. Sonst führe ich mein einsames Wittwer-
leben fort. Ich möchte ihm gerne Valet sagen, doch war ich
noch nicht so glücklich, die Bekanntschaft eines solchen deutschen Frauenzimmer gemacht zu haben, der ich Hand u. Herz
schenken möchte. Sie wissen ja, die Liebe ist keine Waare. Für
eine Amerikanerin passe ich nicht, obwohl ich gerne einräume,
daß es auch wackere Mädchen u. Frauen unter ihnen giebt, die
ein deutsches Herz beglücken könnten; aber es sind eben nur
Ausnahmen. . .

Grüßen Sie herzlich alle Ihre Lieben, auch Hrn. Sauerländer. Diesem bin ich auch eine Kleinigkeit schuldig; es thut mir wehe; aber ich kann nicht helfen. Wäre ich in Philada. vor Auflösung meines Geschäfts gewesen, wäre Alles anders geworden. Sobald ich nur bessere Tage sehe, werde ich Hrn. Sauerl. Alles, oder doch, was ich irgend kann, bezahlen. Er soll mir nicht zürnen, arm bin ich zwar, aber ehrlich. Und in einigen Jahren kann sich auch in meinen Verhältnissen Manches ändern. Einstweilen will ich suchen, von *Sr.* Verlag nach u. nach so viel zu verkaufen, daß ihm indirect schon dadurch bald meine kleine Schuld ersetzt wird. . .[38]

On the nineteenth of October, 1843, Franksen and C. F. Wesselhöft announced in the *Anzeiger des Westens* the opening of their new business on Second Street, between Myrtle and Spruce, with J. G. Wesselhöft as manager. The first five years were difficult and the demand for German books was at best tenuous, not enough to tempt any rival to set up shop. The traveler Alexander Ziegler saw in Wesselhöft a disillusioned man: "Herr Georg Wesselhöft," wrote Ziegler, "der hier die einzige deutsche Buchhandlung besitzt, sich aber ziemlich bitter darüber beklagte, daß die Deutschen wenig Lust zeigten, Bücher zu lesen, noch weniger aber Bücher zu kaufen, war trotz seines körperlichen Unwohlseins für den heutigen Sonntag unser gefälliger Cicerone."[39]

An extraordinary increase in the German population of St. Louis and vicinity (including neighboring St. Clair County, Illinois) took place between 1848 and 1860. *The Saint Louis Business Directory, for 1853-4* listed six German papers, three of them dailies, a German Emigrant Society, a German Benefit Society and German Workingmen's Society, The Society of Freemen (with 300 members), a German Savings Institution, the German Roman Catholic Benevolent Society, St. Vincent's German Orphan Association, and several German bookstores including Wesselhöft's last directory listing—"J. G. Wesselhoeft boot [sic] and medicine store, 79 Market." His business had improved year by year from 1848 to 1853, according to Körner;[40] still the record shows four moves during that time, the first in October, 1849, because of a hundred-percent increase in rent, as Wesselhöft complained.[41] Perhaps he was hurt by the new competition, particularly from Rohland and

Detharding (1848–1851) and Florentin Schuster (1848–1852), for after 1848 he no longer had the market to himself. Early in 1852 Wesselhöft sold his lending library and moved again to new premises.[42]

In September of the same year repeated rumors of his death forced Wesselhöft to make a public statement: "Noch immer am Leben! Man glaubte mich auf der 'Henry Clay' an dem Hudson verbrannt, mit der 'Atlantic' im Erie See ertrunken oder im Mississippi durch einen sogenannten Snag gespießt.—Nun, das geht über's Bohnen lieb.—An Allem kein wahres Wort. Bin glücklich wieder angekommen und dabei eine schöne Auswahl Bilder, Bücher, Schreibmaterialien, Landkarten u. dergl. nach No. 91 Marktstraße gesandt . . ."[43] A year later, in the *Anzeiger* of September 3, 1853, he issued another rebuttal: "Schinderhannes u. Genovefa sind todt, aber Vater Wesselhöft lebt noch!" Proving his point, the bookseller listed a number of new arrivals at his store, imported *Volkskalender,* the latest issues of Joseph Meyer's *Universum* (in a special German-American edition) and *Das Buch der Welt,* a journal of similar content published by Carl Hoffmann of Stuttgart, novels by Scott, Zschokke, and Hackländer, and the works of Schiller "in verschiedenen Ausgaben." But Wesselhöft's professional career was just about over.

Failing health and his son Wilhelm's decision to leave bookselling for farming (he had helped his father in the store for several years) brought the elder Wesselhöft to retirement early in 1854.[44] At leisure now, he paid his adieux to Europe and was warmly welcomed by Zschokke's widow and son. Wesselhöft returned to the United States in 1856 to spend his last years with his daughter Johanna in Mascoutah, near Belleville, Illinois, and with his sister in Hermann, Missouri. There he died on January 12, 1859, his memory alive in the hearts of his children and a few old friends. "Die Masse des Deutschthums in Amerika," commented his son, "kennt nicht mehr den Namen des Mannes, dessen ganzes Ziel und Streben der Hebung des deutschen Elements gewidmet war."[45]

NOTES

1. Gustav Körner, political leader of the Illinois Germans, was elected Lieutenant Governor of that state in 1852. Franz Joseph Grund was a native of Austria who parlayed his undoubted intellectual and personal gifts into a successful political and journalistic career, becoming one of the most influen tial German-Americans of his day. Though held in the highest esteem by Anglo-Americans, Grund evoked some wariness among the Germans because of repeated changes in political affiliation: Democrat in 1836 (he wrote a campaign biography for Van Buren), Whig in 1840 (he did the same for Harrison), Democrat again in 1842, and finally a Lincoln Republican in 1863, the year of his death.

2. These letters shed much light on Wesselhöft's personal life and business activities. Copies were kindly supplied by the *Staatsarchiv* Kanton Aargau, Aarau, Switzerland. Unless specified, biographical facts about Wesselhöft are taken from Körner's account in *Das deutsche Element in den Vereinigten Staaten von Nordamerika, 1818-1848* (Cincinnati: Verlag von A. E. Wilde & Co., 1880), pp. 32-38.

3. Three cousins attended the university in Jena—Eduard, Wilhelm and Robert Wesselhöft. The latter two, who both later emigrated to the United States, played leading roles in the original *Burschenschaft* agitation. A cousin who went to the University in Berlin, Friedrich Johann Frommann, was also involved in the student movement. It was Robert Wesselhöft who composed the letter of invitation to the *Wartburgfest* held on October 18, 1817, sent out to thirteen German universities. The letter is reprinted in Günter Steiger, *Aufbruch: Urburschenschaft und Wartburgfest* (Leipzig: Urania-Verlag, 1967), insert following p. 96. Wilhelm, a physician, and Robert, who studied law in Germany but learned the *materia medica* in Allentown, Pennsylvania from his brother Wilhelm, became influential American exponents of homoeopathic medicine. Both later practiced in New England.

4. Johann Peter Eckermann, *Gespräche mit Goethe . . .* , ed. H. H. Houben (Leipzig: F. A. Brockhaus, 1925), p. 33, entry for June 13, 1823.

5. Johann Heinrich David Zschokke (1771-1848). A humane and enlightened educator whose writings were uniformly popular, whether fiction, moral reflections, history, or the autobiographical *Selbstschau*. His most influential work was the *Stunden der Andacht* which appeared anonymously between 1808 and 1816, and was first collected in book form in 1816. A new edition was issued virtually every year in Europe until 1850. The *Stunden* were written in simple prose, in the undogmatic spirit of a liberal, rationalistic Christianity. Such bourgeois ideals as domesticity, friendship, delight in nature, were praised while deeper problems and cares of life were bypassed. Anathema to conservative Protestants and Catholics alike, the book was attacked as "a work of Satan," the author as "more dangerous to Germany than Voltaire." See Franz Schnabel, *Deutsche Geschichte im neunzehnten Jahr-*

hundert, dritte Auflage (Freiburg: Verlag Herder, 1955), IV, 371-373; and Heinrich Kurz, *Geschichte der deutschen Literatur,* fünfte Auflage (Leipzig: B. G. Teubner, 1870), III, 723a. Zschokke was the father of twelve sons and a daughter. The eldest son, Theodor, became a physician and was a particular friend of Wesselhöft.

6. Johann Georg Ritter (1772-1840) had built a considerable career as bookseller and publisher in the Swabian town of Gmünd. The political reaction and harsh press censorship that followed the Karlsbad Decrees of 1819 forced the closing of Ritter's journal, the *Neue Chronik der Deutschen* (edited by Johann Gottfried Pahl) in 1824. At the age of 52 Ritter emigrated with his family to Philadelphia where he opened a German bookstore and began to print a German newspaper, the *Amerikanischer Correspondent für das In- und Ausland.* Ritter was the first trained and experienced German bookseller and publisher to do business in the United States. After selling his newspaper to Johann Carl Gossler in 1829, and subsequently his printing press to Wesselhöft, he continued his retail book business until his death in 1840.

7. Wesselhöft took over the subscription list of the *Zeitlauf* in October, 1834. Karl J. R' Arndt and May E. Olson, *German-American Newspapers and Periodicals 1732-1955 . . . ,* 2nd rev. ed. (New York: Johnson Reprint Corporation, 1965), p. 578.

8. According to Ludwig August Wollenweber, "Aus meinem Leben," *Mitteilungen des deutschen Pionier-Vereins von Philadelphia,* Heft XIV (1910), p. 3. Wesselhöft's editors were well educated and capable men beginning with Pastor Ernst Ludwig Walz from Karlsruhe. Later editors included Samuel Ludvigh und Maximilian Schele de Vere.

9. *Das deutsche Element,* p. 38.

10. *Alte und neue Welt,* October 20, 1838.

11. Wollenweber, "Aus meinem Leben," p. 3. Schwacke and Schreiber became the owners of the *Alte und neue Welt* in 1843. Schwacke also published the American reprint of Friedrich von Raumer's *Die Vereinigten Staaten von Nordamerika* in 1846.

12. *Ibid.,* p. 4.

13. See Körner, *Das deutsche Element,* pp. 35, 371 (Hahn), 383 (Karl Pankin [*sic*]), 411 (L. [*sic*] Rosenthal). *Das Volksblatt* (Cincinnati), May 7, 1836, mentions G. H. Mittnacht, No. 29 Point Market Street, as Wesselhöft's agent in Baltimore. The *Alte und neue Welt* for October 20, 1838 lists H. L. Reitz as Baltimore agent. On Herder, who opened his branch in August, 1838, and was the first vendor of German books in Cincinnati apart from colporteurs, see *Der deutsche Pionier,* XVI (March, 1885), 519; and *Alte und neue Welt,* September 1, 1838. The addresses given in the text are taken from a Wesselhöft letterhead printed between 1839 and 1841 and found in Peter Kaufmann Papers, Box 6, Folder 21, Ohio Historical Society Library. There are names on this letterhead *not* mentioned by Körner as agencies of the bookstore: C. L. Volz in Pittsburgh; A. Rimmele in Boston; Franksen and [F. C.] Wesselhöft, brother-in-law and brother of J. G. Wesselhöft, in St. Louis.

14. *Alte und neue Welt,* November 11, 1843.

15. Wesselhöft promised to obtain any desired book from Germany within three to four months. He apparently did not deal directly through Leipzig. His printed letterhead (see note 13) listed an agent in Frankfurt am Main, E. Wagner of Stockmar & Wagner, and a forwarding agent, J. C. Peterssen in Bremen.

16. The history of George Rapp's Harmony Society including the episode of Count Leon's arrival, the schism that followed and the ultimate fate of the seceders, is a subject that has occupied Karl Arndt for many years. It was during the 1930's that he found in Germantown, Louisiana the last refuge of the Count and, in an old log cabin that had belonged to Goentgen, the fragments of a fine library. Count Leon, born Bernhard Mueller, arrived in New York in 1831 on his holy mission of "gathering all and uniting all who [wished] to conform to the divine law in keeping with the gospel of Jesus Christ." He and Goentgen had brought along, in Arndt's words, "mathematical and physical instruments and an important library in order to save the quintessence of European literature by transplanting it to North America in a carefully selected collection of books of all sciences and branches of art." This library was transferred to Phillipsburg, Pennsylvania, when the seceders left Father Rapp's colony at Economy, in April, 1832. On August 10, 1833, Count Leon's now bankrupt society at Phillipsburg was officially dissolved. On September 1, the Count and some of the faithful embarked down the Ohio River, a journey that finally led to Germantown, Louisiana. Apparently they took some books with them (those found by Arndt), but most of the library was left behind. See Arndt, *George Rapp's Harmony Society 1785–1847,* rev. ed. (Rutherford, N.J.: Fairleigh Dickinson University Press, 1972), pp. 449, 451, 534.

17. Henry Wadworth Longfellow's copy of this catalogue was kindly made available to me by Kevin B. MacDonnell. On [p. 2] of the catalogue we read: "Die nachstehende schätzenswerthe Bibliothek, welche besonders ein großer Schatz für ein katholisches Seminarium wäre, wünscht man im Ganzen zu verkaufen. Sollte sich aber im Laufe von drei Monaten kein Käufer dazu finden, so soll dieselbe nach den vorstehenden Preisen, vereinzelt werden. . . . Kauflustige belieben sich in portofreien Briefen zu wenden an Dr. J. C. Müller, Petersburgh, Columbiana County, Ohio, und an J. G. Wesselhoeft in Philadelphia." Dr. Müller is no doubt Johann Christoph Müller, chemist, former musical director, and printer for George Rapp's Harmony Society, who seceded with Count Leon. The *Verzeichniß* is fifteen pages long and lists 572 separate entries of exceptional variety; most were in German, but there were a good many sets in Latin and scattered volumes in other languages. The dispersal of the library was recorded by Johann Martin Henni, later Bishop of Milwaukee: "Die reiche, selbst mit den meisten heil. Vätern ausgestattete Bibliothek sah ich auf meiner Durchreise in Pittsburgh, wohin sie durch Ankauf des Hrn. Pettermann, eines der ansehnlichsten Rechtsgelehrten, der erst vor etlichen Jahren zur kathol. Kirche überging, gekommen war. Viele der besten Werke waren schon verkauft." *Ein Blick in's Thal des*

Ohio (München: Gedruckt bey Franz Seraph Hübschmann, 1836), p. 116.

18. Joseph F. Kett, *The Formation of the American Medical Profession* . . . (New Haven: Yale University Press, 1968), p. 136.

19. *Alte und neue Welt*, February 22, 1834.

20. "Das vorliegende Buch," wrote Frommann, "—ein Rückwanderer aus Amerika—hat in seinem Stammlande so viel Beifall gefunden, daß sich im Verlauf dreier Jahre zwei starke Exemplarsendungen aus Amerika und dazwischen die vor zwei Jahren hier gedruckte zweite Auflage vergriffen haben." Hering, *Homöopathischer Hausarzt. Ursprünglich für die deutschen Bürger der Vereinigten Staaten* . . . , Dritte Auflage (Jena: Friedrich Frommann, 1841), p. v.

21. Ebner ran the *Akademische Buchhandlung* associated with the Allentown Academy (its full title: The North American College of the Homoeopathic Healing Art). Behlert, whose name appears with Wesselhöft's on the title page of Hering's *Homöopathischer Hausarzt* (1837) later moved to Philadelphia. See Thomas Lindsley Bradford, *Homoeopathic Bibliography of the United States* . . . (Philadelphia: Boericke & Tafel, 1892), pp. 351, 353, 554.

22. W. Radde in New York was the major supplier of homoeopathic drugs and books in the United States from 1840, when he bought out Wesselhöft's stock, to 1869 when he sold his homoeopathic interests to Boericke and Tafel of Philadelphia. This Philadelphia firm, in turn, was founded in 1843 by C. L. Rademacher, who had been J. G. Wesselhöft's partner from April, 1842 to the dissolution of the business in 1843. Rademacher's store was known as Rademacher and Sheek from 1848 to 1858 in which year it was sold to William Radde, Jr. The younger Radde died in 1862 and the store went to Dr. Francis E. Boericke who joined with Adolph J. Tafel in 1869.

23. Quantities of such colportage were produced in Pennsylvania by Gustav S. Peters in Harrisburg, for example, and later by W. Radde in New York. Philipp Kastner as publisher of the *Lancaster Volksfreund* (Ohio) in 1840 and 1841 printed such old favorites as *Die heilige Genovefa* and this "fliegender Buchhandel" brought in more money than the newspaper. See Friedrich Fieser, "Aus meinen Erinnerungen," *Der deutsche Pionier*, I (November, 1869), 276.

24. A prospectus for the Walz book was printed in the *Alte und neue Welt*, January 4, 1834. An English-language edition was printed in 1835. A companion piece, *circa* 1837, was *Der kleine Amerikaner, ein leichtes Hülfsmittel, zum Elementarbuche der englischen Sprache.* . . . This is advertised in Stephani's *Handfibel* (see note 28 below). For Stohlmann's *Gebetbuch*, see *Alte und neue Welt*, January 1, 1837, and for the *Bettkämmerlein* see John Nicum, *Geschichte des Evangelisch-Lutherischen Ministeriums vom Staate New York* . . . (New York, 1888), pp. 175–176.

25. *Alte und neue Welt*, April 26, 1834, with the note: "(Erscheint am Mittwoch) Preis 6¼ Cts." A copyright English-language edition was also promised.

26. First edition: *Polens Revolution und Kampf im Jahre 1831* (Frankfurt a.M.: In Commission bei Joh. Valentin Meidinger, 1832). Neyfeld was a Cap-

tain in the Polish army who made his way to St. Louis where in 1837 he was co-editor of *Das Westland.*

27. *Allgemeine deutsche Biographie* (Leipzig: Duncker & Humblot, 1898), XLIII, 569.

28. H. Stephani, *Handfibel zum Lesenlernen nach der Lautirmethode . . . Zum ersten Male für die deutschen Schulen Nord-Amerika's zum Druck befördert* (Philadelphia und New York, 1837). 58 pp. A second edition of 62 pages was printed in 1841. Stephani, whose *Handfibel* pioneered the phonic method of teaching German, was a representative of theological rationalism, who in his *System der öffentlichen Erziehung* (Berlin, 1805) came out strongly in favor of state controlled schools and public libraries.

29. Wilmsen's *Deutscher Kinderfreund* was one of the most popular German schoolbooks of the first half of the nineteenth century. Wesselhöft's edition bore the title: *Deutscher Kinderfreund für Schule und Haus. Nach der 146sten Original-Ausgabe besonders für den Gebrauch deutscher Volksschulen Nord-Amerika's zum ersten Male durchgesehen und eingerichtet von einem hier lebenden praktischen Schulmanne. Nebst einem Anhange, enthaltend: Eine kurzgefaßte Geographie von Amerika und insbesondere von den Ver. Staaten, so wie eine kurze Geschichte der Ver. Staaten von Nord-Amerika . . .* (1839), 312 pp. A second edition with a "verbesserte Anhang" was published in 1841 containing 344 pages. The true first American edition of Wilmsen was printed on poor paper by Johann Carl Gossler in 1830 for the Philadelphia German Lutheran congregation of St. Michael's and Zion Church. Wesselhöft made substantial changes in his edition, dropping the section on German grammar, the opening chapter on the human soul, and adding a geography and history of the United States. A chapter titled "Rechten und Pflichten der Unterthanen . . ." (found in the 1830 edition), was obviously unsuitable and the offending "Unterthanen" was replaced by "Bürger."

30. Letter from Wesselhöft to Heinrich Zschokke, dated Nazareth, Pennsylvania, April 13, 1839 and continued from Baltimore, April 28, 1839. *Staatsarchiv* Kanton Aargau, Aarau.

31. *Die Brannteweinpest* was first published in 1837. A German-American edition was issued by Samuel Ludvigh in Baltimore in 1840.

32. Körner, *Das deutsche Element,* p. 42.

33. Wesselhöft reported this itinerary in a letter to Zschokke dated January 26, 1844. *Staatsarchiv* Kanton Aargau, Aarau. The bookseller arrived in St. Louis in December, 1842 and stayed at Camp Spring, a suburban resort owned by his brother-in-law F. Franksen, and his younger brother, Carl Friedrich Wesselhöft. On December 10, the *Wöchentlicher Anzeiger des Westens* ran the following notice: "J. G. Wesselhöft von Philadelphia ist in dieser Stadt angekommen und wird eine kurze Zeit hier verweilen. Er bittet diejenigen, welche eine Bestellung an sein Haus zu machen haben, auf die 'Alte und neue Welt' subscribiren wollen, oder gesonnen sind, aus einer Auswahl mitgebrachter interessanter und nützlicher Werke ein gutes Buch sich anzuschaffen, um ihren gütigen Besuch in Camp Spring.—Cataloge der hier vorräthigen Bücher sind daselbst zu haben und ebenfalls in den meisten

Gasthäusern St. Louis' einzusehen.—Auch sind vollständige Bücher-Catalogue der Handlung von J. G. Wesselhöft u. Co., aus beinahe 2000 verschiedenen Werken bestehend, sowohl im Camp Spring, wie auch bei Herrn A. Olshausen (in der Expedition dies. Bl.) in Augenschein zu nehmen . . ."

34. *Alte und neue Welt,* October 22, 1842.

35. With the March 18, 1843 issue, the *Alte und neue Welt* changed hands. The new publishers were former employees of Wesselhöft, Franz Schreiber and Heinrich Schwacke.

36. This statement is not strictly true. There were before 1843 a few book stores in Ohio that carried German books. In St. Louis a small German bookstore connected with the *Anzeiger des Westens* was managed by Theodor Engelmann from 1837 to 1840, then by Arthur Olshausen until January 7, 1843, on which day the remaining stock was sold at auction. *Wöchentlicher Anzeiger des Westens,* December 31, 1842. When Wesselhöft moved to St. Louis permanently, there was no German bookstore in the city.

37. Not the famous liberal historian who died in 1840. Wesselhöft is perhaps referring to Rotteck's son and namesake who was a lawyer and later a participant in the 1848 Revolution. The younger Karl Rotteck emigrated to America and from 1861 to June 24, 1865, published *Die tägliche Quincy Union* and the weekly *Quincy Tribüne* in Illinois. See Heinrich Bornmann, "Deutsches Zeitungswesen in Quincy," *Deutsch-Amerikanische Geschichtsblätter,* VI (July, 1906), 34.

38. Letter from Wesselhöft to Zschokke, dated January 26, 1844.

39. Alexander Ziegler, *Skizzen einer Reise durch Nordamerika und Westindien* (Dresden: Arnoldische Buchhandlung, 1848), II, 77.

40. Körner, *Das deutsche Element,* p. 37.

41. *Wöchentlicher Anzeiger des Westens,* October 6, 1849.

42. *Ibid.,* February 28, 1852.

43. *Ibid.,* September 18, 1852.

44. The *Wöchentlicher Anzeiger des Westens,* on March 23, 1854, announced a sale of all merchandise "wegen Austritt des Besitzers."

45. Quoted in Körner, *Das deutsche Element,* p. 38.

10. Forgotten Scion of a Famous Family: Carlos von Gagern, Nineteenth-Century Cosmopolitan and Mexican Patriot
Gerhard K. Friesen

Ubi libertas, ibi patria[1]

Even when viewed in the tradition of unusual talent and distinguished public service upheld by the von Gagerns, the career of Carlos is extraordinary in scope and direction. Like Friedrich (1794-1848) an army officer convinced of his political mission,[2] like Heinrich (1799-1880) a persuasive public orator,[3] and like Friedrich (1882-1947) a distinctive writer preoccupied with American themes,[4] Carlos von Gagern (1826-85) has nevertheless remained virtually unknown in his native Germany and abroad. In light of the patriotic and religious loyalty maintained by the Catholic Austrian as well as the Protestant Prussian and Hessian branches of this family, Carlos must have impressed contemporaries as the *bête noire* spoiling this proud record with his active enthusiasm for the young Mexican republic, his rationalistic dissent in religious matters, his commitment to socialism, and his cosmopolitan aspirations. Carlos' spiritual and political iconoclasm as well as the long list of von Gagerns with positively established reputations in the German lands may explain his absence from standard German reference works.[5] Elsewhere, information is erratic and erroneous.[6] A recent attempt by Marianne O. de Bopp to reappraise Carlos von Gagern's Mexican role[7] lacks detailed bibliographic sources and frequently offers inaccurate conjectures rather than factual data. This paper intends to remedy, as far as my sources permit, the dearth of information generally available about the life and work of this remarkable man, Carlos von Gagern.

The von Gagern family traces its origin back to the island of Rügen,[8] where it is first documented in the thirteenth century. A descendant of this oldest of the German branches, Carlos was born on December 12, 1826[9] in the Prussian province of Neumark (since 1945 under Polish administration) near the village of Mantel,[10] in Rehdorf, an estate belonging to his father, the Prussian major Gustav von Gagern.[11] Most consequential for the remainder of Carlos' life was the untimely death of his beloved father in 1834. The lack of firm paternal authority in the further upbringing of the brilliant but unruly youth is evident in his early education; his punctilious guardian von Levetzow,[12] his royalist mother, and his ultraconservative grandparents (with whom he lived in Berlin) all failed to provide the consistent and inspiring guidance Carlos needed. His unbridled exuberance and mischievous delight in challenging authoritarian superiors prompted a succession of *Gymnasien* in Putbus on Rügen, Berlin, Schulpforta near Naumburg, and Zeitz to expel him, although he displayed unusual intelligence and satisfactory industry.

The most decisive influence during Carlos' formative years was Friedrich Ludwig Jahn (1778–1852). While living with his mother's parents in the Friedrichstadt section of Berlin, where he attended the Friedrich-Werdersche Gymnasium[13] until 1842, Carlos decided to join the *Turner* movement. Inspired by his teacher Ernst Wilhelm Bernhard Eiselen (1792–1846), one of the *Turnvater's* most active disciples after he had been officially banished from Berlin and environs, Carlos readily adopted Jahn's steadfast idealism and patriotic candor and coupled it with contempt for the absolutistic regime which blindly persecuted Jahn and like-minded liberals. To Jahn's political principles and uncompromising personality Carlos attributed his lifelong democratic convictions. Nine years after his first participation in the *Turner* activities, Carlos was able to fulfill his ardent hope to meet Jahn in person. Following his relegation from Schulpforta (1843) for flagrantly violating that institution's ban on smoking, Carlos visited his idol in the nearby town of Freyburg an der Unstrut. Although he was astounded by Jahn's lack of personal hygiene and by his calculated rustic simplicity, Carlos' genuine admiration for him was reinforced by this encounter. Accommodating and refreshingly outspoken to the point of vulgarity,[14] Jahn impressed the young admirer with his unorthodox (Germanic-pagan rather than Judaeo-Christian) religious views[15] and his *laissez-faire* educational philosophy. Its radical rejection of restraint and parental responsibility, epitomized in Jahn's statement, "Besser bleibt immer gar keine Erziehung als eine schlechte" (I, 15), struck even the recently relegated youngster as too liberal. The practical application of this peculiar principle and its sad consequences Carlos was able to observe in Jahn's own son Arnold Siegfried, whose lack of formal education led him to operate an Unstrut ferry boat before he emigrated to America[16] after his father's death.

Notwithstanding Jahn's aberrant foibles, Carlos departed from Freyburg as his faithful apostle. In following Jahn's advice that he continue his interrupted studies at the not too distant town of Zeitz, Carlos was to spread the *Turner* gospel of a modern *Kalokagathia* in his new environment. He did so with amazing results. Soon after his arrival in Zeitz, he persuaded the director of the *Gymnasium* to have gymnastics added to the curriculum.[17] Other local schools followed suit, and along with the discipline came its credo, the brotherhood and equality of all, as formulated by one of Jahn's missionaries: "Der deutsche Turnplatz hat es nicht mit Söhnen von Beamten, Gelehrten, Kaufleuten, Handwerkern u.s.w. zu tun, sondern lediglich mit jungen Bürgern, deren Kräfte naturgemäß entwickelt werden sollen. Der Turner bringt auf den Turnplatz nichts als sich selbst, rein und abgestreift von jedem Lebensverhältnis. Daher ist völlige Gleichheit aller Turner und gleiche Teilnahme an allen Übungen das erste Gesetz des Turnplatzes."[18] Modeled after the *Burschenschaft* at the neighboring University of Jena, a student fraternity was organized in Zeitz, complete with colorful insignia, poetry, and drinking ritual. To climax all these achievements, of which he proudly informed Jahn, Carlos organized a *Turnfest* in the adjacent town of Pegau (1844) with the enthusiastic participation of the entire community. Inebriated with his success and the revolutionary sentiments of this time—"Herwegh steckte mir in allen Gliedern" (I, 24) —Carlos castigated before an applauding audience of 6,000 people the anachronism of German political particularism, concluding with his own tetrastich:

> Sagst Du, die Schlange sie lebt, wenn Du sie in Theile zerstücket,
> Weil jedes einzelne Glied krampfhaft sich reget und zuckt?
> Werft in das Feuer zumal eure bunten Pfähle und Marken,
> Und aus der Gluth wird erstehn, *ein* und *lebendig* das Reich.
>
> (I, 24)

The Prussian minister of education reacted swiftly by having him expelled, and denunciation brought about the demise of the Zeitz fraternity. Jahn implored Carlos to remain true to his conviction, regardless of all adversities. And although Carlos' subsequent career did not allow for continued active participation in the *Turner* movement, he adhered to its beliefs as he understood them.

After his *Abitur* in the Pomeranian town of Stargard (1845), Carlos' mother and guardian decreed he should study law in Berlin and concurrently serve as a one-year volunteer in the artillery-guards. While reluctantly doing his military duties as sergeant, he neglected his studies of an academic discipline he considered stagnant and archaic amidst the liberal currents of the *Vormärz*. Frederick William IV's rule had disappointed all hopes which progressives had initially vested in his ascension to the Prussian throne (1840). Instead of granting a constitution, he accentuated the feudal class structure and crushed any true or apparent opposition. In this atmosphere of political frustration, a number of intellectuals in 1844 founded the literary club *Rütli*,[19] whose very name was programmatic. Among its members were the writers Leopold Arends, Louise Aston,[20] Stephan Born, Carl Beck, Ernst Dohm, Friedrich Saß, Carl Gaillard,[21] Rudolf Genée,[22] Rudolf Gottschall,[23] Robert Griepenkerl, Rudolf Löwenstein, and Heinrich Ulke;[24] and the composers Hermann Krigar and Hieronymus Truhn. To qualify for membership, candidates were expected to offer proof of their creativity; for this purpose Carlos composed a lengthy philosophical poem entitled "Atheismus," depicting God as man's creation, in the vein of Ludwig Feuerbach's *Wesen des Christenthums* (1841): "Der Mensch schuf Dich nach seinem Ebenbilde,/Du bist Geschöpf, Dein Schöpfer, Gott, bin ich" (I, 37). The youngest of the members, Carlos was chosen to write the *Jubelhymne* for the *Rütli*'s 1846 anniversary. Set to music by Krigar and embellished by Scholz's arabesques, Carlos' poem in the most solemn style exhorted his fellow Rütlians to emulate the Swiss under Wilhelm Tell:

> Armes Volk, geknechtet so tief,
> Auf zum Streit! die Sturmesglocke rief
> Auf zum Streite und Siege auch Dich.
> Scharf sei das Schwert jetzt in unserer Hand,

Groß der Muth, unzertrennlich das Band,
Das uns umschlingt und ewiglich. (I, 51)

Such Schillerian pathos was, however, not the typical tone among
these "platonic revolutionaries" (I, 39); an expression representative of their generally skeptical if not cynical attitude was Löwenstein's famous "Ballade von der Freifrau von Droste-Vischering,"[25]
a witty travesty on the 1844 Trier exhibition (sanctioned by the
Prussian government) of the robe allegedly worn by Christ. The
poem had its pictorial counterpart in Ulke's likewise popular drawing. Indicative of the *Rütli* members' generally satirical orientation
is the fact that the club's weekly bulletin was actually the predecessor of the journal *Kladderadatsch*, of whose four founders three
were Rütlians.[26]

Opposition to the Prussian state provided the basis for the
Rütli's sympathies with others of similar persuasion. From his
Swiss exile Ferdinand Freiligrath sent manuscripts of his newest
political poems. Rütlians associated freely with a circle of Young
Hegelians named *Die Freien*,[27] including the brothers Bruno and
Edgar Bauer and Max Stirner, who offered readings from his anar-
chist treatise *Der Einzige und sein Eigenthum* (1845). Some *Rütli*
members, including Carlos von Gagern, also attended meetings of
the recently founded Berlin *Handwerkerverein*, "eine Bildungs-
stätte für heranwachsende Revolutionäre, nicht bloß des Arbeiter-
standes, sondern aller Berliner Gesellschaftskreise."[28] Here journeymen returning from abroad, particularly from Paris, acted as the
harbingers of organized socialism.[29] Like kindred associations then
being established in the German lands, this club functioned primarily as an *Arbeiterbildungsverein*, in keeping with the aims and
methods expressed in such early Marxist writings as *Zur Kritik der
Hegelschen Rechtsphilosophie* (1843–44) and *Die heilige Familie*
(1845). In the absence of any legally constituted political parties
at this time, Marx and Engels considered *Lese-* and *Diskussions-
vereine* the most effective organizations for the propagation of
socialism.[30]

Of considerable consequence to Carlos' later career was his
personal acquaintance with Alexander von Humboldt, who lived
only two doors away from him.[31] Always a fatherly friend of
talented young men, Humboldt recognized Carlos' intellectual

promise and predicted a brilliant future for him. While appreciating Humboldt's scientific stature and his personal kindness, Carlos found him evasive in his opinions on religion and politics, two matters of greatest concern to young Carlos. Some of his Mexican activities were admittedly motivated by his desire to trace Humboldt's reception in the country whose future he had prophetically charted and brought to the attention of modern Europe in his book *Essay politique sur le royaume de la Nouvelle Espagne* (1811). And although he found that Mexicans justly held Humboldt in high esteem, Carlos took the pains to document Humboldt's human shortcomings, which he saw as courtly obsequiousness in his correspondence with government officials and vanity for failing to acknowledge all the assistance received in collecting data for his scientific works.[32]

In the fall of 1846, Carlos accepted an invitation by his brother-in-law, the famous Japanologist Philipp Franz von Siebold (1796–1866), to come to The Hague.[33] A colonel on the general staff and government advisor in Dutch-Japanese affairs, von Siebold hoped that Carlos would conclude his law studies and then specialize in oriental languages to become a Japanologist under his guidance. Until he resumed his study of law at the University of Leyden in the spring of 1847, Carlos assisted his brother-in-law in the evaluation of source material for a book on Japan. During these months Carlos received sufficient training to be of service to the Japanese legation in Vienna some thirty years later. As a result of his exposure to oriental art and folklore, Carlos later published his own translation of a Japanese fairy tale (in which he discovered a striking resemblance to *Von dem Fischer un syner Fru* as recorded by the Grimm brothers) along with a theory pertaining to the ethnological significance of folk tales. A good command of Latin and his rapid acquisition of Dutch (facilitated by his knowledge of Low German and English) enabled Carlos to obtain a law diploma by the end of 1847.[34] One year of fairly intensive academic pursuits failed, however, to dull Carlos' political perceptiveness. The scandals involving the House of Orange during his Dutch sojourn strengthened his antimonarchistic attitude, and Carlos seems to have made a heroic effort to arouse his fellow students in Leyden from their traditional preoccupation with wine, women, and song to political alertness by propagandizing the same ideas as in the *Rütli*.

Near the end of 1847 Carlos left for Paris, where he wasted no time in calling on another of his idols. He was, however, completely disappointed by Georg Herwegh's apathy and smugness. Through Alexander von Humboldt's intercession,[35] Carlos was granted an audience with Duchess Hélène of Orleans (the former Princess of Mecklenburg-Schwerin), wife of Ferdinand of Orleans, the eldest son of Louis Philippe, on the eve of the February Revolution which swept away the July monarchy. There is no evidence that Carlos took any part in the Paris uprising. That he welcomed it follows from the distichs with which he described France in the spring of 1848:

> Stets hat der gallische Hahn zuerst den Morgen geahnet,
>   Alle Völker sein Ruf stets aus dem Schlummer geweckt;
> Aber zuerst auch stets auf der Freiheit Altar geblutet,
>   Sühne der eigenen Schuld, doch zur Erlösung der Welt.

(II, 173)

The recently appointed Commissioner for the Département de Basses Pyrénées invited Carlos to accompany him to his new territory. Carlos accepted and used his time in the border region to study Spanish and Basque. An adventurous spirit rather than political persuasion made him accept a secret mission on behalf of the *Carlistas* in their effort to overthrow the regime of Isabella II. Carlos' attempt to gain the support of the opportunist general Baldomero Espartero for the *Carlista* cause failed, and he was nearly executed for conspiracy and high treason. An appeal by the Prussian embassy ultimately brought about his release from several months of captivity in October 1848 on the condition that he would never re-enter Spain.[36]

A lasting result of his Spanish adventure was Carlos' disillusionment about the true character of so-called great men and his distrust of their roles as recorded by historians. His experience with Espartero merely typified the impressions Carlos generally gained from his subsequent encounters with a number of famous contemporaries:

> Er erschien mir durchaus unbedeutend, und Alles, was ich später von ihm in Erfahrung brachte, hat mich in der Ansicht bestärkt, daß er nichts weiter war, als eine glänzende Mittelmäßigkeit in jeder Beziehung, als Militär sowohl wie als Politiker. Er glich, wie so manche von der Geschichte, dieser

ewigen Lügnerin, als groß gepriesenen Männer der Pauke, die an-
geschlagen, desto stärker tönt, je größer der innere hohle Raum;
oder, wie ein rumänisches Sprichwort sagt: Leere Fässer machen
den größten Lärm. . . . . Der Glaube an die historische Wahrheit
empfängt einen starken Stoß, wenn man Gelegenheit hat, sogenannte Männer im Schlafrock zu sehen. Man gelangt da leicht zu
der Überzeugung, daß die Größer vieler, ja der meisten unter
ihnen, nur eine Talmi-Größe ist, die ihren Ursprung dem glücklichen Zusammentreffen verschiedener Zufälligkeiten verdankt.

(I, 130–131)

His acquaintance with three leading French political figures
upon his return to Paris in October of 1848 served to reinforce
Carlos' distinction between the historical process and its human
agents. The historian Friedrich von Raumer, whom Carlos had frequently met in the home of his grandparents, had been sent to
Paris as the representative of the Frankfurt Assembly. In this
capacity he introduced Carlos to Eugène Cavaignac (President of
the Executive Committee which had replaced the provisional
government), Alphonse de Lamartine (a member of the same
body), and Louis Napoleon (then an undistinguished deputy of
the legislature). Less than two months later, Carlos witnessed the
latter's triumphant inauguration as President of the French Republic and the beginning of his exploitation of the Napoleonic myth.

In order to counteract Carlos' all too evident liberalism, his
mother and guardian insisted that he should become an officer,
and in early 1849 he was assigned as lieutenant to an infantry
battalion stationed in Breslau.[37] Repelled by the limited learning
and reactionary outlook of his fellow officers (a situation he later
found faithfully typified in Friedrich Spielhagen's 1864 novel *Die
von Hohenstein*), he discharged his daily duties without overcom-
ing his dislike for the Prussian military.[38] At night, however, he
served as president of a "hochrother Arbeiterverein" (I, 166). An
episode in this connection illustrates that he did not consider
radical egalitarianism incompatible with aesthetic sensitivity. When
it was brought to his attention that some members called him
"Aristo" because of his habitually well-manicured white hands,
he addressed a meeting in these words:

Auch ich, meine Freunde, bin ein rückhaltloser Anhänger
der allgemeinen Gleichheit; ich will sogar, daß sich diese bis auf

die Hände erstrecke. Nur kommt es darauf an, in welcher Weise dies bewerkstelligt werde. Sie kommen von der Hobelbank, Sie von der rußigen Schmiedeesse, Sie haben soeben erst den Pechdraht fortgelegt oder andere ähnliche Arbeiten vorgenommen und dabei die Hände sich beschmutzt; ich bin von meinem Schreibtisch aufgestanden, wo ich höchstens Gelegenheit hatte, mir einige Tintenflecke zu machen. Bevor ich mich jedoch hierher begab, habe ich mir die Hände gewaschen; Sie haben es nicht gethan, und daher die Ungleichheit. Was ist nun richtiger, um dieselbe herzustellen? Daß ich mir die Hände wieder beschmutze, damit sie den Ihren, oder daß Sie sich waschen, damit sie den meinen gleich werden? (I, 167)

With his twenty-fourth birthday on December 12, 1850, Carlos attained his majority under Prussian law. He promptly quit the army and married Elvira Schneider, daughter of the ophthalmologist and physician to the king of Württemberg, Dr. Joseph Schneider.[39] Upon the recommendation of Gustav Adolf Wislicenus,[40] Carlos was elected speaker of the *Freie Gemeinde* in Zeitz, where he delivered his inaugural address on May 24, 1851.[41] Carlos' rhetorical talent and unorthodox religious views qualified him for his new position. Although he had been reared in a pious family, attending Schleiermacher's Dreifaltigkeitskirche in Berlin, Carlos was early repelled by the austerity of Lutheranism, and his emotional antipathy soon developed into an intellectual one. He partook of confirmation only to oblige his family, and his "no" in response to the credo was drowned by the "yes" of the other candidates. After successively studying stupendous amounts of Protestant, Catholic, and Judaic literature, he found their Scriptural bases and dogmas wanting. Ludwig Feuerbach and David Friedrich Strauß merely verified his conclusions. In an 1845 diary entry, "Pete summa, Deo juvante!" he quickly changed *Deo* to read *Fortuna* (I, 178). It is possible that he became acquainted with the *Lichtfreunde* at this time.[42]

In accordance with his own religious views, Carlos de-emphasized the role of the Bible as divine revelation, although he referred to it in his sermons where it was convenient. But in this function it became merely one of many equally authoritative sources in furthering man's belief in himself. What Carlos and others like him preached in Prussian Saxony and the Thuringian *Kleinstaaten*[43] was a pragmatic humanitarianism with a pronounced social and pedagogical orientation.[44] Since most members of his congregation were workers and poor artisans, Carlos organized a cooperative association whose buying power reduced the cost of food, fuel, and raw materials for all members.[45] This successful venture induced others to join the congregation. Nevertheless, constant surveillance, withdrawal of assembly privileges, and relentless prosecution by the authorities were followed by the eventual disbandment of the Zeitz congregation. And although he had been acquitted of charges including *lèse-majesté,* high treason, and blasphemy, thanks to his own brilliant legal defense in a Naumburg court, Carlos was officially advised to leave Prussia. He decided to emigrate to America.[46]

After a stormy fifty-nine-day voyage from Hamburg (during which, since there was no physician aboard, he delivered an emigrant mother's child), Carlos arrived in New York on July 4, 1852. Although rationalist Freethinkers had formed American associations since the 1820's and *Lichtfreunde* had congregated in the United States since the 1840's,[47] no organization of this kind existed in New York when Carlos arrived there,[48] and the notoriously inadequate remuneration of American *Gemeindesprecher*[49] was hardly an incentive for capable men to vie for such a position. Carlos chose to write *Novellen,* poetry, and political articles for the recently founded *Kriminalzeitung.* His journalism, however, did not satisfy his higher ambitions, and any hopes he might have for an active political role he saw frustrated by the contempt of native Americans for the "green" and "damn Dutchman" (I, 210). Rising Know-Nothingism and "amerikanische Gleichheitsflegelei" (I, 207) instilled in him no desire to seek the citizenship of that country. And the sudden assimilation of German aristocrats and recent revolutionary leaders "in den Vereinigten Staaten, dem *receptaculum* so vieler problematischer Naturen und verfehlter Existenzen" (I, 208) horrified him.[50] Last but not least, the "niggerhafte *Yankee-doodle*" (II, 259) struck him as the epitome of musical tastelessness.[51]

Thus ailing with many of the classical symptoms of the mainly imaginary malady of many a nineteenth-century *Amerikamüde,*[52] Carlos resolved to leave the United States, although the economic conditions in the spring of 1853 were excellent.[53] After a brief trip to Niagara Falls, he followed the Mississippi route to New Orleans and sailed to Veracruz, where he landed on July 15.

Apart from his disenchantment with the United States, it was Carlos' old affinity for everything Spanish—particularly the language, "die schönste der Welt" (I, 215), and baroque architecture—that attracted him to Mexico. Furthermore, the new Mexico which had evolved since its colonial period was almost unknown abroad,[54] and in its continuing quest for political identity Carlos sensed adventure and opportunity. In New Orleans he had made the chance acquaintance of Manuel Payno, a distinguished Mexican statistician and later minister of finance, who had provided him with several letters of introduction. One of these led to an interview with Minister of War Tornel, who proposed that Carlos join the Mexican army. Despite his previous aversion to the military, Carlos accepted in the belief that his service would benefit the cause of republicanism in Mexico. Following a series of examinations, he was appointed captain in the corps of engineers. Mexican citizenship seems to have been granted concomitantly. As instructor at Chapultepec military college, where he was also commander of a company, he was able to follow his own inclination and act in a broad educational rather than exclusively military function. He attempted to remedy what he considered the basic flaw in the scientific training of future officers, "denn wie bei allen damaligen Unterrichtsanstalten der Republik wurde nach wie vor nach spanischer Schablone auch in dieser Anstalt der Hauptwerth auf die Kräftigung des Gedächtnisses gelegt; man begnügte sich mit einem oft gedankenlosen Auswendiglernen der ‚Texte', d.h. der Lehrbücher" (I, 255). Apart from reforming teaching methods, Carlos aimed at counteracting the characteristic stoic passiveness among the largely illiterate native Mexican population by instilling in the soldiers a sense of self-esteem and national purpose. Thus he saw the positive role of the Mexican army as a "Lebensschule . . . in welcher die Sitten geläutert, der Charakter gefestigt, Energie, Pünktlichkeit, Ehrenhaftigkeit, Selbstaufopferung, Ausdauer und Disciplin geschaffen und genährt werden müßten" (I, 256).

In command of another company at Chapultepec was Miguel Miramón, who impressed Carlos as an undistinguished capricious twenty-year-old captain who had memorized the infantry manual. With this knowledge and ruthless opportunism he soon rose rapidly through the various ranks and a few years later usurped the Mexican presidency.

Like other Mexicans, Carlos was willing to tolerate General Santa Anna's use of extraordinary executive powers, constitutionally sanctioned in February 1853, for the sake of national progress. But Santa Anna's enlightened despotism rapidly grew into a full-fledged dictatorship, which he had formalized in the December 16, 1853, decree arrogating the presidency for life along with the title of serene highness. In this atmosphere of ostentatious pseudo-courtly ritual and wanton waste of public property, Santa Anna sought more German officers as instructors for his army, and the Mexican ambassador to Berlin was asked to recruit them. When Santa Anna, by way of complementing Carlos for his achievements at Chapultepec, offered to make Carlos his personal adjutant, Carlos declined by replying, "Dispénseme Vuestra Alteza, no sé ser ayuda de cámara" (I, 238). Santa Anna's displeasure effected Carlos' transfer in the spring of 1854 to the Isthmus of Tehuantepec, where he participated in surveying the terrain for a projected railroad. Before his departure from Mexico City, he was made a regular member of the *Sociedad de geografía y estadística*.

In the first year after his arrival in Mexico City, Carlos participated in the social life of the local German colony, composed chiefly of merchants. As their exclusively economic interest in Mexican affairs became evident, he dissociated himself from them and later in his *Apelación* criticized their ingratitude toward Mexico. Although he had made a rational choice in accepting Mexican citizenship, he had to concede that the emotional ties with his native country were too strong to be severed. This sentiment he expressed in a hastily composed poem, which he read as part of the German community's reception for the soprano Henriette Sonntag, when she arrived in the capital on a concert tour in early 1854:

Getrennt vom theuren deutschen Vaterlande
Durch weite Meere, tausende von Meilen,
Sind doch zerrissen nicht die alten Bande,
Und oft zur Heimath die Gedanken eilen.
Wie sie bewegt, ob Freude oder Schmerzen,
Ein Echo findet es in unserm Herzen. (I, 308)

For Carlos her visit was especially moving because, as a fifteen-year-old, he had been enamored with this friend of his family in Berlin. The news of her sudden death in Mexico City on June 17, 1854, reached him in Veracruz, on his way to the Isthmus. Her husband relied on Carlos to arrange for the transport of her coffin to Europe.

Following his Isthmus assignment, Carlos supervised the fortification of San Juan de Ulúa and Veracruz (1854–56). While two former Prussian officers under his command died of the *vómito prieto* (yellow fever), he survived, thanks to the efforts of a friend, the ethnographer Dr. Hermann Behrendt. Carlos took no active part in the growing opposition to Santa Anna and his eventual overthrow. The governor of Veracruz designated Carlos as temporary adjutant to conduct Santa Anna aboard the ship that took him to his exile in Venezuela (August 17, 1855). Carlos' lack of political partisanship in the ensuing *pronunciamentos* and factional strife constituting the early Reform period did not make him immune to its repercussions. In 1856 he lost his command of the engineers in Veracruz and was sent to the state of Yucatan without any official duties. Besides surveying the topography for another railroad, he used this time to study the indigenous Maya culture. As the political intrigues intensified, he left for Havana, where he assisted Santa Anna's wife while the ex-dictator lived on the Danish island of St. Thomas.

Carlos' presence in the United States is not otherwise documented for 1857, but it can be inferred from the fact that he celebrated his twenty-fifth masonic anniversary in 1882.[55] According to Kunwald, he had quit the Mexican lodge *Paz y Concordia* to be received into the lodge *Schiller* in Brooklyn.[56]

In the spring of 1858, Carlos returned to Mexico City via Tampico to offer his services to the conservative government of Zuluaga. Toward the end of the year Carlos was promoted to lieutenant colonel and put in command of a battalion of sappers in Toluca, which was considered an elite unit. His efforts to educate his officers and train his soldiers were cut short by orders to join the war against the Juarist faction. In the battles of Calamanda and San Cosme in early 1859, Carlos and his sappers distinguished themselves, and at Tucubaya the battalion played a key role in defeating the Juarist forces outside Mexico City on April 11,

1859. When the new president, Miramón, ordered the execution of fifty-three captured officers at Tacubaya, Carlos submitted his resignation. Miramón refused to accept it, and Carlos was sent on a scientific mission to the state of Oaxaca. When he returned in 1860 and repeated his request, Miramón had him arrested. Together with Francisco Zarco (editor of the influential *Siglo XIX*), Manuel Zamacona (a member of the legislature and later ambassador to Washington), and several high-ranking officers, Carlos was held prisoner in a former monastery near the capital until Christmas Eve 1860, when the Revolution swept away the Miramón government. Carlos dated his decision to cease being a nonpartisan in the political struggles of Mexico from this year: "Ich wurde gleichzeitig nach reiflicher Überlegung und genauer Kenntniß-nahme der für einen Ausländer schwer zu verstehenden politischen Verhältnisse des Landes Parteigänger, mich selbstverständlich der bis dahin nur oberflächlich von mir gekannten und vielleicht nicht immer richtig gewürdigten freisinnigen Partei anschließend" (I, 287).[57]

After Juárez was elected to the presidency in June 1861, he appointed Carlos to deal with matters of colonization and the preparation of a Mexican map, in the ministry of public works led by Carlos' close friend Ignacio Ramírez. Simultaneously, Carlos developed plans for a program of higher education involving the establishment of a kind of *Realgymnasium,* which he submitted to Juárez. The specifics included the proposed redesignation of the former Archbishop's Palace into a *Colegio de la Reforma.* Such a concept was too radical even for the anticlerical Juarists to realize, and Carlos was instead reappointed to the military college. As its Scientific Director, he was given the authority to reorganize its curriculum and teaching methods according to the principles of his proposal.

Before assuming his new post, Carlos wrote his *Apelación de los mexicanos a la Europa bien informada de la Europa mal informada,* which he dedicated to Benito Juárez. The book appeared in early 1862 in Mexico City,[58] printed by Ignacio de Cumplido, whose presses also produced the widely read liberal newspaper *El Siglo XIX.*[59] Carlos' aim was to correct the mistaken image of Mexico then current abroad, particularly in view of the intervention by several European powers. Britain, France, and Spain had signed a convention agreeing on the joint occupation of Veracruz in order to exact restitution of economic losses resulting from the Mexican civil strife. The first foreign detachments were arriving as the *Apelación* was being written, and this explains the haste in which the book was obviously authored.[60]

Most Europeans, Carlos maintains, were still relying on Alexander von Humboldt for their information on Mexico: "Aun los Europeos mas illustrados y menos mal dispuestos respecto á México, lo conocen casi esclusivamente por la obra de Humboldt."[61] The book therefore charts the problematical course of Mexico's recent history—emphasizing, however, the progressive achievements since its independence from Spain—and presents a long catalogue of outstanding Mexicans in the arts and sciences.[62] Unveiling the mercenary motivation underneath the foreign power's formal pretexts for intervening in Mexican affairs, Carlos castigates not only these hostile parties but capitalism as the ruling force of his century. "El padre yankee dice á su hijo al despedirlo de la casa paterna, y en forma de benedicion: 'Make money, my son, honestly, if you can, but in every case make money.'. . . He aqui en pocas palabras el resúmen de la moral del siglo XIX, en América, como en Europa, en Inglaterra, Francia y España, como en México."[63] As the *sistema regenerador*[64] Carlos advocates socialism, as yet little known in Mexico and too often confused with communism.

The book found considerable resonance in Mexico and abroad. The Mexican press praised it as a patriotic accomplishment, and at a banquet General Paz toasted Carlos as the most Mexican of all Mexicans. English and French translations of the book followed, and the French government had it confiscated. The former Mexican consul general in Paris was charged with being its author and was acquitted only because of Carlos' written testimony.

In keeping with his decision to participate politically, Carlos became a regular contributor to the *Siglo XIX*. One of his outspoken articles questioned the integrity of the prime minister, Manuel Doblado, who promptly had Carlos deposed from office, stripped of his rank, and banished from the capital. As a result of Carlos' appeal to Juárez, these measures were countermanded and replaced by a nominal fine ultimately waived by Juárez. To be out of reach of Doblado's wrath, however, Carlos chose to serve as a government engineer and later as secretary of the state Querétaro. In the latter function one of his duties was to have the leaders of a pro-French army conspiracy executed on June 23, 1862. He was also the chief editor of the government's newspaper, *La bandera nacional,* until he obtained permission to join the army against the large-scale invasion by European troops.

Before rejoining the military, Carlos became the first non-native Mexican ever to deliver a formal oration at the official celebrations of the anniversary of Mexican independence. On the night of September 15, 1862, his fervently patriotic address expressed the determination of the Mexican people to resist any foreign invaders and concluded with an emotional prediction: "México ecsistirá y será libre, y grande y feliz, é iniciará con su triunfo el de la idea democrática en el orbe entero!"[65] His audience was ecstatic, and Carlos immediately had to make a similar speech to the thousands gathered outside the Iturbide theater.

On October 27, 1862, Carlos left Mexico City to become chief of staff under General Patoni, a friend of his in command of a brigade at Quecholac, near Puebla. Carlos' appointment was no coincidence, for he and Patoni were fellow members "einer vom früheren Minister Ignacio Ramírez . . . und von mir gegründeten geheimen politischen Verbindung, welche sich über die ganze Republik ausdehnte und alle hervorragenden Männer der Fortschrittspartei in sich vereinigte. Als Aufgabe hatte sie sich gestellt, die radikalen Prinzipien überall zur Geltung zu bringen und ihren Mitgliedern Positionen zu verschaffen, in denen sie für dieselben erfolgreich wirken könnten." (II, 35–36). In his off-duty hours, Carlos continued his journalistic contributions for *El Siglo XIX;* and for *El fuerte de Guadalupe,* an army bulletin, he wrote a series of patriotic articles. On the assumption that many French soldiers in the invasion forces did not agree with the political ambitions of Napoleon III, Carlos composed a proclamation in French, promising fair treatment and rewards to deserters of the invading armies. This propaganda move was moderately successful.

When the command of a sapper battalion became vacant, Carlos was able to resume his former position. Against Carlos' and other officers' advice, the Mexican commander-in-chief Gonzáles Ortega persisted in fortifying Puebla as his stronghold against the onslaught of the superior French expeditionary force. Carlos and his *zapateros* played a conspicuous role in the defense of Puebla during the murderous sixty-two-day siege.[66] When Puebla capitulated on May 17, 1863, the Mexicans became prisoners of war, and all captured officers were marched to Veracruz and shipped to France. Soon in control of the Mexican capital, the French established a puppet government that was to make Maximilian Emperor of Mexico.

Via the Bermudas and Brest, Carlos was taken to the town of Evreux in Normandy for internment. To supplement the meager subsistence rendered by the French government to its internees, Carlos gave English lessons. Within the town of Evreux, Carlos enjoyed considerable freedom of movement and was hospitably received by the town's *haute-volée*. His acquaintance with the local Prefect Janvier de la Motte gave him insights into the extensive corruption and moral hypocrisy of the political leadership under Napoleon III's reign. Despite a sudden fad of jewelry and nightcaps *à la mexicaine,* French ignorance about Mexico was manifest. At their arrival in Evreux, the Mexican officers were gazed upon like exotic animals. Even educated Frenchmen expected all Mexicans to be semisavage barbarians. When Carlos was introduced to the Duchess of Persigny, she could not help exclaiming, "Mais mon dieu, vous n'êtes pas brun du tout!" (II, 132). Such notions Carlos later found prevalent elsewhere: "Diese komische Auffassung von dem Aussehen der in Frankreich internirten mexikanischen kriegsgefangenen Offiziere bildete indessen keine Ausnahme von der Regel in der französischen Gesellschaft" (II, 133).

With a minority of fellow officers he successfully resisted French efforts to win their allegiance to Maximilian and the Mexican faction backed by Napoleon III; of the 500 officers captured at Puebla, only a quarter remained true to the Republic of Mexico. For this loyalty Carlos was later awarded the first class of the order *Constancia y Patriotismo,* which was created solely to recognize officers that had upheld the republican cause throughout the five-year period of foreign intervention. This distinction entitled the bearer to first preference in consideration for public office. In response to French subversive attempts, Carlos on September 13, 1863, had a memorandum conveyed to Napoleon III, predicting the imminent failure of the French involvement in Mexican affairs. During Napoleon's visit of Evreux, Carlos tried unsuccessfully to obtain a private audience with him. Before departing for Mexico, Maximilian summoned Carlos to Paris in March 1864 to offer him a high position in his government. Carlos rejected it, and at Maximilian's request drafted a detailed exposition of the present Mexican situation, stressing the fictitious nature of the plebiscite which the French had prompted the Mexican puppet government to stage in support of Maximilian's emperorship. Carlos concluded this memorandum with a prophetic premonition about Maximilian's Mexican venture: "Ich fürchte, Eure kaiserliche Hoheit werden den Versuch mit Ihrem Kopfe bezahlen" (II, 344). With the approval of Carlos' compatriots in Evreux, this document was sent to reach Maximilian in London. In light of this, Siebold's offer, in May 1864, to intercede with Maximilian (whom he knew well) on Carlos' behalf was, of course, anticlimactic.

From Evreux, Carlos had been corresponding with Neffziger, chief editor of the liberal *Le Temps* in Paris, to whom he passed on letters he received from Mexico. When Neffziger's journal, using information from Carlos, publicized the authorities' active subversion among interned Mexican officers, the French government saw itself compelled to set all of them free, without further conditions, on July 17, 1864.

Upon his release from French captivity, Carlos went to Paris, where he resided in the military quarter, on the Avenue de la Motte Piquet, near the Champ de Mars. Lacking the money necessary for returning to Mexico (the Juarist government, in its continuing struggle against Maximilian's regime, was unable to provide any), Carlos had to earn it as a writer. For the *Revue du monde colonial, asiatique, et américain,* he wrote a series of articles entitled *Le Mexique contemporain* in order to clarify the French misconception of his adoptive country. In addition to tracing the circumstances leading to the European intervention, Carlos criticized the views which Michel Chevalier (then a member of the French Senate) had expressed in his book *Le Mexique, ancien et moderne* (1863). In attacking Chevalier's hero worship of men like Cortez, Carlos defined the cult of so-called great men as a contemporary idolatry of success, even if it is criminal—a thinly veiled allusion to the rise of Napoleon III. And in contrast to Chevalier's justification of the French interference in Mexico as a historic mission to protect the Latin against the Anglo-Saxon race,[67] Carlos asserted that Mexico's problems were internal and largely attributable to an as yet incomplete amalgamation of its races.

Noirot, the editor of the *Revue,* introduced Carlos to a number of influential Parisian *littérateurs,* among them Alexander Dumas *père* and the scholar-publisher Ambroise Firmin Didot. For Didot's *Nouvelle biographie générale,* then in progress, Carlos prepared a number of biographical sketches.[68] He also gained access to circles frequented by members of the radical left-wing opposition to Napoleon's government and became acquainted with Léon Gambetta, Louis Garnier Pagès, Ernest Picard, Jules Simon, and Adolphe Thiers. The liberal republican Jules Favre, a consistent critic of Napoleon's foreign policy, Carlos regularly supplied with information received from the Juarists, and Carlos' gratification came from the consternation Favre's speeches based on this material caused among the supporters of Napoleon in the French legislature.

In the spring of 1865, Miramón, who had accepted a command in Maximilian's army, asked Carlos to accompany him on an inspection of Prussian armaments. Hoping that he might dissuade Miramón from such an allegiance, Carlos obliged. Although this hope proved illusory, Carlos was able to visit his relatives in Berlin. Here, as in France, he found the crassest ignorance concerning republican Mexicans.[69]

In the summer of 1865, Carlos boarded an English steamer in Liverpool, bound for New York. The voyage reinforced his long-standing resentments against Anglo-Saxons. In spite of his emphatic condemnation of national and racial prejudices elsewhere (e.g., I, 321–322), he firmly believed in a long list of disagreeable characteristics shared by Britishers and Americans alike.

Ich muß allerdings eingestehen, daß ich im Allgemeinen kein Freund der angelsächsischen Race bin, ohne indeß ihre vielfachen Vorzüge, namentlich ihre in der go ahead-Theorie wurzelnde unermüdliche Thatkraft zu verkennen. Es heißt wohl, man brauche selbst den vornehmen Russen nur zu kratzen, damit der Tatare zum Vorschein komme. Bei vielen Engländern und Yankees genügt es, sie mit irgend welchen Spirituosen innerlich anzufeuchten, eine Operation, die sie mit besonderer

Vorliebe an sich selbst vornehmen, und sofort wirst Du sie sich in ihrer ganzen angeborenen Brutalität entpuppen sehen. Häufig ist dazu nicht einmal eine solche Anfeuchtung nöthig. Ihr Mangel an Idealismus, ihr geringes künstlerisches Verständniß, ihre Unfähigkeit, zu singen oder auch nur sich wahrhaft für Musik zu begeistern—der von ihnen zur Schau getragene Enthusiasmus für berühmte Sänger, Sängerinnen und Virtuosen ist nichts als Modesache und gehört zum rein äußerlich guten Ton— machen sie mir antipathisch, nicht zu sprechen von ihrem steifen Wesen, ihren, namentlich was Religion anbetrifft, conservativen Ideen, ihrer maßlosen Selbstsucht und der verletzenden Überhebung über alle anderen Nationen, die sich charakteristisch auch darin kundgiebt, daß sie ihr liebes Ich stets mit großem Buchstaben schreiben, es gern an die Spitze des Satzes stellen und unnöthig oft wiederholen, so daß aus ihrer Rede unaufhörlich das breite Ai (I) hervorklingt. Ein betrunkener Russe, auch wenn er den niederen Ständen angehört, zeigt sich gemeiniglich gutmüthig, er geht sogar so weit, Dich zu umarmen und zu küssen, was freilich ebenfalls lästig fällt; ein betrunkener Goddammer hingegen, sei er selbst von der besten Gesellschaft, wird leicht ausfallend, schlägt gern Alles um sich her in Stücke und ist jeden Augenblick bereit, sich die Rockärmel aufzuschlagen und Dir in Boxerstellung herausfordernd gegenüberzutreten. Angenehmer sind mir die Engländerinnen und Amerikanerinnen, schon ihrer dem Ohre wohlthuenderen Aussprache des Englischen und ihrer feineren Manieren wegen; außerdem sind die letzteren im Allgemeinen entscheidend gebildeter als die Männer, weil diese von Jugend an Geld machen müssen. Am Unerträglichsten zeigen die Angelsachsen sich auf Reisen; liebenswürdiger sind sie im eigenen Lande. . . .

Wenn die Verse:
   „Wo man singt, da laß Dich ruhig nieder,
   Böse Menschen haben keine Lieder"—
Wahrheit enthalten, so ist es nicht gerathen, unter Engländern und Yankees Platz zu nehmen. Dennoch mußte ich es an Bord zwei Wochen lang in ihrer um so ungemüthlicheren Gesellschaft aushalten, als wegen der Schwierigkeit, einander auszuweichen, es kaum möglich war, sich ihr zu entziehen. (II, 257-259)[70]

At this time, the United States was the only major power continuing to recognize the Juárez government as legitimate, and New York was a haven for a great number of liberal Mexicans awaiting a favorable turn of events in their country. One of them was Zarco, whom Carlos taught German during the next several months, while he was trying to obtain sufficient funds for returning to Mexico. Although he saw some positive changes in the American opinion of immigrant Germans as a result of their role in the Civil War, Carlos found little to endear them to him. The Germans in the United States, he concluded, were losing what little education, social grace, and idealism they had. The few exceptions he was willing to make to this rule were the people with whom he associated: Friedrich Kapp, Franz Sigel, and Adolf Douai. The latter two were both active in the German-speaking free congregations.[71] An old friend of Carlos, Douai was director of the German high school and a minister of the *Freie Gemeinde* in Hoboken, which he had helped to found on February 19, 1865.[72] Its executive included Varnhagen von Ense's energetic niece Ottilie Assing, whose humanitarian dedication Carlos greatly admired; to demonstrate her radical egalitarianism, she had formed an intimate friendship with a negro and former runaway slave.

Carlos served as an occasional *Sprecher* for the free congregations in Hoboken,[73] Newark, Brooklyn, and New York. Here he met Karl Heinzen in the fall of 1865, then on one of his frequent lecture tours. Heinzen's blunt manners as well as his hatred of everything related to the *Turner* (ironically, Carlos saw in his exterior a resemblance with Jahn) and the military initially offended Carlos. But in subsequent discussions they discovered that their radical republicanism and atheism were very similar. Both held that the United States was not a model republic as long as it tolerated the presidency (Heinzen referred to the president as a "König im Frack"—II, 279), and after Carlos concluded one of his addresses with the lines

Warum streckst Du in Noth gekettete Hände gen Himmel,
Spannst das schleppende Wort vor die beflügelte That?
Mensch, der droben ist taub für alle Gebete des Schwachen,
Nur wer stark, wird erhört, denn bist Du stark, hilfst Dir selbst.

(II, 283)

Heinzen demonstratively expressed his full agreement.

In December 1865 and January 1866, Carlos published a number of articles on Mexico in the New York German press; in another publication of this period he insisted that masonic lodges should disregard prospective members' religious views.[74]

Following an unprofitable meeting with General Grant (arranged by the Mexican ambassador), Carlos left New York for Matamoros via Chicago, St. Louis, New Orleans, and Galveston. In St. Louis the local military commander introduced him to General Sherman, and in New Orleans Carlos expressed his and fellow officers' gratitude to General Sheridan for providing a steamer to transport them to Matamoros. Soon after his arrival in July 1866, Carlos was appointed secretary of the state of Tamaulipas, in charge of military administration. To an article in the *Rio Grande Courier* (published in Brownsville, Texas) which falsely named Carlos as a supporter of the presidential ambitions of General Ortega, Carlos responded with a *dementi*. He declared that he favored no particular personality, Juárez included, and that he merely endeavored to further the cause of the Republic.

Because he failed to align himself with the local governor's *pronunciamiento* against Juárez, Carlos was imprisoned. He would have been executed if his masonic distress signals had not been noticed by an officer, who helped Carlos to escape.[75] By a circuitous route, he reached the army of General Mariano Escobedo, who put Carlos in charge of his engineers. After assisting in quelling the Tamaulipas rebellion, Carlos accompanied Escobedo to Monterey, where he effected the release of seven captured Austrian officers in return for their word of honor to leave Mexico forthwith; only one of them reneged and was later captured at Querétaro.

Escobedo advised Carlos to ask Juárez for a command in the central Mexican states, and after a journey through numerous war-ravaged settlements, Carlos met the President in Durango, in early January 1867. Having read the Brownsville article but not Carlos' rejoinder, Juárez granted him a frosty reception. Carlos accompanied him to the town of Zacatecas, where both narrowly escaped capture by imperial troops. Following recuperation from an attack of delirious fever, Carlos accepted from Juárez the command of a newly organized battalion in the state of Michoacan. With this unit Carlos took part in the siege of Querétaro. The opposing army was commanded by Miramón, who directed one assault against a sector thinly manned by Carlos' troops, capturing his adjutant von Glümer, a former officer in the Prussian guards.

After the fall of Querétaro on May 15, Carlos obtained permission to see Maximilian, whom he considered a tragic victim of Napoleon's machinations rather than a heinous enemy. In Maximilian's poems and career Carlos detected a sustained idealism that he deeply admired. Since it had been rumored that Juárez would never execute a fellow mason, Carlos wanted to ascertain whether Maximilian was one. His three-hour visit with the ex-emperor convinced him that Maximilian was no mason. Remembering Carlos' memorandum, Maximilian told him, "Baron Gagern, Sie sind ein guter Prophet gewesen."[76] Carlos could not bring himself to observe Maximilian's and Miramón's deaths by a firing squad on June 19, 1867.

On July 1, 1867, Carlos witnessed Juárez' triumphant return to Mexico City. Having resigned his field command, he became a critical observer of the self-congratulatory cult in the government and of the President's measures to prolong his term of office. Juárez, Carlos sensed, was no longer the friend of the people but was lusting for dictatorial power. Together with three other radical republicans, Carlos founded the journal *El Constitucional,* whose first issue was published on August 1. His angry editorials against Juárez' policy provoked the minister of war into having him assigned to the refortification of Perote. When in 1868 Carlos asked to be released from all military duties in order to assume the office of state secretary in Veracruz, he was charged with a fault in technical procedure and imprisoned for months. Acquitted by a military tribunal which also acceded to his request for a discharge, he was accused of libeling the minister of war and arrested again. He nevertheless persevered in his journalistic attacks against the government. A radical club, *La Convención Progresista,* made him its delegate, and *in absentia* a district of the state of Veracruz elected him to the Mexican congress. As a fellow member of congress, Carlos' friend Zarco (who had resumed his editorship of *El Siglo XIX*) in the fall of 1869 delivered a speech to uphold Carlos' mandate. When a second military tribunal finally freed him, Carlos returned to his post in Veracruz. But the warning that a new intrigue was planned against him and possibly his life caused Carlos to leave Mexico in January 1870. Via New Orleans and New York he went to Europe. Letters from friends in Mexico warned him against returning to Mexico under Juárez.

Carlos' role and sympathies during the Franco-Prussian War are not documented but can be inferred from his later attitude toward Bismarck's Empire and his immediate return to America, where he renewed his association with Douai[77] and other radicals remaining unreconciled with the German state. From the summer of 1871 until the spring of the following year Carlos lived in New York, where he joined the editorial staff of *Die neue Zeit*. Contributors to this weekly included such left-wing intellectuals and atheists as Ludwig Büchner, Adolf Douai, Georg Herwegh, Georg Friedrich Kolb, and Carl Voigt. Douai, since the publication of *Das Kapital* (1867), had become an ardent disciple of Karl Marx and was among the first to popularize his doctrine in America.[78] Douai's earlier denouncement of Karl Heinzen[79] coupled with the latter's personal dislike of Marx[80] pitted *Die neue Zeit* against Heinzen's *Pionier* for more than competitive reasons. It is probable that these circumstances affected Carlos' relationship with Heinzen, whose diatribes against Marx and the First International Carlos criticized in his editorials.[81] The ensuing polemics and his harsh review of Heinzen's novel *Der Editoren-Kongreß* embroiled the two in a literary feud that ended their earlier amity. Although Carlos continued to admire Heinzen for his candor and unwavering identification with radical causes,[82] he faulted Heinzen for feeding his personal vanity as a kind of atheistic pope and for lacking a truly cosmopolitan orientation. Heinzen's psychological flaw, according to Carlos, was that he could not accept the invective he so freely dispensed.

At the North American *Turnfest* in Brooklyn in the fall of 1871, the executive of the German-American *Turner* Association asked Carlos to formalize their manifesto to the American people. While he was conscious of surpassing Jahn's principles in scope (particularly his stolid Germanism), Carlos felt that he was merely adjusting them to the exigencies of a new era. Thus he saw the broad modern relevance of the *Turner* program as a humanitarian heritage, and in this spirit he stressed its universal role:

Auf socialem wie auf politischem wie auf religiösem Gebiete strebt ein Theil der Menschheit, der bessere, der edlere, der am meisten erleuchtete, mit niemals früher in so hohem Grade bewiesener Kühnheit, sich zu befreien von den Banden der durch Jahrhunderte langes Bestehen geheiligten Vorurtheile; wo immer es sich darum handelt, Verbesserungen anzubahnen, auf Grundlage der Vernunft und zum Zwecke der Vermehrung des allgemeinen Wohles: da sollen die deutsch-amerikanischen Turner in erster Linie stehen, fest entschlossen, nicht nachzulassen in ihrem Ringen, bis sie den endlichen Sieg erlangt, bis sie durchgeführt haben, was nach freier Forschung sie als wahr und gerecht erkannt. . . . Wir wollen ein Ende zu bereiten suchen dem Zustande des Krieges Aller gegen Alle, welcher der der heutigen Gesellschaft ist, und ihn ersetzen durch den eines harmonischen Zusammenwirkens ihrer verschiedenartigen Elemente. . . . Man kann nicht Sklave sein auf einem Gebiete und frei auf einem anderen. Ein politisch freisinniger Mann muß auch religiös freisinnig sein. Ist er das Letztere nicht, so darf man auch seiner politischen Freisinnigkeit nicht trauen. Dasselbe gilt in Bezug auf die socialen Grundsätze. Ein wahrer Republikaner, ein überzeugter Freidenker kann sich nicht zum Vertheidiger der gesellschaftlichen Klassenunterschiede aufwerfen. Vor Allem die Turner, welche diese harmonische Entwicklung auch in der gleichmäßigen Ausbildung des Leibes und Geistes suchen, müssen sie zur Darstellung bringen auf den drei Gebieten, auf welchen des Menschen Leben sich bewegt. . . Darum müssen wir unsere Kinder zu freien, sittlichen, starken Menschen erziehen, ohne jedes Vorurtheil in religiöser, politischer und socialer Hinsicht.

Mit solchen Menschen müssen aber die Vereinigten Staaten groß, mächtig und glücklich werden, und durch dieselben, wenn sie dieses Land als Vorbild nehmen, alle Völker der Erde.

Das ist das Ziel des Nordamerikansichen Turnerbundes.

(I, 28-29)

Persona non grata in the Mexico of Juárez and his successor Sebastián Lerdo de Tejada, Carlos spent the remainder of his life in Europe. From 1873 to 1883 he resided mainly in Vienna,[83] where he joined the *Geographische Gesellschaft* and lectured on the Indian population of Mexico in early 1873.[84] His former Japanese studies enabled him to function for the Japanese embassy. Journalism, however, remained his livelihood. Apart from writing for the Austrian Press[85] he served as correspondent for the Russian paper *Golos* during the Balkan War of 1878. Other travels took him to Maximilian's Miramar (1875) and Carmen Sylva's (ps. of Queen Elisabeth of Romania) Bucharest (1877). Concurrent with all these activities was Carlos' vigorous participation in the masonic affairs of the Austro-Hungarian Empire, mirrored in numerous publications.[86]

Masonry for Carlos was identical with the "Humanitätsbestrebungen der Menschheit."[87] This ideal, however, he saw distorted in that most contemporary lodges were observing a mere "Formen- und Phrasenwesen"[88] devoid of deeper meaning, while operating as "Mutual Assurance Companies."[89] Masonry, Carlos adjured his brethren, was to regain the importance it once had in the progress of mankind, which Carlos attributed in large measure to the historic roles played by a number of secret societies. To fulfill a meaningful modern function, masonry should dedicate itself to practical pursuits and bring about enlightenment and enjoyment for all human beings. Carlos advocated specifically the overthrow of capitalism as the immoral exploitation of most men. However socialist Carlos' masonic credo might have seemed, it had an essentially elitist correlative. While the majorities have their basic human rights, Carlos maintained, truth and momentous decisions cannot be reached by plebiscite. "Die große Masse bleibt immer nur Masse. Das *vox populi—vox Dei* ist oft nur eine Lüge gewesen."[90] And: "Nicht Alle sind tauglich zu Allem."[91]

In 1883 Carlos assumed a position as Mexican military attaché in Berlin. Because of friction with the German government, he resigned this post after less than two years. An added motivation may have been the fact that he found no understanding within the Prussian lodges. In Dresden, in January 1884, he began his memoirs, *Todte und Lebende,* whose *Schlußwort* he signed "Am Jahrestage der mexikanischen Unabhängigkeit, den 16. September 1884" (II, 396). Their 1884 publication was followed by the reprint of selected parts in the *Deutsche Zeitung von Mexico* of April 1885.

The two volumes are divided into seventeen chapters, of which sixteen center on famous contemporaries Carlos met up to 1871.[92] The resulting series of encounters,[93] while illustrating certain segments of his own life, leaves biographical lacunae and does not follow a strictly chronological progression. As the critical admirer or (more frequently) the adversary of "great" men, Carlos is far more concerned with the sum of his life and his participation in crucial historical events than with personal details about himself. And the loss of letters and other written records would have made it all but impossible to reconstruct his complete autobiography in the nine months he allotted to these recollections. Their meaning he perceived in retrospect as an idealist's peregrinations in a century dominated by the quest for money and success. In this age of selfish particularism and nationalism, he championed individual and political freedom in the belief that they were destined to bring about a cosmopolitan world:

> Andererseits drängt in allmäliger Entwicklung die Menschheit zum Cosmopolitismus. Das während der letzten Dezennien in Europa wieder zur Herrschaft gelangte Nationalitätenprinzip ist als ein nur zeitweiliges Abweichen von der richtigen Bahn zu betrachten. Mit um so kräftigerer Faust, muß deshalb das Banner hochgehalten werden, welches in strahlenden Lettern das Motto zeigt:
> „Omne solum forti patria ut piscibus aequor."[94]
> —dem Starken ist jeder Boden das Vaterland, wie den Fischen das Meer.
> Oder auch besser, wie ich in der Festrede sagte, welche ich 1862 am Jahrestage der mexikanischen Unabhängigkeit hielt:
> „Ubi libertas, ibi patria."
> —wo die Freiheit herrscht, da ist mein Vaterland. (I, vi)

Combined with repeated references to the lack of liberty, the chauvinism, and the reactionary military in Germany, such an outlook was, of course, anathema to the pride of the Wilhelminian Empire. Indicative of how Carlos' memoirs were received is a brief review in the influential *Deutsche Rundschau* which summarized them as "geschmackloses Prunken mit irreligiösen Ansichten und vaterlandsloser Gesinnung."[95]

In his last years, Carlos' health had been rapidly declining, partly as a result of the frequent changes of climate and war injuries he had sustained in the 1850's and 1860's. His hearing began to fail, and he had difficulties in moving one arm and his right foot. In 1885 he suffered a stroke, and although still suffering from its effects, he delivered the *Festrede* on the tenth anniversary of the lodge *Schiller* in Preßburg (November 15).[96] As correspondent for newspapers in Berlin and Vienna he went to Madrid, where he died of a lung hemorrhage on December 19, 1885.[97]

In spite of his espousal of republicanism and socialist ideas, Carlos retained in heritage and outlook a certain aristocratic reservation. He hoped for the ultimate fusion of democratic ideas and aristocratic forms and was unwilling to accept a dictatorship of the proletariat, "eine neue Aristokratie der schwieligen Faust" (I, 168). This unwillingness to accept a completely consequential egalitarianism became even more manifest in the context of his masonic beliefs. Rhetorically he implied that he saw himself as a proponent of modern chivalry in his efforts on behalf of Mexico:

> Una de los obligaciones de los caballeros de la edad media era la de acudir presurosos á la defensa del hombre injustamente oprimido, y de tomar siempre parte por el debil contra el fuerte, por la víctima contra el tirano.
>
> ¿Acaso esta caballerosidad ha desparecido completamente del mundo?
>
> ¿Y no hay Lafayettes, que desertan de la corte mas corrompida, del pais mas despóticamente regido del mundo, y vienen á ofrecer su espada a una colonia que lucha heróicamente por sacudir el yugo de la metrópoli, y establecer su independencia y con ella el sistema republicano?[98]

With this identification, Carlos may be included in a German tradition whose roots I have examined elsewhere.[99] In the nineteenth century, its literary proponents included Karl Follen, Heinrich Heine, Heinrich Laube, Louis von Arensschild, Karl Gutzkow, Johann Straubenmüller, Robert Eduard Prutz, Ferdinand Kürnberger, and Friedrich Spielhagen. Only Carlos von Gagern, however, was a *Ritter vom Geiste* willing to support his word with his sword.

NOTES

1. *Discourso patriotico pronunciado por el c. Carlos de Gagern en el teatro de Iturbide de Mexico. La noche del 15 de Septiembre de 1862* (Mexico, 1862), p. 3. Here and subsequently, I have not attempted to correct the frequently faulty accentuation found in the Spanish titles and quotations of Carlos von Gagern's writings.

2. At his own request, he was appointed supreme commander of the forces in the campaign against the Baden revolutionaries led by Friedrich Hecker and died in the battle of Kandern.

3. He served as the elected President of the Frankfurt National Assembly 1848–49.

4. A great-uncle of his was the liberal poet Anastasius Grün [ps. of Anton Alexander Maria Graf von Auersperg]. For a survey of Friedrich von Gagern's literary work, cf. Norbert Langer's introduction to Friedrich von Gagern, *Jäger und Gejagte*. Stiasny-Bücherei, Band 32 (Graz und Wien, 1958).

5. An exception is vol. 6 of the *Neue deutsche Biographie* (Berlin, 1964), p. 29, but the two-line mention identifies Carlos erroneously as "ehem. Oberst in *kaiserl.* [my italics] mexikan. Diensten."

6. Friedrich Nippold, *Welche Wege führen nach Rom? Geschichtliche Beleuchtung der römischen Illusionen über die Erfolge der Propaganda* (Heidelberg, 1869), mistakenly lists Carlos as a convert to Catholicism. The *Geschichte der Frankfurter Zeitung, Volksausgabe,* Herausgegeben vom Verlag der Frankfurter Zeitung (Frankfurt am Main, 1911), p. 160, mentions him as one of the feuilletonists. Jack Autrey Dabbs, *The French Army in Mexico 1861-1867. A Study in Military Government* (The Hague, 1963), p. 267, refers to one Carlos de Gagun [sic] as a German officer in the Juarist army. The only Mexican reference work including Carlos von Gagern, the *Diccionario Porrua de historia, biografía y geographía de México* (México, D.F., 1964), p. 571, does not even provide the dates of his birth and his death. This work describes his involvement during the French intervention in Mexico so ambiguously that one might conclude, as did the *Neue deutsche Biographie,* that Carlos von Gagern indeed sided with Emperor Maximilian.

7. "Carlos von Gagern," *Revista Humboldt*, No. 46 (1972), 55–65.

8. Unless otherwise noted, I have followed the two-volume *Todte und Lebende. Erinnerungen von Carlos von Gagern* (Berlin, 1884) for biographical information. References to quotations from this work are given in parentheses.

9. "Todtenschau," *Illustrirte Zeitung,* No. 2218 (January 2, 1886), 10.

10. *Andrees Handatlas* (Bielefeld und Leipzig, 1912), pp. 45–46, shows Groß Mantel (Neumark) situated ca. 70 km NE of Berlin and ca. 60 km N of Frankfurt/Oder.

11. Ludwig Kunwald, "Lebensgeschichte Carlos von Cagern's [sic]. Trauer-

rede gehalten in der von der Loge ‚Schiller,' im Or ∴ Pressburg am 5. Januar 1886, zum Andenken an den in den e ∴ O ∴ eingegangenen Br ∴ Carlos Freiherr v. Gagern abgehaltenen Trauerarbeit," in Carlos von Gagern, *Schwert und Kelle,* Aus dem Nachlasse des Verfassers herausgegeben von M[ichael] G[eorg] Conrad (Leipzig, 1888), p. 11. Kunwald's necrologue suffers from a considerable number of factual inaccuracies.

12. The father of Albert Erdmann Karl Gottfried von Levetzow (1828–1903), who served as President of the Reichstag 1881–84 and 1888–95.

13. Karl Gutzkow, who attended this school 1821–29, describes its intellectual climate as an incongruous mixture of rational philanthropy and Romanticism. He relates how the institution was relocated during his final school year in a building that had previously served as a jail for *Demagogen!* Karl Gutzkows *Ausgewählte Werke,* ed. H. H. Houben, vol. 10 (Leipzig, [1908]), 196–217.

14. Confirmed by Jahn's little-known authorship of a hilarious (in the truest sense of the word) *Vulgar* Latin parody of the Bible, *Oratio archaeologica sacro-bursicosa, pro gradu Doctoris Quomodis.* Cf. W. Fabricius, "Zur Studentensprache," *Zeitschrift für deutsche Wortforschung,* vol. 3 (1902), 93.

15. One fascinating fact in Carlos' account of his meeting with Jahn is not mentioned in any other source. The son of a Protestant minister, Jahn abandoned his study of theology under the spell of Wilhelm Friedrich von Meyern's utopian novel *Dya-Na-Sore, oder: Die Wanderer* (1787). Jahn's name may thus be added to Arno Schmidt's list of famous writers (Chamisso, Clausewitz, Fouqué, Goethe, Jean Paul, Karl May) allegedly influenced by this blueprint for a race-oriented dictatorship. Cf. *Tina oder über die Unsterblichkeit.* Fischer Bücherei, No. 755 (Frankfurt am Main und Hamburg, 1966), p. 32.

16. He became one of the earliest members of the *Turnverein Vorwärts* in Baltimore. Cf. Dieter Cunz, *The Maryland Germans* (Princeton, N.J., 1948), p. 324.

17. Dr. Moritz Kloss, who had just finished his *Turner* training under Eiselen in Berlin, was appointed to the staff. Cf. "Die k. Turnlehrerbildungsanstalt zu Dresden," *Illustrirte Zeitung,* No. 1686 (October 23, 1875), 314.

18. Hans Georg Werner, *Geschichte des politischen Gedichts in Deutschland von 1815 bis 1840.* Zweite Auflage (Glashütten im Taunus, 1972), pp. 60–61.

19. Not to be confused with the *Rütli* established in 1852 (a branch of the *Tunnel*) to which Fontane, Heyse, and Storm (among others) belonged. Cf. *Theodor Fontane und Bernhard Lepel. Ein Freundschafts-Briefwechsel,* ed. Julius Petersen (München, 1940), II, 464.

20. One of the most flamboyant German women authors of her time, Louise Aston (1814–71), née Hoche, was later immortalized in the fifth stanza of the jocose student song "Was der Bruder Straubinger im Jahr des Heils 1848 für Schicksale gehabt hat":

> Zu Schleswig in dem Hollenstein
> Schoß mir ein Dän in Strumpf herein,

Doch ne schöne Hand
Mir die Wund verband,
War aber die emansibierische [sic]
Frau Lydia [sic] Aston.

Bruder Straubinger, incidentally, concludes his globe-trotting in typical Forty-Eighter fashion. The little-known final three stanzas read:

Vom Goldland zu Kalifornien
Schied ich mit großen Zornigen,
Grub da Tag und Nacht,
Hab's doch zu nichts gebracht,
Weil ich an jedem Blaumontag
Eine halbe Million versoffen.

Zu St. Louis in Amerika
Ich auch den großen Hecker sah,
Als er beim Frühstück saß
Und grad die Zeitung las,
Daß sie in Frankfurt einen
Erbkaiser gewählet hätten.

Und jetzt nach diesem Leiden all
Sitz ich am Niagarafall
Und denke bei dem Schaum:
O du schöner Traum
Von der deutschen Einheit
Im Jahr acht und vierzig.

Schauenburgs Allgemeines Deutsches Kommersbuch, 91.–95. Auflage (Lahr, n.d.), pp. 714–715.
   Details of Mrs. Aston's evangelism for free love and her erotic predilection for important men are described by Otto Corvin, *Erinnerungen aus meinem Leben,* Neu durchgesehen und bis zur Gegenwart fortgesetzt. Dritte Auflage (Leipzig, 1880), III, 18–20. It is surprising that Mrs. Aston's fascinating pursuit of women's liberation has not been the subject of any special study.
   21. The author of *Woher und Wohin? Die Auswanderung und die Kolonisation im Interesse Deutschlands und der Auswanderer* (Berlin, 1849).
   22. In his *Zeiten und Menschen, Erlebnisse und Meinungen* (zweite Auflage, Berlin, 1899), pp. 31–43, Genée (1824–1914) offers the only other account of the *Rütli* which I have been able to find. It corroborates and complements von Gagern's recollections. Genée considers the satirical criticism of this group comparable to the "dance on a volcano" preceding the French Revolution. Hans Zopf and Gerd Heinrich's *Berlin-Bibliographie,* Veröffentlichungen der Historischen Kommission zu Berlin, Band 15 (Berlin, 1965) does not even mention the *Rütli.*
   23. Von Gagern and Genée both identify him as one of Mrs. Aston's paramours. From the sober tone of Geheimrat von Gottschall's brief mention of her and the *Rütli* in *Die deutsche Nationalliteratur des neunzehnten Jahr-*

hunderts (dritte vermehrte und verbesserte Auflage [Breslau, 1872], IV, 299, and II, 272, resp.), one would not suspect that he had dedicated to her his youthful dithyrambic love poems *Madonna und Magdalena* (1845).

24. After taking part in the Berlin uprising, during which he was wounded and captured, Ulke (1821-1910) emigrated to the United States in 1849. He settled in Washington, D.C., as a portrait painter and naturalist. Some of his patrons were Charles Sumner, John Sherman, Carl Schurz, Edwin Stanton, Mrs. Jefferson Davis, and Ulysses S. Grant. According to Mantle Fielding, *Dictionary of American Painters, Sculptors, and Engravers* (New York, 1965), p. 378, his portraits of various secretaries of war are owned by the Department of Defense, and his portraits of the secretaries of the treasury are housed in the Treasury Department; his portrait of General Grant is found in the White House. Ulke is credited with having established the largest known collection of American beetles, later acquired by the Museum of Natural History in the Carnegie Institute, Pittsburgh.

Von Gagern, who states that he met with Ulke several times in the U.S. (I, 43), relates that his painting "Der Tod Lincoln's" was based on the fact that the mortally wounded President was carried into Ulke's Washington quarters, across from Ford's Theater. Otto von Corvin, IV, 407, similarly links Lincoln's death with Ulke's lodging. None of the books on Lincoln's assassination available to me, however, make any mention of Ulke.

25. Listed as an anonymous poem by recent anthologies, e.g., *Der deutsche Vormärz. Texte und Dokumente,* ed. Jost Hermand (Reclams Universal-Bibliothek Nr. 8794-98 [Stuttgart, 1969], pp. 157-158), and *Gedichte 1830-1900,* Nach den Erstdrucken in zeitlicher Folge herausgegeben von Ralph-Rainer Wuthenow, *Epochen der deutschen Lyrik,* Band 8. dtv Taschenbuch No. WR 4022 (München, 1970), pp. 270-271. For the correct authorship, cf. Kurt Stephenson, "Redakteure des 'Kladderadatsch'–ihr Echo im Studentenlied," in *Darstellungen und Quellen zur Geschichte der deutschen Einheitsbewegung im neunzehnten und zwanzigsten Jahrhundert,* vol. 7 (Heidelberg, 1967), 25.

26. Ernst Dohm (editor), Rudolf Löwenstein (poetry), and Wilhelm Scholz (caricatures). The magazine appeared from 1848 until 1944.

27. Genée, p. 28, and Eduard Bernstein, *Die Geschichte der Berliner Arbeiter-Bewegung. Ein Kapitel zur Geschichte der deutschen Sozialdemokratie* (Berlin, 1907-10), I, 2. Occasional visitors of *Die Freien* were Friedrich Engels, Hoffmann von Fallersleben, Ludwig Feuerbach, Karl Marx, and Arnold Ruge. Cf. Andrew R. Carlson, *Anarchism in Germany,* Vol. 1: *The Early Movement* (Metuchen, N.J., 1972), p. 54.

28. Stephan Born, *Erinnerungen eines Achtundvierzigers,* zweite Auflage (Leipzig, 1898), p. 23.

29. Born, p. 30. Cf. also Ernst Schraepler, *Handwerkerbünde und Arbeitervereine 1830 bis 1853* (Berlin, 1971), p. 54.

30. Manfred Häckel, "Arbeiterbewegung und Literatur," in *100 Jahre Reclams Universal-Bibliothek, 1867-1967. Ein Beitrag zur Verlagsgeschichte* (Leipzig, 1967), p. 385.

31. Humboldt occupied a first-floor apartment in a small house at 67 Oranienburger Straße, behind a customs shed, in the less than fashionable "Siberian" district of North Berlin. Cf. Douglas Botting, *Humboldt and the Cosmos* (New York, 1973), p. 229.

32. In particular the contributions made to the *Essai . . . Espagne* by Patoni, father of the Mexican general José María Patoni, who became an intimate friend of Carlos von Gagern (I, 65). None of the works on Humboldt which I have seen makes mention of the elder Patoni.

33. He had married Carlos' eldest sister, and in her honor named an oriental flower he had discovered *Helenablume* (I, 87). Carlos' youngest sister was married to General von Egloffstein, *Oberstallmeister* in Weimar (I, 313).

34. My inquiry concerning particulars of this degree remained unanswered by the University of Leyden.

35. Humboldt's last visit in Paris was in January 1848. Botting, p. 267.

36. Carlos' involvement in this affair is especially incongruous in view of the fact that Prince Felix von Lichnowski, who had served in Spain as adjutant general under the pretender Don Carlos before returning to Prussian service, was lynched as an arch-reactionary in the 1848 Frankfurt uprising.

37. Possibly as *Portepee-Unteroffizier* or *Fähnrich* (ensign), since he mentions only his silver sword-knot (I, 161) but not his rank. Albert Hans, *La guerre du Mexique selon les mexicains* (Edition revue et augmentée [Paris et Nancy, 1899], p. 31), states that Carlos served as second lieutenant in the Prussian *artillery*.

38. This aversion had probably been fostered early by views prevalent among the Berlin gymnasts. One of their songs was (Werner, p. 48):

> Es hat der Held und Kraft-Ulan
> Sich einen Schnürleib umgetan,
> Damit das Herz dem braven Mann
> Nicht in die Hosen fallen kann.

39. Kunwald, p. 15.

40. As a theology student and Burschenschafter, Wislicenus (1803–75) had been imprisoned 1824–29 and devoted this time to a close study of the Bible. Rationalists and Young Hegelians were also re-examining the validity of the Scripture and its bearing on church dogma, and David Friedrich Strauß' *Das Leben Jesu* (1835) came as an expression of skeptical ideas many had been harboring. Wislicenus detailed their implications for Protestant theologians in his 1844 Köthen lecture *Ob Schrift? Ob Geist?*, rejecting the authority of the Bible in favor of the Hegelian *in uns lebendige Geist* and *Zeitgeist*. Since 1841 known as *Lichtfreunde* and *protestantische Freunde*, earlier dissenters under Pastor Uhlich in the Prussian province of Saxony rallied around Wislicenus, and the movement gained such growing support from the clergy and the public that the Prussian and Saxon governments outlawed any meetings of the *Lichtfreunde*. Widespread opposition to this measure resulted in a conditional reversal by the Prussian *Toleranzpatent* of March 30, 1847, and some

268 / GERHARD K. FRIESEN

forty *Freie Gemeinden* totaling ca. 7,000 members rapidly constituted themselves. Although the 1848 Revolution brought about unconditional constitutional freedom for them, they did not increase substantially until 1849–50, when many served as forums for liberal ideas which could no longer be publicly expressed elsewhere; total membership of the approximately eighty congregations in this period was ca. 35,000. In 1850, however, the governments enforced new restrictions against such congregations, all of which were considered hotbeds of revolutionary tendencies and socialist propaganda. While the movement was not formally prohibited, legal technicalities furnished the pretexts for incessantly prosecuting its ministers ("Sprecher"). When this policy abated in 1858, most *Freie Gemeinden* had ceased to exist. Cf. Wetzer and Welke's *Kirchenlexikon oder Encyklopädie der katholischen Kirche und ihrer Hülfswissenschaften*, zweite Auflage, vol. 4 (Freiburg/Breisgau, 1886). The Protestant sources I have consulted continue to give a one-sided account of the movement.

41. Ferdinand Kampe, *Geschichte der religiösen Bewegung der neueren Zeit. IV: Geschichte des Deutschkatholicismus und freien Protestantismus in Deutschland und Nordamerika* (Leipzig, 1860), p. 14.

42. Genée (p. 28), a fellow Rütlian, describes the *Lichtfreunde* (whom he joined) as very fashionable among the young intellectuals of Berlin.

43. Their political mismanagement had been the subject of Karl Heinzen's *Ein teutsches Rechenexempel* (presented at a meeting of the Baden revolutionaries on March 1, 1848, in Karlsruhe) demonstrating that six duchies and principalities had to support in excess of forty-five princely drones. Cf. Hans Blum, *Die deutsche Revolution 1848–49* (Leipzig, 1897), p. 102.

44. Blankenburg in Thuringia was the site of the first *Kindergarten* founded by Friedrich Wilhelm August Fröbel (who was also an admirer of Jahn) in 1837. Because his nephew Julius Fröbel in Zürich was suspect as a socialist author and publisher (he emigrated to America in 1849), the *Kultusminister* in 1851 issued an edict forbidding the establishment of schools "after Friedrich and Julius Fröbel's principles" in Prussia. Karl Daniel Adolf Douai (1819–88), one of the most enthusiastic and effective speakers of the *Freie Gemeinden* (cf. Kampe, p. 16) and a close friend of Carlos von Gagern, came to the United States in 1852, and in 1859 created what was perhaps the first American kindergarten, in Boston. None of the books dealing with Douai's American contributions includes this very important earlier phase in his life.

45. Before Hermann Schulze-Delitzsch's efforts towards *Verbrauchergenossenschaften* were realized elsewhere in Germany. Cf. Ernst Grünfeld, "Hermann Schulze-Delitzsch," *Encyclopaedia of Social Sciences*, vol. 13 (New York, 1935), 586. A related enterprise by Max Stirner and *Die Freien* failed in 1845 because they had foolishly chosen a most perishable commodity, milk. Cf. Theodor Fontane, *Von Zwanzig bis Dreissig*, ed. Kurt Schreinert and Jutta Neuendorff-Fürstenau, dtv Taschenbuch No. 6025 (München, 1973), pp. 38–39.

46. Whether his wife and infant daughter accompanied him to America as stated by Kunwald (p. 15) is unclear. In *Todte und Lebende* his wife is not mentioned after the Zeitz events (I, 200).

47. C. F. Huch, "Die freireligiöse Bewegung unter den Deutschameri-kanern," *Mitteilungen des Deutschen Pionier-Vereins von Philadelphia*, Elftes Heft (1909), pp. 2–8.

48. Two such bodies came into existence at the end of 1853. Huch, pp. 13–14.

49. Huch, p. 14.

50. It should be remembered that the so-called Forty-Eighters did not come to the U.S. in significant numbers until 1850 and 1851. Cf. Carl Wittke, *We Who Built America* (Ann Arbor, 1939), p. 193. And since among them were numerous subaltern officers of nobility, it is clear that many of these became "proletarians," according to Wilhelm Heinrich Riehl, *Die bürgerliche Gesellschaft*. 6. Auflage (Stuttgart, 1861), pp. 378–379. There are relatively few Forty-Eighters of aristocratic and military background who attained some distinction in the United States.

51. The irony in Lenau's similar reaction is discussed by Harold Jantz, "The View From Chesapeake Bay. An Experiment with the Image of America," *Proceedings of the American Antiquarian Society* (April 1969), pp. 160–161. Jantz suggests that "Yankee-Doodle" may actually have been eternalized in Beethoven's tune to Schiller's "Ode an die Freude." One Dr. A. Berghaus in his note "Das deutsche Lied in Nordamerika," *Die Neue Welt*, vol. 9 (1884) [n.p.], in turn established the Dutch origin of the text and music of the American song. To be fair, however, it should be mentioned that Carlos also decried Dutch musical ability (I, 110).

52. There can be little doubt that Carlos left Europe with certain anti-American prejudices particularly current among educated Germans at that time. Even his one-time mentor Alexander von Humboldt, while acknowledg-ing his own great renown and popularity in the U.S., believed "die V.St. sind ein Cartesianischer Wirbel alles fortreißend, langweilig nivellirend": *Briefe von Alexander von Humboldt an Varnhagen von Ense aus den Jahren 1827 bis 1858*, ed. Ludmilla Assing, 3. Auflage (Leipzig, 1860), p. 295.

Carlos wrote Gustav Adolf Wislicenus of his disappointments; the latter came to America anyway, in order to avoid imprisonment, in 1853, but in 1856 he returned, "amerikamüde" (I, 201), to Europe.

53. Hermann Schlüter, *Die Anfänge der deutschen Arbeiterbewegung in Amerika* (Stuttgart, 1907), p. 132.

54. The mid-nineteenth-century German image of Mexico was largely shaped by Alexander von Humboldt and Charles Sealsfield. Willibald Alexis in his review of Sealsfield's *Virey* (a novel which focused on the year 1812, al-though from the vantage point of 1828) wrote: "Dieses sein Werk führt uns in eine neue Welt mit *ganz neuen Stoffen*, Menschen, Gegenden; es wird für den künftigen Historiker von großem Werthe sein; nur wünschten wir schon jetzt, wenn der Verfasser eine neue Ausgabe besorgt, daß er dieselbe mit vollstän-digern Noten als die bisherige ausstattete. Ja, er verdiente unsern Dank, wenn er in Kürze daran *eine Geschichte der mexicanischen Parteikämpfe bis in die Gegenwart fortführte. Denn trotz aller Zeitungsberichte, wie wenige Leser wis-sen in diesen verworrenen Verhältnissen sich zurechtzufinden.*" [Italics mine]. "Die transatlantischen Romane des Verfassers der Transatlantischen Reise-

skizzen," *Blätter für literarische Unterhaltung,* No. 77 (March 18, 1841), 312. Similarly, the anonymous reviewer of Sealsfield's *Süden und Norden* in *Der Freihafen,* vol. 5 (1842), 194, spoke of Mexico as "eine fremde neue Welt."

A number of descriptive works appeared subsequently in Germany, including: Eduard Mühlenpfordt, *Versuch einer getreuen Darstellung der Republik Mejico besonders in Beziehung auf Geographie, Ethnographie und Statistik,* 2 vols. Hannover, 1844; W. Stricker, *Die Republik Mexico nach den besten und neuesten Quellen geschildert,* Bibliothek der Länder- und Völkerkunde, 1. Heft. Frankfurt am Main, 1847; A. R. Thümmel, *Mexiko und die Mexikaner in physischer, socialer und politischer Beziehung. Ein vollständiges Gemälde des alten und neuen Mexiko, mit Rücksicht auf die neueste Geschichte nach deutschen, französischen, englischen und amerikanischen Quellen dargestellt,* Erlangen, 1848; A. R. Thümmel, *Neueste Geschichte der Republik Mexiko. Von der Gründung des Freistaates bis zur Eroberung der Hauptstadt durch die Vereinigten Staaten.* Erlangen, 1848; Carl Sartorius, *Mexico als Ziel für deutsche Auswanderung,* Bearbeitet für den Hessischen Zweigverein des Nationalvereins für deutsche Auswanderung und Ansiedlung, Darmstadt, 1850; Adolf Wislizenus, *Denkschrift über eine Reise nach Nord-Mexiko, verbunden mit der Expedition des Obersten Donniphan, in den Jahren 1846 und 1847,* aus dem Englischen übertragen von George M. von Ross, Braunschweig, 1850; Adolf Wislizenus, "Beiträge zur Kenntniß des nördlichen Mexico," *Geographisches Jahrbuch,* Vol. 1. Gotha, 1850; B. von Boguslawski, *Über deutsche Colonisation in Mexico,* Ein Bericht an den Berliner Verein zur Centralisation deutscher Auswanderung und Colonisation, Berlin, 1851; Carl Bartholomäus Heller, *Reisen in Mexiko in den Jahren 1845-1848.* Leipzig, 1853. (Of the various biographical accounts on [Friedrich] Adolf Wislizenus [1810-1889], none name his parents. If he was a brother of Gustav Adolf, it is possible that Carlos von Gagern knew his writings on Mexico.) None of the above works, however, could rival the impact of Sealsfield. Indicative is an 1868 essay on Emperor Maximilian by the liberal polyhistorian Johannes Scherr, who relied on the *Virey* for the characterization of Mexico and the Mexicans. Sealsfield's description, Scherr wrote, "muß in seinen Hauptzügen noch heute als treu und treffend anerkannt werden." Cf. Johannes Scherr, "Das Trauerspiel in Mexico," *Menschliche Tragikomödie. Gesammelte Studien, Skizzen und Bilder,* Neue Volksausgabe, ed. Karl Quenzel (Leipzig, n.d.), II, 359. The continuing currency of Sealsfield's Mexican novels is also evident from selections included in an anthology edited by Leopold and Paul Auspitz, *Meister-Prosa* (Wien und Leipzig [1895]), II, 26-39. Cf. also n. 65, *infra.*

55. August Wolfstieg, *Bibliographie der freimaurerischen Literatur,* Reprographischer Nachdruck der Ausgabe Burg 1911 (Hildesheim, 1964), I, 795, has an entry to this effect (No. 15651):

M[oritz] A[mster], Festarbeit der Loge Schiller, Or[ient] Pressburg, anlässlich des 25 jährigen Maurerjubiläums des Br[uders] Carlos Frh. von Gagern. [Bericht, Rede von J. Weinberger: Eigenschaften und Verdienste des Jubilars um die K[önigliche] K[unst]. Der Zirkel [Organ der Humanitas in Neudörfl bei Wien. Begründet und herausgegeben von Franz Julius Schneeberger], XII (1882), 23-28.

Cf. also Carlos von Gagern, "Ueber Friedrich Schiller," *Schwert und Kelle*, p. 206.

56. Kunwald, p. 22.

57. As mentioned by de Bopp (p. 58), Carlos' previous loyalty to the conservative cause was typical of most Mexican career officers during this period of civil war, who usually recognized the government in control of the capital.

58. The book is signed "México, Febrero 9 de 1862" (p. 86).

59. Karl J. R. Arndt and May E. Olson, *The German Language Press of the Americas 1732-1968. History and Bibliography*, II (München, 1973), 308. At this time, Carlos reports (*Apelación*, p. 62) that all the editors had been or would become ministers.

60. It is divided into six chapters, but there is no Chapter IV, and on p. 83 Carlos states that he wrote the book in less than two weeks.

61. *Apelación*, p. viii.

62. Including the synopsis of the principal Mexican languages by Francisco Pimentel, a work Carlos claims to have translated into French (p. 71). I have not been able to locate this translation.

63. *Apelación*, p. 12.

64. *Apelación*, p. 73. Carlos mentions that he had submitted to Santa Anna's government a related scheme, "un projeto sobre la rehabilitacion moral y intelectual de la raza indígena, pero no encontró entonces ningun apuyo" (p. 75), and he expresses the hope that Juárez would be more attentive to such projects.

65. *Discurso patriotico pronunciado por el c. Carlos de Gagern en el teatro de Iturbide de Mexico. La noche del 15 Septiembre de 1862* (Mexico, 1862), p. 16.

66. Carlos' account of the siege (II, 42-73) offers a wealth of authentic information unknown to Dabbs, and makes it clear that the Mexicans had *not* exhausted their ammunition at the time of surrender, contrary to the claim by Henry Bamford Parkes, *A History of Mexico*, Sentry Edition No. 61 (Boston, 1970), p. 257.

67. The advent of Sealsfield's *Kajütenbuch* in the French translation by Gustave Revilliod could have contributed to this concept. In his preface, Revilliod states, "Les Etats-Unis pénétrant déjà une fois en vainqueurs jusqu'à Mexico [sic] se sont chargés de donner raison à toutes ses prévisions, et rien, pas même les troubles qui arment aujourd'hui l'Amérique du Nord, contre celle du Midi, n'est capable, selon nous, d'arrêter la marche triomphale de la race anglo-saxonne vers le sud." *La Prairie du Jacinto* (Genève, 1861), p. xi.

68. Including those on Rüdiger von Starhemberg, Count Magnus Steenbock, Henrik Steffens, Karl Freiherr vom und zum Stein, Michael Stiefel, and the Struensees. Cf. *Nouvelle biographie générale*, vol. 44 (Paris, 1868), 402-576.

272 / GERHARD K. FRIESEN

69. Jesús Guzmán y Raz Guzmán, *Bibliografía de la reforma, la intervención y el imperio* (México, 1930), I, 244, lists a book I have not seen: Gagern, *Die Franzosische [sic] Expedition gegen Mexico.* Berlin. Imp. [sic] Kommission bei E. S. Mittler und Sohn. En 8°. 1863.

70. It is probable that Carlos had assimilated his own dislikes with a certain Mexican xenophobia, partly derived from the traditional Spanish hatred of *herejes.*

71. For Sigel, cf. Huch, p. 16.

72. Huch, p. 20. A year later, on March 11, 1866, Douai participated in establishing the national *Bund der Freidenker* in New York.

73. In this function he performed the ceremony for the former Lutheran minister Heinrich Toelke's second marriage.

74. "Das spezifisch Religiöse in der Freimaurerei," *Mittheilungen an die Vereine deutsch-amerikanischer Freimaurer,* vol. 1 (1866), 82–90. Reprinted in *Schwert und Kelle,* pp. 36–51. Cf. Wolfstieg, No. 34217.

75. Kunwald, p. 20.

76. Verified by Albert Hans (p. 31), who claims to have witnessed this conversation.

77. Like leading socialists in Germany, Douai opposed the war as harmful to the cause of the international labor movement. Cf. F. Bolte, "Bericht über die Massenversammlung gegen den Krieg, abgehalten zu New-York im Cooper-Institut, 19. November 1870," *Der Vorbote,* vol. 6 (1871), 27–29.

78. Along with Friedrich Adolf Sorge, who was on the teaching staff of Douai's Hoboken German Academy. 1868–70 Douai edited the *Arbeiter Union,* official organ of the German-American radical socialists, and after the founding of the Socialist Labor Party in 1876, he edited its three publications, the *Labor Standard, Arbeiter-Stimme,* and *Vorbote.* On September 20, 1883, Douai appeared as a representative of the Socialist Labor Party of the United States before the Senate Committee on Education and Labor. For his testimony cf. Henry Nash Smith, *Popular Culture and Industrialism 1865–1890,* Anchor Doubleday Book No. AD5 (New York, 1967), pp. 302–314.

79. *Heinzen, wie er ist. Eine Anklageschrift von Adolf Douai,* New York, 1869.

80. Eberhard Kessel, "Die Briefe von Carl Schurz an Gottfried Kinkel," *Beiheft zum Jahrbuch für Amerikastudien,* vol. 12 (1965), 150.

81. Carlos also rebuked Rudolf Lexow, publisher of the *New Yorker Belletristisches Journal* (formerly the *Criminalzeitung* to which Carlos had contributed), for permitting such antisocialist attacks in his journal.

82. Notably Heinzen's advocacy of women's rights, an area in which Carlos also claimed to have been active.

83. Kunwald (p. 21) vaguely mentions that Carlos was in Vienna on a mission for the Mexican government. If he was, this must have been after Porfirio Díaz became President in 1877.

84. The *Bibliographía mexicana de estadística* (México, 1941), I, 134, has this entry:

Gager [sic], Carlos de. *Charakteristik der indianischen Bevolkerung* [sic]. Mexico, 1873.

85. According to Conrad (*Schwert und Kelle*, p. 2), he became an editor for the newly founded *Wiener Allgemeine Zeitung* about 1878.

86. Wolfstieg, III, 165, lists over 50 different articles. Three of them were reprinted in vol. 9 (1881–82) of *Der Long Islander. Sonntagsblatt der Brooklyner Freien Presse:* "Die Erziehung zur Freiheit," *Der Long Islander,* No. 5, Wolfstieg No. 28564; "Primus inter pares," *Der Long Islander,* No. 14, Wolfstieg No. 20349; and "Centralisation," *Der Long Islander,* No. 38, Wolfstieg No. 20292.

87. *Schwert und Kelle,* p. 66.

88. *Ibid.,* p. 197.

89. *Ibid.,* p. 66.

90. *Ibid.,* p. 67.

91. *Ibid.,* p. 69.

92. Two related essays, not included in *Todte und Lebende,* are "Eine Erinnerung an Garibaldi," *Die Gegenwart,* vol. 26 (1884), 195–196, and "Emilio Castelar und die Gewissensfreiheit," *Die Gegenwart,* vol. 28 (1885), 210–211. Conrad (*Schwert und Kelle,* p. 5) relates that Carlos has planned a third volume which was to focus on his masonic involvement.

93. The first and second volumes are designated *Erste Reihe* and *Zweite Reihe* respectively.

94. According to Victor Hamburger, *Sealsfield-Postl. Bisher unveröffentlichte Briefe und Mittheilungen zu seiner Biographie* (Wien, 1879), p. 1, this was also Sealsfield's device.

95. "Todte und Lebende," *Deutsche Rundschau,* vol. 43 (1885), 157.

96. Kunwald, p. 22.

97. Conrad in *Schwert und Kelle,* p. 8. Cf. also "Todtenschau," *Illustrirte Zeitung,* No. 2218 (January 2, 1886), 10. *The Annual Register: A Review of Public Events at Home and Abroad, for the Year 1885.* New Series (London, 1886), p. 201, mistakenly gives the date of Carlos' death as December 22. Kunwald (p. 9) relates that Carlos' only daughter Gretchen committed suicide after being notified of her father's death. From Kunwald's account it can be inferred that a son of Carlos survived.

98. *Apelación,* pp. vi–vii.

99. *The German Panoramic Novel of the 19th Century.* German Studies in America, No. 8 (Berne and Frankfurt/M, 1972), pp. 122–125.

11. Eduard Dorsch and the Civil War
Erich A. Albrecht

Beginning with the year 1861, the German physician Eduard Dorsch, who had fled Germany in 1849 to come to America, started to write a number of highly critical poems which dealt, as Dorsch put it, with *Kriegerische Zeiten,* a collection in longhand which covers the years from 1861 to 1864. The manuscript of this largely unpublished collection can be found in the Newberry Library in Chicago.

The first twenty-seven of the poems are directly or indirectly concerned with the Civil War. Numbers 28 and 29 deal with Emperor Maximilian's Mexican fate and the execution of Robert Blum in the year 1848 on the Brigittenau, respectively. The manuscript collection ends with a section containing six poems in translation only one of which refers to the Civil War. Its title is: "Wie McClellan Manasse nahm."

When Dorsch in 1884 published his best known collection of poems under the title *Aus der Alten und Neuen Welt,*[1] he selected only four of the war-poems for inclusion. They are: "Einem Todten zum Gedächtnis," "Ein Begräbnis am Potomac," "Der letzte Washington," and "Eine unbekannte Leiche." Dorsch must have valued them more highly than the other twenty-three which remained unpublished. Even a casual examination of the titles will show that the collection is not a carefully developed composition but consists of strong emotional reactions to disconnected events that happened around the time of the Civil War.

With certain reservations, what is said by Harold G. Carlson in his M. A. thesis *Eduard Dorsch, His Life And His Works* about Dorsch's first volume of poetry *Kurze Hirtenbriefe an mein Volk, diesseits und jenseits des Oceans,* published in 1851 by E. Magnus, needs to be kept in mind when one reads the poems in *Kriegerische Zeiten:*[2]

[*The Hirtenbriefe*] A small, thin volume of thirty-six pages, it contained sixty-two sonnets, written shortly after he arrived here. They still show the intense revolutionary spirit fostered by the ferment abroad. They are typical products of *"das junge Deutschland."* They rage at the cruelty of political tyrants and at the intolerance of the church. They exhort his compatriots to united action in throwing off these oppressive yokes. The thinker, the iconoclast and revolutionary are predominant here. These poems do not lack a sense of style and form, but are devoid of that rich, lyrical note found in his later works. Perhaps, as Konrad Nies suggested, prose would have served him better here although it is unjust to deny him a genuine poetic enthusiasm.

Since then, Dorsch, formerly a member of the liberal movement in Germany and in the South German revolution had become a well-established and much appreciated M.D. in Monroe, Michigan, whose most useful contribution to his community was the safe delivery of numerous babies. With his wife and his mother to provide for, when the opportunity came to establish himself in Monroe he took it. As far as practical political activity was concerned he did in 1860 join the then Republican party and served as presidential elector from the second Michigan district, supporting Abraham Lincoln. This electorship won him, as his poem "Der letzte Washington"[3] indicates, an invitation to the White House. But otherwise he stayed put.

This, however, did not mean that he would keep silent when what he considered great social, political, or military evils had to be fought.

While most of his targets in the *Kriegerische Zeiten* are political and military men and events, Dorsch did not forget the clergy and the church.[4] As a fervent "Freidenker," the former contributor to the "Lustige Blätter" and the "Leuchtkugeln" describes in a clever but irreverent way the arrival of Jefferson Davis and Horace Greeley at the Gate of Heaven. This being a particularly interesting specimen of Dorsch's satirical writing, the expression of contempt towards the "Rebellenbrut" shows his sometimes excessive rage at prominent individuals, here especially Jefferson Davis and Horace Greeley. The poem begins with a discussion of a heavenly dinner party at which, as requested by the good Lord, "trichinenfreier

Schweinebraten" is served. Rabbis who are reluctantly present at the dinner and cannot refuse to eat portions of the "Schweinebraten" are a source of much amusement for the Lord. After the dinner party, Jefferson Davis and Horace Greeley arrive at the Gate of Heaven. In spite of the touching plea by a Negro the two are, of course, relegated to hell after they have been called a number of harsh and insulting names. Dorsch's treatment of Davis and Greeley raises the important question to what extent they and others, as for instance Simon Cameron, Lincoln's first Secretary of War, deserved the insults and criticism levelled at them. As will be shown later, Dorsch was fairly often right in his criticism, but in the case of Horace Greeley he obviously misinterpreted Greeley's motives and actions.

Dorsch seemed to know only black and white; the gray area of compromise was alien to him. In his poem "Der letzte Washington" he wrote:

> "Kein Kompromiss mehr mit dem Sklavenfrohn
> Kein Zugeständnis! Nein! Krieg bis zum Messer."[5]

Greeley's position is briefly but, it seems, correctly described in Schem's *Deutsch-amerikanisches Conversations-Lexikon:*

Den Führern der Conföderirten gegenüber wünschte er ein mildes Verfahren beobachtet zu sehen. Das Vorhaben, General Lee vor ein Kriegsgericht zu stellen, verurtheilte er daher scharf, und später leistete er für Jefferson Davis Bürgschaft (Mai 1867), wofür er sich von einem Theile der radikaleren Republikaner bittere Vorwürfe zuzog.[6]

After Jefferson Davis and Horace Greeley it is Simon Cameron, mentioned above, who is lambasted by Dorsch. In the poem bearing his name, Cameron is accused of being a greedy "Kriegsgewinnler." To test the correctness of this serious accusation, one contemporary and two later historians have been consulted. Friedrich Kapp called Cameron "weniger ein Staatsmann als ein geriebener, die Richtung der öffentlichen Meinung vorausspürender Politiker";[7] Bruce Catton writes about Cameron: "The word was out that Pennsylvanians with good connections were getting a good deal from Secretary Cameron; it was said that 'there is already evidently much feeling between Lincoln and Cameron' and that

Lincoln had received so many complaints about Pennsylvania contracts that he intended to have the manner examined."[8]

Kinder but similarly sharp is James B. Fry's characterization of Cameron:

> The talents of Simon Cameron, Lincoln's first Secretary of War, were political, not military. He was a kind, gentle, placid man, gifted with powers to persuade, not to command. *Shrewd* and skilled in the management of business and personal matters, he had no knowledge of military affairs, and could not give the President much assistance in assembling and organizing for war the earnest and impatient, but unmilitary people of the North.[9]

All three sources prove that Dorsch's term "Kriegsgewinnler" was indeed correctly applied to Cameron.

It would be wrong to call Dorsch a vicious critic since he, like many of his countrymen, German immigrants, Forty-Eighters, and others, was deeply, one might well say passionately, concerned with the great issues of his time, especially the conflict between *slavery* and *freedom*. Slavery in his time called forth the strongest emotion and the angriest language and sometimes unfair criticism. What some German critics did not consider was what is best expressed by Dieter Cunz in his article "The Maryland Germans in the Civil War":

> The concept of slavery stood in the sharpest contrast to their [the Germans'] liberal and progressive ideas. Naturally they knew nothing of the specific American background, and the economic conditions, which for a certain period had made slavery understandable and pardonable; what they did observe was the horror of slavery as judged from the standpoint of their ideals and theories.[10]

As far as Dorsch was concerned it was also a matter of impatience and regret over opportunities missed. Of Washington he writes in "Der letzte Washington":

> ". . . die Macht war sein,
> Die Sklaverei für immer ausgeschlossen,
> Wenn er gewollt. Er aber wollte Frieden
> Und hat sich mit der Halbheit gern beschieden."

After a visit to the White House on Washington's Birthday on February 22, 1862, Dorsch writes in the same poem:

> "Wir schauten all die Herrlichkeit mit an,
> Wir liessen uns im Weissen Hause drängen,
> Die Hand zu schütteln mit dem langen Mann;
> Wir horchten in des Capitoles Gängen
> Auf Worte, die, verloren dann und wann,
> Wir eifrig suchten in den Sinn zu zwängen,
> Den unsre Meinung ihnen gern geliehen,
> Und diese war: *sogleich* das Schwert zu ziehen."

The line about drawing the sword at once refers to Lincoln's attempts to find ways other than military action to avoid the complete break-up of the Union. In a letter written in August 1862 Lincoln wrote to Horace Greeley that he considered it to be his main task to save the Union, not to abolish slavery or to preserve it. If to preserve the Union it was necessary to abolish slavery, it would be abolished; and if slavery must remain in existence to preserve the Union, it should be so. This declaration of Lincoln and his delaying actions concerning slavery and war were bound to agitate the radical abolitionist Dorsch.

How deeply Dorsch felt about the abolition of slavery is shown by his repeated treatments of this problem. In a long poem, called "Europa und Amerika," personified Europe warns Columbia to be firm in regard to slavery and freedom in general. False friends, southerners, and others seek to destroy the ideals of freedom. Immigrants from Europe, it is claimed in the poem, are going home, disappointed by corruption. Europa is deeply concerned, but America re-assures her that slavery will be abolished and freedom will prevail.

In the poem "Einem Todten zum Gedächtnis" Dorsch in 1861 visualizes the effect that John Brown's fight and his death will have on the people of the North. While what Dorsch calls the sacrificial death of John Brown did have a great effect on many readers, Dorsch again was only conditionally right, if one accepts the opinion of Wilhelm Kaufmann who claims that it would have been better if Brown had not attacked when he did so, since his action delayed a better solution and merely complicated matters.[11] Of course, Kaufmann, writing in 1911, had information at his disposal that was not available to Dorsch.

In still another poem dealing with slavery, entitled "Noch nicht," Dorsch criticises Lincoln's "Not yet" which was, no doubt, uttered in some other form when General Fremont in 1861 unilaterally ordered the freeing of slaves in Missouri whose owners had been guilty of actual hostilities against the Union Army or Union-Government, but Fremont's unauthorized order was quickly rescinded by Lincoln.[12]

That Dorsch's repeated outcries against slavery, well reasoned or not, were not a particular, personal obsession becomes clear when one considers the numerous poems written by German-Americans and Americans, as for instance John G. Whittier's "Eine Feste Burg ist unser Gott," which resembles Dorsch's heart-felt pleas for the abolition of slavery.[13]

The next major targets of Dorsch's pen were the generals and the Union Army as a whole. Of the generals he singled out McClellan, Fremont, Halleck, Blenker, Grant, and Sherman. McClellan is dealt with in the following four poems: "Der neue Fabius Cunctator," "Der westliche Napoleon," "Ein Begräbnis am Potomac," and "McClellan, der Vogelfänger. Anakreontisch." In all of these he is criticised because of his alleged weakness and procrastination, or hesitancy in certain battles, to exploit his success in battle.

Dorsch concentrates on one defect in McClellan's conduct as a military man. Most likely Dorsch never had the kind of information that would have enabled him to see McClellan's other, positive, qualities. A passage in Lücke's *Der Bürgerkrieg der Vereinigten Staaten* concludes with the same kind of criticism we find in Dorsch's poems but gives credit for his masterly organization of the Union Army under his command.[14]

Still the *Cunctator* quality or defect must have been strong in McClellan, as the following parodistic *McClellan's Soliloquy,* written by a Daughter of Georgia, shows:

> Advance, or not advance; that is the question!
> Whether 'tis better in the mind to suffer
> The jeers and howlings of outrageous Congressmen,
> Or to take arms against a host of rebels,
> And, by opposing, beat them?—To fight—to win—
> No more; and by a victory, to say we end
> This war, and all the thousand dreadful shocks
> The flesh's exposed to—'tis a consummation

Devoutly to be wished. To fight, to win,
To beat! perchance to be beaten;—ay, there's the rub.
After a great defeat, what would ensue!
When we have shuffled off the battle-field,
Must give us pause; there's the respect
That makes calamity a great defeat.
But shall I bear the scorn of all the North,
The "outward" pressure, and Old Abe's reviling,
The pangs of being scoffed at for this long delay,
The turning out of office (ay, perchance,
When I myself might now my greatness make
With a great battle)? I'd not longer bear
To drill and practise troops behind intrenchments,
But that the fear of meeting with the foe
On dread Manassas, from whose plains
Few of us would return—puzzles my will,
And makes me rather bear the evils I have,
Than fly to others which are greater far.
These Southerners make cowards of us all.[15]

While contemporary and near contemporary sources seem to justify Dorsch's criticism of McClellan, more recent studies, such as Bruce Catton's, make it clear that Generals Scott and McClellan's alleged hesitancy was largely due to the realization that their armies were in a miserable state of preparation and training. Risking battle with them meant disaster, as it did at Bull Run.[16]

In the poem "Der verlorene Führer" Dorsch uses language which might have invited a libel suit from Fremont, the subject of the poem, had he ever seen it. Dorsch declares that Fremont had died "wie ein Bube." The poem was written in 1864, Fremont died in 1890. To Dorsch he had died in 1864 when he had changed sides politically and when he, as Dorsch puts it, had turned into a rich aristocrat and had sidled up to the "Sklavenbarone." Here Dorsch writes during the heat of a political battle. After reading "Der verlorene Führer" one is inclined to think that Dorsch was wise in not publishing most of his anthology *Kriegerische Zeiten.*

The generals Halleck, McDowell, Grant, Sherman, and Blenker are dealt with or briefly referred to in the poems "Quos ego," "Nach der Schlacht bei Bull Run," "Aus Vicksburg," "Der letzte Kampf," and "Der westliche Napoleon." In "Quos ego," written

on March 4, 1862, Halleck is accused of unmilitary weakness, in
not ordering the execution of confederate soldiers who have been
convicted of sabotage. Halleck's lack of forcefulness is confirmed
in a biographical sketch in Schem.[17] In the last four lines of the
poem "Nach der Schlacht bei Bull Run," Major General Irvin
McDowell is quoted as saying:

> Ich wäre verrathen und verkauft,
> Fing ich nicht jetzt schon zu laufen an,
> Denn ich bin lahm, auch reisst's mich im Ohr
> Und wer in der ersten sich nimmt in Acht,
> Der spart sich auf für die zweite Schlacht.

In Otto Eisenschiml und Ralph Newman's account of "The First
Big Battle of the War" it is reported that General McDowell
"admitted his defeat in a manly and straightforward manner."
There is no indication that McDowell cowardly ran to save himself
for another day.[18]

The poems "Aus Vicksburg" written in July 1863 and "Der
letzte Kampf" written in the fall of 1864 celebrate the brilliant
leadership of the generals Grant and Sherman. Neither of them is
the main subject of the poems mentioned. But they show that
Dorsch was happy to praise where praise was due. Of Grant he
writes in "Aus Vicksburg":

> Die Thaten von unserem Ulysis Grant
> Wer könnte sie würdig beschreiben?

One should note the words: ". . . von *unserem* Ulysis Grant." They
indicate, as other passages do, Dorsch's complete identification
with the American cause. Unlike some of his famous countrymen,
he was not interested in glorifying the German element in the
Union Army. If that had been his intention he would not have
introduced the name of Brigadier General Ludwig Blenker in his
poem "Der westliche Napoleon." In this poem Dorsch writes:

> Da kam Herr Lincoln selber,
> Hurje!
> Und rief: "Macht vorwärts, Kälber,
> Jup, jup, heide!
> Die schönste Zeit ver-Blenker-t ihr,
> Statt dass die Bein' ihr schlenkert hier,

Und euch besauft in voller Ruh,
Marschiert einmal auf Richmond zu,
He, he!

As far as Dorsch's information went, Blenker was another *Fabius Cunctator,* the label attached to McClellan by Dorsch. Actually Blenker had done well in several battles. In a somewhat flowery way Kapp states: "Es war bei Bull Run, wo die Blenkerische Brigade die Ehre der amerikanischen Waffen und die Bundeshauptstadt rettete."[19] It seems surprising that Dorsch did not make Blenker's love for pomp and circumstance the target of one of his satirical poems, of which Carl Wittke writes knowingly.[20] But, as stated above, Dorsch was an impatient and critical man. Whatever delayed or hindered the Union Army angered him and made him cry out.

Lest it be thought that Dorsch dealt in his Civil War poems only with high ranking generals and politicians, the two poems: "Der letzte Mann von Beaufort" and "Auch ein deutscher Held" need to be mentioned. The first of the two gives a long-winded humorous, satirical account of the reactions of one drunken soldier, not a German, to the battle of Beaufort:

Fort Walker hüben, Fort Beauregard drüben,
Vertheidigt durch mächtige Columbiaden,
Von deutschen Artilleristen geladen,
Die was sie in Deutschland gelernt, hier üben,
Verwehren den Eingang der Flotte nicht.

Lines three and four must be read against the important fact that both the Confederate Army as well as the Union Army gained very much by the presence of numerous European- especially German-trained officers and enlisted men. Colin Ross quotes the great Confederate General Lee as stating: "Ohne die Deutschen wäre es eine Kleinigkeit die Yankees zu schlagen!"[21] Of course not all German-American soldiers were included in General Lee's statement. One of the non-heroes is portrayed in a very humorous manner in Dorsch's poem "Auch ein deutscher Held." The introductory lines refer to the fact that "Wilsons Creek und Mumfordsville verkünden deutschen Ruhm." But the real "hero" of the poem is a drunken German soldier who risks his life for his comrades by being willing to drink a fair amount of captured applejack which his comrades fear has been poisoned by the Confederate soldiers on fleeing their camp. The applejack turns out to be safe, and a great alcoholic feast takes place during which the hero is honored as "sans peur et sans reproche."

In his poem "Lebendig begraben" Dorsch describes an after-the-battle scene in which Union soldiers pick up wounded and dead soldiers and officers. They eventually find the seemingly lifeless bodies of two colonels. They bury the first one. They place the second one into an open grave; although not showing a recognizable mortal wound, he is evidently dead, but, about to be covered by the necessary quantity of earth, suddenly comes to life and utters the words—"John, wo ist die Pulle."

The Union Army, like all armies, had its quota of drunkards, cowards, and quitters. It was also, as most Civil War historians know, an army plagued by much sickness and disease. Dorsch, the doctor of medicine, refers to the prevalence of typhus, dysentery, and other troubles stemming from an irritated *Darmkanal.* He was also aware of the miserable lack of equipment, weapons, uniforms, and horses. In the first poem of his collection *Kriegerische Zeiten* he enumerates, in addition to the health problems, the presence of lice and the lack of decent food. Rancid bacon and beans often were the only items of food available, and water the only potable liquid. The shortages are recorded and bemoaned in the *Klagelied eines sehr Gemeinen von Broadheads erstem Michigan Kavallerie Regiment* and the poem called *Der Michigan Volontär.*

More serious than the problems of sanitation, missing equipment, bad food, and lack of weapons was, in Dorsch's opinion, treason and bad leadership. In his poem *Roth, Weiss und Blau* appear the lines:

> "Der rohe Tau ist Heldenbluth
> Das hier vergossen der Verrath."

The poem recalls what happened "Auf dem Schlachtfeld von Balls Bluff, Ende Februar 1862" and refers to rumors that were possibly or very likely planted by Confederate agents in the army led by General McClellan. A detailed account of the battle of Balls Bluff, which led to a very large and entirely unnecessary loss of the lives of Union soldiers, is described by Lücke in a manner which lends substance to Dorsch's reference to *Verrath.*[22]

Since most of Dorsch's poems have as subject matter events that took place during the first half of the Civil War, they, by necessity, dealt with a considerable number of ills and shortcomings, of which treason was one of the worst and the most serious. The Union Army was indeed in a sorry state but Generalfeldmarschall Moltke's claim that the Union Army and the Confederate Army were "two armed mobs chasing each other around the country," was not justified.[23] By 1863 the Union Army had turned into what might be called a regular army with capable leaders for whom Dorsch found generous words of praise. He, of course, never intended to write a history of the Civil War in verse. Whatever he wrote, whether it was negative or not, came from the pen of a man who was a devoted citizen of his adopted country.

Lack of space does not allow here a complete evaluation of Dorsch, the poet, the man, and the capable physician. A reading of the following sources will make it clear that his contributions to the making of Michigan and the United States as a whole were considerable and lasting: John Andrew Russel, *The Germanic Influence in the Making of Michigan* (University of Detroit Press, 1927); the already mentioned dissertation of Carlson about Dorsch; the particularly positive biographical sketch in the *Dictionary of American Biography* (ed. by Allen Johnson and Dumas Malone), vol. 5 (1946); and the recent study of Robert E. Ward entitled "Eduard Dorsch and Otto Roeser. German-American Poets in Michigan," *Michigan Heritage* (Winter 1969).

NOTES

1. Eduard Dorsch, *Aus der Alten und Neuen Welt*. Gedichte. New York, The International News Co., 1884. 360 pages.

Since the limitations of space allowed only a few of the poems to be given or discussed in detail, the titles of all twenty-seven shall follow here. The titles are preceded by the page numbers of the manuscript.

1) p.	1–4	Der Michigan Volontär. Juny 1861.
2)	5–8	Simon Cameron.
3)	8–12	Klagelied eines sehr Gemeinen von Broadheads erstem Michigan Kavallerie Regiment.
4)	13	Nach der Schlacht bei Bull Run. Am 28. July 1861.
5)	15–26	Der letzte Mann von Beaufort.
6)	27–30	Einem Todten zum Gedächtnis, den 1. Dezember 1861.
7)	31–39	Ein Schmetterling.
8)	40–43	Der neue Fabius Cunctator.
9)	44–45	Ein Begräbnis am Potomac, den 2. Februar 1862.
10)	46–51	Auch ein deutscher Held, den 15. Februar 1862.
11)	52–56	Quos ego, den 4. März 1862.
12)	57–63	Der letzte Washington. An Washington's Geburtstag, den 22. Februar 1862.
13)	64–65	Roth, Weiss und Blau. Auf dem Schlachtfelde von Balls Bluff, Ende Februar 1862.
14)	66–70	Europa und Amerika. Ein politisches Zwiegespräch.
15)	71–75	Der westliche Napoleon.
16)	76–79	McClellan, der Vogelfänger. Anakreontisch.
17)	80–84	Warte, Kröte! den 25. März 1862.
18)	85–93	Die Quelle der Jugend.
19)	94–97	Noch nicht.
20)	98–101	Aus Memphis. Juny 1862.
21)	102–105	Lebendig begraben. Siehe N.Y. Tribune 24. Juny 1862.
22)	106–109	Eine unbekannte Leiche.
23)	110–116	Die Nemesis. den 25. July 1862.
24)	117–121	Aus Vicksburg. July 1863.
25)	122–127	Der letzte Kampf. Herbst 1864.
26)	128–132	Der verlohrene Führer. Im Sommer 1864.
27)	133–140	An der Himmelsthür. (Juni 1864).

2. The Carlson statement was taken from the text given in the *Michigan History Magazine*, vol. 20 (1936), p. 416.

3. The text of this poem can be found in Dorsch's: *Aus der Alten und Neuen Welt*, pp. 114–118.

4. Dorsch, *Parabasen*. Milwaukee, 1875.

5. MS pages 133–140.

6. Alexander J. Schem, *Deutsch-amerikanisches Lexicon* [etc.], 4. Band (New York, 1871), p. 755.

7. Friedrich Kapp, *Aus und über Amerika. Thatsachen und Erlebnisse* (Berlin, 1876), 2. Band, p. 211.

8. Bruce Catton, *The Coming Fury*. Vol. One of the Centennial History of the Civil War (New York, 1961), p. 400.

9. In Ned Bradford, *Battles and Leaders of the Civil War* (New York, 1956), p. 26.

10. In: *The Maryland Historical Magazine*, XXXVI (1941), 394.

11. Wilhelm Kaufmann, *Die Deutschen im amerikanischen Bürgerkrieg* (München, Berlin, 1911), pp. 14-15.

12. Schem, 4. Bd., p. 453.

13. Frank Moore, *The Civil War in Song and Story* (New York, 1889), p. 148.

14. Martin Lücke, *Der Bürgerkrieg der Vereinigten Staaten, 1861-'65* (St. Louis, Mo., 1892), p. 112.

15. Moore, p. 358.

16. Catton, p. 439.

17. See: Henry Wager Halleck in Schem, 5. Bd., p. 122.

18. In: *The American Iliad. The Epic Story of the Civil War as narrated by Eyewitnesses and Contemporaries* (Indianapolis and New York, 1947), pp. 61-69.

19. Kapp, 2. Bd., p. 281.

20. Carl Wittke, *Refugees of Revolution. The German Forty-Eighters in America* (Philadelphia, 1952), pp. 233-234.

21. Colin Ross, *Unser Amerika* (Leipzig, 1940), p. 227.

22. Lücke, p. 114.

23. Moltke's verdict is quoted in a newly published book by Hugh Brogan, ed. of *The Civil War in the Times Report Series* which was not available when this paper was written.

12. The Survival of German Traditions in Missouri
Adolf E. Schroeder

Thomas Hartshorne, arguing persuasively that variation among social, racial, and ethnic groups in the United States is so wide that the idea of a national American character has questionable validity, found nevertheless that "the most striking fact that emerges from a study of American conceptions of the American character during the twentieth century is the remarkable similarity among them."[1] The search for a national character, the attempt to establish the unique qualities which the American experience has produced, has had a profound influence on American life. The concept of the "melting pot," that great crucible of common experience which was to bring about the Americanization, assimilation, and acculturation of all who came to the New World, has been implicit in American thought since colonial times. Unity became a pervasive symbol in a country born of revolution: ". . . join in hands, brave Americans all/ By uniting we stand, by dividing we fall,"[2] a thought at least as old as Aesop. "Union at home's the only way."[3] "From whence we came it matters not/ We all make now one nation."[4] Daniel Webster, melding the ideal upon which the American cause was founded with the concept of a necessary unity, "Liberty *and* Union, now and forever, one and inseparable,"[5] articulated a view already well entrenched in the American tradition by the 1830s.

A unity of purpose, however, was to be difficult to achieve in a multi-ethnic society; and one of the characteristics of the American experience has been the tension created by a pervading desire for unity, a national purpose, an identity as a people on the one hand, and, on the other hand, not only fundamental differences on national and local issues but an equally fundamental need, for many years not acknowledged, to preserve and treasure the presence of an older heritage. Carl Wittke urged the recognition of different cultural ties long before the current interest in ethnicity: "Immigrants . . . brought with them memories and experiences of an older social order. . . . Civilizations much older than our own are mirrored in the folksongs, traditions, customs, and folklore of any immigrant group. It is not a question . . . of relative values. . . . It is a matter of appreciating what there may be of Old World Culture in the soul of even the poorest and most ignorant immigrant. . . ."[6]

There were, of course, some early observers of the American scene who saw not only the accommodation to the new environment that took place in immigrants, the rapid Americanization of their children, and the putting away of the past, but noted the persistence of cultural differences and identification. Timothy Flint observed early that "strong features of nationality are very striking characteristics in this country universally. The Germans, the French, the Anglo-Americans, Scotch, and Irish all retain and preserve their national manners. . . ."[7] Charles Sealsfield, one of the most perceptive European commentators, based his views not only on personal observation and conversations with Americans he encountered but also on his wide reading of national and local newspapers and journals, a careful evaluation of the observations of others, as well as a familiarity with topical broadsides, folklore, and political oratory, which in spite of an almost obligatory hyperbole often catch as few other forms of expression can the spirit and essence of a particular time and place.[8] Sealsfield recognized the elusive nature of the American national character, saw the heterogeneity of American society as one of its most significant aspects, and evoked the diversity of cultures as skillfully as he sketched the boundless variety of geographic and climatic characteristics. He sought to come to terms with whatever was "American" in American life, as others did, anticipating by some years the recognition of the force of the frontier on the development of national psychology; but he realized the intransigent and deep-seated differences in those shaped by different cultural memories and social conditions.

Gottfried Duden discovered in himself a need for what he called "the bond of common memories." "Das Einzige, was ich hier vermisste, war die Nähe befreundeter vaterländischer Familien. . . . Allein was immer fehlen wird, das ist das Band der gemeinsamen

Erinnerungen."[9] This was a theme prevailing well into the twentieth century in Missouri. "The German clings to memories from abroad . . . deep in his heart there is something that cannot be expressed in English. . . ."[10] Or as Walter Hoops said in 1971, in explaining that language was no longer the glue which held the German-American societies together in St. Louis: "It's the social part. The social part of having friends."[11] Whether expressed or not, it was a theme implicit in the provision of German schools for children, the formation of numerous societies, and the preservation of customs and traditions.

The persistence of German culture in Missouri has been reinforced by factors other than the tenaciousness of a sense of common origin: the pattern of German settlement and the development of population clusters in the state; the political and religious orientation of early settlers; geographical and climatic factors which contributed to the wide dispersal of early settlers and then served to isolate rural communities for long periods of time; a significant German participation in the cultural, economic, and political life of the state in both urban and rural areas; and a historical circumstance which has had substantial effect, the strongly pro-Union stance of the German population in a state with deep southern sympathies. The folk memory is long, and in many ways attitudes toward the German presence in Missouri have been shaped as much by the incidents of the Civil War as by the events of the twentieth century, a factor which has contributed in turn to a continuing sense of identity among Missouri Germans.

Although in Missouri, as in lower Louisiana, some of the early settlers intermarried with French families and Gallicized their names, Flint reported that in 1817 when he visited Missouri's first German settlement, established by Joseph Neyswanger who made his way from North Carolina to the White River near Cape Girardeau in 1799, he found it "pure German," with a language less mixed than that in Pennsylvania.[12] Many of those who urged and led settlement to Missouri saw themselves not as new Americans but as new Germans. Duden's vision was: "Wäre einmal eine kleine Stadt in dem Geiste gegründet, den amerikanischen Deutschen als Mittelpunkt der Kultur zu dienen, so würde man bald ein verjüngtes Germanien entstehen sehen, und die europäischen Deutschen würden in Amerika eben so ein zweites Vaterland

haben, als die Briten. Möchte sich doch in Deutschland dafür ein
lebendiges Interesse entwickeln!"[13]

Duden, a lawyer and government official in Mülheim on the
Ruhr, had become convinced that many of the crimes which he
had to prosecute were due to poverty and overpopulation in Germany, and he set out to find in western America a place where
European immigrants would have an opportunity to build a new
life. He arrived in St. Louis in late October, 1824, with traveling
companion Ludwig Eversmann (who was to remain in Missouri),
and in order to acquaint himself with the realities of life on the
frontier bought land in what was then Montgomery County, west
of the river Femme Osage on Lake Creek. Duden lived in Missouri
for almost three years before returning to Germany, where in 1829
he published *Bericht über eine Reise nach den westlichen Staaten
Nord-Amerikas.* . . . Appearing at a time of political unrest and
economic upheaval in Germany, the book, later republished in
1832 in St. Gallen and 1834 in a revised edition in Bonn, gained
a wide readership and was responsible for a surge in immigration
to Missouri; Duden was later criticized by his countrymen and
others for having misled those hoping for a better life on the
western frontier, but as Judge Hugo Muench pointed out in 1913,
he "liess es nicht an wohlgemeinter Warnung fehlen, die aber nur
gern von denjenigen übersehen wurde, die bestrebt waren, bloss die
Lichtseiten seiner Schilderungen in sich aufzunehmen. . . ."[14]

Whether spurred by Duden, letters from relatives already in
Missouri, or by conditions at home, a number of societies were
formed in the early 1830s to emigrate to Missouri. In 1832
Nikolaus Lenau bought shares in the "Ulmer Verein der Aus-
wanderer," a group of two hundred who planned to come to
Missouri.[15] Disillusioned by life in America and the rigors of an
Ohio winter, Lenau never reached the state, but many others did.
The "Berliner Gesellschaft," professional men and wealthy aristocrats and their families, settled in Franklin and Montgomery
counties. Among this group was Baron Wilhelm Johann von Bock,
who founded the little town of Dutzow on Lake Creek, below
Duden's abandoned farm, naming it for his estate in Mecklenburg
and designating all the streets for German poets. Frederick Gustorf
described his visit to the Missouri home of von Bock on August
16, 1836:

"Madame Bock, a very cultured woman, surrounded by her five daughters, greeted me very cordially. I had heard that this was a very hospitable home where all Germans were welcome. This was indeed a fact. The room was decorated with German engravings, a piano, and a small collection of books . . . was filled with young Germans from the cultured classes. . . . They talked about a ball . . . and about the habits and customs of the Americans, which the Germans cannot get used to."[16]

In spite of good coffee served in beautiful cups, "real German cream puffs," and an afternoon of music, Gustorf was not enchanted by life in Missouri. "I cannot believe that women of such culture come here to milk cows." He was further shocked by the living conditions of members of a "settlement of peasants from Osnabrück," but had to concede that their achievement had been substantial: "They settled here on Government land two or three years ago and are the lowest class of German immigrants. By constant diligence and hard work they now have large fields of wheat under cultivation. . . ."[17]

In 1833 the "Solingen Gesellschaft," a contingent of over 150 professional men, merchants, artisans, farmers, and their families, led by Friedrich Steines, arrived and settled east of Dutzow around Augusta and Femme Osage, in Warren and St. Charles counties, in or near New Melle, Warrenton, Marthasville, Holstein and south of the Missouri River at Washington in Franklin County. The "Giessener Auswanderungsgesellschaft" was founded by Paul Follenius and Friedrich Münch, whose original purpose was to establish a model German state in Arkansas. When an advance party returned to Germany and discouraged the plan to settle in Arkansas, it was decided to come to Missouri[18] instead, and Münch, a prolific writer, composed an "Auswanderer Lied" for the new destination:

Auf, in mutigem Vertrauen,/ Fest und brüderlich vereint!
Vorwärts, vorwärts lasst uns schauen
Am Missouri Hütten bauen,/ Wo der Freiheit Sonne scheint!
. . . .
Deutsche Kraft und deutsche Treue/ Ueber Meere flieh'n sie hin.
O, so blühe dann auf's Neue,
Deutsche Kraft und Deutsche Treue/ Am Missouri sollt ihr blüh'n.[19]

The Giessener emigrants traveled in two groups, and the first, led by Follenius by way of New Orleans was plagued by illness and accident and disbanded in St. Louis. After settling the muddled financial affairs of the group, Follenius moved with six of the families to Warren County, near where Duden had lived. Münch led the other group, which came by way of Baltimore and settled in Lake Creek Valley on the other side of Duden's Hill from Follenius. A man who combined practicality with his love of writing, Münch was one of the few "Latin farmers" to succeed at farming.

> "Von den zahlreichen 'lateinischen Farmern,' welche um mich herum wohnten, ging einer nach dem andern zu Grunde, nachdem die von ihnen mitgebrachten Mittel in die Hände der Taglöhner-Familien, welche sich dabei ganz wohl befanden, übergegangen waren. Einige retteten sich noch rechtzeitig in die Städte, wo sie zu anderen Berufsarten übergingen; ich bin fast der Einzige, der seine hiesige erste Heimstätte bis heute behauptet hat."[20]

Gustorf visited a member of the Giessener Society, Professor David Göbel, in early September, 1836, and although Göbel was clearly discouraged about hardships he faced, he had hope for the children of the immigrants: "We old ones will pass away and rot, but our children will have a chance to enjoy a new life in a new country." Gustorf had his own view about that: ". . . how can children get a proper education in a wilderness without schools and other cultural facilities? They will grow up to be ruffians. . . ."[21] In fact, education for the children was a problem on the Missouri frontier, but Münch, who became a schoolmaster from necessity, since there was no one else, and taught both German and American children in his home, reported: "viele meiner Schüler, welche später eine hervorragende Stellung einnahmen, haben niemals einen andern Unterricht genossen."[22]

Second-generation Germans generally prospered in Missouri, and a number of the "Duden followers" and their children achieved considerable prominence in state and local affairs. Writing in 1872, Münch maintained that the life of most of the Germans in Missouri was an improvement over the conditions of those who had remained in Germany. The immigrants had retained their habits of industriousness, developed independence, and contributed substantially to the development of the state, a view in accord with that of later historians.[23] Their lives centered on family and church, and Münch noted that they had preserved their traditional amusements: "Die Deutschen lassen hier ihr Theil von Lustbarkeit sich nicht nehmen; Tanzvergnügen, auch Scheibenschiessen u. dgl. sind hier sogar häufiger als in den deutschen Dörfern und es geht dabei in der Regel insofern anständiger zu, als die Sache nicht, wie so oft bei der deutschen Kirchweih', mit einer allgemeinen Prügelei (der Quintessenz des Vergnügens) endigt."[24]

The substantial settlement of Germans in central Missouri began in the 1830s. Dr. Bernhard Bruns, a native of Westphalia, arrived in St. Louis in the Fall of 1835 and made several trips to explore the interior of the state. In a letter of October 3, 1835 he reported having found a fertile area in Gasconade County, on a river which he called "Mariafluss."[25] There were already several German families in the vicinity, and Dr. Bruns thought the settlement large enough to support a doctor.[26] He returned home for his wife and son, and with two of her younger brothers, Franz and Bernhard Geisberg, came back to the settlement on the Maries River, which soon developed into a center of German Catholicism. In 1836 the first log church was built, and in May, 1838 the Diocese of St. Louis established the parish of Westphalia as a center for missionary work in central Missouri and sent Father Ferdinand Helias, a native of Belgium, to direct the work. Although he had joined the Jesuit order to serve the Indians, Father Helias spent his life in central Missouri, establishing several parishes in Osage County, where groups of Catholics from the Münsterland, the Rhine, and Bavaria had been settling since 1835. The towns of Westphalia, Rich Fountain, Loose Creek, St. Thomas, and others, all between the Osage and Gasconade rivers, were predominantly German, and Father Helias served communities as far west as Cole Camp, where a small group of Germans, apparently traveling on the Missouri River to Franklin, near Boonville, and following the old Santa Fe Trail southwestward, had in the early 1830s settled along Lake Creek in Pettis and Benton counties and founded the towns of Mora and Cole Camp.[27] Letters of Mrs. Bruns and her brothers, preserved by the Geisberg family in Münster, offer a detailed view of early life in the area as groups of new immigrants from

Westphalia, Hannover, and the Rhineland joined the old settlers. The community of Westphalia was a particularly close-knit one and life centered on church activities. Father Helias moved to nearby Taos, where he is buried, and an inscription he wrote on the front page of an old Rich Fountain missal outlines his life and service: "Flandria nos genuit; docuit nos Gallia;/ Roma, Teutonia, Helvetiaque sinus peragravimus omnes;/ Post varios casus, terraque, mariaque labores,/ Sistimus: Et solido fundamine condimus urbem/ Westphalia, septemque sacratas Numinis Adeo."[28]

Although early settlement was concentrated in the eastern and central parts of the state, individuals found their ways farther west. Heinrich Dierking settled in the late 1830's near the present site of Concordia, and delighted with the fertile farm lands wrote his friends in Hannover, who with others from Westphalia and Lippe-Detmold eventually developed a substantial settlement in parts of Saline, Pettis, Johnson, and Lafayette counties.[29] One of the most prominent citizens of early St. Joseph, which was founded by French trader, Joseph Robidoux, was Frederick W. Smith, a native of Prussia, who settled at "Blacksnake Hills" in the Platte Purchase in 1838 or 1839. Smith made the original map of St. Joseph, which he named for Robidoux; served as Captain of the Militia for years and later as Major in the State Volunteers. In 1841 he was appointed first postmaster of St. Joseph, was elected mayor of the city in 1861, and later became judge of the Buchanan County Court.[30]

The largest group to emigrate from Germany was the "Stephan-led Alt-Lutheraner," from Saxony, numbering over six hundred, who arrived in St. Louis in the Spring of 1838. The majority of this group, which was to found the Missouri Synod of the Lutheran Church, whose energetic educational and publication program has had a profound and lasting influence on the state, settled in Perry County, where they founded the towns of Altenburg, Dresden, Frohna, Johannisberg, Paitzdorf, Seelitz, and Wittenberg, and established the "Log Cabin College," which was later to become Concordia Seminary. A congregation was also established at Union-town, and a number of professional men, artisans, and merchants chose to remain in St. Louis, where they founded Trinity Lutheran Church.[31]

Group emigration from other areas of the United States continued, as those who had come to the older states to establish German communities found that their children were forgetting their native language and customs and adopting the ways of the Anglo-American majority. The *Anzeiger des Westens,* St. Louis' first German newspaper, reported in 1835 that there were still families coming from Pennsylvania in the belief that they would find a German state in Missouri.[32] One of the more enthusiastic, energetic, and determined of these groups, and the one that was perhaps to be the most successful in establishing and maintaining a German tradition was the "Deutsche Ansiedlungs-Gesellschaft zu Philadelphia," which had been founded to create a colony that would be German in every respect. On December 6, 1837, seventeen members arrived on the last boat of the season and made their way to the lovely area on the Missouri River which had been selected for the site of the town, named Hermann, in honor of Arminius. Hermann thrived in spite of early difficulties, and by 1839 had a population of 450.[33] German craftsmen constructed there the brick and stone buildings with steeply pitched roofs, the ornamental stone and ironwork, the terraces and gardens they remembered from the "alte Heimat," and within a few years there were German churches, schools, newspapers, musical clubs, a theater, and a Turnverein. Hermann was to become the third largest wine-producing area in the United States, and in 1848 a "Weinfest" was held to celebrate the first grape harvest. A parade, led by a wagon drawn by two white horses transporting Bacchus, crowned with grape leaves, and the brass band wound past the vineyards so that all might see the richness of the harvest.[34] Not surprisingly, the area along the Missouri River from St. Louis to the mouth of the Gasconade was known as the "Missouri Rhineland."

About 1840 German Catholic families began settling in Ste. Genevieve County, in the area of New Offenburg and Zell, and in 1848 Father Angelo Hypolite Gandolfo began the St. Joseph's Catholic Church at Zell, one of the earliest examples of the impressive churches built in Missouri by German stone masons.[35] Ste. Genevieve itself, although strongly French, had a prominent German population which contributed substantially to community life. The business practices of "Butcher Operle" of Ste. Genevieve must have been welcomed, for it is reported that the larger the family and the smaller the income, the larger the cut of meat for less the price.[36]

Missouri's most successful experiments in utopian communities were those founded by Wilhelm Keil in the 1840s in Shelby and Adair counties. The initial colony, Bethel, a tract of 2,560 acres[37] in the North River Valley in north Shelby County was particularly prosperous and within three years the population exceeded 600.[38] The group, mainly from western Pennsylvania and eastern Ohio, composed primarily of former members of Georg Rapp's Harmony Society and German Methodists, developed its own religious philosophies and rituals. Keil, whose magnetic and compelling personality was an essential element in the stability and strength of the community, served as pastor and head of the Colony, which celebrated church holidays such as Easter, Pentecost, and Christmas but abolished the rites of baptism and confirmation. A harvest festival was celebrated, and Keil's birthday, March 6, was marked with a feast, held in the big upstairs hall of his residence, Elim, to which the whole community marched, preceded by a brass band and a "Schellenbaum." In 1855 Keil left Bethel to establish Aurora Colony in Oregon, his 75-wagon train carrying the body of his oldest son, who had been promised before his death that he would be able to go West with the others. The Missouri colony was governed from afar during Keil's lifetime, but upon his death in December, 1877 steps were taken to dissolve the communal society and individual ownership of property was restituted in June, 1879.[39]

By the middle of the nineteenth century the German presence was strong in Missouri, in St. Louis, along the "Missouri Rhineland," and farther westward. A German school had been opened in St. Louis in February, 1837 with Friedrich Steines as first teacher, a year before the city's first public school was established. On July 4, 1847 Emil Mallinckrodt wrote his brother Eduard in Dortmund: "One hears much Low German in the streets and markets and all Germans are without exception well off. They own one-third of St. Louis. . . . Missouri is now becoming Germany for America. . . ." He reported that property purchased in April had almost tripled in value in six weeks, predicted that St. Louis would be bigger than London, and foresaw a prosperous and peaceful future.[40] In 1850 St. Louis, with a total population of 77,465 had 23,954 German born,[41] and in 1858 Münch in describing the most important cities in the state estimated that Germans comprised approximately one-eighth of the entire population. Some towns like Augusta and Washington were almost entirely German, and in Hermann "vergisst man, dass man sich in einem nicht-teutschen Lande befindet." Other cities with substantial German population were New Madrid, Cape Girardeau, and Hannibal; St. Charles was half-German; Jefferson City, the capital, with a population of 3,000, was half German; Warsaw, partly German. And on the extreme western part of the state, Weston was over one-third German and St. Joseph, with about 7,000 population, had almost 2,000 Germans.[42] In Kansas City a German "Schulverein" was formed in 1859 by the Kansas City Education Society, a group with over a hundred members, whose purpose was to establish the first "public school" in the city for non-denominational German-English instruction.[43]

Although many of the German settlements were farming communities, German artisans and tradesmen were widely dispersed in Missouri before the Civil War, not only in those areas strongly German but also in other cities and settlements. German stonemasons worked on the new capitol of the state in 1840,[44] and by the middle of the century brickmaking in many areas was controlled by German immigrants. Pottery was a craft dominated by German-trained workmen; wineries were being established, sometimes on farms; and, as Duden had predicted, breweries prospered in St. Louis. Limestone and brick were used for building and what Charles van Ravenswaay, who has made an extensive study of German arts and crafts in Missouri, has called the "Missouri German vernacular style" of brick buildings was developed. Dwellings graced with handwrought hinges and "Haussprüche" and distinctive barns with carving and other decorations, became a part of the Missouri landscape. In Washington, as well as Hermann, the houses were built to the street with large gardens in the back. Churches, both the richly decorated Catholic and the plain but graceful Evangelical Lutheran, were placed on hills or in the most prominent places available. Gravestones with German inscriptions were made from the local "cotton rock," and many Catholic cemeteries had wooden and wrought iron crosses made by the local blacksmith.[45]

The development of music organizations, theater groups, and

social and cultural clubs was strongest in St. Louis,[46] where the first Oratorio Society was formed in 1839; the first theater production was in 1842, Schiller's *Räuber*. The Thalia Society produced plays from 1846–1849, and the "Sängerbund" formed a dramatic section which began presenting plays in 1852. Heinrich Börnstein, publisher and editor of *Anzeiger des Westens,* founded the "Philodramatische Gesellschaft" in 1853, and in 1859 a permanent theater, the "St. Louis Opern Haus," opened with Goethe's *Egmont.* A Schiller week was held the same year, commemorating Schiller's 100th birthday. However, such activities were not limited to St. Louis. Hermann, which had never had a single strong religious orientation, led with theater and music groups, and in 1854 two members of Hermann's "Erholung" took scenery and costumes from their theater to Washington to help organize a "Theaterverein" there, which a year later moved into its own building.[47] Washington had a Thalia Society in 1855, and Augusta's "Harmonie Verein" was founded in 1856 (a library was established in 1858). There were active Turner societies in most "German" cities and towns, and German newspapers established in towns across the state before the Civil War.

German folk celebrations were a part of life in nineteenth-century Missouri. A "Vogelschiessen" was reported by Gert Göbel to have taken place on July 4, 1840 at Washington, he thought most likely the first of its kind west of the Mississippi, causing great amazement among the American settlers. The traditional target for such a match was a wooden bird with outstretched wings, intended to represent the imperial German eagle. "Der Vogel war ganz ordnungsgemäss mit Krone, Ring, Scepter, Reichsapfel und Fahne ausgerüstet, lauter Dinge, die den Amerikanern ganz unverständlich waren. . . ."[48] Different prizes were offered for shooting off various parts of the body, and the marksman who shot down the last part was declared "Schützenkönig," an honor he held for the year. Göbel remarked that to a German, accustomed to the exacting protocol of the championship shooting matches, this first Missouri "Vogelschiessen" might have seemed unorthodox, but the traditional celebration and dance followed the shooting competition.

The part the Germans played in the Civil War in Missouri, particularly in St. Louis, was a major one. There were Germans

who were slave-owners, including Eversmann, who had come to
Missouri with Duden, and Emil Malinckrodt; and some immigrants
were Southern sympathizers as a lavishly illustrated broadside of
some twenty-four stanzas, a parody of Bürger's "Lenore," demonstrates. A satirical view of the November, 1860 dispatch of the
Missouri Volunteer Militia to guard the Kansas border against the
"Jayhawkers," it mocks pro-Union officials and German militia
equally:

> Herr Stewart fuhr um's Morgenroth,/ Empor aus schweren
>   Träumen:
> Kreuz-Donnerwetter! Schwerenoth! Ich darf nicht länger
>   säumen.
> Jetzt gilt's Governor, fasse Muth! Montgomery, die Teufelsbrut,
> Bedroht Missouri's Grenzen. . . .

The officials were corrupt, the soldiers reluctant, and the ballad
suggested that Stewart, who had "invented the war," have as his
epitaph "Da liegt der Hund begraben."[49]

However, there is no doubt that the Missouri Germans were for
the most part pro-Union, although Bethel colonies remained
neutral. Enlistment records in the Adjutant General's Office in
Jefferson City show that many of the Union Army clerks were
German and that enlistees from all sections of Germany and of all
occupations joined the Union. About thirty of the most prominent
members of the Augusta "Harmonie Verein" enlisted following
Lincoln's first call for volunteers and were instrumental in taking
Camp Jackson and thus "holding Missouri to the Union."[50]

The Camp Jackson incident resulted in a number of anti-German broadsides and songs in St. Louis which have survived in
various manuscript and printed versions. In the fray that ensued on
May 10, 1861 when Federal officers, noting the presence of Confederate flags in the Camp and fearing its loss, determined to take
it, the crowd which gathered along the streets was fired upon, and
Confederate balladeers were quick to place the blame on the
Germans.

> When the Dutch surrounded Camp Jackson. . . .
> To drive us from the Happy Land of Canaan
> The people gave three cheers/ For Davis volunteers

Which raised the Heßians [sic] indignation
They fired upon our brothers
Killing sisters, wives and mothers. . . . .[51]

The song ends with the hope that the Dutch will soon be driven from the Happy Land of Canaan. The intensity of the feeling aroused by the Camp Jackson affair is reflected in "The Capture of Camp Jackson," composed by a member of the Missouri Guards some forty years after the battle, in 1900, which refers to the "imported Dutch."[52]

Of the ten regiments of volunteers raised in St. Louis, nine were largely German. Franz Sigel, a "48'er," was elected Colonel of the third Missouri Volunteers in St. Louis and participated in the battles of Wilson's Creek and Pea Ridge. Since the latter was the most important battle that took place in the Ozark region, General Sigel became the German immigrant most widely sung about in Missouri. A fragment of an old song was collected by Vance Randolph in 1939: "Oh, who is Price a-fightin'? He's fightin' now I know/ It surely must be Sigel/ Cause I hear the cannons roar."[53]

"General Sigel's Grand March," composed and "respectfully dedicated" to Sigel was published in St. Louis, and Poole's "I'm Going to Fight Mit Sigel" became so well known that a parody was used as an army bugle call[54] and the title was used by Tony Pastor in his "Song of Song-Titles." A few of the songs of the War in Missouri are favorable to the Union and German forces—one urges "Stand back, boys, and give the Dutch room. . . ,"[55] but more common were the broadsides and songs in which the German forces lost, in defiance of actual fact. In 1904 a fragment was sung by an old janitor in the State Capitol: "Sterling Price he wheeled his men about/ And cut the Dutch into Sauerkraut."[56] A stanza of a Missouri version of "Root, Abe, or Die" became widely dispersed in the oral tradition in the state and was preserved in "ballet books" and scrapbooks well into the twentieth century: "Twas there that Lyon bit the dust and Siegle ran away/ Just as he did at Carthage upon a former day. . ."[57] "Joe Stiner" and "Joe Slinsworth," versions of the same song, recount the Missouri campaigns with some basis in fact and much satire on German drinking habits. In a period of comic and minstrel songs in which stereotypes of ethnic groups provided inspiration both to frontier wits and city broadside makers, the German's accent, his food preferences, and, above all, his love of lager beer were mercilessly parodied. The lager beer was a particular sore point in a rural society, settled by Southern protestants, and a later song from an Ozark manuscript collection states ". . . the Dutchmen in this town/ They like their lager beer/ They drink it in the night and in the morning. . . ."[58] And in the "Hell Bound Train," heard by Vance Randolph at a Revival Tent Meeting: "The tank was full of lager beer/ And the Devil himself was the engineer."[59]

During the 1860s German-Americans gained considerable prominence in local and state government. Dr. Bruns was mayor of Jefferson City during the Civil War,[60] and Bek reports that the boarding house in the capital where senators and representatives took their meals became known as the "German Diet."[61] During the next twenty years immigration continued and group settlement still occurred. A community in the western part of the state, primarily composed of Germans who had first stopped in Ohio and Indiana, was established in 1872 by Isaac Neuenschwander at Lowry City in St. Clair County,[62] and at Christmas time in 1873 a group of seven German Lutheran families from Minnesota arrived and purchased property on the fertile Spring River prairie in Lawrence County, founding the town of Freistatt and the next year establishing a church.[63] In St. Louis, as German immigration increased, German societies and organizations proliferated, eventually numbering over 300.[64] Although the very number of societies mitigated against unity, as did the geography of the city, spread out along the river, the population dispersal, and the fact that German instruction was discontinued in the public schools after the school board election of 1887,[65] the German tradition persisted: German language publications, including the prestigious *Westliche Post,* with which both Carl Schurz and Joseph Pulitzer were associated, prospered, German organizations abounded, and German customs endured.

H. E. Krehbiel observed that "music entered more deeply into the life of the German people than that of their neighbors,"[66] and this is reflected not only in the thriving musical societies in the cities but by individuals and families who perpetuated musical traditions and carefully preserved and treasured German song books. One *Handschrift* in St. Louis contains traditional ballads and songs current orally in Germany in the late nineteenth century,[67] and a booklet, *Lieder für die Deutsche Volkswehr,* contains not only folksongs but such political ballads as "Russland steck die Pieke ein" and "Pressfreiheit und Galgen."[68] Older people interviewed within the last year still remember fragments of children's songs and other songs from their youth. In the rural areas, although immigration had virtually ceased by the end of the century, folk customs and traditions were still maintained. Around the turn of the century the custom of the "Gastbitter," who invited guests to an approaching wedding, was practiced in several communities. His horse gaily decorated, carrying a staff to which everyone invited would attach a ribbon, the "Gastbitter" rode from house to house and farm to farm with his message. A former resident of Howard County remembers that everyone kept ribbons in the house for this purpose and that the "Gastbitter" was a colorful sight. At each stop he recited a lengthy invitation in verse, making up in earnestness what it lacked in poetical skill, describing in great detail the enormous amount of food and drink that was to be available for the wedding guests. His account of the distance he had traveled and the hardships he had endured to bring the invitation was usually so eloquent that he would receive a glass of wine or other refreshment while the ribbon was being attached to his staff.[69] In the Saxon Lutheran area of Perry County the "Bräutigamsführer" was the one delegated to ride around and invite the wedding guests.[70]

Although most of the farmers and craftsmen spoke in their regional dialects, informants reported that most songs and poems were in high German, as Bek, who participated in a Low German Marriage Feast in the Concordia area in the early 1900s and collected several "Hochzeiter" poems, demonstrated: "Hier bin ich her gesandt,/ Werde ein Brautbitter genannt/ In diesem Hause bin ich wohlbekannt?/ Hier nehme ich meinen Hut und Stab/ Und setze meinen Fuss darein/ Das ich möchte willkommen sein. . . ."[71]

Bek noted that the "Hochzeitbitter" carried a pistol which he discharged in the air at each house and included a description of other ritual practices—a chain placed across the path, requiring the groom to pay a "ransom" to proceed, and the mock struggle in which the married women ensnare an unmarried girl in the tablecloth used at the feast. He discovered that it was customary for the man sent to take the bride to the wedding to recite a poem and found other evidences of the preservation of old cultural and social customs. Münch believed "doch wird ein besseres Hochteutsch, als allgemein auf dem Lande in Teutschland gesprochen";[72] there was nevertheless some language corruption as a version of the invitation to the wedding, "Hochtit," sent by a resident of Florissant shows: "Nu stürt jo Hund und holt jo Mund/ denn de Hochtit Nötiger kommt rund/ Guten Tag im Gatier,/ Jetzt sind wir hier/ Un nem uk mein Hütken ab un/ Gruz jo all to Hus."[73]

The first World War saw the official abolishment of the use of the German language in Missouri and elsewhere. Although in St. Louis prior to the War there had been understanding and acceptance of the emotional commitment of the German-American community, which Carl Schurz had in 1904 called the "hyphen" between America and Germany,[74] there was an increasing hostility to German organizations, and the German-American Alliance disbanded in 1918 and contributed its treasury of $30,000 to the Red Cross.[75] By common consent German singing ended at the "Liederkranz" in April, 1918.[76] As G. K. Renner has shown,[77] the Citizen's Dry Alliance capitalized on the emotional issue of the war and the German background of the major brewing interests to further the cause of temperance, and an advertisement in the *Springfield Daily Leader* of November 4, 1918 urged that a "dry vote is a vote against the Kaiser . . . a vote for Democracy." On July 12, 1918 the Missouri Council of Defense adopted a resolution which was publicized throughout the state, declaring its opposition to the "use of the German language in the schools, churches, lodges and in public meetings of every character," and its belief that "the . . . adoption of English by all patriotic German organizations is a national duty . . . and will be regarded by loyal Americans as the clearest evidence of loyalty. . . ."[78] The resolution urged restraint from violence, and in fact the only serious incident that occurred in Missouri took place after the war in August, 1919, in Jackson, when the publisher of the *Deutscher Volksfreund* was forced by returned soldiers to promise not to print German any more to save his press from destruction.[79] As in other states there were some place name changes. Although Bismarck in St. François successfully resisted attempts to change its name to "Loyal,"[80] in Gasconade the town of Potsdam was changed to Pershing.[81]

Such examples indicate the force of the pressures in American society that have encouraged the acculturation of European ethnic groups, manifested both in the assimilative expectations of the majority group and the urge of second- and third-generation "hyphenated" Americans to escape the ethnic stereotypes in American humor, song, folklore, and nativist rhetoric. A particular tension developed in Missouri during the Civil War which was not lessened by the two World Wars. Reporting on the National Sänger-fest held in St. Louis in 1964, the Chairman of the Reception Committee noted that considerable adverse feeling toward the festival became evident. There were several reasons for this, but "There was a deep-seated and silent factor always present. This was the . . . issue of 'things German.' This always seems to be a . . . factor, from the next of kin, to associates, and neighbors."[82]

One of the results of this societal pressure has been the continued decrease in the public use of the German language. Arndt and Olson found that before the outbreak of World War I there were three daily, 25 weekly, and 12 monthly German publications in Missouri.[83] At present there is only one newspaper, the *Deutsche Wochenschrift,* published in Omaha and St. Louis, which serves to keep the Missouri German community informed of cultural events and meetings. Of the many publications previously issued by the churches, only *Der Lutheraner* still appears, although the Concordia Publishing House publishes *Tägliche-Andachten* on a bimonthly schedule and in 1971 it republished *Liederperlen,* a hymnal, by popular demand. Churches in St. Louis, Freistatt, and Concordia still offer services in German; in Hermann, ironically, confessions are heard in German, but the priest answers in English. Although the only communities in Missouri which can be considered bilingual enclaves today are those established by Amish and Mennonite groups now moving into central and western Missouri from Maryland and Pennsylvania, the language has persisted, and in communities such as Freistatt, Westphalia, Cole Camp, Concordia, and Altenburg it has been found that residents over forty can often speak German and that younger people can understand it.[84]

Missouri's German heritage also survives in the architectural and decorative arts, place names, customs, and folklore. Van Ravens-waay has discovered evidences of German craftsmanship present in many buildings along the Missouri River, including churches,

dwellings, barns, and places of business. A record of the survival of
the arts and crafts of the early German settlers of the Missouri
River Valley was undertaken by the WPA Index of American
Design Project, and facsimile renderings of pottery, domestic
utensils, and furniture, originally deposited in the Metropolitan
Museum of Art, are now preserved by the Index of American
Design in the National Gallery of Art. Such museums as that maintained by the Missouri Historical Society in St. Louis have collected examples of German craftsmanship for study; museums in
Hermann, Jefferson City, Westphalia, and other cities preserve
artifacts from the early days of settlement which demonstrate the
ways in which German-trained artisans adapted their crafts and
skills to the needs of the region and the materials available around
them.

Germany has given more place names to Missouri than any
other country, and these cities, towns, churches, schools, and
crossroads remind of the origin of those who "caused barren hill-
sides to blossom with grape vines and fruit trees, and opened large
farms in the midst of dense forests," and through whose efforts
"villages and towns sprang up where solitude had previously
reigned, and the liberal arts began to flourish. . . ."[85] Except
during the Civil War period the German population of Missouri has
not been politically unified, but a cultural loyalty has remained
to the present time and is manifest both in the urban areas such
as St. Louis where societies and organizations serve to perpetuate
and promote the language and traditions among the younger
people and in rural communities where the customs of the household and farm and the traditions of the holidays are practiced.
Wooden shoes made by parents and grandparents and medicinal
"Alpen-Kräuter" ordered from Germany are vividly recalled by
many young Missourians; church and social gatherings are popular
in both urban and rural areas, and musical societies flourish,
perhaps more vigorously than in Germany.[86] As faith in the
efficacy or desirability of the melting pot concept decreases and
ethnic consciousness increases, the old German traditions which
were displaced within the last few years by more modern amusements are being revived. Bethel has reinstated its Harvest Festival;
St. Nicholas appears on December 6 in several Catholic communities; and in Lutheran Perry County sweets are distributed

early in December to the children, although time has obscured the meaning of the custom.[87] "Fastnacht" is celebrated, and until 1972 "Wurstjäger" made their rounds in Rhineland, Missouri. The "Wurstjäger" Dance as well as other traditional songs and dances are still taught and performed at Hermann's annual "Maifest." Although no evidence was found that "shooting in the New Year" is still practiced, the German community of Ste. Genevieve has always participated prominently in the "Gui-annee" or "the run" on New Year's Eve, and versions of the "Gui-annee" survive in French, German, and English.[88]

Andrew Greeley has observed that ethnicity "seems to touch on something basic and primordial in the human psyche,"[89] and the celebration of the Bicentennial has created a resurgence of interest in the achievement and contribution of the many ethnic groups which make up the United States. Efforts are underway in many areas of Missouri to document family, church, and community history and to record and preserve not only the social and cultural history but also the folkloristic evidences of a German tradition which survives in the practices and beliefs of the people. The enormous social, cultural, economic, and political effect of the German immigration to Missouri has been long recognized, and current investigation shows that there are many communities in the state which retain their character, flavor, and individuality as German settlements. Further study of these communities can lead to a better understanding of the immigrant experience in a key midwestern state.

NOTES

1. Thomas L. Hartshorne, *The Distorted Image* (Cleveland: Case Western Reserve University, 1968), p. 187.

2. "The Liberty Song" [1768] in Frank Moore, ed., *Songs and Ballads of the American Revolution* (New York: D. Appleton & Co., 1856), p. 39.

3. "New Yankee Doodle" (New York: J. Hewitt [1798]). Sheet Music.

4. "Platt and Liberty," quoted by Dixon Ryan Fox, *The Decline of Aristocracy in New York* (New York: Harper & Row, 1965), p. 115.

5. Daniel Webster, "Second Speech on Foote's Resolution" [January 26, 1830] in *The Writings and Speeches of Daniel Webster*. 18 vols. (Boston: Little, Brown & Co., 1903), VI, p. 75.

6. Carl Wittke, *We Who Built America. The Saga of the Immigrant* (Cleveland: Western Reserve University, 1939), p. 362.

7. Timothy Flint, *Recollections of the Last Ten Years* (Boston: Cummings, Hilliard & Co., 1828), p. 236.

8. Karl Postl, writing anonymously or under various names, including C. Sidons and Charles Sealsfield, published in Stuttgart, London, Philadelphia and Zürich during 1827–1846. The first complete critical edition of Postl's work, which will include new biographical and bibliographical studies, is currently being published in twenty-eight volumes by Georg Olms in Hildesheim under the editorship of Karl J. R. Arndt.

9. Gottfried Duden, *Bericht über eine Reise nach den westlichen Staaten Nord-Amerikas und einen mehrjährigen Aufenthalt am Missouri (in den Jahren 1824, 25, 26, and 1827), in Bezug auf Auswanderung und Ueberbevölkerung* (Elberfeld: Sam Lucas, 1829), p. 230.

10. *Central Blatt & Social Justice*, St. Louis, II (April, 1909), p. 9.

11. Walter Hoops, Interview, August 17, 1971, by Irene Cortinovis. University of Missouri-St. Louis, Archive and Manuscript Division.

12. Flint, *Recollections*, p. 232.

13. Duden, *Bericht*, pp. 235–236.

14. Hugo Muench, "Aus dem Kapitel: 'Deutsche Ansiedlungen in der Umgebung von St. Louis,' und 'Lateinische Farmer'," *Deutsche Geschichtsforschung für Missouri* (Sedalia), I (Oktober 1913), 35.

15. Carl Hepp, ed., *Lenaus Werke*. Kritisch durchgesehene und erläuterte Ausgabe (Leipzig und Wien: Bibliographisches Institut, n.d.), I, xxxv.

16. Fred Gustorf, ed., *The Uncorrupted Heart*, Journal and Letters of Frederick Julius Gustorf 1800–1845 (Columbia, Mo.: University of Missouri Press, 1969), p. 134.

17. Ibid., p. 131.

18. Friedrich Münch, "Das Leben von Paul Follenius," *Erinnerungen aus Deutschlands trübster Zeit* (St. Louis & Neustadt/Haardt, 1873), pp. 57–71.

19. Hugo Muench, p. 40.

20. Friedrich Münch, "Sonst und Jetzt (et haec meminisse juvabit)," *Der Deutsche Pionier,* IV (September 1872), 231.

21. Gustorf, *The Uncorrupted Heart,* pp. 139–141.

22. Friedrich Münch, "Sonst und Jetzt," p. 230.

23. Perry McCandless, *A History of Missouri, 1820 to 1860.* The Missouri Sesquicentennial Edition, Volume II (Columbia, Mo.: The University of Missouri Press, 1972), p. 40 states: "As a whole, the German immigrants were a stable, hard-working people. For those with an agrarian background, Missouri's cheap and productive land offered a real opportunity, and they took advantage of it. The Germans tended to stay put; . . . land passed from father to son . . . family stability arose within the German communities. They were . . . good farmers. . . . German merchants, craftsmen, and professionals—classes that were to provide valuable contributions to Missouri life—concentrated . . . in St. Louis."

24. Friedrich Münch, "Welchen Einfluss auf das sittliche Leben unserer hiesigen deutschen Bevölkerung hat deren Versetzung aus der alten in die neue Welt bisher gezeigt?" *Der Deutsche Pionier,* III (Januar 1872), 341.

25. A map appended to N[icholas] Hesse, *Das westliche Nordamerika,* in besonderer Beziehung auf die deutschen Einwanderer in ihren landwirtschaftlichen, Handels- und Gewerbeverhältnissen (Paderborn, 1838) designates the river "Mariafluss," while the map in Alphonso Wetmore, *Gazetteer of the State of Missouri* (St. Louis: C. Keemle, 1837), With the latest additions and surveys from the Office of the Surveyor General, February 1837, calls the stream "River Maria," and on p. 73 makes reference to water power on "the Mary's." However, Robert L. Ramsay, *Our Storehouse of Missouri Place Names* (Columbia, Mo.: University of Missouri Studies, vol. 26, No. 3, 1954), p. 9, reports that his research had shown that the word was originally "Marais" or marsh and had nothing to do with girls named Marie, as folk etymology would have it.

26. Bernhard Bruns, Letter dated St. Louis, October 3, 1835. Unpublished correspondence of Dr. Bruns and of his wife, Henriette, née Geisberg, was graciously made available by Mrs. Carla Schulz-Geisberg of Nienberge, Germany.

27. J. G. Brühl, "Die deutschen Ansiedlungen in Pettis, Morgan, und Benton Counties, Missouri," *Der Deutsche Pioneer,* I (Nov. 1869), 269–273.

28. *Sacred Heart Parish, 1838–1938* (Jefferson City, Mo.: Midland Printing Co. [1938].), p. 20.

29. William G. Bek, "Survivals of Old Marriage Customs Among the Low Germans of West Missouri," *Journal of American Folklore,* XXI (1908), 60.

30. *History of Buchanan County and St. Joseph, Missouri From the Time of the Platte Purchase to the End of the Year 1915* (St. Joseph, Mo. [n.d.]), pp. 306–307.

31. P. E. Kretzmann, "The Saxon Immigration to Missouri, 1838–39," *The Missouri Historical Review,* XXXIII (January, 1939), 157–170. Hereafter cited as *MHR.*

32. *Anzeiger des Westens* (13. Nov. 1835) as cited by Ernst A. Stadler, "The German Settlement of St. Louis," *Midcontinent American Studies Journal*, VI (Spring, 1965), 19.

33. Samuel F. Harrison, *History of Hermann, Missouri* (Hermann, Mo., 1966), p. [27]; Anna Hesse, *Centenarians of Brick, Wood and Stone* (Hermann, Missouri, 1969), p. [5].

34. Anna Hesse, "Notes from the Pageant; The Arts and Crafts of Early Hermann" [n.d.]. Distributed at Missouri Historical Preservation Meeting in Hermann, October 18, 1969.

35. [Charles van Ravenswaay], "German Architecture," in *Missouri, A Guide to the "Show-Me" State*, compiled by workers of the Writers Program of the Works Project Administration in the State of Missouri (New York: Hastings House, 1954), p. 185.

36. Ralph D. Killian, "The Melting Pot" [n.d.], Western Manuscripts Collection, University of Missouri-Columbia. Mr. Killian reports that Butcher Duerr of Perryville and Butcher Buehler of Warsaw, both from the same province as Butcher Operle, had the same characteristics when it came to selling their meat.

37. William G. Bek, "A German Communistic Society in Missouri," *MHR*, III (October, 1908), Part I, pp. 52–74.

38. Roger Grant, "Missouri's Utopian Communities," *MHR*, LXVI (October, 1971), 25.

39. Bek, *MHR*, III (January, 1909), Part II, p. 121.

40. Letters of Emil Mallinckrodt to his brother Eduard. Emil Mallinckrodt Papers, Missouri Historical Society, St. Louis.

41. Sister Audrey Olson, "The Nature of an Immigrant Community: St. Louis Germans, 1850–1920," *MHR*, LXVI (April, 1972), 343. In this award-winning study, Sister Olson reports that since the census for 1880, which gives a résumé of the history of St. Louis, and the official figures for 1850 census returns differed, she tabulated the manuscript census returns for 1850 and arrived at the figure cited.

42. Friedrich Münch, *Der Staat Missouri, geschildert mit besonderer Rücksicht auf teutsche Einwanderung* (New York: Farmers' & Vine Growers Society, 1859), p. 204.

43. A. P. Scheuermann, "Die Deutschen gründeten die erste Schule in Kansas City," *Deutsche Geschichtsforschung für Missouri*, I (1914), 136–137.

44. Raymond C. Backes, "Catholicism in Capital City, 1828–1913." M.A. Thesis, St. Paul Seminary, St. Paul, Minnesota, 1956, p. 9.

45. Charles van Ravenswaay, "The Arts and Crafts of German Settlers Along the Lower Missouri River. A Regional Culture Surveyed." 1975. 552 pp. Typescript. Manuscript belonging to Mr. van Ravenswaay who prepared the work after long study of the arts of early America.

46. Carl Waldemar and Ed. C. Buechel, *Das deutsche Theater in St. Louis, 1842-1892*. Zur Eröffnung des Germania Theaters den Freunden der deutschen Bühne gewidmet (St. Louis, August, 1892), 19 pp.

47. Anna Hesse, "Notes from the Pageant."

48. Gert Goebel, *Länger als ein Menschenleben in Missouri* (St. Louis: C. Witter [1877]), p. 83.

49. Broadside. "Schauderhafte Beschreibung der erstaunlichen Heldenthaten, Die unsere tapfern Stadtsoldaten Im Krieg mit Kansas thaten!" Missouri Historical Society, St. Louis.

50. Carl Wencker to R. A. Hoffmann, "History of the 'Augusta Harmonie Verein,'" February 2, 1906, Missouri Historical Society. That participation of Germans "held Missouri to the Union" is questioned by historians but believed by many Missourians.

51. Group of Civil War Ballads, ca. 1861. Case Family Papers, Missouri Historical Society.

52. Camp Jackson Box, Missouri Historical Society.

53. Vance Randolph, *Ozark Folksongs*, 4 vols. (Columbia, Mo.: State Historical Society of Missouri, 1946-1950), II, p. 250.

54. John F. Poole, "I'm Going to Fight Mit Sigel." Library of Congress, Music Division; Hans Sperber, "Bugle Calls," *Midwest Folklore*, I (1951), p. 169.

55. Henry M. Belden, *Ballads and Songs Collected By the Missouri Folk-Lore Society* (Columbia, Mo.: University of Missouri Press, 1955), p. 373.

56. Ibid., p. 355.

57. Ibid., p. 361.

58. Townsend Godsey Collection of Folk Song, March 16, 1949. Western Manuscripts Collection, University of Missouri.

59. Randolph, *Ozark Folksongs*, IV, p. 23.

60. Lawrence Lutkewitte, "Civil War Mayor of Capitol City," *The Daily Capital News and Post Tribune*, Jefferson City, Mo. (June 21, 1931).

61. William G. Bek, "The Followers of Duden," *MHR*, XIX (January, 1925), 350.

62. Esther Tompkins, "Valley Center (formerly German Valley) United Church of Christ, 1873-1973," (Lowry City, Mo., 1973).

63. "A Brief History of Lawrence County, Missouri, 1845-1970," *Lawrence County History* (Mount Vernon, Mo. [1970]), p. 61.

64. Audrey Olson, p. 352.

65. Selwyn K. Troen, *The Public and the Schools* (Columbia, Mo.: University of Missouri Press, 1975) gives an excellent review of the controversy over German in the St. Louis schools in "The Strategy and Politics of the Melting Pot," pp. 55-78.

66. Henry Edward Krehbiel, Introduction to *Songs of Germany*. Collected and edited by Max Spicker (New York: G. Schirmer, 1904), p. iii.

67. Emil Lipp Collection, University of Missouri-St. Louis, Archive and Manuscript Division.

68. *Lieder für Deutsche Volkswehr*, V. Heft (Braunschweig: Oehme und Müller, 1848), 15 pp.

69. Interview with Mr. & Mrs. Casper Buersmeyer, Jefferson City, Mo., May 24, 1974.

70. Interview with Dr. Theodor Fischer, Altenburg, Mo., March 16, 1973.

71. William G. Bek, *JAF*, XXI (1908), 64–65.

72. Friedrich Münch, *Der Staat Missouri*, p. 77.

73. MS sent by Miss Marie C. Goldbeck, Florissant, Mo., June, 1974.

74. Dieter Cunz, *The Maryland Germans* (Princeton, N.J.: Princeton University Press, 1948), p. 395 quotes Schurz.

75. *St. Louis Republic*, April 14, 1918, Part II, p. 1.

76. *Globe Democrat*, St. Louis, April 27, 1918, p. 5.

77. G. K. Renner, "Prohibition Comes to Missouri, 1910–1918," *MHR*, LXII (Summer, 1968), 363–397.

78. *Final Report of the Missouri Council of Defense* to His Excellency, Honorable Frederick D. Gardner, Governor of Missouri (St. Louis: C. P. Curran, 1919), p. 61.

79. *The Missouri Cash-Book* (Jackson, Cape Girardeau County, September 4, 1919).

80. Gertrude M. Zimmer, "Place Names of Five Southeast Counties of Missouri," typewritten M.A. Thesis, University of Missouri, 1944, p. 26.

81. Frank T. E. Weber, "Place Names of Six South Central Counties of Missouri," typewritten M.A. Thesis, University of Mo., 1938, p. 85.

82. Music Papers, Missouri Historical Society, St. Louis.

83. Karl J. R. Arndt and May E. Olson, *German-American Newspapers and Periodicals, 1732–1955* (Heidelberg: Quelle & Meyer, 1961), pp. 237–280.

84. Investigations and interviews were undertaken 1973–1975 by the writer and students in German Honors courses at the University of Missouri-Columbia. The interest, enthusiasm, and substantial contribution of Barbara Beermann, Robert Brady, Betsy Garrett, Carol J. Miller, Lisa Monsees, J. Michael Smith and others are gratefully acknowledged.

85. *History of St. Charles, Montgomery and Warren Counties, Missouri.* Written and compiled from the most authentic Official and Private Sources (1885). Reprinted (St. Louis: Paul V. Cochrane, 1969), p. 106.

86. Walter Hoops, Interview [n.d.], by Margaret Sullivan. University of Missouri-St. Louis, Archive and Manuscript Division. He reports that his sister was "flabbergasted to see those German singing societies and picnics that we went to," since she "had not seen things like that" since she was a child.

87. Letter from Lester Golz, Frohna, Mo., April 10, 1973.

88. Ida M. Schaaf Collection in Music Papers, Missouri Historical Society; *Ste. Genevieve Herald*, Bicentennial Edition (August 17, 1935).

89. Andrew Greeley, *Why Can't They Be Like Us?* America's white ethnic groups (New York: E. P. Dutton, 1971), p. 42.

13. Die deutsch-brasilianische Schule, ein Werk der Selbsthilfe
Karl Fouquet

1. EINLEITUNG

Unter deutsch-brasilianischer Schule verstehen wir die Gesamtheit der durch deutsche Einwanderer, deren Kinder und Enkel in
Brasilien geschaffenen Bildungsstätten, von der kleinen Schule im
Urwald an bis zu Oberrealschulen, Lehrerseminaren und Fach-
schulen. Als deutsch gelten die Einwanderer aus der Mitte, dem
Südosten und dem Osten Europas, die sich zur deutschen Sprach-
und Kulturgemeinschaft bekannten oder noch bekennen, insbesondere also die "Reichsdeutschen" aus dem von Bismarck geschaffenen Reich, die "Österreicher" aus den Ländern der habs-
burgischen Monarchie, die Schweizer deutscher Sprache und die
"Russlanddeutschen" aus den Gebieten des Zarenreiches. Der Begriff "deutsch" trägt bei den folgenden Betrachtungen keinen
politischen Ton.

Diese Schule entwickelte sich im Lebensraum des brasilianischen
Volkes, dem früheren Kaiserreich und der heutigen Bundesrepublik
Brasilien. Das Volk aber bestand zu Beginn des 19. Jahrhunderts,
von dem wir ausgehen, aus den Nachkommen der seit 1500 eingewanderten Portugiesen, der seit 1550 eingeführten afrikanischen
Sklaven, aus Indianern als den Ureinwohnern und aus Mischlingen
der drei Gruppen. Als der Prinzregent von Portugal, der spätere
König Dom João VI., auf der Flucht vor Napoleon I. im Jahre
1808 eine Exilregierung in Rio de Janeiro einrichtete und die bis
dahin dem internationalen Handel verschlossenen Häfen des
Landes den Schiffen befreundeter Nationen, das heißt zunächst
den Gegnern Frankreichs, öffnete, begann der Zustrom von
Fremden oder Ausländern, unter denen alle Einwanderer außer
den Portugiesen zu verstehen sind. In der Reihenfolge ihrer Ankunft in mehr oder weniger starken Strömen waren es vor-

nehmlich Deutsche, Spanier, Italiener, Polen und Japaner. Aus ihnen und dem alten Stamm der Kolonialbevölkerung bildete sich das heutige brasilianische Volk. Zu den während der Zeit der Entdeckung lebenden 1 bis 2 Millionen Eingeborenen gesellten sich rund 2 Millionen Portugiesen, 3,6 Millionen Afrikaner, 310,000 Deutsche, 600,000 Spanier, 1,540,000 Italiener, 190,000 Japaner und 760,000 Ausländer verschiedener Herkunft. Die Zahl der rund 3,6 Millionen Einwohner von 1819 wuchs bis 1974 auf 100 Millionen an. Bewundernswert ist die Leistung des kleinen Portugal, das eines der größten Reiche der Gegenwart schuf und ihm den Stempel seiner Sprache und Gesittung aufdrückte. Der Einfluß der Fremden und ihrer Nachkommen äußert sich mit zunehmender Kraft in der Wirtschaft und der Politik wie im gesellschaftlichen und geistigen Leben, jedoch ohne das nationale Gefüge zu lockern.

Die Einwanderer bevorzugten den kühleren, subtropischen Süden des Landes, die Deutschen insbesondere die Staaten Rio Grande do Sul, Santa Catarina, Paraná, São Paulo und, trotz seines heißen Klimas, Espírito Santo. Von vereinzelten Vorläufern abgesehen, ließen sie sich seit 1808 nieder, zuerst als Kaufleute und Handwerker in einigen Hafenstädten und seit 1818 auch als Landwirte und Handwerker auf dem Lande. Marksteine in der Geschichte ihrer städtischen und ländlichen Kolonien bildeten die Gründung der Gesellschaft "Germania" (1821) in Rio de Janeiro, eines noch bestehenden Klubs, die Anlage der Kolonie São Leopoldo in Rio Grande do Sul im Jahre 1824 und die Entstehung der Kolonien Blumenau und Dona Francisca, jetzt Joinville, in Santa Catarina um 1850. Die gegenwärtig im Lande verwurzelten Deutschen und Deutschstämmigen werden auf 2 Millionen geschätzt, also auf zwei Prozent der Gesamtbevölkerung. Mehr als die Hälfte von ihnen lebt in den beiden südlichsten Staaten des Landes. Ihre zahlenmäßig größten und wirtschaftlich wie kulturell wichtigsten städtischen Gruppen sind die von São Paulo und Pôrto Alegre.

Ihrer wirtschaftlichen und sozialen Lage nach gehörten die deutschen Einwanderer der Jahrzehnte bis um 1850—von bedeutenden Ausnahmen abgesehen—den am wenigsten begünstigten Schichten der Bevölkerung ihrer Heimat an. Mit den "Einundfünfzigern," den 1851 eingetroffenen Fremdenlegionären, freiheitsbegeisterten Kämpfern für das "ungeteilte" Schleswig-Holstein, die den "Achtundvierzigern" in Nordamerika gleichzustellen sind, begann der Zustrom von Angehörigen des gebildeten Bürgertums. Er hielt bis in unsere Tage an. An seinem Pegel verzeichneten sich weitere Höhepunkte nach dem Ersten Weltkrieg, in den Jahren 1933–1939 mit der Ankunft der Emigranten aus dem nationalsozialistischen Reich und nach 1953 mit der Übersiedlung von Fachleuten aus der Bundesrepublik Deutschland, die zum Aufbau der einheimischen Industrie mit Hilfe ausländischer Unternehmen benötigt wurden.

Daß die Deutschen arm ins Land gekommen seien, ist eine weit verbreitete, durch Verallgemeinerung entstandene Legende. Zwischen Armen und Reichen stand die überragende Zahl derjenigen, die auf eigene Kosten reisten und die erforderlichen Mittel besaßen, um sich ihrem Stand entsprechend neu einzurichten. Fast alle verfügten über berufliche Ausbildung. Eine weitere Legende besagt, daß sie kamen, um die Freiheit zu suchen. Auch das gilt nur für eine Minderheit. Freiheit und Unfreiheit hüben und drüben hielten sich die Waage; sie waren jeweils nur anderer Art.

Im Wirtschaftsleben zeichneten sich die deutschen Einwanderer und ihre Nachkommen durch ihr Handwerk aus, das sie später, hauptsächlich gemeinsam mit den Italienern, zur bodenständigen Industrie fortbildeten, auch als Kaufleute und "Kolonisten," d.h. kleinere Landwirte auf eigener Scholle. Ihr Hauptverdienst im sozialen Leben war die Bildung eines gesunden Mittelstandes zwischen den Großgrundbesitzern und deren Sklaven und Knechten. Dies geschah, nachdem Einwanderer von den Azoren in den beiden Südstaaten ohne bleibenden Erfolg vorgewirkt hatten, und seit den siebziger Jahren des 19. Jahrhunderts unter kräftiger Mithilfe anderer Einwanderer, allen voran der Italiener, Portugiesen und Polen, sowie seit zwei Generationen der Japaner. In der Politik und—mit mehr Erfolg—in der Verwaltung traten sie in wachsender Stärke zunächst in den Munizipien, später in den Bundesstaaten und schließlich auch in der Landesregierung hervor. Im Jahre 1974 wurde erstmals ein Brasilianer deutscher Abstammung Bundespräsident, General Ernesto Geisel. Ihm waren je ein Präsident tschechischer und italienischer Herkunft vorausgegangen.

Wissenschaft und Kunst (mit Ausnahme der kirchlichen) darbten infolge einer selbstsüchtigen Politik des Mutterlandes Portugal bis um das Jahr 1808, das Jahr der großen Wende. Sie entfalteten sich dann, anfangs zögernd, später in rascherem Zug und haben heute eine beachtliche Höhe erreicht. Universitäten und Hochschulen, selbständig bestehende Fakultäten, Forschungsinstitute, höhere Schulen, Pflegestätten der Künste und unternehmungsfreudige Verlage für Bücher, Zeitschriften und Zeitungen beweisen das. An dieser Entfaltung waren die Ausländer und ihre im Lande verwurzelten Nachkommen aufs regste beteiligt, unter ihnen in vorderster Reihe die Deutschen mit ihren Forschern, Professoren und Lehrern, ihren Künstlern, Schriftstellern, Journalisten, Ärzten und Ingenieuren. Führend und wegweisend bewährten sich seit der Frühzeit auch Kirchen und religiöse Gemeinschaften. Etwa zwei Drittel der deutschen Einwanderer waren evangelisch, ein Drittel war katholisch und ein geringer Teil mosaischen Glaubens.

In dem Jahrhundert nach 1808, genauer nach dem Beginn der stärkeren Einwanderung um 1824, entstand, blühte und verging die deutsch-brasilianische Schule vor diesem geschichtlichen Hintergrund.

2. SELBSTHILFE IM ÖRTLICHEN BEREICH

Die Deutschen, die sich in Brasilien niederließen, verfügten im allgemeinen zum mindesten über Volksschulbildung. Das traf bereits für die schlichten Handwerker und Landleute der ersten Jahrzehnte zu und gilt in höherem Maß für die später Erschienenen. Eine Eingabe der Siedler von São Leopoldo RS an Kaiser Dom Pedro I. vom 1. September 1825, also 13 Monate nach der Ankunft des Vortrupps aufgesetzt, enthält die Unterschriften von 135 Männern [15]. Da die Zahl der Bewohner der Kolonie an jenem Tag nicht feststeht und sich nur auf etwa 800 schätzen läßt, von denen drei Viertel Kinder und Frauen gewesen sein dürften, vertreten die 135 Unterzeichneten rund die Hälfte der Männer. Unter ihnen befanden sich 107 des Schreiben kundige, also vier Fünftel.

Hier wie bei anderen Gelegenheiten fällt es schwer, den Prozentsatz der Analphabeten einwandfrei festzustellen, ganz abgesehen davon, daß der Begriff als solcher in einzelnen Ländern und zu verschiedenen Zeiten unterschiedlich bestimmt worden ist. Wir gelangen darum nur zu annähernd richtigen Werten, die genügen müssen und auch genügen. Von der Stichprobe São Leopoldo

1825 gehen wir auf die für uns wichtigsten Auswanderungsländer in Europa in den achtziger Jahren des 19. Jahrhunderts über, zeitlich in die Mitte unserer Wanderbewegung. Der abgerundete Prozentsatz der Analphabeten unter den Rekruten betrug 1881 in Russland 79, Italien 48, Österreich ohne Ungarn 39, in der Schweiz 2,5 und im Deutschen Reich 1,6. Dort fiel er bis 1890 auf 0.5 und in einzelnen Gliedstaaten, wie Württemberg und Sachsen, auf 0.01 [10]. Entsprechend dürfen wir uns die Zahl der Schriftunkundigen unter den deutschen Einwanderern vorstellen. Um 1920 galt bei ihnen eine übrigens ehrenwerte ältere Frau aus Masuren als ein weißer Rabe.

Im Gegensatz hierzu waren zu Beginn des 19. Jahrhunderts nur wenige Brasilianer des Lesens und Schreibens kundig. Es gab weder Volksschulen noch Mittelschulen. Die führenden Familien der Grundbesitzer und höheren Beamten ließen ihre Kinder von Geistlichen und Privatlehrern unterrichten und schickten die Söhne zum Studium an europäische Universitäten, zumal nach Coimbra. Die Sorge der Behörden wegen dieser unbefriedigenden Lage schlug sich seit 1822, dem Beginn der politischen Selbständigkeit, nur langsam in Gesetzen und Verfügungen nieder, und diese blieben zumeist ohne Wirkung, da es an Geld für den Betrieb von Schulen, an fachlich vorgebildeten Lehrern und an Verständnis im Volke fehlte.

In Niterói RJ wurde 1835 ein Seminar zur Ausbildung von Volksschullehrern eröffnet; elf Jahre später folgte São Paulo, schon damals einer der Mittelpunkte geistigen Lebens, mit einem weiteren Seminar, das jedoch in zwei Jahrzehnten seines Daseins nur 40 Diplome ausstellte, und endlich im Jahre 1875 wiederum São Paulo mit dem Lehrerseminar, das unter dem Namen Escola Normal Caetano de Campos bekannt ist. Es hat den ersehnten Wandel im Schulwesen des ganzen Landes eingeleitet. In Rio entstand 1838 ein Gymnasium, das den späteren Gymnasien und Kollegs zum Vorbild dienen sollte. Es trägt den Namen seines eifrigen Förderers, Kaiser Dom Pedros II. Die ersten Universitäten wurden in São Paulo im Jahr 1934 und in Rio 1935 gegründet. Ihnen waren bedeutende juristische und medizinische Fakultäten und Polytechnische Institute vorangegangen. Seitdem nimmt die Zahl der Universitäten, selbständigen Fakultäten und Hochschulen in einem Maße zu, das die Besorgnis vorausschauender Männer erregt. Das *Statistische Jahrbuch von 1961* gab bereits 1,236 an [*19*].

Trotz außerordentlicher Fortschritte in den letzten Jahrzehnten leidet der Unterricht auf allen Stufen noch an der Bevorzugung des Wissens vor dem Verstehen und Können, an übertriebenem Auswendiglernen, einer allgemein zugestandenen Oberflächlichkeit und dem Streben vieler Schüler nach einem "Diplom," das ihnen gesellschaftliches Ansehen verleiht und damit wichtiger erscheint als im Beruf verwertbare Kenntnisse. All diese Mängel sind erkannt, und seit den dreißiger Jahren bemühen sich die Regierungen ernstlich, sie zu beseitigen. Beachtliche Mittel werden eingesetzt, ausländische Hilfe wird einbezogen, und die amtlich geförderte Stiftung MOBRAL—Movimento Brasileiro de Alfabeticacão, brasilianische Bewegung mit dem Ziel zu alphabetisieren—nimmt sich vornehmlich der Erwachsenen an. Nach amtlicher Statistik betrug der Anteil der Schriftunkundigen im Jahre 1872 79% der Bevölkerung über 14 Jahren und im Jahr 1970 nur noch 19%. Der Leser findet nähere Angaben in den unter den Belegen verzeichneten Artikeln von Hermann M. Görgen [*13*] und Vereza Coutinho, zur Zeit Kulturattaché an der Brasilianischen Botschaft in Bonn [*11*].

Die Behörden ihrer Heimatstaaten blieben in Kontakt mit den Portugiesen, Spaniern, Engländern und Franzosen, die sich in den Jahrhunderten europäischer Kolonialherrschaft in überseeischen Ländern ansiedelten, was auch für die nach Sibirien ausgewanderten Russen zutraf. Die deutschen Auswanderer hatten keinen Kontakt mit den Behörden ihrer zahlreichen Heimatstaaten. Wenn sie, nach dem Wort Bismarcks, ihr Vaterland abstreiften wie einen alten Rock [*9*], verzichteten sie auf politische Bindung. Sie ließen damit auch Schule, Kirche und die Einrichtungen zur Pflege von Wohlfahrt und Geselligkeit zurück. Auf brasilianischem Boden vermißten sie diese. In den ländlichen Kolonien—nicht in den städtischen, die eigene Wege gingen—baten sie um Hilfe für Schule und Kirche, und die Behörden bis hinauf zur Zentralregierung in Rio de Janeiro bemühten sich zu helfen. Das läßt sich an vielen Beispielen nachweisen. Diese verfügten jedoch, wie wir bereits wissen, weder über Geldmittel noch Lehrer für den Unterricht. Ihre Hilfe blieb Stückwerk. Das Land konnte den Neulingen nicht bieten, was es aus der Kolonialzeit her selbst nicht kannte und was der alte Kern des Volkes erst später, während der Verschmelzung mit den Ausländern, durch die Arbeit vieler Geschlechter zu erwerben begann. Im Ganzen betrachtet war, was nun geschah, von Ort zu Ort und von Generation zu Generation das Gleiche und doch im einzelnen verschieden. Es wurde beeinflußt von dem Bildungsstand der Siedler, der Einsicht und dem guten Willen führender Männer und Frauen, dem Bekenntnis der Kolonisten und ihrem Verhalten gegenüber den Kirchen, dem Wohlstand oder der Armut einer Kolonie, von ihrer Verkehrslage und, nach dem Sturz des Kaisertums im Jahre 1889, von zahlreichen Schulgesetzen und Verfügungen.

Im allgemeinen fanden sich in jeder neuen Kolonie bald Familien zusammen, die für Schule und Kirche sorgten. Sie stellten ein Haus bereit, wenn das nicht die Kolonisationsgesellschaft tat, und suchten einen Lehrer. Der war oft ein "Neudeutscher," ein Einwanderer, der noch keine passende Arbeit gefunden hatte und annahm, was sich ihm bot, um dann alsbald eine besser bezahlte Stellung zu erlangen oder sich selbständig zu machen. Sein Gehalt war kärglich. Er leistete gelegentlich zugleich die Dienste des Pfarrers, oder der Pfarrer, bei den Evangelischen von seiner Frau unterstützt, gab im Nebenamt den Unterricht. Auch Handwerker und Kolonisten, die den Härten ihres Berufs im Urwald nicht gewachsen waren, wurden Lehrer. Manche unterrichteten aus Neigung, und zu diesen gehörten Männer und Frauen von höherer Bildung. Die Zahl der Lehrer, die in Europa und später, als die einheimischen Präparanden und Seminare entstanden, im Lande ausgebildet wurden, war gering. Nach und nach aber bildete sich ein Stand tüchtiger Erzieher, die sich durch Hingabe an ein Ideal ausgezeichnet und ihrem Beruf zu Ansehen verholfen haben.

Die Schulen waren in der Mehrzahl einklassig, d.h. alle Schüler der aus verschiedenen Jahrgängen gebildeten Abteilungen wurden in einem Raum unterrichtet. In der Regel gab es nur zwei oder drei Abteilungen. Der Unterricht beschränkte sich auf Schreiben, Lesen, Rechnen, Religion, sowie die Grundlagen der Erdkunde und Geschichte der alten und neuen Heimat. Die portugiesische Sprache galt von Anfang an und allenthalben als die zweite Sprache, aber es fiel schwer, ihr gerecht zu werden, besonders wenn der Lehrer selbst als Neuling im Lande sie nicht kannte. Dann geschah es, daß die Kinder sich eben so wenig mit einem

"Brasilianer" verständigen konnten wie die eingewanderten Eltern. Dennoch lag kein Versäumnis vor, selbst nicht von Seiten der Behörden; keiner konnte über seinen Schatten springen.

In Rio Grande do Sul und Espírito Santo unterhielten die Kirchengemeinden zahlreiche Schulen, die als Gemeindeschulen bezeichnet wurden. Neben ihnen bildeten sich, besonders in konfessionell gemischten Siedlungen, Vereinsschulen. Die Mitglieder der Vereine verpflichteten sich zu Monatsbeiträgen oder Sachleistungen oder gewährten dem Lehrer freien Tisch. Die Beziehungen zwischen Kirche und Schule waren bei großer Mannigfaltigkeit eng und sind es geblieben, zumal in den eben erwähnten Staaten. In Santa Catarina, Paraná und São Paulo überwogen die Vereinsschulen. Nur ausnahmsweise setzte sich auf dem Lande eine Schule als privates Unternehmen eines Lehrers oder Pfarrers durch.

Das Gedeihen fast aller Schulen wurde dadurch beeinträchtigt, daß ihnen in der Regel weder eine sie beaufsichtigende Behörde noch eine sonstige Stelle vorgesetzt war, die sie beraten, Achtung fordern oder im Notfall erzwingen konnte. Die Freiheit des Einzelnen innerhalb einer Siedlungsgemeinschaft ließ neben der Tüchtigkeit auch der menschlichen Schwäche genug Raum sich auszuwirken. Wer seine Kinder nichts lernen lassen wollte, behielt sie zu Hause. Geizige zahlten kein Schulgeld, und Streitsüchtige entzündeten allzuoft Hass und Feindschaft. Dennoch hat die Kolonieschule ihre Aufgabe erfüllt. Sie hat verhindert, daß die Nachkommen der Einwanderer als Analphabeten aufwuchsen und bewirkt, daß sie diejenigen Kenntnisse erlangten, die sie als Kolonisten und Handwerker brauchten. Aus der Kolonieschule sind zahlreiche Männer hervorgegangen, die sich als Kaufleute und Fabrikanten, als Lehrer und Geistliche hervorgetan und die ihr Teil zu dem viel bewunderten Aufschwung Südbrasiliens beigetragen haben.

Das an Zahlen gemessene Verhältnis zwischen Regierungsschulen und Privatschulen—der amtlichen Bezeichnung für alle nicht von Behörden unterhaltenen Schulen—sei an einigen Beispielen aus Koloniezonen verdeutlicht: im Munizip São Leopoldo bestanden um 1858 14 öffentliche und 34 private Schulen mit 244 bzw. 1,081 Schülern [7]; im Jahre 1917 im Munizip Blumenau 10 staatliche und 113 private mit 520 bzw. 5,011 Schülern und im Munizip Joinville, gleichfalls im Jahr 1917, 5 staatliche und 64 private Schulen mit 303 bzw. 3,238 Schülern [14]. Ernesto Pellanda stellte derartige Leistungen der Selbsthilfe im Kampf gegen das Analphabetentum heraus, indem er auf die aus deutschen Siedlungen hervorgegangenen riograndenser Munizipien Estrêla, Lageado, São Leopoldo und Santa Cruz verwies. Dort betrug 1924 der Prozentsatz der Analphabeten unter den Eheschließenden durchschnittlich 7.5 [17]; im ganzen Land betrug er um die gleiche Zeit 52.

Höhere Schulen entstanden in einigen aus Kolonien hervorgegangenen Kleinstädten und in größeren Städten, wo sich nach und nach Gruppen deutscher Einwanderer zusammenfanden. Auch hier gingen bedeutende Anregungen von der Geistlichkeit aus. Die frühesten Ansätze lenken wiederum den Blick nach São Leopoldo. Dort wurden 1867 eine evangelische und im Jahre darauf durch deutsche Jesuiten eine katholische höhere Schule eröffnet. Für das Jahr 1972 lassen sich allein in Verbindung mit der Evangelischen Kirche Lutherischen Bekenntnisses in Brasilien 21 staatlich anerkannte Gymnasien und Kollegs nachweisen [6]. Ein brasilianisches Gymnasium umfaßt vier Jahrgänge, die an fünf der Grundschule anschließen und ein Kolleg weitere drei Jahrgänge. Darüber hinaus unterhält diese Kirche neben anderen höheren Bildungsanstalten ein Lehrerseminar, ein Proseminar mit den Klassen Untertertia bis Obersekunda zur Vorbereitung auf das Studium der Theologie und eine theologische Fakultät. Aus der eben erwähnten katholischen Schule in São Leopoldo gingen ein Priesterseminar und eine Universität hervor. Neben den Jesuiten beteiligten sich Weltgeistliche und Angehörige anderer Orden wie Franziskaner, Benediktiner und Frauenorden an dem Ausbau des Schulwesens auf allen Stufen. Über ihr Werk im Verband der gesamten katholischen Kirche Brasiliens unterrichten unter anderem die umfangreichen Bände der kirchlichen Jahrbücher von 1958 und 1960 [5; 4]. Mit den Kirchen wetteiferten die zumeist paritätischen Vereine. Ihnen gelang der Aufbau von Bildungsanstalten, die etwa deutschen Realschulen entsprachen (in Pôrto Alegre, Santa Cruz RS, Blumenau, Joinville und Curitiba) und von Oberrealschulen, deren Abgangszeugnisse zum Studium an deutschen Universitäten berechtigten (in São Paulo und Rio). Einen vorzüglichen Einblick in den Betrieb eines solchen Vereins gewähren die Jahresberichte der Oberschule in São Paulo, des heutigen Colégio Visconde de Porto Seguro, über die Jahre 1923 bis 1938.

In diesen höheren Schulen war die Unterrichtssprache deutsch und die zweite Sprache, die nach Kräften gefördert und zumeist von Luso-Brasilianern gelehrt wurde, das Portugiesische. Einige unterhielten gleichzeitig ein Gymnasium mit portugiesischer Unterrichtssprache nach brasilianischem Lehrplan.

3. SELBSTHILFE IM WEITEREN RAHMEN

In nahezu allen Siedlungen schwanden die Schwierigkeiten, die sich den Pionieren entgegenstellten, bereits während der ersten Jahrzehnte nach der Gründung. Der Kolonist erfreute sich seines Besitzes; der Handel, das Handwerk und die sich entfaltende Industrie verhalfen vielen Familien zu Wohlstand und selbst zu Reichtum. Diese Vorgänge vollzogen sich in den zahlreichen städtischen und ländlichen Niederlassungen weder gleichzeitig noch gleichmäßig, aber doch derart, daß allenthalben die führenden Männer sich gegen Ende des 19. Jahrhunderts vor die Wahl gestellt sahen, entweder die Schulen in der bisherigen Weise fortzuführen, ihre Söhne und Töchter auf die zum Teil weit entfernten brasilianischen höheren Schulen oder gar nach Deutschland zu schicken, oder mit vereinten Kräften ihre bescheidenen Schulen den wachsenden Anforderungen und bestehenden Möglichkeiten entsprechend auszubauen. Das erste hätte für die Nachkommen ein kulturelles und wirtschaftliches Absinken bedeutet, das zweite einen Verzicht auf die Überlieferung und, in jedem Falle, die Entfremdung der Kinder von ihrer Heimat. Der dritte Weg erschien als der schwierigste, aber als der einzige, der sicher zu einem allgemein anerkannten Ziel führte; nämlich, der Jugend in ihrer Gesamtheit die Bindung zur überlieferten Kultur der Familie und zur brasilianischen Heimat zu erhalten, sie als pflichtbewußte Staatsbürger zu erziehen und ihr die freie Bewegung in zwei Sprachen zu ermöglichen, der deutschen und der portugiesischen. Dies sollte ihr eine zusätzliche Kraft geben und ihr die Aufgabe erleichtern, Mittler zwischen der Heimat der Väter und ihrer eigenen Heimat zu sein, zum Wohl beider.

Diese Gedanken wurden nicht überall klar erfaßt, sie äußerten

sich jedoch in unzähligen Worten und Taten und bestimmten das
Bemühen, das wir nunmehr darstellen und das Lehrer, Geistliche
und Eltern verband. Als Mittel zum Zweck erkannten diese den
Zusammanschluß der Lehrer—und damit bis zu einem gewissen
Grad auch der Schulen—über die Ortsgrenzen hinaus, ihre wirt-
schaftliche Sicherstellung und die Ausbildung im Lande geborener
Lehrer unter Mithilfe von Erziehern aus Deutschland, Österreich
und der Schweiz.

Den ersten Schritt tat der "Deutsche (später: Deutsch-brasilianische) Katholische Lehrerverein von (für) Rio Grande do Sul."
Er trat 1898 als ein Kind des ersten Riograndenser Katholiken-
tages ins Leben. Seine kräftigsten Förderer waren Patres der Gesellschaft Jesu und Weltgeistliche, sein Organ war seit 1900 die
Lehrerzeitung. Unter Einsatz seines Vermögens schuf der Verein
ein Seminar, das 1919 in Arroio do Meio eröffnet und später nach
Hamburgerberg verlegt wurde. Wie die anderen, nach ihm entstandenen Lehrervereine, suchte der katholische Lehrerverein
sämtliche in Betracht kommenden Lehrer seines Gebiets als Mitglieder zu erfassen, sie auf Haupt- und Bezirksversammlungen
durch Sing-, Spiel- und Filmfahrten in persönliche Verbindung zu
bringen, durch Vorträge, Lehrproben und Fortbildungskurse zu
fördern, ihnen Lehr- und Lernmaterial in beiden Sprachen zu vermitteln und sie durch Mitarbeit an den nach 1900 entstandenen
Fürsorgekassen vor Not bei Krankheit und im Alter zu schützen.
Das Gefühl der Standesehre wurde gepflegt.

Drei Jahre später entstand der "Deutsche Evangelische Lehrerverein von Rio Grande do Sul." Die beiden Brüder stritten sich
selten, traten mit zunehmendem Alter in fruchtbaren Wettbewerb,
halfen sich gegenseitig und hielten endlich als Glieder des Landesverbandes Deutsch-Brasilianischer Lehrer gute Kameradschaft. Im
Jahre 1902 erschien die *Allgemeine Lehrerzeitung für Rio Grande
do Sul* als Monatsschrift des Vereins, 1908 wurde eine Sterbekasse
eingerichtet, 1912 eine Pensionskasse, der auch die Versorgung von
Witwen und Waisen oblag, und 1913 wurde in Santa Cruz das
"Deutsche Evangelische Lehrerseminar für Rio Grande do Sul"
gegründet. Es siedelte 1926 nach São Leopoldo über, wo es sich
sehr gut entwickelte. Um die Wende der dreißiger Jahre zählte es
bereits über 50 Seminaristen, Söhne und Töchter von Handwerkern, Landwirten, Lehrern und Pfarrern, die fast alle im Land

geboren waren. Sie wurden zur Zweisprachigkeit erzogen. Die weitere rege Tätigkeit des evangelischen Lehrervereins entsprach der des katholischen.

Schwierigkeiten bereitete der Zusammenschluß im Staat Santa Catarina. Dort hielten die beiden großen Siedlungsgruppen um Blumenau und Joinville einander das Gleichgewicht. Jede erhob Anspruch auf Führung. Um 1910 entstand in Blumenau ein "Deutscher Schulverein für Santa Catarina," der *Mitteilungen* herausgab, und nach dem Ersten Weltkrieg regten sich zeitweise mehrere Vereinigungen in Joinville, Blumenau, Brusque und Florianópolis, die in den "Deutschen Lehrerverein von Santa Catarina" aufgingen. Zwei Präparanden, eine bereits vor 1914, leisteten Gutes im kleinen Kreis, verloren jedoch ihre Daseinsberechtigung mit dem Aufblühen der Seminare in São Leopoldo und Hamburgerberg.

Der "Deutsche (später: Deutsch-brasilianische) Lehrerverband Paraná" in Curitiba erblickte seit Beginn der zwanziger Jahre seine vornehmste Aufgabe in der Hilfe für die weit verstreuten Schulen im Innern des Staates und in der Werbung für die Ruhegehaltskasse in Rio. Umfangreiche Reiseberichte von Mitgliedern des Vorstandes überliefern ein Bild von den damaligen Zuständen "auf der Kolonie."

Besonders genau sind wir über den "Deutschen Lehrerverein São Paulo" durch dessen Protokollbücher aus der Zeit von 1916 bis zur abschließenden Vorstandssitzung im August 1938 unterrichtet. Er trug zuletzt den Namen "Hans-Staden-Verein." In Anpassung an das Zeitgeschehen stellte er verschiedene Aufgaben als vordringlich heraus, unter diesen den Ausbau des Büchereiwesens und des Kulturfilmdienstes. Er betreute vorübergehend auch Schulen in anderen Bundesstaaten. São Paulo trug seit 1927 nebenbei die Last der Verwaltung des Landesverbandes, ähnlich wie Rio die der Ruhegehaltskasse.

In der damaligen Bundeshauptstadt entstand 1920, wie in allen Staaten außer Rio Grande, fast allein aus dem Antrieb der Lehrerschaft die sechste Vereinigung dieser Reihe, der "Deutsche Lehrerverein Rio de Janeiro." Er betrachtete die Staaten Rio, Espírito Santo und Minas Gerais, sowie den Norden, als Arbeitsfeld. Sein Sorgenkind war Espírito Santo, wo nach einem seiner Berichte aus dem Jahr 1931 die Rückständigkeit so groß war, "daß die drastischen Einzelheiten sich für eine Veröffentlichung wenig eignen."

Wir übergehen kleinere Unternehmen, wie die jährlichen Geldsammlungen zur Unterstützung von Schulvereinen, die sogenannten Schulhilfen, mehrere Ansätze zur Schaffung von Lehrerseminaren in Gestalt von Präparanden oder von Hilfskassen und die Tätigkeit der Verlage von Schulbüchern in beiden Sprachen und wenden uns den beiden umfassenden Organisationen zu, die in wenig mehr als anderthalb Jahrzehnten ihres Bestehens das Werk der Selbsthilfe krönten, der Ruhegehaltskasse und dem Landesverband.

Der Plan für die "Ruhegehalts- und Hinterbliebenenfürsorge-Kasse für deutsche Lehrer und Lehrerinnen in Brasilien," kurz RHK genannt, lag bereits 1920 vor. Ihn auszuführen wurde möglich, als die beiden großen Schulen in Rio und São Paulo ihn billigten. Die Gründung erfolgte 1921. Bald bildeten sich, unter tatkräftiger Leitung des Zentralvorstandes in Rio und in enger Verbindung mit den Lehrervereinen, deren Vorsitzende mit den Direktoren der Seminare den Vorstand bildeten, Bezirksstellen in den vier südlichen Bundesstaaten. Schulvereine, Firmen und Freunde schlossen sich als Förderer an. Die älteren kleinen Kassen, wie die des Evangelischen Lehrervereins, gliederten sich ein. Schon nach zehnjährigem Bestehen waren 392 Mitglieder angeschlossen; 32 erhielten ein Ruhegehalt. Das Vermögen wuchs schnell an. Für 1935 wurden als Ziel 1,000 Contos de Réis angestrebt, und 1938 betrug es rund 2,000 Contos, was einer Million Mark nach damaligem Kurs entsprach. Die Zahl der Mitglieder war auf etwa 450 angewachsen. Zuverlässige Angaben über den letzten Stand fehlen, da die Akten der Geschäftsstelle ein Opfer des Krieges wurden. Noch im Jahre 1938 beschloß der Vorstand auf Grund des Dekrets 383 der Bundesregierung vom 18. April, auf das wir zurückkommen, nach Befragen seiner Rechtsberater, die Mitgliedschaft auf Reichsdeutsche zu beschränken und die ruhegehaltsberechtigten brasilianischen Staatsangehörigen im Verhältnis zu ihren Beiträgen auszuzahlen. Damit verlor die Kasse ihren Sinn, und die Auflösung war eingeleitet. Was ein derartiges Unternehmen zu jener Zeit bedeutete, läßt sich im Hinblick auf die Tatsache verstehen, daß die brasilianische Sozialgesetzgebung erst um 1930 einsetzte und 1935 wirksam wurde.

Auch der "Landesverband Deutsch-brasilianischer Lehrer," die letzte der großen Vereinigungen, geht in seinen Anfängen auf das Jahr 1920 zurück. Aus verschiedenen Gründen nahm er seine Tätigkeit jedoch erst 1927 auf. Nach seinen Satzungen trug er paritätischen Charakter und diente dem Zweck, das deutsch-brasilianische Schulwesen zu fördern und die Belange der Lehrer nach Kräften zu vertreten, vornehmlich durch Fühlungnahme mit den brasilianischen Schulbehörden, durch Anschluß an den Verband der Deutschen Auslandlehrer und den Verein für das Deutschtum im Ausland, sowie durch Unterstützung der Ruhegehaltskasse und Schaffung einheitlicher, den brasilianischen Verhältnissen angepaßter Lehrbücher. Mitglieder des "Landesverbandes" waren die Lehrervereine, die 10 Prozent ihrer Mitgliedsbeiträge an ihn abführten. Die Hauptversammlungen fielen mit den jeweils mehrere Tage dauernden "Schultagen" zusammen und gingen allmählich in sie über. Den Vorstand bildeten die Vorsitzenden der Lehrervereine, die Direktoren der Seminare und der Vorsitzende der Ruhegehaltskasse, so daß beide Vorstände miteinander verzahnt waren. Der Vorsitzende wurde vom Schultag gewählt, der Sitz der Verwaltung war São Paulo. Insgesamt wurden seit 1920 sechs Schultage einberufen, die mit wachsender Beteiligung in São Paulo, Pôrto Alegre, Rio, Curitiba, wiederum Pôrto Alegre und zuletzt, im Jahre 1933, in Blumenau abgehalten wurden. In Blumenau trafen sich rund 350 Lehrer, Vertreter der Behörden, der Kirchen und der Schulvereine.

Während der Jahre des Aufbaus 1927 und 1928 entstanden die einzelnen Abteilungen. In enger Verbindung mit mehreren Verlagen sorgte die Lehrmittel-Abteilung für die Verbilligung von Büchern, Wandbildern, Karten und Globen und die unentgeltliche Belieferung bedürftiger Schulen. Die Stellenvermittlung wurde stark in Anspruch genommen. Sie gab zeitweise gedruckte Rundschreiben heraus, wirkte dann aber erfolgreicher Hand in Hand mit den Lehrervereinen, deren Zeitschriften und den Seminaren. Den Lehrern, die nicht von ihrer deutschen Heimatbehörde beurlaubt waren, wurden Beihilfen zur Erholung im Land oder in Europa gewährt, durchschnittlich sechs im Jahr und mindestens in der Höhe des Betrages der Schiffspassage bei Reisen ins Ausland. Dem Aufbau von Schulbüchereien und öffentlichen Leihbüchereien galt die Tätigkeit des Bücheramtes. Für die Verbreitung guter Filme setzte sich seit 1935 der Kulturfilmdienst ein, dessen Mit-arbeiter mit ihren 20 Vorführgeräten zahlreiche Reisen bis in die entferntesten Kolonien unternahmen. Rundbriefe und ein lebhafter Briefwechsel hielten den Verkehr mit den angeschlossenen Vereinen und den weit von einander getrennt wohnenden Mitgliedern des Vorstandes aufrecht. Karteien der Schulen und der Lehrer ermöglichten den Überblick über das Ganze und den Einblick in die örtlichen Verhältnisse.

Reiches Urkundenmaterial lieferten die Fragebogen, die seit 1928 gemeinschaftlich mit den Gliedvereinen, den Seminaren und einem Verlag entworfen, an sämtliche Schulen versandt und von ihnen in der großen Mehrzahl auch ausgefüllt wurden. Im Archiv des Hans-Staden-Instituts sind, sich wiederholende Ausfertigungen aus verschiedenen Jahren einbegriffen, fast 1,300 Kopien erhalten. Sie beziehen sich auf 800 bis 900 Schulen und weisen, ergänzt durch Listen verschiedener Art, für die Zeit um 1930 1,038 Schulen nach, 564 in Rio Grande do Sul, 297 in Santa Catarina, 61 in Paraná, 33 in São Paulo, 67 in Espírito Santo und 16 in weiteren 5 Staaten. Nach den Schätzungen von Lehrervereinen und Bezirksstellen wurden rund 250 kleine Schulen nicht erfaßt. Wir können hiermit als Gesamtzahl 1,300 ansetzen.

Die umfassende Arbeit, die hinter diesen Zahlen stand, ließ sich neben- und ehrenamtlich in Freistunden und während der Ferien nur leisten, da die Beteiligten für das Ziel begeistert waren. Das gilt in gleicher Weise für beruflich vorgebildete Lehrer, wie für Laien und Geistliche, für Landeskinder unter ihnen, zumeist auf der Kolonie tätig, wie für die jungen Seminaristen und Akademiker aus dem deutschen Sprachgebiet in Europa, die an den städtischen Schulen wirkten. Als mit dem Gedeihen des Verbandes und seiner Glieder die Verantwortung wuchs, regte der Vorsitzende schon 1929 an, einen Leiter zu berufen, der sich seinen Pflichten hauptamtlich widmen könnte, und als das nicht geschah, legte er, schwer erkrankt, acht Jahre später sein Amt nieder. Der nunmehr gewählte Geschäftsführende Vorsitzende übernahm den Auftrag, das verheißungsvoll begonnene Werk auszubauen, die vorhandenen Mängel nach Möglichkeit zu beseitigen und ein Schulsystem zu schaffen, welches das staatliche—wennschon in bescheidenem Maße—weiterhin ergänzen, ihm Lasten abnehmen und unter gegenseitiger Anregung Hilfe im Kampf gegen das Analphabetentum und Mängel in seinem Unterrichtswesen leisten sollte.

Unsere Darstellung wäre unvollständig ohne einen Hinweis auf die Hilfe, die das deutsch-brasilianische Schulwesen aus dem Ausland erfuhr, ähnlich wie das der italienischen und polnischen Einwanderer. Die Daheimgebliebenen empfanden es als Pflicht, die Angehörigen in der Fremde—oft waren es Geschwister, Kinder oder Enkel—nicht gleichgültig ihrem Schicksal zu überlassen, und es war nichts weiter als menschlich, daß sie die Beziehungen zu ihnen aufrecht erhielten. Hiermit verbanden sich im einzelnen vielerlei Zwecke: geschäftliche für denjenigen, der sie als Schrittmacher des Handels betrachtete; konfessionelle für den, der sich ihnen als Glaubensbrüdern verbunden fühlte; wissenschaftliche für den Forscher, dessen Feld sich im 19. Jahrhundert über die ganze Erde ausdehnte, sowie künstlerische und kulturelle jeder Art. Auch der Wunsch, der eigenen Sprache ihre Geltung zu erhalten, spielte eine Rolle. Nicht zuletzt wurde den Ausgewanderten die Aufgabe zugedacht, als Mittler zwischen den Völkern zu dienen. Was deutscherseits fehlte, waren politische Ziele. Vor 1870 verfügten die Kleinstaaten nicht über die Macht, Weltpolitik zu treiben, und das Reich Bismarcks und Kaiser Wilhelms II. fühlte sich gesättigt in dem Bewußtsein, nach langer Zerrissenheit den größeren Teil des Volkes in einem Staat geeinigt und dadurch den Frieden in Europa gesichert zu haben. Nur zögernd folgte es in Afrika und Ozeanien der Kolonialpolitik Englands, Frankreichs und Hollands auf den Spuren der ältesten Kolonialmacht Portugal. Dies bedeutet nicht, daß nicht gelegentlich ein Außenseiter sich politischen Träumen überlassen hätte. Entscheidend war, daß keiner von ihnen Widerhall fand.

Ob und in welcher Weise amtliche Stellen in Österreich und der Schweiz sich der Schulen in Brasilien angenommen haben, ist nicht bekannt. Wennschon, dann nur in bescheidenem Maß. Anders im Reich. Dort wirkte seit der Jahrhundertwende der Verein für das Deutschtum im Ausland, der VDA. Er beschränkte sich ausdrücklich auf kulturelle Ziele und insbesondere auf die Pflege der deutschen Sprache, vergab Studienbeihilfen, unterstützte Schulen, versandte Bücher und versuchte darüber hinaus zu helfen, wo er in der Not angesprochen wurde. Der Gustav-Adolf-Verein unterstützte seit 1842 evangelische Gemeinden und deren Schulen, während seit 1871 der Sankt-Raphaels-Verein sich der Katholiken annahm. Der wissentschaftlichen Erforschung des Auslanddeutschtums widmete sich von 1917 an das Auslands-Institut in Stuttgart. Neben ihnen entstanden und vergingen kleinere Vereinigungen ähnlicher Zielsetzung und gleichfalls ohne politisches Gepräge.

Das Reich trieb bis 1918 keine auf das Ausland gerichtete Kulturpolitik. Gelegentlich gab ein Fürst privatim einer Kirchengemeinde, einem Hilfsverein oder einer Schule der Ausgewanderten eine Spende. Erst unter dem Eindruck der Verluste an Land, Menschen, Sachwerten und kulturellen Einrichtungen durch den Ersten Weltkrieg und unter dem Druck des Versailler Vertrages fühlte sich die Weimarer Republik veranlaßt, nach dem Vorbild anderer Staaten, Kulturpolitik zu treiben, d.h. im Ausland um Verständnis und Freundschaft zu werben. Das geschah durch die üblichen und, zumeist unter Voraussetzung der Gegenseitigkeit, zwischenstaatlich anerkannten Mittel. So erhielten manche Schulen Beihilfen durch die Botschaft in Rio und durch Konsulate; Lehrer wurden auf Anforderung größerer Schulen aus dem heimatlichen Dienst auf eine Reihe von Jahren beurlaubt; der Landesverband empfing eine jährliche Beihilfe insbesondere zur Verbilligung der Lehrmittel, ausdrücklich auch der in portugiesischer Sprache; Urlaubsreisen wurden begünstigt, und die Ruhegehaltskasse wurde nach Maßgabe ihrer eigenen Leistungen gefördert. Das Reich änderte nach 1933 nichts an dieser Politik. Die Landesgruppe der Nationalsozialistischen Partei versprach den Lehrerverbänden, sich jeglicher Einmischung in das Schulwesen zu enthalten und den Bund der nationalsozialistischen Lehrer in Brasilien auf Reichsdeutsche zu beschränken, als eine Standesvereinigung zur Vertretung beruflicher Interessen ihrer Angehörigen bei heimatlichen Schulbehörden. Das Versprechen wurde gehalten. Nur wenige Lehrer und Vorstände setzten sich bei einigen Gelegenheiten darüber hinweg und leisteten dadurch in einer Zeit politischer Erregung beider Völker einem seit Generationen angewachsenen Mißtrauen Vorschub.

4. GEGENZÜGE

Wir haben uns bemüht, das Denken der Deutschen und ihr Handeln zu verstehen und wollen nun versuchen, in gleicher Weise dem der Brasilianer gerecht zu werden. Hierzu bedarf es einer weiteren Erinnerung an die Geschichte dieses jungen und stolzen

Volkes. Entdecker und Eroberer des Landes waren die Portugiesen. Ihnen gelang es durch kühne Erkundungszüge und durch Abwehr mächtiger Feinde, der Franzosen, Holländer und Spanier, die Grenzen bis zu dem jetzigen Verlauf auszudehnen. Es gelang ihnen aber auch, wie nur selten einer dünnen Herrenschicht, ihre Sprache und Gesittung auf die beherrschten Massen zu übertragen. Das waren im Anfang die ihren Niederlassungen benachbarten Indianer und bald darauf außerdem die aus Afrika eingeführten Sklaven. Im Jahre 1819, als dieser Vorgang zwar noch nicht abgeschlossen, aber doch gesichert war, betrug nach einem Ministerialbericht die Bevölkerung des Landes, wie bereits erwähnt, 3,617,500 Seelen; davon waren 843,000 Weisse (Portugiesen), d.h. 23% von der Gesamtzahl. Die schwer errungene sprachliche Einheit wurde indessen in den Augen vieler Brasilianer, wenigstens für die vier südlichen Staaten, noch einmal in Frage gestellt, als sich die um jene Zeit begonnene amtliche Werbung von europäischen Einwanderern auswirkte. Bis um 1930 ließen sich dort rund vier Millionen Menschen nieder, und unter ihnen waren kaum ein Drittel Portugiesen. Im Gegensatz zu den indianischen Eingeborenen und den Afrikanern gehörten diese Fremden alten Kulturvölkern an, die sich ihrer Überlieferung bewußt waren. Ferner war im Lauf des 19. Jahrhunderts die konfessionelle Einheit des brasilianischen Volkes verloren gegangen; neben die katholischen Kirche waren die evangelische und kleinere religiöse Gruppen getreten. Die Unterschiedlichkeit der rassischen Herkunft bereitete zwar bei der Toleranz der Brasilianer in diesen Fragen und infolge einer entsprechenden Gesetzgebung keine Gefahr, aber die Unsicherheit der Lage in anderen Ländern, in Nordamerika, Europa, Afrika und Südostasien beunruhigte verständlicherweise. Separatistische Regungen hatten seit der Erklärung der Unabhängigkeit das staatliche Gefüge erschüttert; das Bewußtsein einer gemeinsamen, wennschon kurzen Geschichte hatte infolge der mißlichen Schulverhältnisse die breiteren Schichten des Volkes noch nicht erfaßt. Als einziges Band der Einheit war die portugiesische Sprache verblieben, und dieser Umstand mußte um so höher bewertet werden, als ein Blick auf das politisch zersplitterte und in sich verfeindete Europa genügte, die traurigen Folgen eines verbissenen Nationalitätenkampfes erkennen zu lassen. So lag es nahe, daß manche Brasilianer eine Gefahr heraufziehen sahen, und für verborgene

Gefahren hatten schon ihre Vorfahren in Portugal stets ein feines Empfinden bewahrt. Brasilien war auf Einwanderer angewiesen und warb um sie mit allen ihm verfügbaren Mitteln, aber es wünschte keine Minderheiten.

Hieraus erklärt sich das Weitere, wenn wir berücksichtigen, wie tief alle Völker durch die politischen Leidenschaften unseres Jahrhunderts berührt worden sind. Wir wollen jetzt aber für viele einen Mann sprechen lassen, der maßgeblichen Einfluß auf die Entwicklung ausgeübt hat. Was er von Santa Catarina sagt, gilt im wesentlichen auch für die Nachbarstaaten und für das ganze Land. Es ist Ivo D'Aquino, Professor für Verfassungsrecht an der Juristischen Fakultät in Florianópolis und seit 1937, während der Regierung des Gouverneurs und späteren Bundesinterventors Nereu Ramos, Minister für Justiz, Erziehung und Gesundheit des Staates Santa Catarina. Er berichtete als Minister eingehend über die Nationalisierung des Unterrichts unter politischen Gesichtspunkten [8]. Sein Buch geht auf einen in der Rechtsfakultät in Curitiba gehaltenen Vortrag zurück. Das politische System, zu dem er sich bekennt, ist die viel angefeindete und von São Paulo und anderen Staaten durch Waffengewalt erfolglos bekämpfte Diktatur von Getúlio Vargas, 1930–1945, insbesondere in ihrer Form seit 1937. Der Titel "Nationalisierung des Unterrichts" ist das in jener Zeit viel gebrauchte Kennwort für die Maßnahmen gegen das sogenannte ausländische Schulwesen. Es artete auch zum Schlagwort aus.

Ivo d'Aquino betrachtet diese Nationalisierung als an sich durch die (autoritäre) Verfassung von 1937 gerechtfertigt. Um aber auch dem Gewissen von Soziologen und Juristen Genüge zu tun, beruft er sich auf Fachleute, und unter diesen auf den amerikanischen Philosophen und Pädagogen John Dewey, den er in portugiesischer Übersetzung zitiert: "Der Staat ist an die Stelle der Menschheit getreten, das Weltbürgertum dem Nationalismus gewichen, den Bürger und nicht den 'Menschen' heranzubilden ist das Ziel der Erziehung geworden." Im Folgenden betont er, daß in Brasilien das Recht des Bodens gelte, nicht das des Blutes, daß demnach jeder im Lande Geborene Brasilianer sei und als solcher sprechen und fühlen müsse (S. 7–11).

Alle zwischen 1911 und 1931 in seinem Staat erlassenen Gesetze, die der Verbreitung der Landessprache in den ausländischen

Kolonien dienen sollten, beruhten laut d'Aquino auf zwei Grund-
fehlern: Sie unterschieden zwischen Privatschulen in diesen Kolonien und Privat- und Regierungsschulen in denjenigen Gebieten, in
denen das Portugiesische bereits herrschte, und sie bezeichneten
als ausländisch solche Schulen, in denen Brasilianer unterrichtet
wurden, wo doch die Schüler fast alle im Lande geboren seien.
Eine unverständliche Nachlässigkeit habe dazu geführt, daß die
Gesetzgeber unbewußt den Samen des Problems sprachlicher Minderheiten (minorias raciais) ausstreuten. Aber angesichts unserer
politischen Ordnung gebe es keine Luso-Brasilianer, Deutsch-
Brasilianer, Italo- oder sonstige (Bindestrich-) Brasilianer, denn die
brasilianische Staatsbürgerschaft (cidadania) sei unteilbar und un-
terschiedslos (homogênia). Als Beispiel für die früheren Unter-
lassungen führt er das Dekret vom 28. Januar 1931 an, das eines
der strengsten und umfassendsten gewesen sei. Es erkläre in seinem
3. Artikel diejenigen Schulen als ausländisch, in denen Kinder unter
14 Jahren in einem Fach oder in mehreren Fächern in einer
fremden Sprache unterrichtet werden. Aus diesem Dekret, das bis
1938 in Kraft geblieben sei, ergebe sich unter anderem, daß Ausländer als Volksschullehrer zugelassen werden konnten; daß der
Leiter einer Schule, wenn es (außer dem Lehrer) einen gab, zwar
das Portugiesische fließend sprechen mußte, daß ihm aber eine
mangelhafte Aussprache und ausländischer Akzent nachgesehen
wurden; ferner, daß die Schüler zwar verpflichtet waren, die Na-
tionallieder zu lernen, es ihnen aber weder verboten war, ausländische Lieder und Hymnen zu singen, noch sich in der Schule
einer fremden Sprache zu bedienen. So habe der Gesetzgeber
ganze Generationen brasilianischer Kinder dem Einfluß von
Fremden ausgeliefert, und so sei es nicht zu verwundern, daß
fremde Regierungen—unmittelbar durch ihre Konsulate oder mit-
telbar durch im Lande entstandene Kulturvereinigungen, die geistig
aus ausländischen Quellen genährt würden—alle diese Schulen
unterstützten und dem Körper der Nation das Gift eines gefährlichen (fremden) Volksbewußtseins (racismo) einflößten (S. 12-
18).
   Professor d'Aquino fährt fort, die (liberale) republikanische
Verfassung des Landes von 1891, in der die Rechte der Persönlichkeit als geheiligt betrachtet worden seien, sei der Nationalisierung
nicht günstig gewesen. Die unter Getúlio Vargas in Kraft getretene

Verfassung von 1934 habe bereits versucht, den Unterricht in der Volksschule den nationalen Forderungen entsprechend umzubilden, aber die Rücksicht auf die Wähler in den in Betracht kommenden Staaten haben das verhindert. In Santa Catarina würde beispielsweise der geschlossenste Teil der Wählerschaft, der des Itajaítales, welcher ein Viertel der Gesamtheit umfaßte und die Landessprache nicht kannte oder sich ihrer im täglichen Leben nicht bediente, niemals Gesetze gebilligt haben, die seine völkischen Überzeugungen (convicções raciais) aufs tiefste verletzt hätten. Von diesen seien die Wähler durchdrungen gewesen infolge der planmäßigen und zähen Propaganda der Agenten im Solde Berlins. Erst die (nach Auflösung des Kongresses und der Parteien oktroyierte autoritäre) Verfassung von 1937 habe ein wirksames Vorgehen ermöglicht (S. 18-25. Zum Verständnis: Analphabeten sind nicht wahlberechtigt. Daher fiel die Wählerschaft der Zonen ausländischer Kolonisation mit ihrem niedrigen Prozentsatz von Analphabeten so stark ins Gewicht.)

Jetzt hätten die Regierungen der drei südlichen Staaten fast gleichzeitig erkannt, daß keine Schulen fortbestehen dürften, die kein nationales Empfinden kennen und den moralischen und politischen Bestand der Nation bedrohen (atentatórias à continuidade moral e política da Nação). In Santa Catarina sei die Gefahr am bedrohlichsten, weniger in den polnischen und ukrainischen Siedlungen, auch kaum in den italienischen, wohl aber in den deutschen, wo folgende Umstände zur Absonderung beitrügen: Der geschlossene Widerstand gegen jeglichen Einfluß, der den Bräuchen und dem Volksbewußtsein der Bewohner entgegenwirke; die planmäßige, gelenkte und kräftige Propaganda von Leuten, die diesen Zustand erhalten wollten; die geldliche Hilfe und Unterstützung durch die deutsche Regierung und deutsche Organisationen oder diesen angeschlossene inländische Verbände; kirchliche Handlungen und Gottesdienste in deutscher Sprache; Zeitungen, Zeitschriften, Kalender und Bücher in deutscher Sprache und schließlich das Fehlen oder die Wirkungslosigkeit von Staats- und Bundesgesetzen (S. 25-32).

Es würde zu weit führen, wollten wir die folgenden Textteile des Buches, Seiten 32-58, in gleicher Weise exzerpieren. Auch ist es nicht unsere Aufgabe, Irrtümer des Verfassers zu berichtigen. Es genügt zu wissen, daß er sich weiterhin mit der evangelischen

Kirche und den Schul- und Lehrervereinen befaßt, die sich zu einem einzigen Vorsatz und einem gemeinsamen Ziel verbunden hätten, nämlich die in Brasilien geborenen Nachkommen von Deutschen einzudeutschen (germanizar), und daß er gegen die nationalsozialistische Propaganda auftritt, um sich zuletzt den Maßnahmen der catarinenser Regierung zuzuwenden. Von den im Jahre 1937 vorhandenen 661 privaten Lehranstalten seien 1938 noch 113 und 1941 noch 72 erhalten geblieben (diese ohne fremdsprachlichen Unterricht). Für jede geschlossene Schule sei sofort eine staatliche oder munizipale eingerichtet worden.

Es erübrigt sich auch, die Maßnahmen der catarinenser Regierung einzeln darzustellen. Als Beispiel diene nur, was das Dekret 301 vom 24. Februar 1939 vorsah (S. 51–54 und 78–90). Es diente zur Unterdrückung des passiven Widerstandes und verpflichtete die bis zu drei Kilometern von einer Schule entfernt wohnenden Erziehungsberechtigten, die in Brasilien geborenen Kinder im Alter von 8–14 Jahren zum Unterricht zu schicken. Um der Behörde die Überwachung zu ermöglichen, mußte sich in den Koloniezonen jeder Erziehungsberechtigte einen amtlich eingetragenen "Schulausweis" (quitação escolar) ausstellen lassen, mit Passbild, Personalangaben einschließlich der der Staatsangehörigkeit, Angaben über Namen und das durch behördlichen Ausweis belegte Alter jedes Kindes, Ort, Schule und Klasse. Im Falle der Behinderung eines Kindes durch Krankheit wurde eine ärztliche Beglaubigung verlangt. Kein Kind durfte länger als drei aufeinander folgende Tage unentschuldigt fehlen. Streng verboten war der häusliche Einzel- oder Gruppenunterricht. Zur Überwachung waren Schulinspektoren, Schulleiter, Lehrer und Steuereinnehmer verpflichtet. Die Strafen für Vergehen gegen das Dekret, in einer langen Reihe von Artikeln, Paragraphen und Absätzen festgelegt, bestanden aus zum Teil schweren Geldbußen und der Aberkennung bürgerlicher Rechte, wie die Anstellung im staatlichen und munizipalen Dienst, Empfang von Geldern aus behördlichen Kassen, gleichviel aus welchem Anspruch, Kauf von Stempelmarken (ohne die damals keine Quittung gültig war) und Erhalt irgend welcher amtlichen Bescheinigungen. Beamte und Angestellte, die gegen diese Bestimmungen handelten oder sie nicht beachteten, wurden entlassen.

Soweit Ivo d'Aquino. Zum besseren Verständnis haben wir

unserem Auszug in Klammern einige Ausdrücke des Originals und Erklärungen beigefügt. Die in dem Text wiederholt vorkommenden Wörter raça, racista und racismo beziehen sich nicht auf den biologischen Begriff Rasse, sondern auf Volk, Volkstum und Sprachgemeinschaft. Im übrigen haben die Schwierigkeiten der Übersetzung und die Unklarheit mehrerer Begriffe beiderseits zu Mißverständnissen geführt, ungewollten und gewollten. Zur Klärung solcher, das Leben der Nation berührenden Begriffe, trug neuerdings der Rechtsgelehrte Ataliba Nogueira durch eine beachtenswerte kleine Schrift bei [16].

Die seit 1937 in den drei Südstaaten erlassenen und vorbereiteten Verfügungen wurden in den Jahren bis 1941 durch mehr als 20 Dekrete der Bundesregierung grundsätzlich bestätigt, erweitert und auf das gesamte Land ausgedehnt. Diese Dekrete betreffen die Abwehr ausländischen Einflusses, die Auswahl der Einwanderer, ihre Verteilung zwecks schneller Nationalisierung, ihre und ihrer Nachkommen Eingliederung in das nationale Leben und insbesondere die Erziehung der Jugend. Wir beschränken uns auf das Wichtigste, soweit es unser Thema unmittelbar berührt und halten uns dabei an die vorzügliche, amtlich herausgegebene Sammlung dieser Dekrete von Konsul Maurício Wellisch, dem ehemaligen Leiter der Technischen Abteilung des Einwanderungsamtes [21]. Grundlegend war das bereits erwähnte Dekret 383 vom 18. April 1938. Es verbot den im Lande lebenden Ausländern, sich politisch zu betätigen und betraf hauptsächlich die Zweigstellen der Auslandsorganisation der Nationalsozialistischen Partei, NSDAP, und die der Faschistischen Partei. Den Ausländern blieb erlaubt, Kultur- und Wohltätigkeitsvereine zu unterhalten, vorausgesetzt, daß diese keine Beihilfen von fremden Regierungen, von Institutionen und Privatpersonen im Ausland erhielten und keine geborenen und eingebürgerten Brasilianer und Kinder von Ausländern zuließen. Der 4. Artikel dehnt die Verbote auf Schulen und sonstige Erziehungsanstalten aus, die von Ausländern oder Brasilianern oder von Vereinigungen gleichviel welcher Nationalität unterhalten wurden. Zuwiderhandelnde verlieren ohne weiteres auf 5 Jahre die öffentlichen Ämter, die sie etwa ausüben und können des Landes verwiesen werden. Nach dem Dekret 406 vom 4. Mai 1938 ist das Portugiesische die (alleinige) Unterrichtssprache in allen Landschulen, sind Lehrbücher ausschließlich portugiesisch abzufassen und darf Schülern unter 14 Jahren keine Fremdsprache gelehrt werden. Die Schulen sind von geborenen Brasilianern zu leiten. Keine Kolonie, kein Verein, und keine Firma in einer Kolonie darf einen ausländischen Namen tragen. Das Dekret 3.010 vom 20. August 1938 enthält die Ausführungsbestimmungen, mit Zusätzen und einem Anhang 286 Artikel im Umfang eines Buches. Die fünf Tage später erschienene Verfügung 1.545 verpflichtet die Behörden des Bundes, der Staaten und der Munizipien und alle staatlich beaufsichtigten Körperschaften im Rahmen ihrer Zuständigkeit zur völligen Anpassung der von Fremden abstammenden Brasilianer beizutragen, unter anderem durch den Unterricht und durch Eingliederung in patriotische Vereine. Zu den Pflichten der Behörden und der erwähnten Körperschaften gehören, außer zahlreichen weiteren: Die Einziehung zum Militärdienst so vieler Söhne von Ausländern wie möglich und zwar in Kasernen außerhalb ihres Wohngebietes; die Beaufsichtigung der Koloniezonen, wenn nötig durch geheime Inspektion; die Versetzung nachlässig vorgehender Beamten; die vormilitärische Ausbildung an höheren Lehranstalten; die Leibeserziehung der Schüler durch Offiziere und Unteroffiziere. Brasilianern unter 18 Jahren wurde die Ausreise grundsätzlich verboten, und verboten wurde fernerhin der Gebrauch fremder Sprachen in Amtsräumen, Kasernen und in der Predigt. Druckschriften in fremden Sprachen mußten im voraus beim Justizministerium angemeldet und durften nur mit dessen Genehmigung und nach Entrichtung einer Gebühr veröffentlicht werden.

In Einzelheiten wurden diese Maßnahmen nach dem Eintritt Brasiliens in den Krieg am 11. August 1942 Deutschen, Japanern und, mit Einschränkung, auch Italienern und deren Nachkommen gegenüber ergänzt und verschärft. Einige Bestimmungen wurden später gemildert und andere aufgehoben. Eines der Ergebnisse bestand darin, daß die sogenannten ausländischen Schulen in den drei Südstaaten sofort und in den übrigen Staaten bald danach aufhörten zu bestehen. Die Lehrerverbände traf schon 1938 das gleiche Geschick.

5. ERGEBNIS

Geschichtliche Vorgänge der Vergessenheit zu entreißen, wie oben geschehen, erhält erst dann einen Sinn, wenn die Frage nach dem Warum und dem Wie sich durch Fragen nach den Auswirkungen und nach einer Lehre für die Zukunft ergänzen läßt. Wir stellen auch diese und werden versuchen, sie aus der Perspektive von nahezu vier Jahrzehnten kurz zu beantworten. Über das Geschehen selbst haben wir aus dem Erleben seit der Kindheit und der späteren Mitarbeit in verantwortlichen Stellen berichtet, unter Zuhilfenahme der Literatur und erreichbarer Quellen. Zu diesen gehören die bisher nicht ausgewerteten Akten des Landesverbandes und Protokollbücher [1; 2; 3]. Weltanschauungen, Staatsraison und Recht berührende Erörterungen schalten wir aus. Wer solche wünscht, kann die als verbindlich geltende *Allgemeine Erklärung der Menschenrechte* der Vereinten Nationen vom Jahre 1948 und ihre Ergänzungen zu Rate ziehen.

Über das, was Schulen und Verbände unter Opfern geleistet und erstrebt haben, geben die Abschnitte 2 und 3 Auskunft. Zusammenfassend sei wiederholt, daß sie dem Staat kulturelle und soziale Aufgaben abgenommen haben, die als solche noch nicht erkannt waren oder mit den vorhandenen Mitteln nicht bewältigt werden konnten. Sie wirkten als Pioniere. Die langwährende Abgeschlossenheit der Koloniezonen von anderen Landesteilen war geographisch und durch die mangelhaften Verkehrswege bedingt. Die portugiesische Sprache zu erlernen war den sich selbst überlassenen Einwanderern und ihrem Nachwuchs vielfach unmöglich. Es sind keine Fälle bekannt, daß sie in Gruppen oder einzeln Widerstand geleistet hätten. Im Gegenteil, sie bemühten sich um die Landessprache. Die Schulen erzogen künftige Staatsbürger zu Treue und Pflichterfüllung. Der Erfolg zeigte sich nicht nur bei der überdurchschnittlich lebhaften Beteiligung an den Wahlen, wo es im munizipalen und einzelstaatlichen Leben zumeist um saubere Verwaltung ging, er zeigte sich auch in der Art, wie diese Bürger ihre Steuern entrichteten und wie sie Freiwillige zur Verteidigung des Landes stellten. Auch hierbei haben die Deutschen und Deutschstämmigen nicht hinter ihren Mitbürgern anderer Herkunft zurückgestanden. Das hebt z.B. der Franzose Jean Roche hervor, ein objektiver Zeuge: "Aus der Geschichte der Zeit (der beiden Weltkriege, in denen 'Deutschland und Brasilien sich als Feinde gegenüberstanden'), aus den Urkunden erfahren wir, daß es (unter den Brasilianern deutscher Herkunft) weder Drückeberger noch Verräter gegeben hat. Das heißt, sie haben sich als gute brasilianische Bürger verhalten" [18].

Die Nationalisierung wurde seit 1937 mit Härte durchgeführt, wie Ivo d'Aquino selbst bekennt (S. 53). Sie griff tief in das tägliche Leben der Betroffenen ein. Die Leistungen der Selbsthilfe wurden dabei nicht beachtet, geschweige denn gewürdigt. Ihr wurde ein Sinn unterlegt, der ihr fremd war. Am schwersten wurde jedoch die Diskriminierung ganzer Volksteile empfunden, die sich keiner Schuld bewußt waren. Zumal nach dem Eintritt des Landes in den Krieg spielten sich traurige, häßliche Szenen ab, die wir in unserer Geschichte gern entbehrt hätten. Das Ergebnis aber ist, daß die jüngeren Generationen die Sprachen ihrer Vorfahren vielfach nicht mehr verstehen oder doch im Umgang nicht mehr gebrauchen. Sie sind einsprachig portugiesisch geworden. Bei den Brasilianern deutscher Herkunft haben sich in abgelegenen Landstrichen Mundarten besser erhalten als die Hochsprache.

Der unvoreingenommene und leidenschaftslose Beobachter erkennt in den Massenwanderungen ein notwendiges Geschehen. Wenn er sein Herz mitsprechen läßt, was er sollte, wird er den Wandernden wie den Völkern, aus denen sie kommen und zu denen sie gehen aus den Mühen und Opfern der Bewegung einen möglichst reichen Segen wünschen. Daß Brasilien aus der Einwanderung seit Beginn des 19. Jahrhunderts einen für seine Zukunft entscheidenden Gewinn gezogen hat, ist eine allgemein anerkannte Tatsache. Es fragt sich nur, ob sein Vorteil nicht noch beachtlicher gewesen wäre, und sein Ansehen nicht noch mehr gewonnen hätte ohne die Strenge des Vorgehens, und wenn es den kulturellen Beitrag der Einwanderer ebenso hoch veranschlagt hätte wie den materiellen. Viel ist für immer verloren, aber manches läßt sich durch Umkehr zu liberalerem Denken, für das Anzeichen vorliegen, und durch entschlossenes Handeln noch retten.

QUELLEN

1. *Akten des Landesverbandes Deutsch-Brasilianischer Lehrer* einschließlich Briefwechsel mit den Lehrervereinen, den Seminaren und der Ruhegehalts-kasse, 1924-1938.

2. *Fragebogen* (fast 1.300) für Schulen, zumeist herausgegeben unter Be-fürwortung des Landesverbandes von Pastor Georg Schmeling, Pater Theodor Amstad S.J. und dem Verlag Rotermund & Co., um 1930.

3. *Protokollbücher des Deutschen Lehrervereins São Paulo und der Ruhe-gehaltskasse Bezirk São Paulo, 1916-1938*, 4 Bände.

4. *Anuário Católico do Brasil 1960*. Publicado pela Conferência Nacional dos Bispos do Brasil. II Edição. Petrópolis. Editôra Vozes. 1.287 S.

5. *Anuário dos Religiosos do Brasil*. Publicação da Revista da Conferência dos Religiosos do Brasil. Rio, 2a edição 1958. 2 Bände, 439 + 602 S.

6. *Jahrweiser für die evangelischen Gemeinden in Brasilien*. São Leopoldo, 1973, S. 217.

7. *Revista do Arquivo Público do Rio Grande do Sul*. Nos. 15-16, 1924, Pôrto Alegre, S. 456.

8. d'Aquino, Ivo: *Nacionalização do Ensino. Aspectos políticos*. Florianó-polis, Imprensa Oficial do Estado, 1942, 189 S. — Mit Texten von Dekreten, Übersichten, Statistik.

9. *Bismarck im Deutschen Reichstag, 26. 6. 1884. Nach Max Klemm: Was sagt Bismarck dazu?* Berlin, Scherl, 1924, Bd. I, S. 213. Nachweis von Dr. Helmut Springstubbe, Hamburg, 1975.

10. *Brockhaus Konversations-Lexikon*. 14. Aufl. 1893, Bd. 1, S. 572.

11. Coutinho, Antônio Carlos Vereza: "Bemerkungen zur Kultur- und Erziehungspolitik Brasiliens." In: *Zeitschrift für Kulturaustausch*. Institut für Auslandsbeziehungen, Stuttgart, 1974. 24. Jg., 4. Viertelj., S. 49-53.

12. Fouquet, Carlos: *Der deutsche Einwanderer und seine Nachkommen in Brasilien 1808-1824-1974*. São Paulo, Instituto Hans Staden; Pôrto Alegre, Federação dos Centros Culturais "25 de Julho," 1974, 264 S., ill.

13. Görgen, Hermann M.: "Der brasilianische Kreuzzug gegen das An-alphabetentum." In: *Deutsch-Brasilianische Hefte*, Bonn 1974, Jg. 13, Nr. 5, S. 300-319.

14. Koch, Herbert: "Das deutsche Schulwesen in Brasilien." Langensalza, 1923, S. 19. (*Manns Pädagog. Magazin Heft* 948).

15. Löw, Ulrich: "Ein Orden für den Kolonie-Inspektor." In: *Serra-Post Kalender*, Ijuí RS, 1974/75, S. 71-77. Mit Faksimile der Handschrift in der National-Bibliothek, Rio.

16. Nogueira, Ataliba: "A Nação." In: *Revista da Faculdade de Direito da Universidade de São Paulo, ano LXVI-1971*, S. 77-96.

17. Pellanda, Ernesto: *A Colonização Germânica no Rio Grande do Sul 1824-1924. Repartição de Estatística do Estado do Rio Grande do Sul*, Pôrto Alegre, Livraria do Globo, 1925, 195 S., ill.

18. Roche, Jean, Professor an der Universität Toulouse, Leiter des dortigen Instituts für Luso-Amerikanische Studien, Verfasser von grundlegenden Arbeiten über die deutsche Kolonisation in Rio Grande do Sul und Espírito Santo. "Unterredung mit Evelyn Berg." In: *Correio do Povo*, Pôrto Alegre, 28. 7. und 4. 8. 1974.

19. Rosenthal, Erwin Theodor: "Brasilianisches Hochschulwesen." In: *Zeitschrift für Kulturaustausch*, Stuttgart, 1962, Heft 4, S. 301-304.

20. Strothmann, Friedrich: "Die jährlichen Hauptversammlungen des Deutschen Evangelischen Lehrervereins von Rio Grande do Sul 1901-1926." In: *Allgemeine Lehrerzeitung für Rio Grande do Sul*, Pôrto Alegre, Sept. 1926, S. 5-9.

21. Wellisch, Maurício: *Legislação sôbre estrangeiros. Anotada e atualizada.* Rio, Ministério das Relações Exteriores. Serviço de Publicações 11. Imprensa Nacional, 1941; LI + 275 S.

14. Hermann J. Oberth.
The Father of Space Travel:
American Perspectives
Peter Horwath

When Professor Karl J. R. Arndt accepted a position at Clark University in Worcester, Mass., in 1950, he was already well-established as a scholar with great promise of further achievements to come. Because of his monumental publications since, he has become a member of the intellectual *crème de la crème* that has traditionally distinguished his Alma Mater. Clark University has been internationally known almost since its foundation in 1887 for its scholars, scientists, and inventors. G. Stanley Hall (1844–1924) did pioneering work there as an educator and psychologist, and it was during Hall's tenure as President of Clark University that honorary degrees were conferred upon Sigmund Freud and Carl Gustav Jung on the occasion of Freud's lectures there in 1909. A second notable person whose name is associated with Professor Arndt's institution is the endocrinologist Gregory G. Pincus (1903-67) who is probably best known for his work with M. C. Chang, J. Rock, and C.-R. Garcia in the development of the birth control pill.[1] Clark University, however, is more than the importer of the "couch" or the incubator of the "pill," it is also the cradle of modern rocket experimentation. In 1958 Wernher von Braun was awarded an honorary degree by Clark University. The developer of the V-2 Long-Range Rocket (A-4) and of Saturn V paid high tribute to the memory of Clark University's most distinguished alumnus, Robert H. Goddard (1882-1945).[2] In the years 1914-1943, Goddard had also been a professor of physics at Clark University. During his first years there, he commenced rocket experiments, and in 1919 he published a thin treatise, *A Method of Reaching Extreme Altitudes.* Three years later, Goddard received a letter from Heidelberg urgently requesting him to mail to the sender his "books" dealing with "the problem to pass over the atmosphere of our earth by means of a rocket."[3] The writer of this letter of May 3, 1922 was Hermann Julius Oberth, a 28-year-old (former) doctoral candidate at the University of Heidelberg. Through newspapers, Oberth had learned that he was not alone in the field of rocket research. On July 19, 1923, Goddard received a 92-page monograph entitled *Die Rakete zu den Planetenräumen* (München u. Berlin: R. Oldenbourg, 1923). In an appendix Oberth discussed Goddard's 1919 paper, the reception of which he had acknowledged on June 12, 1922. This is the day on which a somewhat bizarre interaction between American and German rocket research started. History, however, vindicated the old wisdom that "all is well that ends well," for the end was a good one, indeed.

Hermann J. Oberth was born on June 25, 1894 in Hermannstadt (Rum. Sibiu), Siebenbürgen (Transylvania), then a city of the multifaceted Austro-Hungarian Empire. He is a *Siebenbürger Sachse*, one of the "Saxons" of Transylvania who are said to have the world's oldest democracy. H. J. Oberth was one of three children of Dr. Julius Gotthold Oberth and his wife Valerie Emma, née Krasser. The family was Lutheran. Oberth's father, a successful surgeon, was the director of the county hospital in Schässburg (Rum. Sighisoara).[4] Here, in the "Rothenburg of Transylvania," young Hermann attended the Bischof-Teutsch-Gymnasium. Jules Verne's (1828–1905) imaginary accounts of moon flights set the 11-year-old youth's imagination ablaze, and at sixteen he familiarized himself with the basics of propulsion. In June of 1912 he made his *Matura*, receiving a prize in mathematics. World War I interrupted his studies at the University of Munich. In 1913 he had matriculated there as a student of medicine, but his real interest was with rocket flight. As an infantryman in the Austro-Hungarian army, Oberth saw action for about a year on the Russian front. Wounded, he was transferred to the Twenty-Second Field Ambulance Unit stationed in Schässburg. Problems pertaining to space technology and space medicine, e.g., the effects of (simulated) weightlessness, kept him occupied. At the youthful age of twenty Oberth had already succeeded in mathematically defining the most important relationships between fuel consumption, air resistance, gravitation, attained velocity, attained height, and duration of travel. As late as 1919, Goddard maintained the impossibility of expressing these relationships mathematically. By 1917 Oberth had conceived of a long-range rocket 25 m in length and 5 m in diameter which, propelled by alcohol and oxygen, was to have had a payload of 10 tons. The War Ministry in Berlin promptly rejected the submitted design of the so-called "England-Rakete" as fantasy.

Having been discharged after the war with the rank of sergeant-major, H. J. Oberth resumed his studies at the University of Klausenburg (Rum. Cluj). With the transfer of *Siebenbürgen* to Rumania, he became a Rumanian citizen. In 1918 he married Mathilde Hummel who bore him, in a happy marriage, four children. Only with great difficulties did he receive permission to leave for Germany in 1919 where he was to study at the Universities of Munich (1919-1920), Göttingen (1920-1921), and Heidelberg (1921-1922). The University of Heidelberg rejected his dissertation (1922) on rocket-design. Oberth decided to partially underwrite the publishing expenses of his study, and it appeared in 1923 as *Die Rakete zu den Planetenräumen.*[5] In this epochal best-seller, the author described the essential elements of the giant rockets of our own era. Supporting his theories with mathematical explanations, Oberth maintained that rockets could be built which would reach such immense speeds that they would escape the earth's gravitational pull, thereby allowing interplanetary travel within a few decades. Such flights would be manned (probably without harm to the passengers) and economically useful. Independently, Oberth had arrived at conclusions similar to Goddard's. In 1925 a second edition of his book appeared; it was the same year in which Oberth became acquainted with the pioneering work of Konstantin E. Tsiolkovski (1857-1935). Oberth freely acknowledged priority of Tsiolkovski and Goddard in deriving certain equations underlying rocketry. A considerably enlarged third edition, *Wege zur Raumschiffahrt*, appeared in 1929. Goddard became also acquainted with this edition. It contained design concepts for immense interplanetary vehicles utilizing clustered liquid-propelled motors. In the discussion of electric propulsion and the ion rocket, Oberth was some 30 years ahead of his contemporaries. The book won for Oberth the first annual Robert Esnault-Pelterie-André Hirsch Prize (10,000 francs) which enabled him to finance his research on liquid-propellant rocket engines.

In autumn 1928 Fritz Lang was directing a movie for the UFA, called *Die Frau im Mond,*[6] and Oberth was engaged as a scientific advisor. To heighten the effect, the now standard count-down in reverse was done for the first time. On the day of the film's premiere, an actual rocket was to be launched and expected to reach an altitude of 40 km. During an experiment (1929), however, the rocket exploded and Oberth lost the sight of his left eye. Nevertheless, much new and valuable information was gained from the experiments. In the meantime, the *Verein für Raumschiffahrt*[7] had become interested in the project. Oberth continued his experiments at the *Chemisch-technische Reichsanstalt* with the help of three assistants, one of them being an 18-year-old student (1930) by the name of Wernher von Braun who, at the age of 24, became the Technical Director at the new rocket center at Peenemünde. Having been successful with liquid rocket motors, Oberth returned to Mediasch in Transylvania to resume his teaching.

From 1938 to 1940, H. J. Oberth was a professor at the *Technische Hochschule* of Vienna, where he worked on liquid-propellant rockets. He did similar work subsequently (1940-1941) in Dresden. In 1940 he had become a German citizen. Between 1941-1943 he was a consulting engineer working at the A-4 project at Peenemünde, and in 1943-1945 he was assigned to developing an ammonium-nitrate anti-aircraft rocket with the *Westfälisch-Anhaltische Sprengstoff A.G.* located near Wittenberg.

At the end of the war, Oberth was detained for four months in an American interrogation camp. In 1949 he went to Switzerland where he had the opportunity to continue his experiments. In 1950 the Italian Admiralty asked him to complete the solid-propellant ammonium nitrate anti-aircraft rocket at La Spezia. In the meantime, both the United States and the Soviet Union were drawing heavily on the V-2 engine design in developing large rocket motors.[8]

In June 1955, Wernher von Braun invited H. J. Oberth to join him in his work on rockets in the USA. Until June 1956, Oberth was associated with guided missile work at the U.S. Army Redstone Arsenal in Huntsville, Alabama. Thereupon he worked for two years with the U.S. Army Ballistic Missile Agency in the same place. On October 4, 1957, the Soviet Union successfully placed *Sputnik I* into orbit around the earth. (W. v. Braun's requests for permission to orbit a satellite had up to this moment been denied.) When the U.S. Navy's Vanguard projects failed, von Braun and his associates received the go-ahead. On February 1, 1958, a Jupiter C rocket (development begun in 1955) placed *Explorer I* into orbit.[9] The measurements taken by this satellite led to the discovery of the "Van-Allen-Belt" (cf. the ceremonies on October 27, 1961 at Iowa Wesleyan College when both H. J. Oberth and J. A. Van Allen were given honorary degrees).

In November 1958 Oberth returned to Germany; he was 64 and approaching retirement age. Despite interventions by several persons, Oberth could not get a U.S. pension because he had not been a civil servant long enough. Oberth, moreover, was by now too old to stay on.[10] The possibility of receiving a modest pension existed in West Germany.

Viewing the contribution of the three great modern pioneers in rocketry (Tsiolkovski, Goddard, and Oberth), Dr. Ernst Stuhlinger, Oberth's immediate superior in Huntsville, stated that "the works of the three masters appear to us in retrospect as three summits in the history of space travel. The three contributions confirm and complete each other. Each achievement, however, forms a supporting and decisive foundation-pillar for the ensuing development of space flight."[11] Oberth himself has contributed 95 concepts and ideas to rocket technology—that is, by far the greatest number.[12] The concepts of the "Rückstoßprinzip" and of the "Stufenprinzip" are intimately associated with Oberth's work. The fact that relatively few tragedies have marred the rocket program also bespeaks a great feat, a feat which in many respects is H. J. Oberth's.[13]

The *XXIII. Raumfahrtkongress der Hermann-Oberth-Gesellschaft* met in Salzburg on June 25–29, 1974. On the opening day, H. J. Oberth's birthday was celebrated. Dr. A.-F. Staats, the President of the H.-O.-G. (formerly, *Deutsche Raketen-Gesellschaft*), read the following handwritten birthday letter[14] which Oberth's most famous student, Wernher von Braun, had forwarded to him:

Alexandria, Virginia

Herrn

    Prof. Dr. Ing. e. h. Dr. hc. Hermann Oberth

      Feucht/Bayern

Lieber Hermann!

Es tut mir von ganzem Herzen leid, daß es mir nicht möglich ist, bei Deiner 80. Geburtstagsfeier in Salzburg zugegen zu sein. Ich höre aber, daß unser gemeinsamer Freund Eberhard Rees[15] kommen wird. Eberhard's amüsante Festreden sind berühmt, und Du kannst Dich auf einiges gefaßt machen!

Der Zufall will es, daß ich gerade heute die von dem Kriterion-Verlag in Bukarest herausgebrachte Neuauflage Deines Buches "Wege zur Raumschiffahrt" zugesandt bekam. Alle Historiker des Weltraumfluges sind sich darüber einig, daß mehr als irgend ein anderer Faktor dieses Buch und sein Vorläufer "Die Rakete zu den Planetenräumen" den wirklichen Anstoß zu der praktischen Verwirklichung dieses großartigen Menschheitsvorhabens gegeben haben. Es waren Deine Inspiration und Deine analytische Vorarbeit, die die latenten Kräfte mobilisierten und die verschiedenen Gruppen von Experimentatoren in aller Welt auf den Plan brachten. Du weißt, daß diese beiden Bücher und der Umstand, daß ich als junger Student im Jahre 1930 für Dich arbeiten durfte, auch mir selbst den Leitstern meines Lebens gegeben haben.

Nur wenigen Erfindern und Bahnbrechern der Technik ist es vergönnt, die Triumphe ihrer Pionierarbeit noch selbst erleben zu können. Du konntest nicht nur Augenzeuge des Starts von Apollo 11 und der glücklichen Rückkehr der ersten Menschen vom Mond sein, sondern auch von den vielfältigen wissenschaftlichen Erfolgen von Skylab hören, das ja auch auf einem Konzept beruhte, das Du bereits vor einem halben Jahrhundert entwickelt hattest.

Ich hoffe, daß es Dir und Deinem guten Engel, der Tilly, vergönnt sein möge, noch viele Jahre in guter Gesundheit unter uns zu sein. Auch wenn zur Zeit von der Raumfahrt weniger gesprochen wird als vor ein paar Jahren, so sind wir uns doch in der Gewißheit einig, daß ihre wertvollsten Beiträge zum Wohle der Menschheit noch bevorstehen.

Dein getreuer
Wernher von Braun

Dr. Ernst Stuhlinger, Associate Director for Science, NASA, George C. Marshall Space Flight Center, wrote down some memories and observations on December 17, 1974 for this article:

My first encounter with Hermann Oberth, although not in person, dates back to 1929. As a 15-year-old schoolboy, I read in a magazine that Professor Oberth was proposing a rocket flight to the moon, and back to earth, with several people on board. Photographs were shown of several rocket engines he had built and tested. This prospect for future space flight impressed me deeply, although I did not know at that time that I would spend the better part of my life working on rockets and space flight. In 1943, I had the greatest pleasure of meeting Professor Oberth personally in Peenemünde, Germany, where he helped develop the V-2 rocket. Shortly before I met him, I had read his book *Die Rakete zu den Planetenräumen* which impressed me deeply because of its style of elementary power and prophetic boldness. Professor Oberth is a born teacher; his statements are always very clear and persuasive. Many of his arguments begin with the simple words 'as we have learned in school . . . ,' and then he continues quoting basic facts of physics which lead quickly to the point he wishes to make. Undistracted by doubters and other people with lesser knowledge, he has fought for his ideas of rockets and space flight for 70 years now and he has been gratified with the fulfillment of many of his early dreams. In his discussions of technical and scientific aspects of rocketry, and of the applications of rockets and space flight for human needs, Professor Oberth appears to be without emotions, except for his passion for honesty. When he meets a dishonest person, his reactions can be cynical and even harsh, sometimes lacking the diplomatic finesse which is indispensable if one wishes to win an argument with a dishonest person. A little anecdote, undoubtedly true, illustrates this feature of Professor Oberth's character. In 1944, Professor Oberth lived with many colleagues in a sort of community house in Peenemünde. Food was rationed and very rare. Each person had his own little store of sugar for his cooking needs. Professor Oberth stored his sugar box on an open shelf in the community kitchen. One day, it was stolen. Professor Oberth put a note on the bulletin board, reading like this: "The person who stole my sugar should be advised that the sugar was poisoned. The poison leads to a slow death. Only I have the antidote. The thief is advised to contact me to receive the saving antidote. Signed H. Oberth." The next day, another note was seen close to the first one: "Dear Professor Oberth, thank you for your well-meaning advice. Unfortunately, it came too late. The sugar tasted fine. Greetings from the other world."

Professor Oberth's belief in absolute honesty is borne out by his fervent recommendation that each politician should first promise that he will remain honest throughout his political career, and then should be connected to a lie detector during each of his political speeches.

Students of rocketry and space flight have always recognized and acknowledged Professor Oberth as one of the most important, or perhaps even the most important, pioneer in this field of modern technology. Among his major contributions are the thermodynamic analyses of rocket engines; quantitative design studies of hydrogen-oxygen rocket motors, near-earth and space trajectories of rockets, satellites, and spacecraft, optimization studies of trajectories and missions, studies of control and guidance systems, studies of many detailed mechanical design features of rockets and spacecraft, and many others. Even at an early time of his work, he emphasized practical uses of rockets, satellites, and spacecraft. Observations of the earth, communication satellites, satellite astronomy, and manufacturing under weightlessness of space were mentioned in his first book published in 1923. With untiring effort, he worked out many mathematical details for his designs. When I asked him one day whether he had derived a specific equation in one of his books, he simply said: "I derived all equations in all my books; at the time when I wrote them, there were no publications where these derivations could be found."

Professor Oberth joined the U.S. Army Ballistic Missile Agency in Huntsville, Alabama, in June 1955; he left the U.S.A. for Germany in November 1958. During the three and one-half years in the American rocket and space program, he engaged in theoretical studies of trajectory optimization, stability of orbits, multi-stage projects, application of rockets to planetary exploration, advanced spacecraft and propulsion systems, and plans for future space missions. He was a quiet, taciturn scientist; if a colleague asked him for some advice, however, he took great pains in providing as much information and help as possible. For those who had close working contact with him, he will always be the great prophet of space flight, with a clarity and boldness unparalleled in our profession. Among the three Fathers of Space Flight, Tsiolkovsky, Goddard, and Oberth, Hermann Oberth is certainly the one who applied his genius in the broadest way to all the technical, scientific, and human aspects of space flight. In fact, there is no portion of this wide area of human endeavor to which he has not made substantial and even decisive contributions.

Dr. George C. Bucher, Deputy Associate Director for Science (NASA), knew Professor Oberth very well during his stay in the U.S.A. He contributed the following observations (November 8, 1974), trip report (October 30, 1961), citation (kudos), and newspaper-excerpt: "Generally speaking, Professor Oberth was a somewhat retiring individual during the years that I was closely associated with him. He was somewhat hampered by a less-than-complete mastery of the English language, but by his very nature he worked largely alone on his research and did not 'squander' his time in discussions on nontechnical matters. In other words, he tended to be a 'loner' but was always cordial to those he came in contact with."

TRIP REPORT TO
IOWA WESLEYAN COLLEGE, MT. PLEASANT, IOWA
FOR AWARD OF DOCTOR OF SCIENCE DEGREE TO PROF. OBERTH
October 26–28 1961

The undersigned was privileged to accompany Professor and Mrs. Hermann Oberth from Huntsville to Mt. Pleasant, Iowa where Professor Oberth received an honorary Doctor of Science degree from Iowa Wesleyan College. Travel was by air from Huntsville to Chicago and by train from Chicago to Burlington, Iowa. The party was met at the train by officials of Iowa Wesleyan College and members of the press.

The ceremonies were held on Friday, October 27, the same day on which the first SATURN was fired. The program for the day included a tour of the new Adam Trieschmann Hall of Science at the college, a luncheon for the distinguished guests and associates of the college, an afternoon program for dedication of the new Hall of Science and awarding of honorary degrees, a ribbon cutting at the Hall of Science, and a dinner for the guests and associates of the college. In the morning Professor Oberth was given a specially conducted tour of the Hall of Science. He was seated, together with Mrs. Oberth, at the head table during luncheon. Just prior to the luncheon Mr. Walter Hecker of Cleveland, Ohio joined the Oberths and remained with the party for the rest of the day. At the dedication program Professor Oberth was awarded the honorary degree of Doctor of Science. The citation was read by President Chadwick of Iowa Wesleyan College. A copy of the citation is attached for your information. Any lack of accuracy in the citation was more than compensated for by the warmth and sincerity with which President Chadwick presented it. Upon acceptance of his degree, Professor Oberth was given a prolonged standing ovation. He was the only degree recipient to be so honored by the audience. For those who knew Professor Oberth and the history of his life, it was a tender and unforgettable occasion to witness the awarding of his first and only Doctor's degree. The entire audience, and Professor and Mrs. Oberth were visibly impressed. Seven honorary degrees were presented, including one to Mr. S. S. Kresge, head of the dime store company, and one to Robert Sarnoff, Chairman of the National Broadcasting Company. Dr. James A. Van Allen, an alumnus of Iowa Wesleyan, was the principal speaker after the awarding of the degrees. At the evening dinner Professor Oberth was invited to comment. He thanked the college for his degree, stated that he was impressed with the new science building, was proud to be an honorary alumnus of the college, and wished future success for the college in all its endeavors. As we returned to the motel after dinner, Mrs. Oberth affectionately addressed her husband as "Herr Doktor" and he beamed with pride.

Dr. and Mrs. Van Allen send their personal regards to Dr. von Braun and Dr. Stuhlinger and their other acquaintances at MSFC. Mr. Hecker also sends his regards and expression of satisfaction that Professor Oberth had finally received his degree.

All officials of Iowa Wesleyan College were extremely gracious and spared no effort in making the trip pleasant and memorable. The college would be extremely honored if Dr. von Braun would be able to visit some day.

The day following the ceremonies the undersigned accompanied Professor and Mrs. Oberth to Chicago where they were met by relatives and friends. They plan to spend approximately five days in Chicago, then go to Cleveland for a few days to visit more friends and relatives, then to El Paso, then to Convair in San Diego, and finally to visit their son in Fair Oaks, California.

If further details of the trip are desired the undersigned may be reached at 876-4935.

George C. Bucher
Assistant to Director
Research Projects Division

Distribution:
Dr. von Braun   (M-DIR)
Dr. Rees   (M-DEP-R&D)
Dr. Stuhlinger   (M-RP-DIR)
Dr. McCall   (M-DIR)
Mr. Dannenberg   (M-SAT-DIR)

HONORARY DEGREE CONFERRED OCT. 27, 1961, by PRES. J. RAYMOND CHADWICK UPON HERMANN OBERTH

HERMANN OBERTH, born in Hermannstadt, Siebenbürgen, Rumania, 1894, receiving his German citizenship in 1941; EDUCATED in the elementary school and Gymnasium in Schässburg, passing his Maturit Examination in 1912, followed by three years of study in Munich before and after World War I, also one year each in Göttingen, Heidelberg and Klausenburg, receiving in June, 1923 the title of "Secondary Professor" in mathematics and physics, and in 1938 the title of "Professor" from the Institute of Technology in Vienna; EFFECTIVE TEACHER, first at Schässburger Gymnasium and Obergymnasium in Mediasch, Siebenbürgen, and later as a private teacher having at one time Dr. Wernher von Braun as his pupil; WORLD-FAMOUS PIONEER IN THE FIELD OF ROCKETS, publishing his first work—*The Rocket to the Planets* in 1923, the first book to treat the theory of rockets as applicable to space flight in a profound, comprehensive and scientific manner, followed by a second more elaborate work—*Ways to Outer Space Travel*—in 1929, in which he demonstrated beyond doubt the possibility of outer space travel, thus becoming along with Professor Goddard of America and Professor Ziolkovsky of Russia, one of the three great rocket pioneers of the world, and now the only one of the three still living; IMAGINATIVE AND BRILLIANT AUTHOR, as demonstrated by the aforementioned works, as well as many others including: *The Electronic Spaceship* (1950), *Errors in the Rocket Development* and *Man into Space* (1954), *The Mooncar* (1957) describing the means of transportation needed to get around on the surface of the moon; RECIPIENT OF NUMEROUS CITATIONS AND HONORS from many lands, including

Rumania, France, Austria, Germany, England, Denmark, Switzerland, Greece and America, culminating with a Herman Oberth award (a bust in bronze) by the Huntsville section of the American Rocket Society in 1960, given to the most distinguished outer space scientist, in recognition and appreciation of his five years of creative services with Dr. von Braun's scientific group in Huntsville, Alabama; OUTSTANDING PROPHET whose prophesies have come true; DISTINGUISHED PROFESSOR without a degree, we deem it a great honor at Iowa Wesleyan, a College with many notable scientists among her graduates, to award you your first and only degree and to welcome you as an HONORED ALUMNUS; therefore, upon the recommendation of the Committee on Honorary Degrees, and by vote of the Board of Trustees, I, by virtue of the authority vested in me as President of Iowa Wesleyan College, confer upon you the honorary degree of Doctor of Science with all the honors, rights, privileges and responsibilities thereto appertaining.

Molly Scholes of *The Hawk-Eye* (Burlington, Iowa, Sunday, October 29, 1961, p. 33) gave the following account: "But the man who received a standing ovation when he received an honorary *Doctor of Science* degree was Dr. Hermann Oberth, of Germany, called the 'granddaddy of rocketry'.

Oberth, a tall, husky man with white, wavy hair and a mustache, beamed with a touch of embarrassment and modesty at the crowd's reception when his degree citation was read.

Debt to Oberth

He is the man to whom Dr. Wernher von Braun has said he owes his decision to make space flight his life's work. Oberth is the only one living of the early rocket pioneers. It was Oberth's dissertation on rockets that was rejected in 1921, but which later became the basis for much of the U.S. rocket work. Many of his ideas were used in the first V-2 development.

Some of his notions, such as a giant space mirror, are still to be developed. Such a mirror could be used to increase the amount of habitable land by reflecting sunlight or sun energy to wastelands, Oberth said.

Oberth said such ideas eventually will bring the world's peoples together.

'Some of these tasks are of such magnitude to accomplish that scientists will have to work together rather than fighting,' he explained.

But will they work together? Oberth shrugged. 'I hope so,' he said.

Dr. Mitchell R. Sharpe, the historian at the George C. Marshall Space Flight Center, offered (December 20, 1974) a telling bit of personal observation:

"I remember a curious analogy he made one time. When someone said that the huge rockets proposed in the mid-50s were too complex to fly, Oberth pointed out that his automobile had six cylinders and his lawn-mower only one. However, the auto always started and the lawn-mower never did!

A somewhat unkind, but wholly true observation of Oberth's lack of practical experience in astronautics was made by a colleague who said, 'If Oberth wants to drill a hole, he first invents the drill press.' The man was a theoretician, no doubt about it."

Mr. Mitchell R. Sharpe was also the Associate Editor of *Space Journal,* an astronautical quarterly written for the layman. Published in Huntsville for several years, the first issue was dedicated to Oberth. The cover carried his portrait. Oberth's contribution to I/1 (Summer 1957) was on space construction techniques. Since Oberth's article "Some Future Astronautical Considerations" (pp. 14-16) is not listed in any bibliographies consulted, I am gladly following Mr. Sharpe's recommendation to include it *in toto* (minus illustrations). A few months after the first issue of *Space Journal* had appeared, the Soviet Union orbited unexpectedly (October 4, 1957) *Sputnik I,* a 22.8 inch diameter sphere, containing a tracking beacon and three scientific experiments![16]

It is curious to read Professor Oberth's conclusion: "I think that by the year 2,000 we shall have developed space travel techniques!"

SOME FUTURE ASTRONAUTICAL CONSIDERATIONS
By Hermann Oberth

The first man-made earth satellite will soon circle the earth. This satellite, and succeeding ones, will be small (not larger than a basketball), and will carry nothing more than a few instruments. Larger satellites, equipped with elaborate automatic instrumentation, will follow, and by means of ultra-high-frequency radio, will transmit information to the earth.

Even now, experiments are being conducted at Randolph Air Force Base, Texas to ascertain what the human body can withstand. From these experiments, engineers will determine those points in the construction of ferry rockets and manned satellites which will require special attention. This work will be completed in five to ten years.

The next step forward will depend on information concerning cosmic rays and cosmic dust which we shall have gained from unmanned satellites. Space technique can then follow either of the two courses. I should like to call these "the course of the thick walls," and "the course of the thin walls." Space travel will be possible in either case.

On earth there are people who live 9,000 feet (and, of course, even higher) above sea level. If we consider the 9,000-foot altitude as an example, the protection afforded these people from cosmic rays and dust by the atmosphere above them would be duplicated in a space vehicle by a layer of liquid air seven meters thick. Naturally, it will not be necessary to use liquid air as a protective layer, since the same effect can be obtained with a one-foot-thick outer shell of lead over a nine-inch-thick shell of aluminum. A third, or innermost, shell consisting of one-half inch beryllium will complete the effect. Observation ports will also consist of three layers. Beginning with the outermost, or exterior, layer, there will be foot-thick flint glass, then a nine-inch layer of crown glass, and finally, one-half inch of plexiglass. The space traveler could spend all of his life in such a protected area, without danger from cosmic rays and dust. This is the course which I call "the course of thick walls," a course which, I hope, will not be necessary, since the human body may very well be able to withstand cosmic rays.

If the human body is able to withstand these rays, the space vehicle's walls can be made of very thin and light material, so that few "secondary" rays would be encountered. For protection against cosmic dust, the vehicle walls may be constructed along the lines suggested by Dr. von Braun (a protective shell placed around the whole at a distance of one or two inches). When cosmic particles strike this outer shell their high speed will cause most of them to heat and evaporate. The diminished force of the remaining particles will not be sufficient to damage the inner or actual vehicle wall. This will be the technique of the "the thin walls."

Thus, astronautical technique will take one of the two following courses:

1) In the case of the thin walls, construction materials will be obtained right from the earth, and large orbital space stations will be built. Perhaps large mirrors of metal foil will be used to influence the earth's climate. Soon electrical space ships, such as those suggested by me in 1928 and further developed by Dr. Ernst Stuhlinger, will be built. These will not be launched from the earth, but will be capable of leaving an orbital station with ease. They will use little fuel, and with them we shall easily be able to rise to 22,000 miles. A station orbiting at this altitude will complete its path once each day, and could be controlled to remain over the same spot on earth continually.

Large telescopes could keep an accurate "eye" on the earth in order to ascertain, for instance, that countries are actually keeping their disarmament promises; or, photographs could be obtained to counter Russian propaganda concerning so-called benefits to be derived from the Russian way of life. These stations could also serve television by acting as reflective relay stations for television waves. Likewise, communications will be improved, in that radio waves can be beamed and concentrated, thus allowing literally thousands of messages to be transmitted and received at the same time. In addition to this we can carry on many scientific experiments, and last, but certainly not least, we shall be able to reach other heavenly bodies with our electric space ships.

2) On the other hand, space technique will take an entirely different course should the human body prove incapable of withstanding cosmic rays for periods of little more than an hour. This should be the minimum time, since the human body can withstand X-rays which are ten times as strong as cosmic rays for a duration of at least 20 minutes. In this case, space vehicles with small thick-walled cabins will be launched, and we shall try as quickly as possible to build an atomic powered electric space ship with which to obtain materials from the moon. We might even bring an astroid into an orbital path around the earth, and get our materials from it. These materials would be used for the protective walls of any further space shelters for men.

The second course will not be as simple as the first course mentioned, but in any case, I think that by the year 2,000 we shall have developed space travel techniques.

IV

Dr. George C. Bucher mentioned the difficulty Professor Oberth had with English. So did others, and this, to strike a humorous note, inspired a special language even for the personnel of the Air Force Air Command Research and Development Command in Baltimore. The following lists some terms from an unofficial "English-German Glossary" being circulated widely in the late 50s:

Engineering—Das aufguefen grupe
Project engineer—Das schwettenoudter
Wind tunnel—Das huffenpuffen grupe
Computing—Das schlidenruler grupe
Security—Das schnoopen bunche
Planning—Das schemen grupe
Structural test—Das pullenparten grupe
Contract administrator—Das tablegepaunder grupe
Nuclear research—Das whizkidden grupe
Facilities—Das deskgeschoven bunche
Support equipment—Das garterbelten grupe
Those with responsibility—Das ultzerenbalden grupe
Guided missile—Das sientifiker geschtenwerkes firenkrakker
Rocket engine—Firenschphitter mit smoken-und-schnorten
Liquid rocket—Das skwirten jucenkind firenschpitter
Guidance system—Das schteerenwerke

Celestial guidance—Das schruballische schtargazen peepenglasser mit komputerattachen schteerenwerke

Pre-set guidance—Das senden offen mit ein pattenbacker und finger gekressen schteerenwerke

Control system—Das pullen-und-schoven werke

Warhead—Das laudenboomer

Nuclear warhead—Das eargeschplitten laudenboomer

Hydrogen device—Das eargeschplittenlaudenboomer mit ein grosse hollengraund und alles kaput.

NOTES AND ACKNOWLEDGMENTS

1. Dr. Pincus's association with Clark U. encompasses the years 1938-45. In 1930, he was a student at the *Kaiser-Wilhelm-Institut* in Berlin.

2. W. v. Braun is the Chairman of the International Sponsors of the Robert Goddard Library Program at Clark U.

3. "When I was now publishing the result of my examinations and calculations, I learned by newspaper, that I am not alone in my inquiries . . ." (*The Papers of Robert H. Goddard*. Vol. I: 1898-1924. Ed. by Esther C. Goddard and G. Edward Pendray. New York: McGraw [n.d.], p. 485).

4. While Schässburg was the "Schulstadt" of the "Saxons," Hermannstadt (before 1223: Sibinburc; 1935: 21,000 Germans of a population of 46,000) was their cultural and political center. These "hospites theutonici," or "Flandrenses" were of lower Rhenian and Moselle-Franconian stock, and they had been called into the land by Hungarian kings to further mining, and to protect the Transylvanian passes against southern invaders. The first "Saxons" arrived 1150; the Teutonic Knights under Hermann v. Salza established themselves in Transylvania in 1211! The "Siebenbürgen Sachsen" of the Carpathian highlands, and the "Donauschwaben" in the Pannonian Plain contributed substantially to the social and economic fabric of South-Eastern Europe.

5. Oberth had written his dissertation in the Winter of 1921-22. At the end of October 1922 he submitted the manuscript to Oldenburg, and on June 8, 1923, the printed version was available in the bookstores (according to information received from Prof. Oberth, May 6, 1975).

6. On June 3, 1931, H. L., Fine Arts Theatre in Boston sent Goddard the following invitation: "It is our pleasure to present a Boston premier of an astronomical semi-scientific film called *By Rocket to the Moon*. This film was made at the UFA studios in Germany and was directed by Fritz Lang in collaboration with Professor Oberth, the German rocket experimentor.

We are enclosing a courtesy card to attend the opening performance which is to be on Saturday, June 6, at one o'clock.

We are looking forward to your presence" (*The Papers of R. H. G.*, Vol. II, 1925-37, p. 798).

7. Following the example of the *VfR*, the *American Interplanetary Society* was founded in 1930.

8. On April 15, 1955, W. v. Braun and 40 of his associates became U.S. citizens. In 1952 there were 117 Germans in Huntsville. Initially, 112 of W. v. Braun's engineers and scientists were removed to the U.S.A. See William-Epstein: *Rocket Pioneers on the Road to Space* (1955), H. Gartmann: *The Men Behind the Space Rockets* (1956), and K. D. Huzel: *Peenemünde to Canaveral* (1962).

9. J. B. Medaris. *Countdown for Decision* (1960).

10. I am indebted for this and for other information (e.g., concerning *The*

Papers of R. H. G., Vols. I–III) to Dr. Fred C. Durant, III, Assistant Director, Astronautics, Smithsonian Institution.

11. Ernst Stuhlinger, "Raumfahrt in Vergangenheit und Zukunft," *Astronautik: Organ der Hermann-Oberth-Gesellschaft*, III (1974), 70. (My translation) This is the key-note speech which Dr. Stuhlinger gave at the *XXIII. Raumfahrtkongress der H.-O.-G.* (Salzburg, June 25–29, 1974).—Prof. Stuhlinger (b. 1913 Niederrimbach) was at the Guided Missile Division, Fort Bliss, 1946–50; and at the Army Ballistic Missile Agency, Huntsville, 1950–60. In his capacity as Director of Research Projects, he was then the superior of Oberth.

12. This information has been gained from the text of a speech, "Aus dem Leben Hermann Oberths: 'Dichtung' wird 'Wahrheit'," which Dr. A.-F. Staats gave at Garmisch. Dr. Staats kindly let me have a copy of his address, and the information is found on p. 7.

13. A.-F. Staats sees in this fact Oberth's greatest achievement (*ibid.*, p. 8). Selected U.S. references: Walters, H. B. *H. O.: Father of Space Travel* (1962); Newlon, Cl.: *Famous Pioneers in Space* (1963); Von Braun-Ordway: *History of Rocketry and Space Travel* (1967); Stoiko, M.: *Pioneers in Rocketry* (1974); *Newsweek* (24:18 3 Jl '44); *TIME* (44:48 10 Jl '44); *UN World* (6:9 N '52); *N Y Times* (p. 13 7 Jl '55); *US News* (39:16 15 Jl '55); *Sat R* (39:42 1 S '56 por); *Cur Biogr Yrbk* ('57:416–18 '58 por); *Newsweek* (71:12 25 Mr '68 il pors); *Electronic N* (14:18 28 Jl '69); *The Enc Am* ['73] ("Rocket"); *Coll Enc* ['74] ("Oberth," and "Rocket"); *The N Enc Brit: Microp* ['74] ("Oberth"); *The N Enc Brit: Macrop* ['74] ("Rockets . . ."); the most recent German biogr.: Hans Barth. *H. O.: Der Vater der Raumfahrt*. Bucuresti: Kriterion Vlg, 1975.

14. Dr. von Braun sent me a copy of his birthday-letter, and gave me permission to use it for the present study. He is now VP, Eng. and Devel., Fairchild Industries, Germantown, Maryland.

15. Dr. Eberhard F. M. Rees, a graduate of the *TH* of Stuttgart, was 1970–73 Director, Technical, NASA-MSFC. In 1956–60, he was Deputy Dir., Developm. Operations Div., Army Ball. Miss. Agency. At the *XXIII. Raumfahrtkongress*, Dr. Reese talked on "Die Bedeutung des Skylab-Programms für die weitere Entwicklung der Raumfahrt."

16. Contributors (I/1): B. Spen. Isbell (Editor-In-Chief), R. E. Jennings, W. v. Braun (2), Fr. L. Whipple, E. Stuhlinger, D. M. Popper, E. W. Woolard, A. Howard, Jr., and Y. Lybrand; portrait study by A. L. Herrmann. G. Stanley Hall was Wundt's first American student.

15. Some Remarks About German-American Relations
Heinrich Meyer

If a young man wanted to speak of his own experiences, even in so personal a place as a Festschrift, he would no doubt be censored for being subjective and forgetting what a scholar ought to say. But time takes care of a great deal. As the young man gets older and finally old, as his own experiences become so to say historical because they are no longer those of the younger generations, subjective observations become documentary and therefore worthy of scholarly attention. When I came to this country in 1930 and still when I published my Texas-German novel, *Konrad Bäumlers weiter Weg,* in 1938, conditions and the general outlook on life, professional concerns and prospects, political and personal needs, economic advantages and difficulties were so enormously different that they are no longer clear to one's own mind unless one makes an effort to compare the nineteen thirties with the nineteen seventies. Just two examples. When I went to Washington in 1932 and visited the Library of Congress I received a pass to the entire library except for the rare book room, where the Volbehr collection was being housed. In roaming over the building, perhaps as the only such person, I ran into Charles Martell who was the original designer of the Library of Congress classification and who used to take me out for lunch every day and generally bought me a Partagas into the bargain. Cars were so rare yet in Washington that I was tempted to make a shortcut to the left where streets and avenues meet, and when a policeman blew the whistle and saw my Texas plate he waved me on and said "Hi, pardner, you are accustomed to the wide open spaces!"

The originator of the Union catalogue was another friend of those days. He had come as an immigrant and tried to make a living by printing calling cards in an alley. It occurred to him to see the Congressional Librarian and to suggest that the handwritten cards, which were still in my time the majority, be printed, and thus got something going which now can never end. His name was Ernest Kletsch, and I will never forget that he told me he used to sleep on park benches and in box cars and that, if I should get into such a situation, I should always collect enough old newspapers to cover myself against the cold. The Volbehr collection, incidentally, was a large collection of incunabula which the German book trade had brought together and which Congress authorized to purchase, which President Hoover signed into law as one of his last official acts. There have not been many such good bargains since. But then a postcard at the time cost 1 cent and a letter 2 cents, which indicates the rate of inflation we have since incurred. My salary as an instructor at Rice Institute, as it was called at that time when it was one of the richest universities and charged no tuition whatsoever, was $2,500, and the top salaries of H. A. Wilson, Radoslav A. Tsanoff, and Griffith C. Evans were between $7,000 and $8,000, which in purchasing power was easily above most professional incomes in the 1970s. And this was the time when I first came to know Karl Arndt.

At that time and for a while longer, one could quickly meet nearly all major professors of German at the Modern Language Association meetings, and one *did* meet them. There usually were but two or three in any department, and nobody found anything amiss when one of us, as I did in St. Louis in the midthirties, gave two talks at the meeting. One man could easily hear all talks and report about them in the *Monatshefte,* as Senn did about this meeting. The majority were on a *Du* basis, and these old personal relations remained alive. When I had what used to be called the "Meyer case" against the United States Government in a suit to revoke the citizenship of a non-native, things had changed a good deal. But Arndt, who was about to leave for an assignment in Europe, caused Louisiana State University to offer me his professorship temporarily until his return. Having just settled down in Pennsylvania to put *Organic Gardening* on a more reputable base, I had to refuse the offer, but I ought perhaps to mention that it was the only such offer which then reached me. Since the case was, of course, recorded when it was decided by Joseph C. Hutcheson, Jr. of the Fifth Circuit in my favor, I need not dwell on it, although it would form a very interesting aspect of German-American rela-

tions of a certain kind. But the case brings me back to the ante-
cedents which will be the chief content of this contribution: what
was it in the first place that brought a young Germanist to this
country at that time?

I will first tell of my own case and then take up that of another
young man, a Swiss student, who came to the United States around
the time of the war between the states and left a most absorbing
record of his sojourn in California and Nevada. As my psychology,
if that is what we can call it, was not much different from his, the
distance of 1975 from 1930 as well as from 1865 becomes even
more noticeable, and this is after all what this little essay attempts
to illustrate in order that the currently young and those whom this
may reach later have at least some guide for understanding the not
so distant and recent past.

It must seem fantastic to a contemporary student that a young
man of twenty-four, as I was when I was first offered the instruc-
torship at Rice in 1928, would be so uninformed about America
that he more or less assumed it to be on the whole the country of
Sealsfield, Gerstäcker, Ruppius, Pajeken, etc. Most likely, even
today the first two names came to the knowledge of German boys
as authors of children's versions of America books, but I still read
them in the original editions together with the novels of Balduin
Möllhausen which had kept appearing till the time of my birth,
though Möllhausen had started in the days of Alexander Humboldt, who wrote an introduction to his first great book and whose
secretary and heir became Möllhausen's father-in-law. After all, it
must be remembered that life and customs in my childhood hardly
differed from those of 1840 or, for that matter—at least for those
who lived in the country—from those of 1740. It was the ordinary
church-bound outlook, largely pre-industrial. Even as electrically
minded a city as Nürnberg, where Schuckert had developed the
electromotor industry, was only then starting to instal a few
Bogenlampen, while a man with a fuse on a pole went about to
light the gas lamps in the street. In our house we still used a
petroleum lamp, and candles for the other rooms when needed.
And telephones, cars, aeroplanes were altogether new. We had seen
the first Zeppelin with the same awe as Halley's comet and found
it most amusing when our neighbor, Professor Gradl, acquired a

car and loaded it with his painting utensils and started cranking it until finally it got going. The first aeroplane moved me to tears when it flew over the *Stadtpark* across from us in about 1914, so unusually shaking was this human achievement then. Thus it is not surprising that I more or less assumed—for I can hardly say that I thought about it at all—that the United States would be on the whole somewhat like the country Cooper, Sealsfield, Gerstäcker, Ruppius, Pajeken, and even Karl May depicted. The *Karl-May-Jahrbuch* of that day, edited by the father of the present director of the Karl May Verlag (whom everybody came to be aware of as the chess referee in the Spassky-Fisher match in Iceland), used to have pictures of the Rocky Mountains, including "Mount Winetou." We assumed therefore that such a mountain existed and that, accordingly, most of the Winetou story would be pretty close to reality too.

I had, of course, passed beyond my early childhood plans when the reading of Gerstäcker's *Jagd- und Streifzüge* suggested that I might as well provide for my own future in America by laying in a powder horn, a bullet mold, and a rifle, but the underlying urge to come to America was undiminished just the same and thus remained tinged with an utterly unrealistic romanticism as to what America would be like. Emigrating to Texas meant, as quite a few well-meaning contemporaries told me, a rough life for which I had best buy a six-shooter at the earliest opportunity. In fact, I often stood in front of a gun shop and wished I had the money to buy one, as it were, *auf Vorrat*. It then turned out to be quite different, of course, but strangely enough there was still enough of the pre-industrial America left, especially during the depth of the Depression, to make it quite easy for me to collect actual data about events a generation before, some of which I put into my novel.

A few figures in it are by no means fictional, and the descendant of one of these, Dr. Engelhardt, made it a point to secure copies of this book for his children. Incidentally my pen-name was partly calculated to make the unwary Germans under Hitler think of *Houston* Stewart Chamberlain and thus to be induced to buy the book in which I made front against racism by transposing matters back to early Texas days. But—again a sign how close the ties with the past still were—the descendants of Sam Houston, among them Mrs. G. C. Evans, wife of the distinguished mathematician mentioned above, did not like the taking in vain of the hallowed fore-bear by *H. K. Houston Meyer*. Neither did they like to hear of Houston's life among the Cherokees, to be sure. As I have told before, my novel was not submitted to the Reichsschrifttums-kammer, because Dr. Kilpper, the director of the Deutsche Ver-lags-Anstalt, readily saw that it did not fall under German law, as it was not written by a German nor translated into German. Re-ferring to my propaganda purpose and to actual data is not to sug-gest at all that the book is documentary. In fact, most of it is freely invented, and the hunchback in it owes his origin to Charles Laughton in the part of Quasimodo of Notre Dame, just as the charming French girl to whom my hero was married, derived from Mrs. Hodges, wife of a cherished friend and colleague at Rice. Yet if all is looked at and found, Joe Gallegly at Rice was perhaps closer to the old West, whose life he led and lore he preached, than any other contemporary except possibly the fellow Oklahoman of Hodges, Will Rogers.

With these background facts and reminiscences before us or rather behind us, I must say a word about Sealsfield, the subject of Arndt's life-long, though not exclusive studies. Not only did I in my childhood dislike Sealsfield (though *Der Kampf ums Block-haus* was one of the early stories I read), but I never was able to feel that he described real people. At any rate, whatever little Sealsfield may have had to do with my wanting to go to America, he had nothing to do with my wanting to stay here. None of this is meant to disparage the critical edition of Arndt, but I hope that sooner or later one of his or my students will discover the much richer opportunities, barely touched by Preston A. Barba, my one-time predecessor at Muhlenberg, which Möllhausen offers. How many of his sketches are still at the Smithsonian? I wonder. How do the later romantic versions of his novels compare with the earlier factual reports about the dislocation of the Indians through the white man's incursions? How does his picture compare with the pictures others drew earlier and later? How for instance does the Hubert Howe Bancroft series, which incidentally served me in good stead for my novel (as did a five-volume set, *Texas and the Texans*) relate events which the German visitors and travelers record in their works? No doubt, Bancroft and his inestimable collections in California record much of the regional history in minute detail, but they are after all "rough data," as the current term has it, and not necessarily adequate as a reflection of the total social reality. How, for example, would we weigh the fictional California of Bret Harte against the picture which Bancroft and his collaborators developed on the basis of records? This has puzzled me ever since I used Bancroft and others for atmosphere and data, but I have come to an answer only now and therefore have undertaken this paper.

At the time when Hemmann Hoffmann came to this country, no German Swiss would have objected to being included under the title of this essay; and even today most writers in German, born in Switzerland, appear in the history of German literature, so that Switzerland never had to set up a professorship for Swiss letters in the United States. But the fact remains worth emphasizing that Hemmann Hoffmann is a Swiss and I am glad of it, for I could turn to a Swiss librarian and get some help. Dr. Salfinger, of the Öffentliche Bibliothek der Universität Basel, who has often helped me most generously, again came to my assistance with extracts and copies of articles, from which the following facts are taken: "Mitten im Kränzewinden auf das große Schützenfest 1844 wurde uns ein gesunder Knabe geschenkt, den wir zum Andenken an das Ereignis Hemmann tauften," is the first pertinent fact, taken from an autobiography of Hemmann's father, Theodor Hoffmann-Merian, edited by Alfred Altherr in Basel 1889. Dr. Salfinger adds for our information that the name alludes to Hemmann Sevogel, "der Oberhauptmann der Basler, der in der glorreichen Schlacht bei St. Jakob 1444 fiel; das Schützenfest war gleichzeitig die Jahrhundertfeier jener Schlacht." The death notice in the *Basler Nachrichten* tells us that Hoffmann was active in the insurance business, in church activities and all kinds of good works, had five children of whom one lived till 1940 in California, and died in 1904. The book he wrote must have been quite successful, for Dr. Salfinger found three editions mentioned: 1871, 1874, 1879. (I own the first edition: *Californien, Nevada und Mexico. Wanderungen eines Polytechnikers.* Basel. Schweighauserische Verlagsbuchhandlung 1871. IV, 428 pages.)

The family was obviously well off, for when young Hemmann received a letter from a relation in California, inviting him to come over and take up the position the cousin was giving up for another, his father accompanied him to Le Havre in a first class compartment. This was on January 16, 1864, and the young *Polytechniker* listed the temperature as 16° Reaumur below zero (-4° F), and gives his first character portrait when he says: "Wir saßen in Pelz und Wolldecken behaglich eingehüllt im Ersten-Class-Coupé." Even at 4 below zero he is comfortable in an unheated train. The charm of his report is that whatever happens he is always comfortable and at peace with the world. As a student of technology he was much impressed by the powerful engine of the Bremen steamer *Amerika* which worked with 800 HP and required thirty-one men to service. It is amusing to find his description of New York, where he had relatives who showed him around, but we will not stop to report about it. It seems to me that the book might well be translated and sold with considerable success, especially if illustrated with contemporary material. He took a boat in New York and sailed south, "nichts bemerkend von dem blutigen Bruderkampf, der in gleicher Breite am Festland tobte." They evade all other ships, land in Aspinwall, and cross the Panamanian area by train. Everything is described in lively detail, just as Hubert Howe Bancroft described his crossing at an earlier date, only that Hoffmann is a businessman and technician and can report about the financing and the organization of the companies and their work, but he is just as open to the wonders of the tropical nature which, of course, was all wonderfully new to him.

There were adventures of all sorts, like being stopped in mid-ocean by a ship of the same line, and then having to undergo a search because it had been reported that they carried seditionists on board. Finally he arrives in San Francisco, March 12, rents a wooden cabin and equips himself appropriately, but the promised opening in an assay office did not materialize, because the cousin did not give up his own position. For the speculations he had engaged in had failed. Of course, we get again a thorough picture of San Francisco, the work of an assayer, the composition of the population, and thus learn, for example, that the Spanish element was still distinguished or that the Indians worked as peaceful people among the whites, etc. He is a good observer: "An Sonntagen wird in der Regel zwischen 11 und 1 Uhr sogenannter Gottesdienst gehalten, ferner Abends von 8 bis 11 Uhr; diese Abend-gottesdienste sind die besuchteren, man geht dahin anstatt in's Concert oder in's Theater." But when the cousin defaulted, he took the steamer to Sacramento on May 6, furious about being not even seen off: "Nun wußte ich, daß ich allein in der Welt stand und daß ich auf Niemanden hier, als auf mich selbst angewiesen sei. Dabei plagte mich einigermaßen das Gewissen, denn ich handelte der bestimmten Vorschrift meines lieben Vaters ganz zuwider; er hatte mir verboten nach den Minen zu gehen und mir anbefohlen, bei irgend welchen Widrigkeiten auszuharren und seine Hülfe in Anspruch zu nehmen." Having seen many return from the mines, derelict and miserable, he had no illusions whatsoever about a fortune in California, but was easily distracted by a lady who had accompanied a friend and overlooked the signal and thus was still on board when the ship was well under way. He found her desperation so amusing that he was able to see his own situation in a more cheerful frame of mind.

Arrived in Sacramento, he has barely time to get on a train, then in the mailcoach, day after day, unable to talk because of the horrible noise of the coaches, pulled by six horses over the most miserable roads. "Anfänglich war unser Vehikel ordentlich vollgepfropft mit zwölf unglücklichen Passagieren, Herren und Damen, die sich zwischen ihre Koffern(!), Nachtsäcke und Schachteln so gut einducken mußten, als es eben ging. Man mußte gezwungen in derjenigen Position verharren, in welche man beim Einsteigen versetzt wurde; es brauchte ein langes Studium, um mit Marter und Mühe einmal ein Glied rühren zu können." But finally they reach Placerville, then Carson and Silver City, "eine Bretterstadt, die wie ein hinausgeworfenes Kartenspiel, planlos und verworren durch das Hochthal zerstreut liegt." Then on to Virginia, "dem damaligen Hauptort von Nevada-Territory.—Virginia war schon eine sehr ansehnliche Stadt, mit allen Schöpfungen der Civilisation ausgestattet, steinerne Häuser, Kirchen, Collegien, Theater, größere industrielle Werke, aller Art Geschäftshäuser, alles nagelneu, als hätte man die ganze Stadt in einer Nürnberger Schachtel hierher gebracht und in diesem Gebirgsthale aufgestellt." But the mail coach moves on, and only three passengers are left. All stages are registered day after day, and in fifty-eight hours he spent 125 miles on a steamer, 22 on the railroad and 334 miles in the mail coach, to arrive on May 10, 1864 in Austin, Nevada.

It may be time to stop for a moment and look up Austin in Bancroft's works. Volume XXV contains the history of Nevada, Colorado, and Wyoming (San Francisco, 1890). We find there that in April, 1863 a hotel, newspaper, and post office were added to the new city, that a pony express was started for the various mines, and that Wells Fargo and Co. established an express office, which in 1865 carried treasure from the mines to the tune of $6,000,000. Three banking houses were in operation. "Men of the learned professions flocked there, and Austin was that anomaly of modern times, a city in the midst of a wilderness, grown up like a mushroom, in a night. It was incorporated in 1875, and disincorporated in 1881." The man whom Hemmann met is, however, not mentioned by Bancroft. He was the superintendent of the Reese-River-Mines and lived in a dwelling which is described as half house, half cave. "Ich glaubte eher vor Reineckes Palast—Malepartus—zu stehen, als vor demjenigen des Superintendenten der hochgepriesenen Reese-River-Minen. Dieser Mr. Roberts, ein stämmiger, bärtiger, gesunder Amerikaner aus dem Staate Maine gebürtig, hieß mich willkommen, nahm von meinem Introductions-schreiben Kenntnis und musterte mich vom Kopf bis zum Fuß.—Seine erste Frage war: 'Bringen Sie Geld mit von der Company in San Francisco?' Als ich dies verneinte, zogen dichte Wolken über seine Stirne und das Gewitter fand seine Entladung in einem derben Fluche." The cousin, of course, had failed to provide the wages, and what was most puzzling: why had he sent him on this expensive expedition to mines which obviously were to be abandoned?

"Doch mein Entschluß war bald gefaßt, tüchtig die Arbeit anzupacken, wo sie sich finde und Mr. Roberts wacker an die Hand zu gehen. Trotz ihrem wirschen und rohen Äußeren sind die Leute in den Minen in der Regel tüchtige Kerls, die das Herz am rechten Fleck haben. Sie machen zwar wenig Complimente und gehen ihren eintönigen Weg, sind aber dabei zum größten Theil von einer kindlichen Treuherzigkeit, von der man in den großen Städten keinen Begriff hat."

Hemmann thus settles down and stays with Mr. Roberts in the one-room cave-cabin which was all at once kitchen, dining room, bedroom, office, and "salon." The detailed description follows. We have reached page 66 and 360 more to go. I hope the reader will be enticed by these excerpts to read on. Each page is equally goodnatured, fresh, alive, decent and rich in observations of the natural and social scene, of people and their activities and new enterprises. The news from the east about the progress of the war between north and south gives occasion for celebrations; and Hemmann's obvious practical gifts, and healthy activity made him a useful member of the frontier communities in which he managed to keep busy. He built breweries and acted as brewmaster, but he also bought mining shares, and even managed to pick sound ones so that at the end he comes off with a profit, although he barely survived the expedition in the end. For going home by way of Mexico he fell into a fever and might have died if he had not been placed into a hospital where Catholic sisters nursed him back, much amazed at his not being a "Christian" like themselves. Again a thirty-day ocean voyage, landing in France: "Ohne Aufenthalt setzte ich meine Reise bis nach Basel fort, wo ich am 15. Januar 1868 gegen acht Uhr Abends glücklich anlangte. Das Herz pochte mir allerdings laut genug, als ich vor den beleuchteten Fenstern meiner väterlichen Wohnung stand und die Klingel zog. Es war auf Jahr und Tag exact vier Jahre seit meiner Abreise. Meine kleine Schwester, die aber derweil groß geworden, öffnete mir die Thüre. 'Ist's möglich!' rief sie aus, und dann so laut sie es vermochte die Treppe hinauf: 'Der Hemmi isch do! Der Hemmi isch do!'—Eine Secunde später lag der vielgereiste Polytechniker glücklich in den Armen seines Vaters und seiner Schwestern." And herewith ends the report.

I hardly need to say more about the writer and his writing, which is so rich and so far above the fabrications, or whatever one wants to call the books, of Sealsfield that one might easily have thought that Hoffmann was a distinguished writer and Postl a mere amateur. But what is especially pleasant to me is the obvious fact that Hemmann Hoffmann was not only a very good writer, a very solid character, and a very fine observer, but that he was such a lovable man who flows over with good will and good cheer. When I had digested his report and used it in a seminar in comparison with similar reports and other texts by Möllhausen, Gerstäcker, Griesinger, Moritz Busch—best known for his books on Bismarck—and other *Gartenlaube* authors who had been in the United States and were continuing to write about it or from it, then I came away with a feeling that Hoffmann depicted the America I also had come to discover. And what is even more surprising, he depicted the same world and the same characters in the same spirit I had long since come to like and admire in Bret Harte. To be sure, he did not romanticize the holdupmen or the gamblers, but from where he was he probably did not see too much of this phase of life anyway. He was on the actual frontier, as the comparison between Bancroft's history and Hoffmann's diary must have indicated, and gamblers and such were not likely to make their appearance in such places where the amenities were slight and wealth only a prospect. As a document of history and as a piece of writing, Hoffmann's memoirs ought to be taken up by all who enjoy genuineness and the past of this country.

It is customary now to show one's superiority over one's forebears by finding them too "bürgerlich," too little ready for that great thing, Revolution or Anarchy, etc. It is accordingly only natural that one makes money from books which ridicule the past and find its literature funny or *kitschig.* A favorite is, of course, the "Familienblatt" *Die Gartenlaube.* Since I have mentioned it as a favorite source for German-American relations, 1 will conclude with a few remarks on this periodical which, in its time, was the most widely read magazine in the entire world. Those who regard it as too tame now must have been very careless in their scholarship, else they could not have missed the fact that its founder and editor, Ernst Keil, had constant trouble with the censor and was, in fact, one of the leading political forces of 1848 and German liberalism. The best essay about him is by the great Wilhelm Ritter von Hamm, a neighbor and friend of Liebig, who ended up as an Austrian administrator. He also gave the best report about Lasalle and about Gerstäcker, all to be found in *Gesammelte kleine Schriften,* herausgegeben von Dr. Leo Pribyl. 2. Band. Wien, Pest, Leipzig. Hartlebens Verlag 1881. Most or some of these essays had first appeared in the *Gartenlaube* and other periodicals. Why should the family be denigrated anyhow? But apart from current superiorities we must recall a few facts here.

When there was no energy shortage and no population explosion, when California ranked behind Alabama and Mississippi with a population of 1,485,053 and Florida had a mere 528,542, and the entire United States added up to only 76,149,386, which are the figures given for 1900, the family was not only the emotional and political and social basis of life, but also its economic foundation. With one kerosene lamp in the average house, the family would *have to* sit around the table and read or knit or talk. If they had the *Gartenlaube,* they had far more reliable and objective reports than any current weekly in German is offering today. But here we are not concerned with the extraordinary reporting job about wars abroad and visits with the great and the small, we would only point out that the *Gartenlaube* reached right into the midst of the war between the Russians and Turks and thus notified its correspondents through its own pages about its wishes. When someone looked for a relative in America or a lost parcel anywhere, he asked for help in the *Gartenlaube,* and more likely than not obtained it within a few weeks.

It must be remembered that at that time life proceeded decently and rather equitably. One got the mail to Europe in a week and not in six weeks, which it now requires, and the kings could move about trustingly without having to fear kidnapers or assassins. The few attempted assassinations in the civilized countries were regarded as a professional hazard, as King Umberto of Italy once said: "Sono gli incerti del mestiere" (those are the hazards of the métier of being a king). But we saw our kings and crown princes and liked them and were sure they did not waste taxes like our bureaucrats who always start with getting new offices set up for themselves. The kings were so trusting that Ludwig of Bavaria could not even get away when the revolution broke until the tires were fixed on the one available car. Whether this is a mere function of a thinner population or reveals a different moral and social standing of all may remain a question. But if one wanted to find out what other parts of the world were like, one could look at the *Gartenlaube* and get reports from experts and suitable wood engravings to illustrate the scenery.

This is where authors like Gerstäcker, Moritz Busch, and such come in. To mention at random a few such articles I open a few volumes. The 1877 edition has four pages about Buffalo Bill, because the previous year had contained an article about the massacre on the Little Bighorn, several articles about Lasalle, and another on Cornelius Vanderbilt dated from New York. Vanderbilt had just died in his eightieth year. Moritz Busch, who wrote about

Bismarck during the war, also gave his recollections about the Mormons; someone else describes an afternoon in Philadelphia; others report about their investigations and controlled experiments with spiritist figures. The number of smaller items on America is also considerable. The next year contains the first publication of the famous life of Robert Blum by Hans Blum, unbeknown to our great literary critics of *Bürgertum* and *Familienpusselei*. This time Moritz Busch writes about Lothar Bucher, whom some called "Bismarcks rechte Hand" and who had gone to England when the government sentenced him for his political opinions in 1848. Other topics concerning America include: Bayard Taylor; a report about birds in Illinois, monasteries in Mexico; tramps; pilgrim fathers; the "Allgemeine deutsche Unterstützungsgesellschaft" in San Francisco; American horses; the heating of Lockport, N.Y.; the technicalities of American newspaper publishing and selling; a German-American invention for pianists. The heirs of one Heinrich Agethen who died in San Francisco are being sought through the good offices of the *Gartenlaube* as well. Just in passing, a piece of "Lebenserinnerungen einer Matrone" tells of an evening with Thackeray. Among the American reporters appears Theodor Kirchhoff, who had emigrated there and died in San Francisco in 1899. He tells of social life, gambling, etc. in the 1880 volume, which moreover contains articles on presidential elections, oil wells, German labor associations in America, and much else, and, by the way, also the history of the *Sozialdemokratie* by Mehring, which had been started the year before. In 1900, Cronau writes about the Galveston disaster and about the Palatinate victory on the Mohawk (1757), but, on the whole, Africa and China were now in the news more than America. So it would be easy to make a list of the *Gartenlaube's* contributions to German-American understanding.

When I wrote my novel, I was told by those who had experienced those years in this country that a great change in outlook toward Germany came in the mid-nineties when English propaganda became more and more violent about the unwelcome competitor and new colonial rival. This must have escaped the visiting professors as well as most of those already settled in American universities. It probably did not become manifest as yet in the university environment which only recently had adopted the

German patterns. But then visiting professors always see the hosts in a more rosy light than those in less glamorous positions. This is no doubt one reason for the relative dullness of most of the books written by bright and even prominent professors, who wrote of their days in America at that time. They all offer the same general vague impressions and hardly get behind the surface, but again this is a theme which much deserves further investigation.

It may be appropriate to conclude with a few more personal recollections by *this* professor. When I came to Rice, it had about 1500 students. The President had one secretary, the Registrar and Bursar each had three assistants, the Dean was the American historian and later ambassador to Portugal and Bolivia, Caldwell, who had only office hours a few times a week and no secretary. Neither did any department have clerical help. Rice was surely not burdened with administrative personnel and expense. When I took the trip to Washington I mentioned before I stopped one afternoon at Duke University to see what the German Department there was doing. I came to a wooden building and asked the first man I saw. "I am the German Department," said he, "I am Dean Wanamaker." We chatted a little, then he suggested that I meet President Few, who had got the money from the Dukes on which the college was to be expanded into a university. I was a young fellow of twenty-eight, but the President seemed not to mind this at all; he showed me around in person and had me admire the chapel, which I seem to recollect as the only major structure then standing. It would hardly be possible for a casual visitor today to have such easy access to such important people as university presidents nor would they feel free to dangle their long legs like Dr. Few and to chat about their success as money-raisers to a complete stranger. "What will you do if I now go and tell Doris Duke?" I asked him even then, and he grinned and said: "I'd say you were a liar."

German-American relations have many more facets, of course, than I have here been able to list, but since some of mine struck me as interesting and characteristic of the last time when America was free and easy, I have put them down for the record.

16. The Case for German-American Literature
Robert E. Ward

One might not expect that a history of any body of literature requires a defense before it is to be written. Yet such is the matter before us. Whereas European scholars have long recognized the importance of studying German *Auslandsliteratur,* American scholars have been content to interpret and reinterpret, in a fashion bordering on literary-historical chauvinism, only those bodies of literature which represent the official language of other nations and provinces. French-Canadian literature has received ample treatment, and Mexican and Chicano writings currently enjoy the attention of literary scholars. Yet German-American literature, which represents the largest body of non-English North American literature, has received only scant treatment.[1]

This gap in the history of foreign language literature produced on the North American continent is no doubt due in part to the propensity among literary historians to opt for the *dulce* and *utile* in the literary art. Their preference is thus for the genius of the great masters such as Goethe and Schiller, rather than works which perhaps have more cultural significance for the study of social, political, religious, and economic phenomena than to art for its own sake. Bound up in his partiality for aesthetics and value judgments as to what is "humanely useful" and humanistically significant, the American literary historian, most notably the Germanist, has, through arrogance, ignorance, or indifference, turned away from German-American literature.

Thus, it has remained for the cultural historian and ethnic studies specialist to sort out from the huge storehouse of American literature in the German language those works which best serve his investigative purpose. While so doing, he has made a strong case for various classes of German-American literature, e.g., historical and theological works, philosophical and political treatises, ethnographic essays and travel sketches, and biographies and autobiographies. But German-American imaginative or creative literature remains largely untapped. To this class of literature belong the many poems, plays, novels, novellas, and short stories which, although not frontrunners in literary style and stylistics, embody an aesthetic which values the particularized investigation of human behavior as an end in itself.

German-American poetry and prose fiction represent attitudes toward experience which are literary manifestations of the philosophies of self-determination and self-development. As such, they form with varying degrees of intensity differing literary consequences which are dependent upon the historical circumstances of America as a whole, and German-America as one of its parts. Professors Wellek and Warren maintain that it is the business of the literary historian to interpret the devices (e.g., symbols, metaphors, myths, metonymy) of the poet, dramatist, or novelist, since it is through them that suggestion is turned to definition.[2]

And what of the philological aspects of German-American literature? Is it not a breach of duty on the part of American Germanists to fail to assist the sociologist, the cultural historian, and the ethnologist to whom the subtle nuances and dialectal peculiarities of the novelist or poet may be of great importance?

It is clear that German-American literature has a four-fold significance. In one sense, it can be considered as an extension of the literary activity of German-speaking mother countries produced on foreign soil. In this perspective, then, it has profound import for the study of German literature itself. Secondly, the study of German-American literature will reveal and document the subtle ways in which German-American writers exert influence on their contemporaries and possibly on their literary confrères who wrote in English. Thirdly, the influence of English-language American writers on their German-American literary confrères presents a contrast that has considerable significance for the study of cross-cultural relations in American literary and philosophical thought. And lastly, the investigation of the literary products of the two distinctive types of German-American writers, namely those born abroad and those born here, will reveal an important chapter in the history of foreign cultural phenomena and their influence in America. A certain by-product of a comprehensive investigation of

German-American literature is the discovery of writings which might become an effective tool in motivating the American student to choose the German language as part of his educational curriculum. There is certainly no harm in exposing the American student to some of the grammatically and structurally correct German-American literary works and to the fact that the German language, spoken by millions of Americans since the seventeenth century, is not foreign to the American environment.

Since the main task is to study and interpret the creative expression of all German-language writers who have carried on the German and the American literary traditions on United States soil, our definition of a *German-American* must eschew considerations of U.S. citizenship or even long-term residence. A German-American writer, then, is that person who composed literature in the German language while residing in the United States, or who writes of his experiences there.

It is not difficult to make a case for German-American literature if one views it simply as *Auslandsliteratur* or *Trivialliteratur* as has generally been done by European literary historians. But our thesis is that the study of German-American literature is of greater significance when viewed as the literary expression of the carriers of German traditions, customs, and attitudes in the United States. Thus, the scope of German-American literature takes on even greater horizons. The argument may then be proffered that the definition of this body of writing should be expanded to include the English-language works of German-speaking immigrants and their descendants who have maintained ties to the German ethnic community. Ancillary jurisdiction may then be had on *all* works, irrespective of language and the author's personal ties to the German heritage. Indeed, a great many of the German-American writers also wrote creative works in English. There are also several German-American immigrants and descendants of German-speaking immigrants who wrote wholly or predominantly in English, e.g., Herman Hagedorn and Theodore Dreiser. If our definition is thus broadened to include English-language works, it must be limited to certain types of writing. The question is, where does one draw the line?

Since German-American literary works in the German language have not been comprehensively studied and by virtue of linguistics are easily identifiable, it appears expeditious and desirable to focus our efforts on a history of German-American literature in the German language. It is for this reason that we shall confine our present discussion to such works only. Our qualified definition, then, of German-American literature must exclude the once popular "scrapple English" writings of Charles Follen Adams, Kurt Stein, and others, which are only imitative of German.

The author of this essay has compiled bio-bibliographical data on some 3,000 writers of German-language imaginative or creative literature in the United States since the latter part of the seventeenth century.[3] Approximately 5 percent of them were born and raised in the United States, and nearly 6 percent of them were children when they came to this country. Thus, some 11 percent of the writers investigated have had substantially little personal contact with non-American German-speaking settlements and countries. The total number of works composed by all German-American writers in this study exceeds 30,000, excluding the thousands of literary products which have appeared in German-language periodicals here and abroad.[4] German-American literature is also to be found in hundreds of anthologies, including at least 60 which are wholly or mainly German-American.[5]

To attempt to categorize German-American literature according to schools or movements would be premature at this point, since relatively few works have been carefully studied. A prodigious approach to such categorization would be to compare the schools and movements of both German and American literature with those discerned in German-American literature. Zimmermann, Jockers, and Spuler divide German-American literature into characteristic periods.[6] Their brief surveys conclude that there is continuity of periods, but that movements and schools do not exist. This thesis should be tested, for so much German-American literature remains to be studied that any conclusion regarding periods, schools, or movements must be tentative at the present.

Professor Pochmann has outlined the development of German-American literary prose and poetry.[7] His thesis is that the prose must be analyzed in its stages of development, from simple letters or reminiscences of the early immigrants to memoirs and histories, followed by polemics, then stories, followed by novels and plays. The epic poetry should also be considered in this light. It should be apparent from the discussion that follows here that such a clear-cut division is not appropriate. We can, however, agree with Pochmann's theory that the lyric poetry appears to have its roots in the early hymnals and the folksong tradition of the German-speaking colonists of seventeenth-century America.

The first major representative author of German-American imaginative prose and poetry was Franz Daniel Pastorius, leader of the Germantown, Pennsylvania settlement, who composed German works there as early as 1690. His poem, *Gegen die Negersklaverei* is one of the earliest protests against involuntary servitude in the colonies. The mystic Johannes Kelpius wrote German hymns and religious poetry at his Pennsylvania wilderness retreat as early as 1694, and J. Conrad Beissel became one of America's most prolific seventeenth-century mystics and hymnists. Under Beissel's direction, the Ephrata Community in Pennsylvania became the center for German Protestant monasticism in America and for original hymns and choral music in the colonies. The poem *Das Raben-Geschrey,* was composed in 1776 by Andreas Schneeberger, mystic and founder of the Snowhill Monastic Society. The major work of the Harmony Society (1785–1847) contains hymns whose style is tinged with mysticism. Hymnals are the major contribution of the various religious groups of this early period, especially the Mennonites, Dunkers, Schwenkfelders, Lutherans, and Moravians.

The seventeenth and eighteenth centuries are also marked by the publication of travel books and sketches containing poetic descriptions of the American landscape and relating the conditions in the American colonies and settlements. A handful of poetry is to be found in the German-American newspapers, almanacs, and calendars, ranging from doggerel verse to odes and ballads. Of particular interest are the poems by the Hessians and other German-speaking mercenaries as well as those by German-Americans among Washington's troops. Patriotic recruiting poems, and works celebrating General Washington and the American struggle for independence, and moralizing and satirical maxims abound. In 1729, Georg Michael Weiss' *In der Americanischen Wildnüss* appeared. This work represents the first tract by a Reformed minister in America. From 1741 to 1743, Count Nikolaus Ludwig von Zinzendorf (pseuds.: Bruder Ludwig; Ordinarius Frater; Ludwig von Thurnstein) authored hundreds of German verses on American themes. After arriving in America in 1741, Johann Christopher Friedrich Cammerhof became the creator of the "blood and wound" imagery in Moravian poetry. Another notable poet of this period is Justus H. C. Helmuth whose hymns and elegiac verses rank among the best of the eighteenth century. In the 1750s, Dr. Abraham Wagner translated Latin, Greek, and Bohemian works into German. Considered the most significant of the Schwenkfelder poets, Wagner carried on a correspondence with Tersteegen. An important translation of J. T. V. Braght's influential work was done by Johann Heinrich Müller (Henry Miller, J. H. Miller).

Translations were made of Thomas Paine's writings and other patriotic and political works during the Revolutionary War period. Significantly, Johann Peter Müller (also known as Peter Miller and Bruder Jaebez) translated the Declaration of Independence into German at the request of the Continental Congress. It was published in a Philadelphia German newspaper before the English original was printed in the local press.

The period following the War for Independence through the first three decades of the nineteenth century is marked by religious didacticism and concern for the effects of the war and the question of statehood. The major works are hymnals, lyric poetry, and non-fictive prose. Some of the themes treated by writers of this period are the plight of the redemptionists, slaves and Indians, public hangings, epidemics and disease, the emergence of new industries, the hard winters suffered by the settlers, the exploitation of children, and the New England bias against the foreign element.

Late eighteenth-century dramatizations were performed by members of the Mosheimsche Gesellschaft. Published in Göttingen in 1781, the anonymous play, *Der hessische Officier* appears to have been written by someone who had been in America during the revolutionary period. Probably the first plays written by a German-American are the tragedies and comedies of Gustav Anton Freiherr von Seckendorff (pseud.: Patrick Peale) which appeared shortly after the turn of the century. Also popular during the early 1800s were Seckendorff's romances and poems.

As a result of the reprisals following the Wartburgfest and the Hambacher Fest, many political émigrés came to America's shores.

They were soon followed by the Forty-Eighters. Whereas German-American literature had been chiefly the child of the seventeenth- and eighteenth-century mystics and Protestant religious sects, its growth and popularity now was largely dependent on *Die Grauen* and *Die Grünen,* most of whom had university educations and experience in writing.[8] Not a few of these political radicals and exiles were journalists and editors of German-language periodicals. With their arrival, the German-American press ceased being a step-child. Aside from the ever popular hymnals and religiodidactic tracts, most of the writings of the first half-century appeared in German-American periodicals. Thereafter the publication of German-American writings in book form thrived, reaching its peak at the close of the century.

In the 1830s, Charles Sealsfield's (real name: Karl Anton Postl) German-American works originated the German transatlantic and exotic novel. Friedrich Gerstäcker's stories appeared in the late 1840s. But few of the other early nineteenth-century German-American prosaists, e.g., Karl Follen, Klemens Hammer, Franz Lieber, Wilhelm Wagner, chose this genre. In 1850, August Gläser, J. M. Reinhard, and N. Schmitt published the anonymous novel, *Die Geheimnisse von Philadelphia.* Like Eugène Sue's earlier *Mystères de Paris* (1842–43) it served as the model for a number of urban mystery novels.[9]

Often called the "German Cooper," Heinrich Balduin Möllhausen was probably the most widely read German-American novelist of the 1860s and 1870s with his adventure tales and travel books. Otto Ruppius was famous for his treatment of the German greenhorn in America, and Friedrich Armand Strubberg (pseud.: Armand; Farnwald) became popular for his sensational novels and stories appealing to youth. The frontier, Wild West adventures, the lonesome prairie, the Indian, and the gold prospector were popular themes in the writings of hundreds of minor German-American authors as well, including several who settled or were raised in Texas.[10]

The emigration novel enjoyed popularity both here and abroad. Its predecessor was the travel book which had considerable influence on German emigration to the New World. Although generally written in a journalistic fashion, many travel books and sketches of the late eighteenth and early nineteenth centuries contain beautifully written passages which border on creative literature. A notable emigration novel of this period is Karl Ludwig Haeberlin's (pseud.: H. E. R. Belani) *Die Auswanderer nach Texas* (1841). Novelist Georg Asmusen is recognized for his beautiful travel sketches, and poet Karl de Haas for his *Nordamerika, Wisconsin. Winke für Auswanderer* (1846), a book which is credited with greatly promoting emigration to that state. Therese Albertine Louise Robinson's (pseud.: TALVJ) popular short story, *Die Auswanderer* (1852) appeared in English translation in 1853.

Ethnographic sketches and stories also enjoyed a vogue among German-American and German readers, particularly in the latter half of the nineteenth and early twentieth centuries. Gustav Brühl (pseud.: Kara Giorg) was a prolific writer of ethnological works, and was equally at home in poetry about Mexico, Central America, and America's primeval forests. Malvina Doris Elisabeth Lampadius (pseud.: Gretchen Licht) published studies and lectured widely on the American Negro and Indian. Southern planters and their mulatto mistresses are frequent characters in the works of this period. The defenseless Negro slave is often the subject of cruelty on the part of his own race, usually a Negro overseer who vents his desire for revenge for his own mistreatment and societal alienation on other members of his race.

The German-American characters are generally depicted as friends and defenders of the Negro. They are characterized as free of racial prejudice toward the Negro and Indian, and the intolerance of their Anglo-American contemporaries forges a common bond among the German immigrant and other minority groups.[11] Another recurring theme of German-American prose fiction is the exotic European or Creolean appreciation for music, literature, and the fine arts in contrast to the Anglo-American lack of aesthetic sense and preoccupation with materialism.

The Civil War is also a frequent theme of late nineteenth-century fiction. In addition to fictive works which generally favor the North over the South, a substantial body of Civil War memoirs exists. Friedrich Adolph Harter's *Erinnerungen aus dem amerikanischen Bürgerkriege* (1895) was a best seller. Edmund Märklin's *In Sattel und Meeresgrund* (1880) is recognized as one of the best written books of Civil War memoirs. A common theme of the memoir-novel is the political background of the Forty-Eighter and his trials and tribulations in America. In *Hierarchie und Aristo-kratie,* Friedrich Hassaurek (pseud.: Heinrich Fiedler) relates his longing for Vienna and states in his preface that this work was expressly written for German-Americans whom he wishes to give a true picture of the social conditions that led to the Revolution of 1848. Several of the themes identified by Condoyannis have considerable currency with those of contemporary American authors: trials of a suspect in prison for months or years awaiting due process of law, the police spy system, and the evils of a ponderous bureaucracy.[12] Hassaurek's hero is the people of Vienna. The collective hero is a common device in the early fictive works of the Forty-Eighters.

Condoyannis also points to the Sunday blue laws and Jesuit intrigue as common themes in German-American fiction. Emil Klauprecht's German-American characters are convinced that the Catholic Church wants to dominate the world and that its priests go to great lengths to get their hands on legacies. Irish Catholics and Jewish characters are also frequent targets in German-American prose fiction.

The concern of German-American fiction writers of the nineteenth-century for minute details of physical appearance and landscapes, and their stress on the past life and ancestors of their characters (especially the exotic types) are reminiscent of the continental German writers of Poetic Realism. Although Klauprecht, Hassaurek, Adolf Douai, and others lack the poetic prose talent of Theodor Storm or Adalbert Stifter, like these great regionalists, they ask us to accept their characters' often implausible actions. German-American fictional characters are frequently poorly drawn and lack shading.

Some of the recurring characters of nineteenth-century German-American fiction are the pioneer clergyman, the hunter, the rancher, the swindler, the entrepreneur, and American and German-American historical personages. Perhaps the most frequent stock character is the incompetent immigrant who is unequal to the struggle for existence imposed on him in the American environment. Closely allied to this character is the figure of the German-speaking immigrant who tries to hide his origin.[13] Another recurring theme is the failure of marriages between Germans and other nationalities in America. Sealsfield and Strubberg make use of the conflict-of-nationalities theme, and the Anglo-American contempt for foreigners is frequently met in Klauprecht's works.

An extremely popular figure among the fiction writers is the detective. In addition to the urban mystery novels, German-American imitations of the dime detective thrillers became quite popular during the latter half of the nineteenth and the early part of the twentieth centuries, especially those written by F. G. Ahrens, Karl Alfred Theodor Alisat, Philipp Berges, and Rudolf Lexow.

Sketches of German-American city life remained popular through the nineteenth and early twentieth centuries, and were largely drawn by liberal writers, e.g., Johann Rittig, Caspar Stürenberg, and Adolf Schaffmeyer. The conservatives, on the other hand, were more conditioned by their rural environment which, according to Condoyannis, was usually a church-dominated community. The social tendency of German-American prose fiction is appropriately represented by the writings of political emigrés, e.g., Douai, Mathilde Anneke, Reinhold Solger, Willibald Winckler, Samuel Ludvigh, and scores of Forty-Eighters and those exiles who fled Germany after the passage of the strict anti-Socialist laws in 1878. Although some of them underwent a political metamorphosis after arriving here, a number of them remained enthusiastic supporters of Karl Marx. Whereas the feuilleton and political pamphlet were their chief weapons, their political and social propaganda is discernible in their fictive and poetic works as well.

The nineteenth century was the great period of Turner poetry and essays. The original purpose of the Turners was to propagate socialism in America; later they concerned themselves chiefly with physical fitness, education, and the support of nationalism in the German fatherland. Their poetry generally exhibits a great love for Germany and disillusionment with the contemporary form of government there.[14] In their prose, the Turner writers dwell largely on American politics, slavery, socio-economic questions, and the "tyranny of organized religion." They are especially vehement in their attacks on the Catholic Church which opposed the Forty-Eighters' support for Lincoln. Ardent collectivists were also the backbone of the Freie Gemeinden, Freimännervereine, and Freidenkervereine whose representative writers attacked capitalism and promoted support for labor groups.

A major chapter of German-American literature is the conflict between the writings of the conservative-oriented religiodidactics and those of the liberals and far-leftists. Characteristic of both groups is their interest in relatively innocuous themes. The desire to entertain is characteristic of two major conservative fiction writers, Frank Grether and J. J. Messmer, both of whom strongly opposed socialism.

Another interesting topic to be studied when making a case for German-American literature is the influence and activity of the various religious publishing houses, especially in the areas of children's literature and the Victorian era writings for adults, e.g., the Wartburg Publishing House in Chicago, the Eden Publishing House, the Concordia Publishing House, and the Louis Lange Publishing Co.—all in St. Louis. The German publications of the Reformed Church's Deutsches Verlagshaus (later known as the Central Publishing House) in Cleveland and the Methodist Book Concern in Cincinnati were also widely circulated. A considerable body of non-religious literature was written by German-American pastors, priests, and rabbis, which should be treated in my comprehensive study of German-American literature.[15]

There were several prolific and influential women among the German-American writers of the last century. Mathilde Anneke, the wife of communist writer Fritz Anneke, wrote several novels and treatises in which she espoused radical causes. Therese Robinson, wife of a well-known scholar, wrote a great many novellas and short stories. She is perhaps best known for her treatise on McPherson's forgery of the ballads of the ancient bard, Ossian. Fernande Richter (pseud.: Edna Fern) was acclaimed as one of America's outstanding German writers in 1908. Her *Venusmärchen* (1898) blends German-American and other personages into a new and original form. A social activist, she was part of the circle that centered around the writer and reformist, Robert Reitzel. Part of the manuscript to her novel, *Dietrich in Amerika,* was printed in Michael Singer's periodical, *Der Zeitgeist,* and was suppressed during the First World War. Lotte Leser won a prize for her German-American humoresque, *Wie Peter Miffert "nein" sagen lernte,* and was well-known for her novellas, plays, and articles on German-American literature.

Therese Robinson was also noted for her historical writings. There were several nineteenth- and early twentieth-century authors whose historical works are of significance to any serious study of German-American literature. Joseph Linenberger wrote a story on the German Russian emigrants who came to America in 1876 and 1878. Georg Lippard's novel on the American Revolution appeared in Hamburg in 1859. Robert Clemen wrote a history of the Inquisition, and Hermann Scheffauer's novels and essays are an example of the pro-German publications during the World War I period.

The intelligent, lively style of Erwin Rosen in his novel, *Der deutsche Lausbub in Amerika* (1912) should be studied for its effect on German-American readers seeking an escape from the trauma of the anti-German hysteria as a result of the First World War. Published in two volumes, the book reached at least 44 editions by 1922. Lively humor is characteristic of the prose works of Hermann Zagel whose novel *Jack Roostand* (1909–1912) also gained wide popularity among its readers. Although these works are devoid of great literary merit, they are to be valued as representative products of ethnic history. Equally important are the writings of German-American humorists whose works should be contrasted against those of their contemporaries on the European continent. Such a study would lay to rest the myth that German-language literature lacks humor. Often the prose works of German-American authors display pervasive elements of caustic humor and critical satire (see e.g., the works of Berthold Baer, Hugo Tippmann, and Henry Urban).

Frequently humorous and genuinely delightful reading are the writings of German-American dialect authors and poets. Very little has been written on them.[16] Two areas of German-American dialect literature have been the subject of detailed and comprehensive studies, namely Pennsylvania Dutch and Yiddish prose, poetry, and drama. Both of these areas have existed alongside of the main current of German-American literature by virtue of the fact that they are the literary products of two distinct communities whose members are bound together within their respective groups by common ethnic traditions and religious beliefs. The Pennsylvania Dutch have remained essentially apart from the mainstream of American life. And whereas the Jewish community has not done so, its dialect literature has more in common with Slavic cultural influences than with the German. The strongest link between Yiddish and the main body of German-American literature appears to be that of language relationship. Yiddish being a German dialect, its writings may be included among German-American literature, but these have been appropriately treated as a separate body of literary expression. It should be noted, however, that the works of Jewish authors in America written in High German fall within the several categories discussed in this outline.

German-American humor finds an appropriate vehicle in the theatre. Konrad Nies' *Festspiele* satirize the propensity of his contemporaries for "Vereinsmeierei," a theme that remains current. Adolph Philipp was noted for his slapstick street-corner comedies which can be enjoyed even today. The fact that approximately twice as many comedies as tragedies were performed here is indicative of the general taste of audiences who sought less a serious art experience than they did entertainment.[17] In his *Amerikanische Eindrücke* (1906), Ludwig Fulda refers to nineteenth-century drama as the impoverished cinderella of the creative arts in America. And so was the German-American theatre despite the efforts of a handful of talented actors, directors, and theatre managers. Although the German-American stage has been the subject of several investigations, very little has been written on the works of German-American dramatists. This is partly due to the fact that, according to Leuchs, only 5 percent of the repertoire of German-American theatrical groups, Turner performances, and cultural societies consisted of German-American plays.[18] There are, however, a great many pieces worthy of scholarly inquiry, e.g., the tragedies of Ernst Anton Zündt, the social dramas of Wilhelm Rosenberg, and the historical plays of Caspar Butz, P. J. Reuz (pseud.: Otto Welden), Hugo Schlag, and F. G. Ernst.

Comparative studies of German-American poetry are also scarce. Except for a few dissertations and articles dealing with some of the individual German-American poets' works, all of the studies of the main body of German-American poetry dwell more on the lives of the poets than on their lyrical and epic products.[19]

German-American poetry of the nineteenth century may be

divided into four major areas: (1) sentimental lyrics, mainly on homesickness and the difficulty of adjusting to a new environment; (2) lyrical poetry and ballads on patriotic and homespun themes; (3) poems of social protest, most notably by the Forty-Eighters and their sympathizers; (4) lyrical descriptions of North American landscapes. Major poets to be considered are Caspar Butz, Eduard Dorsch, Konrad Krez, Ernst Otto Hopp, and Robert Reitzel. At the turn of the century, the verses of Wilhelm Benignus, Konrad Nies, Georg Edward, Martin Drescher, Max Hempel, and Pedro Ilgen are considered among the best. H. A. Rattermann's "Barbara Brand" qualifies as one of the best German-American ballads, and Max Hempel's "Im Seziersaal" antedates Gottfried Benn's antiseptic poetry.

Prof. Frieda Voigt's study "German Writers in the USA: 1885–1935" critically examines the poems of several other authors.[20] W. L. Rosenberg's polemic, anti-war verses, Otto Sattler's nature descriptions, Albert Gehring's soul-searching lyrics, Henni Hubel's tragic ballads, and Richard Herzfeld's (pseud. Richard Norden) *Silhouetten* (1927) are considered excellent examples of German-American poetry. Drescher (pseud. Flamingo) and Oskar Kollbrunner rank among the "top ten of German-American writers." The powerful ballads and structurally pure lyrics of Kurt Baum make him the foremost German-American poet of the early twentieth century. Friedrich Baltzer, Georg Sylvester Viereck, and others attack the war mongers who persecuted German-Americans. Unlike Viereck, Baltzer defends America's position during the First World War. The contrast of attitudes toward the war and the lives of the German-American citizenry during this period as reflected in German-American literature have not been thoroughly investigated.

Drescher, who has been highly praised by German critics, was an excellent translator of American poetry. An outstanding translator of poetry during the nineteenth century was Karl Theodor Eben (Poe's "Raven"). Karl Knortz's translations of Walt Whitman's works and Frank Siller's German rendition of Longfellow's "Evangeline" deserve recognition. F. G. Ahrens, Hugo Andriessen, Hermann Rosenthal, Wilhelm Dilg, and other German-American writers produced thousands of translations of literary works from English and other languages. Their activity suggests still another problem which has received only superficial treatment—to what extent are German-American writers responsible for introducing English-language and other foreign literary works to European and German-American readers?

During the 1930s, German-American literature declined sharply, reaching a low point in total output which was the natural result of the peaking it had experienced at the turn of the century. This phenomenon is best explained by a study of immigration trends, the Americanization process, and the effects of the first world war. Before the first influx of political émigrés from Nazi Germany, German-American literature as a whole included only a few writers of some international fame. Most of them were novelists (Sealsfield, Ruppius, Strubberg, Gerstäcker, Griesinger, Möllhausen, and Kenkel), whose writings were better received abroad than in this country. In addition to these major representatives of German-American prose fiction, several other German-American writers have been mentioned at least in German literary histories. Thus Georg Asmusen and Philip Berges have been cited as authors of the *Heimatroman.* Johannes Gillhoff has been ranked among the minor writers of the *Dorfnovelle,* and Alfons Paquet is considered a master at journalistic detail. Clara Blüthgen's stories for children place her among the few popular German-language women writers of her day, and Raoul Auernheimer must be considered a minor representative of the Austrian as well as German-American school of literary prose.

The writings of the exile authors and poets who came to America after 1933 do not lend themselves entirely to the definition of German-American literature. Heinrich and Thomas Mann, Erich Marie Remarque, Franz Werfel, Alfred Döblin, Hermann Broch, and other major German exile writers have been elaborately treated by literary historians who recognize their works more for their universality, as products of the German mind, than as peculiarly German-American. What distinguishes them, however, from Sealsfield, Gerstäcker, Ruppius and the others, is the absence of themes in their writings which deal predominately with some facet of the American experience. That is not to say that American themes are totally absent from the works of the major exile writers since 1933. Carl Zuckmayer, for example, has written more than some beautiful lines describing the American landscape. Perhaps the only valid measuring stick, for purposes of qualifying these writers as German-American, is their naturalization application or the extent to which their American residence can be said to have influenced their writing.

Alfred Gong, a talented poet, fled the Nazis as well as the Communists. Nostalgic and tragic accounts of life in and flight from the homeland are contained in the prose and poetry of Transylvanian Saxon writers earlier in the century, and of the Danube Swabians since the 1950s. Studies of German-American works by authors from individual German territories and states may shed light on similarities and differences in their writings.[21] Mimi Grossberg treats recent Austrian writers in America, and Linus Spuler provides insight into the works of Swiss-American authors and poets since the beginning of the twentieth century.[22]

The period between the two world wars is filled with stories of the hardships suffered both in the homeland and in America. Abraham Kroeker writes of his flight from Communist tyranny, and the hardships suffered under the Russian yoke during the years 1921–1924. Felix Smith's novel, *Entwurzelt* (1932) deals with German-Americanism during the period 1920–1931. Themes treating America are found in several talented prose writers since the 1930s, e.g., Joachim Maas, Heinrich Meyer (pseud.: H. K. Houston Meyer), Ralph Wood, Fred Karl Scheibe, Johannes Urzidil, Vicki Baum.

Despite the demise of the German-American press, German-American literature is still alive today. Its major representatives are poets, e.g., Hanns Fischer, Hertha Nathorff, Margarete Kollisch, Dagobert Runes, Kurt Fickert. The love lyrics and other poems of the late Rudolf Voigt place him among the top poets of this century. Like Voigt, both Ernst Waldinger and Rose Auslaender are appreciated in Germany as well as stateside for their keen poetic imagery. Among the few American-born poets, special attention must be focused on Herman F. Brause and Don Heinrich Tolzmann, founders of the Verband deutschsprachiger Schriftsteller in Amerika. Their individualism represents the new direction in which German-American poetry appears headed—one which though it reveres the culture of the poet's "Urheimat," is an expression not of a foreign culture transplanted in America, but rather of American culture with its often obscure vestiges of the

German heritage. Such may also be said for the delightfully fresh lyrics of Russell Gilbert and other Pennsylvania Dutch poets.

Our case for German-American literature has touched upon only a few problems, themes, and writers that merit the attention of the literary historian, especially the Germanist. The time to tell the story of German-American literary endeavor has never been riper than now. On the eve of the American Bicentennial Celebration and at the peak of scholarly involvement in ethnic studies, this facet of the cultural contributions of America's German-speaking immigrants and their descendants remains an unconcluded chapter in the annals of American-German and German-American creative thought and literary expression.

NOTES

1. For an extensive bibliography of secondary literature on German-American writers and their works, see Robert E. Ward, "Dictionary of German-American Literature. Part I." *German-American Studies*, X (Fall, 1975)—in press. Hereafter cited as *Dictionary*.

2. René Wellek and Austin Warren, *Theory of Literature* (N.Y., 1939).

3. Robert E. Ward, "Handbook of German-American Creative Literature," unpublished manuscript.

4. For a bibliography of German-American literary periodicals, see Ward, *Dictionary*.

5. For a bibliography of anthologies containing German-American literature, see Ward, *Dictionary*.

6. G. A. Zimmermann, *Deutsch in Amerika*, 2nd ed. (Chicago, 1894); Ernst Jockers, "Deutschamerikanische Dichtung," *Der Auslandsdeutsche*, XII (1929), 321–26; Linus Spuler, *Deutsches Schrifttum in den Vereinigten Staaten* (Lucerne, 1959–60). Cf. also Spuler, "Von deutsch-amerikanischer Dichtung," *German-American Studies*, I, 1 (1969), 8–16.

7. Henry A. Pochmann, "The Mingling of Tongues," in: *Literary History of the United States*, ed. Robert E. Spiller et al., vol. 2 (N.Y., 1948), pp. 676–693.

8. The terms were used to refer to the political exiles from 1817 to 1848, and the Forty-Eighters, respectively.

9. In 1842, Viktor Wilhelm Fröhlich, a German-American poet and editor of several periodicals, translated Sue's novel for a Cincinnati German newspaper. It later appeared in book form in New York. Dr. J. Frost's *Geheimnisse von Berlin* appeared in Philadelphia six years earlier (1836). See also the urban mystery novels of Heinrich Börnstein, Friedrich Hassaurek, Emil Klauprecht, Theodor Griesinger, and F. Wickede, and George Condoyannis' discussion in "German-American Prose Fiction from 1850 to 1918," (diss. Columbia Univ., 1953).

10. For the Texas-German writers, see Selma Metzenthin-Raunick, "A Survey of German Literature in Texas," *Southwestern Historical Quarterly*, XXXIII, 2 (1929). See also her other studies listed in Ward, *Dictionary*.

11. For the Negro in German-American literature, see Leroy Woodson, "American Negro Slavery in the Works of Friedrich Strubberg, Friedrich Gerstäcker and Otto Ruppius," (diss. Catholic Univ. of America, 1949). On the American Indian, see Preston Barba, "The American Indian in German Fiction," *German-American Annals*, n.s., XI (1913), 143–74.

12. Condoyannis suggests these and other themes.

13. Condoyannis considers the pathetic figure of Karl, the merchant in Klauprecht's *Cincinnati oder die Geheimnisse des Westens* as a typical representative of this character type.

14. The Turner lyric has been treated by Marion D. Learned, "The German-American Turner Lyric," *Report,* Society for the History of the Germans in Maryland, VI (Baltimore, 1892). See also Henry Metzner, *Deutsch-amerikanische Dichtung mit besonderer Berücksichtigung des Turnliedes* (N.Y., 1909).

15. In this connection, see J. E. Rothensteiner, *Die literarische Wirksamkeit der deutsch-amerikanischen Katholiken* (St. Louis, 1922); Robert E. Ward, "Reflections on Some German Poems by Lutheran Pastors in America," *Concordia Historical Institute Quarterly,* LXIV, 3 (Aug. 1972), 114-121.

16. See H. H. Fick, "Die Dialectdichtung in der deutsch-amerikanischen Literatur," *Freidenker-Almanach für das Jahr 1896* (Milwaukee, 1896), 69-94; Karl Knortz, "Die plattdeutsche Literatur Nordamerikas," *Americana Germanica,* VI, 3 (1897), 76-83.

17. See F. A. H. Leuchs, *The Early German Theatre in New York, 1840-1872* (N.Y., 1928) for relevant statistics.

18. Ibid.

19. For an extensive bibliography of secondary works on German-American poetry, see Ward, *Dictionary.*

20. Prof. Voigt's unpublished and uncompleted manuscript was graciously given to me by her daughter after her death. The manuscript consists of notes and bibliographical data on several German-American writers.

21. See, e.g., Robert E. Ward, "Amerikas deutschsprachige Dichter aus Baden-Württemberg," *Badische Heimat,* Heft 4 (Freiburg i.B.: Nov. 1974), 105-110.

22. See Mimi Grossberg, "Biographical and Bibliographical Notes," in: *Austrian Writers in the United States 1938-1968, An Exhibition of the Austrian Institute and the Austrian Forum, Inc.* Pamphlet (N.Y., 1968); Mimi Grossberg, *Österreichs literarische Emigration in den Vereinigten Staaten 1938* (Vienna, 1970); Mimi Grossberg, *Österreichische Autoren in Amerika: Geschick und Leistung der österreichischen literarischen Emigration von 1938 in den Vereinigten Staaten* (Vienna, 1970); Spuler, *supra,* note 6.

17. Six Poems
Fritz Senn

Unterwegs

(Zur Jahrhundertfeier 1974 anläßlich der Ankunft rußland-
deutscher Mennoniten in Nordamerika)

Jahrhundertelang auf Wanderwegen,
    Als suchten wir von Land zu Land
Die Insel mit den goldnen Pflügen
    Von Vancouver bis Samarkand!

Dazu ein unbegrenzt Gefilde
    Mit Saaten rein und Früchten schwer,
Des lieben Gottes fleißige Gilde,
    Ein feingefügtes Bauernheer.

    Und immer Menno in der Mitte,
Mit Bibelbuch und Mosesbart,
    Gerüstet noch nach Pilger Sitte
Mit Hut und Stab zur Weiterfahrt.

    Wann wird die Odyssee wohl enden,
Und wann erreichen wir den Port?
    Und wann entgürten wir die Lenden
Zum letzten Mal am Heimatort?

    An einem Tag da wird's geschehen,
Ein Tag, der kein Ende hat,
    Wenn unsere Augen erspähen
Die Zinnen der ewigen Stadt!

Heimat

Große Höfe waren uns zu Spielplätzen gegeben,
Hunde und Katzen waren unsere trauten Gefährten,
Störche sahen wir langbeinig über den Scheunen schweben,
Stare und Spatzen lärmten und praßten in Maulbeerhecken und
    Gärten,
Und dahinter die Felder, die Steppe, die russischen Lieder,—
Schön war das, schön, das kommt niemals wieder!

So wurden wir groß. Das verwuchs mit uns wie Lunge und Leber;
Manchmal saßen wir am Rande der alten Kurganen,
Wir bestiegen die einstigen Heldengräber
Und träumten von Recken und Rossen und wehenden Fahnen!
Und dahinter die mächtigen Wälder, die unendliche Weite, die
    russischen Lieder,
Schön war das, schön, das kommt niemals wieder!

    An Sommerabenden, mondlichthellen,
    Und in regenschwülen Gewitternächten,
    Rieselten leiser der Lieder Quellen,
    Doch manchmal brachen wie aus dunkeln Schächten
    Der Russen traurige Heimwehlieder,
    An Straßenzäunen bei duftendem Flieder!
    Schön war das, schön! Das kommt niemals wieder!—

Heimkehr

Wenn der Wanderbursche hat die Welt gesehn,
Will er doch zuletzt nach Hause gehn,
Will zuletzt doch bringen einen Gruß
Seinem alten Dorf am Fluß!
Summend geht die Straße er entlang . . .
Da . . . in einem Hof ertönt Gesang,
Spielen, Tanzen, Ringelreihn,
Nachtigallen, Fliederduft und Mondenschein,
Und die Holde, die er sich erkor,
Küßte, herzte und durch Tod im Krieg verlor,
Lange steht er sinnend vor dem Tor. . . .
Weiter schreitet er voraus
Und kommt nun zu seinem Vaterhaus.
Stall und Scheune stehn nicht mehr,
Und das Haus ist ohne Dach und leer,
Türen, Fenster, alle Möbel
Hat verschleppt der Pöbel!
Auf der Beischlagsstufe sieht er sich als Kind,
Neben sich den lieben Sausewind,
Sausewind, den liebsten Hund
Auf dem ganzen Erdenrund,
Der am besten ihn verstand,
und oft zärtlich leckte seine Hand.
Sommers, in der Beischlagsecke,
Ruhten sie auf einer Decke
In der heißen Mittagszeit,
Oh, wie ist das alles weit! . . .

Barfuß, mit zerrissnen Hosenknien,
Sieht er sich ein Wägelchen ziehn,
Vollgeladen mit Kawunen und Melonen,
Obendrauf ein Korb mit grünen Bohnen,
Sausewind läuft nebenher,
Rastet oft und atmet schwer,
Froh, daß es nach Hause geht,
Diesmal wird das Mittag spät!
Auch im Wald sind sie gewesen,
Haben Beeren dort gelesen,

Er ist noch auf einen Baum geklettert,
Plötzlich brach ein Ast, beim Rutschenmüssen
Sind die Hosenknie zerrissen!
Seine alte Mutter wettert,
Abends sitzt sein Mütterchen gebückt,
Während sie die Hosenknien flickt!
Vater schilt und schmust dabei!
Oh, die liebe Kletterei! . . . .

Plötzlich nimmt er seinen Wanderstab,
Und geht zu der Liebsten Grab,
Auf dem Kirchhof, früher wohlgepflegt,
Jetzt kein Grab, das eine Innschrift trägt!
Denkt an Friedrich Rückerts Spruch, den er einst las:
"Über alle Gräber wächst zuletzt das Gras!"

. . . .Wenn ein Wanderbursch nun wieder wandern geht,
Schließt ihn ein in euer Nachtgebet!
Denn wer weiß von seiner Schritte Ziel?
Und die Welt hat dunkler Wege viel!
Einer sucht den Garten seiner Kindheit lang,
Und den Brunnen mit der alten Bank,
Wo die Nachtigall im Sommer sang!
Einer war zu lang auf Wanderfahrt,
Auf derselben sind ergraut ihm Haar und Bart!
Einem blieb von allem Hab und Gut,
Nur der Wanderstab und Wanderhut!
Einer sucht in Herbst und Nebelnacht
Ein vergrastes Grab für seine Lebensfracht!
Wandernd mußte er von Hause gehn,
Wege, die im fremden Land verwehn.

Herbstabend in der alten Heimat

Im Dämmern liegt das Herbstgelände
Von Ruhesehnsucht überhaucht,
Das Feuer ferner Stoppelbrände
Versinkt, verraucht.

Die Herde gleitet von der Weide
Den Ställen zu,
Der Pflüger im verstaubten Kleide
Eilt heim, zur Ruh.

Im Dorfe stiller Abendfriede,
Laternenschein,
Die Hammerschläge einer Schmiede
Schlafen ein.

Ein jeder findet seine Klause
Nach Müh und Not,
Bereitet schon in jedem Hause
Stehn Milch und Brot.—

Wär Frieden zu erwandern in der Welt.
Hier fände ihn verborgen, wer ihn sucht,
Hier unter der Akazien grünem Zelt . . .
Wir zogen fort und ließen Pflug und Feld,
Das Dorf, die stille Bucht.
Und werden, wenn die Dämmrung fällt,
Von alten Bildern heimgesucht:
Die Mütter singen kleine Kinder ein
Und ferne rollt noch irgendwo ein Wagen,
Die letzten Pflüger müssen bald zuhause sein,—
Ein irres Blinken, feuchter Mondenschein,
Die Fenster gehen auf, die alten Uhren schlagen,
Manch Bauer schläft vor seiner Haustür ein.—

Lied des Blinden

Aus Tula kam öfters ein Blinder
Mit der Leier bei uns in Russland ums Haus,
Seine Führer waren zwei Waisenkinder,
Die sahen verlaust und erbärmlich aus.

Von Hunden umkläfft und umlagert,
Ging dieser Bettlerverein,
Zerlumpt und abgemagert
Und bleich wie ein Totengebein.

Der Blinde spielte die Leier
Und sang in tiefem Baß:
„Bitte, gebt uns einen Dreier
Und etwas Kwaß . . .”

Vater spendete einen kupfernen Pottak,
Und für jeden eine Schnitte Brot,
Der Blinde befühlte die Münze—„Wott tak!
Eine Spende nach Christi Gebot”!

Er sang ein Lied zur Leier,
Mit leerem, totem Blick,
Das klang zur Abendfeier
Wie Mozarts *Kleine Nachtmusik*!

Jetzt, da mein Augenlicht immer mehr schwindet,
Ich kaum noch lesen und schreiben kann,
Und die Angst steigt,—daß ich erblindet,
Arm werde wie jener Bettelmann,

Da rückt ganz plötzlich, leise
Das Lied des Blinden aus Tula vor,
Und seine bezwingende Weise
Dringt mir herzergreifend ins Ohr!

Ist der kleine Verein verschwunden,
In Rußlands wogendem Völkermeer?
Noch tönt in Abendstunden,
Das Leierlied aus Osten her.

Und ob der Blinde gestorben, verzogen,—
Und ob seine Leier zerbrach,
Mich trägt sein Lied wie auf Wogen
Durch Dunkel und Ungemach!—

A. Solschenizyn

Mit einem Bleistift ausgerüstet
Betritt er das Lager: zwölf Jahre strenge Haft!
In der dunklen Ecke einer Baracke hat er sich eingenistet,
Auf der rauhen Seite von einem Stiefelschaft
Auf Leinwand schreibt er seine ersten Zeilen,
Er merkt kaum, wie man ihn begafft!
Im stillen denkt er an Stephanus und an seinen Meister,
Der einst schuldlos gelitten auf Sachalin . . .
„Ein Leidloser ist wie ein Erdenkloß, ein Leidender ist ein Rubin!"
Der, den sie einst erschießen wollten
Und später als der Russen Weisester gegolten.
Dann erwirbt er zwei Hefte und kann jetzt schreiben,
Dazwischen muß er im Winter die kalten Hände reiben.
Es friert und stürmt, daß die Baracke kracht!
O wie lang ist eine sibirische Winternacht!
Die Kost ist kärglich, der Mantel Lumpen zumeist,
Ringsum das Land ist verschneit und vereist!
Er ist noch völlig unbekannt.
Er schreibt *Ein Tag im Leben des Iwan Denissowitsch,*
Das seine Berufskollegen verspotten als puren Kitsch,
Dieses elende Schmeichlerheer!
Die täglich schreien, als ob die Wahrheit bloß im Kreml wär!
Sein Darben aber ist mehr!
Das Buch wird gedruckt und Chruschtschow gibt es frei!
Darob im Kreml ein großes Geschrei.
Der Autor gibt seinem ersten Buch
Zum Geleit auf die Reise folgenden Spruch:
„Der Schukows sind viele in der UdSSR,
Dieses Buch wäre Lüge, wenn es anders wär.
Nun, Buch, sei Leib, sei Blut, du schwarze Schrift!
Kein tot Programm steh zwischen Volk und mir!
Nun sei ein Lärm, beschriebenes Papier,
Ein Schrei der Not, der jeden Leser trifft . . ."
So zieht das Buch nun und weckt und mahnt
Die Schläfer und Träumer in jedem Land.

Tabula Gratulatoria

Erich A. Albrecht, University of Kansas, Lawrence
Theodor W. Alexander, Texas Tech University, Lubbock
Karl O. E. Anderson, Clark University, Worcester, Massachusetts
Mariann Hundahl Appley, Worcester, Massachusetts
A. Arnold, McGill University, Montreal, Canada
Raymond E. Barbera, Clark University, Worcester, Massachusetts
John F. Baumann, Forest Park, Illinois
C. Richard Beam, Millersville State College, Pennsylvania
James Franklin Beard, Clark University, Worcester, Massachusetts
Edwin H. Bennett, Worcester, Massachusetts
David P. Benseler, Washington State University, Pullman
Jutta and Eckhard Bernstein, Worcester, Massachusetts
Richard Bigalke, Kenosha, Wisconsin
Norman H. Binger, University of Kentucky, Lexington
James Edward Arndt Blair, Middletown, Connecticut
Ruth M. Blair, Middletown, Connecticut
Bernhardt Blumenthal, La Salle College, Philadelphia, Pennsylvania
Jay F. Bodine, University of Kentucky, Lexington
Peter Boerner, Indiana University, Bloomington
Hermann Boeschenstein, University of Toronto, Canada
Klaus H. Bongart, Wilfrid Laurier University, Waterloo, Ontario, Canada
Frank L. Borchardt, Duke University, Durham, North Carolina
Mrs. Dell J. L. Bush, Bellaire High School, Texas
Robert F. Campbell, Clark University, Worcester, Massachusetts
William Carter, Clark University, Worcester, Massachusetts
Gerhard Clausing, University of Minnesota, Minneapolis
Morris H. Cohen, Clark University, Worcester, Massachusetts
Carl Colditz, Wayne State University, Detroit, Michigan
Marianne Cowan, The City College of New York
William C. Crossgrove, Brown University, Providence, Rhode Island
Jessie C. Cunningham, Sudbury, Massachusetts

Reinhard Czeratzki, Walla Walla College, College Place, Washington
Anita E. D'Angio, Waltham, Massachusetts
Mary H. Dessecker, Buena Park, California
Randall Donaldson, Loyola College, Baltimore, Maryland
Lieselotte J. Dumais, Ludlow High School, Massachusetts
Walter Dumke, Timberlake, Ohio
Edmund F. Eckhardt, Ridgewood, New York
Hildegard Emmel, University of Connecticut, Storrs
Norbert V. Englisch, Waterloo, Ontario, Canada
Hildegard K. Evans, Westminster, California
Gloria Flaherty, Bryn Mawr College, Pennsylvania
Wolfgang B. Fleischmann, Montclair State College, Upper Montclair, New Jersey
Gertrude B. Fletcher, San Diego, California
H. H. Fredette, Oakton, Virginia
Bruno Friesen, Ottawa, Ontario, Canada
Bernard J. Freitag, Council Rock High School, Newtown, Pennsylvania
William Louis Gaines, Institute of European Studies, Chicago, Illinois
Hans Galinsky, Amerikanistische Abteilung, Johannes-Gutenberg Universität Mainz, West Germany
Helmut Germer, Kent State University, Ohio
Linda Goltz, Lincoln Park, New Jersey
Franz X. Groll, Baltimore, Maryland
Walter Werner Gross, Wantagh, New York
Oscar J. Grossmann, Milwaukee, Wisconsin
Diether H. Haenicke, Wayne State University, Detroit, Michigan
Carl Hammer, Jr., Texas Tech University, Lubbock
Arthur M. Hanhardt, University of Rochester, New York
Johanna M. Offner Harsney, Youngstown, Ohio
Sherman S. Hayden, Clark University, Worcester, Massachusetts
Howell J. Heaney, Philadelphia, Pennsylvania
Patricia Herminghouse, Washington University, St. Louis, Missouri
Jacob and Frances Hiatt, Worcester, Massachusetts
Alice C. Higgins, Worcester, Massachusetts
Robert Hitchman, Seattle, Washington
Walter Höllerer, Technische Universität Berlin, West Germany
Hans E. Holthusen, Evanston, Illinois

Peter Horwath, Arizona State University, Tempe
Agnes Hostettler, Queens College, Charlotte, North Carolina
Frederick H. Jackson, Wilmette, Illinois
Ruth L. Jeismann, Elgin Community College, Illinois
John Jeppson, Worcester, Massachusetts
Walter J. Johnson, Norwood, New Jersey
Hartmut M. Kaiser, Clark University, Worcester, Massachusetts
Otto H. Kappus, Baltimore, Maryland
Josef M. Kellinger, Wilson College, Chambersburg, Pennsylvania
John F. Kennison, Clark University, Worcester, Massachusetts
Gunther Kison, South Bend, Indiana
Heinz Kloss, Institut für Deutsche Sprache, Mannheim, West
    Germany
Fred Kluetmeier, Greenfield, Wisconsin
Fred W. Koehler, Baltimore, Maryland
Hans J. Koehler, Los Gatos, California
William A. Koelsch, Clark University, Worcester, Massachusetts
H. P. Kraus, New York, New York
John T. Krumpelmann, Baton Rouge, Louisiana
John G. Kunstmann, The University of North Carolina, Chapel
    Hill
Gertrud Lackschewitz, Missoula, Montana
Mrs. Arnold Lake, Wantagh, New York
Klaus Lanzinger, University of Notre Dame, South Bend, Indiana
Richard H. Lawson, San Diego State University, California
Ursula D. Lawson, Athens, Ohio
Dwight E. Lee, Clark University, Worcester, Massachusetts
Wolfram K. Legner, George Washington University, Washington,
    D.C.
Johanna Leisher, DeBary, Florida
Kurt E. H. Liedtke, San Francisco State University, California
Otto R. Lies, Holden, Massachusetts
E. Lindenschmidt, Robbinsville, New Jersey
Otto Löhmann, Marburg, West Germany
William S. Lyon-Vaiden, McDonogh School, Baltimore, Maryland
William H. McClain, The Johns Hopkins University, Baltimore,
    Maryland
Marcus A. McCorison, Worcester, Massachusetts
Amelia M. McDonald, Thermopolis, Wyoming

Charles W. Mann, University Park, Pennsylvania
Martin R. Martzall, Denver, Pennsylvania
Christian Sophus Mass, Baltimore, Maryland
Penny G. Mattern, Worcester, Massachusetts
Margarete Maria Meade-Hartelt, Cedar Rapids, Iowa
E. Mertens, Hildesheim, West Germany
Mrs. Almut H. Metzroth, Greenfield High School, Massachusetts
Heinrich Meyer, Nashville, Tennessee
Beatrix Moore Meyer-Burghagen, Deerfield Beach, Florida
Hans Mollenkott, Northern Valley Regional High School, Old
    Tappan, New Jersey
Merriam Moore, Ridgefield High School, Connecticut
Carl-Heinz Most, Rochester, Minnesota
Manfred Mumper, Los Angeles, California
George J. Mundt, Colgate University, Hamilton, New York
Gert Niers, Bricktown, New Jersey
Mira Niessner, Brooklyn, New York
Henry W. Nordmeyer, The University of Michigan, Ann Arbor
Roger C. Norton, State University of New York, Binghamton
Rudolph F. Nunnemacher, Clark University, Worcester, Massa-
    chusetts
Winifred L. O'Grady, Boston, Massachusetts
May E. Olson, Corvallis, Oregon
Donald Palmerino, Palmer, Massachusetts
Charles A. Partin, E. Grand Rapids High School, Michigan
Daniel Paul, Grand Blanc, Michigan
Kenneth F. Pedersen, German American Societies of Milwaukee,
    Inc., Wisconsin
Bernard G. Peter, Baltimore, Maryland
Helmut F. Pfanner, Durham, New Hampshire
Gertrude Powers, Clark University, Worcester, Massachusetts
Mr. and Mrs. Francis W. Pramschüfer, Jr., Baltimore, Maryland
Gerhard Rauscher, University of Wisconsin, Milwaukee
Dona Reeves, Southwest Texas State University, San Marcos
Anita C. Reichard, Ashland College, Ohio
Joseph R. Reichard, Oberlin College, Ohio
Robert D. Richardson, Jr., University of Denver, Colorado
Gisela F. Ritchie, Wichita State University, Kansas
Walter L. Robbins, University of Cincinnati, Ohio
John A. Robinson, Baltimore, Maryland

Robert R. Robinson-Zwahr, Lubbock, Texas
Josef Roggenbauer, University of Maine, Orono
Ernst Rose, New York University
Anton K. Rumpf, Cleveland, Ohio
Jeffrey L. Sammons, Yale University, New Haven, Connecticut
Wilmer D. Sanders, Winston-Salem, North Carolina
John F. Schank, Fullerton, California
Erica E. Schnur, Mars Area High School, Pennsylvania
Adolf E. and Rebecca B. Schroeder, Columbia, Missouri
Arthur R. Schultz, Middletown, Connecticut
H. Stefan Schultz, Durham, North Carolina
Wilhelm and Mary Seeger, Caledonia, Michigan
Albert Seemann, Towson, Maryland
Lester W. J. Seifert, The University of Wisconsin, Madison
Harriet D. Semke, Westmar College, Le Mars, Iowa
Richard K. Seymour, University of Hawaii, Honolulu
Pamela G. Shriver, Berwick, Pennsylvania
John R. Sinnema, Baldwin-Wallace College, Berea, Ohio
Margret Sloane, Alameda, California
Herbert B. Smith, Pomona College, Claremont, California
Ingeborg H. Solbrig, University of Iowa, Iowa City
John M. Spalek, State University of New York at Albany
Jack M. Stein, Harvard University, Cambridge, Massachusetts
Erich W. Steiniger, Oxford, Ohio
Hans Steinitz, New York, New York
Carol M. Strauss, Worcester, Massachusetts
Hilda Täubel-Giles, Lee's Summit, Missouri
Rita Terras, Connecticut College, New London
Jack Thiessen, University of Winnipeg, Manitoba, Canada
Royal L. Tinsley, Jr., University of Arizona, Tucson
Don Heinrich Tolzmann, University of Cincinnati, Ohio
Walter Tomforde, East Northport, New York
William Topkin, Clark University, Worcester, Massachusetts
Frank Trommler, University of Pennsylvania, Philadelphia
Anthony J. D. Uzialko, Bethlehem, Pennsylvania
Robert Van Dusen, McMaster University, Hamilton, Ontario, Canada
James A. Vaupel, Capital High School, Olympia, Washington
John A. Wagner, M.D., Baltimore, Maryland
Seymour Wapner, Clark University, Worcester, Massachusetts

Frederick S. Weiser, Hanover, Pennsylvania
John J. Weisert, University of Louisville, Kentucky
Glenn Welliver, DePauw University, Greencastle, Indiana
Wen-Yang Wen, Clark University, Worcester, Massachusetts
Richard D. Wetzel, Chesterhill, Ohio
W. Bruce White, University of Toronto, Erindale College, Mississauga, Ontario, Canada
Robert Bray Wingate, Harrisburg, Pennsylvania
Ruth Grosvenor Woodis, Worcester, Massachusetts
Frank H. Woyke, Southbury, Connecticut
Carrie-May Kurrelmeyer Zintl, Baltimore, Maryland
Richard A. Zipser, Oberlin College, Ohio

Adelphi University Library, Garden City, New York
The Library, The University of Alberta, Edmonton, Canada
Assumption College Library, Worcester, Massachusetts
Mikkelsen Library, Augustana College, Sioux Falls, South Dakota
I. Gibson Hopkins Library, Austin College, Sherman, Texas
Ritter Library, Baldwin-Wallace College, Berea, Ohio
Öffentliche Bibliothek der Universität Basel zu Handen, Switzerland
The Library of Bethany and Northern Baptist Theological Seminaries, Oak Brook, Illinois
Bennington College Library, Vermont
Bibliothèque Nationale, Paris, France
John Carter Brown Library, Brown University, Providence, Rhode Island
Brown University Library, Providence, Rhode Island
Ellen Clarke Bertrand Library, Bucknell University, Lewisburg, Pennsylvania
The Library, California State University, Fresno
Logue Library, Chestnut Hill College, Philadelphia, Pennsylvania
The Public Library of Cincinnati and Hamilton County, Ohio
Robert Hutchings Goddard Library, Clark University, Worcester, Massachusetts
Carl B. Ylvisaker Library, Concordia College, Moorhead, Minnesota
Carleton College Library, Northfield, Minnesota
Carleton University Library, Ottawa, Canada
West Library, Central Bucks High School, Doylestown, Pennsylvania

Cornell University Libraries, Ithaca, New York
University of Dayton Library, Ohio
Detroit Public Library, Michigan
Stoxen Library, Dickinson State College, North Dakota
Perkins Library, Duke University, Durham, North Carolina
The Library, Eastern Montana College, Billings, Montana
Elgin High School Library, Illinois
Evanston Township High School Library, Illinois
Franklin and Marshall College Library, Lancaster, Pennsylvania
The University Libraries, The University of Georgia, Athens
The Library, Georgia Southern College, Statesboro, Georgia
Goethe House Library, New York
Niedersächsische Staats- u. Universitätsbibliothek, Göttingen, West
    Germany
Julia Rogers Library, Goucher College, Towson, Maryland
Harvard College Library, Cambridge, Massachusetts
Helsinki University Library, Finland
Hilo College Library, University of Hawaii at Hilo
Willard J. Houghton Library, Houghton College, New York
University of Houston Library, Texas
Henry E. Huntington Library and Art Gallery, San Marino, Cali-
    fornia
The Main Library, Indiana University, Bloomington
The University of Iowa Libraries, Iowa City
The Library, Iowa State University of Science and Technology,
    Ames
Ithaca College Library, New York
Milton S. Eisenhower Library, The Johns Hopkins University,
    Baltimore, Maryland
Kent State University Library, Ohio
Chalmers Memorial Library, Kenyon College, Gambier, Ohio
Krauss Library, Lutheran School of Theology at Chicago, Illinois
Krauth Memorial Library, Lutheran Theological Seminary, Phila-
    delphia, Pennsylvania
Miami University Libraries, Oxford, Ohio
Millersville State College Library, Pennsylvania
The Library, Minneapolis Public Schools, Minnesota
University of Minnesota Libraries, Minneapolis
The Newberry Library, Chicago, Illinois

Harriet Irving Library, University of New Brunswick, Fredericton,
Canada
Stadtbibliothek, Nuernberg, West Germany
Niagara University Library, Niagara University, New York
Ohio Wesleyan University Library, Delaware, Ohio
University of Oregon Library, Eugene
Bodleian Library, Oxford University, England
State Library of Pennsylvania, Harrisburg
University of Pennsylvania Libraries, Philadelphia
Free Library of Philadelphia, Pennsylvania
Library Company of Philadelphia, Pennsylvania
Princeton University Library, New Jersey
Russell Sage College Library, Troy, New York
A. S. Alexander Library, Rutgers-The State University, New Bruns-
wick, New Jersey
Rolvaag Memorial Library, St. Olaf College, Northfield, Minnesota
Skidmore College Library, Saratoga Springs, New York
University Library, University of Southern California, Los Angeles
Stanford University Libraries, California
Victoria College Library, Toronto, Canada
Wake Forest University Library, Winston-Salem, North Carolina
The Library, Wartburg College, Waverly, Iowa
Reu Memorial Library, Wartburg Theological Seminary, Dubuque,
Iowa
University of Washington Libraries, Seattle
The Library, Western Reserve Historical Society, Cleveland, Ohio
Wheaton College Library, Norton, Massachusetts
Wieland-Archiv, Biberach an der Riss, West Germany
Wilfrid Laurier University Library, Waterloo, Ontario, Canada
Forrest R. Polk Library, University of Wisconsin, Oshkosh
University of Wisconsin-Milwaukee Library
The Library, University of Wisconsin-Platteville
Wisconsin Lutheran Seminary Library, Mequon
Thomas Library, Wittenberg University, Springfield, Ohio
The University of Wyoming Library, Laramie

American Antiquarian Society, Worcester, Massachusetts
American Historical Society of Germans from Russia, Lincoln,
Nebraska

Concordia Historical Institute, St. Louis, Missouri
Germanistic Society of America, New York
German Society of Pennsylvania, Philadelphia
Historical Society of Mecklenburg Upper Canada, Rexdale, Ontario, Canada
The Historical Society of Pennsylvania, Philadelphia
The Historical Society of Western Pennsylvania, Pittsburgh
Institut für Auslandsbeziehungen, Stuttgart, West Germany
The New York Historical Society
State Historical Society of Missouri, Columbia

John F. Kennedy-Institut für Nordamerikastudien, Freie Universität Berlin, West Germany
Department of German, Bryn Mawr College, Pennsylvania
German Department, University of California at Irvine
German/Classics/Russian Department, California State University, Sacramento
Department of German, University of Florida, Gainesville
Department of Germanic Languages and Literatures, The University of Michigan, Ann Arbor
Department of German and Russian, Michigan State University, East Lansing
German Department, Middlebury College, Vermont
German Graduate School, Millersville State College, Pennsylvania
Amerika Institut der Universität München, West Germany
Institut für Deutsche Philologie der Universität München, West Germany
German Section, Department of Modern and Classical Languages, University of New Mexico, Albuquerque
Department of Germanic Languages, University of North Carolina, Chapel Hill
Department of German, Northwestern University, Evanston, Illinois
Department of German, Wilfrid Laurier University, Waterloo, Ontario, Canada
Germanistisches Institut an der Universität Wien, Austria
Department of Modern and Classical Languages, University of Wyoming, Laramie

Annor Wood Products, Ltd., Waterloo, Ontario, Canada
Aufbau, New York
Buchzentrum L. Heidrich, Vienna, Austria
Danube Swabian Association of Southern California, Downey
Frauenhilfsverein der Deutschen Gesellschaft von Maryland, Baltimore
German-American National Congress, Chicago, Illinois
German-American National Congress, Group #16, Indianapolis, Indiana
German Consulate General, New York
German Information Center, New York
German National Tourist Office, New York
Pazifische Rundschau, Vancouver, British Columbia, Canada
Stern Magazine, New York
Walter J. Johnson, Inc., Norwood, New Jersey

With special gratitude we wish to acknowledge the generous support of this publication by the Consulate General of the Federal Republic of Germany, Boston.